ESSENTIAL COLLEGE CONCEPTS

A POST-COLLEGIATE REVIEW OF IDEAS, PHRASES AND QUOTATIONS THAT YOU SHOULD HAVE LEARNED IN COLLEGE, BUT PROBABLY DIDN'T

D0861638

in American History, Anthropology, Art, Economics, Historiography, Literary Concepts, Philosophy/Religion, Political Science, Psychology, Science and Sociology

William W. Tilden

Plaine Style Press
Berkeley

Plaine Style Press
P.O. Box 7172
Berkeley CA 94707
essentialcollegeconcepts.com

Library of Congress Control Number

ISBN 978-0-692-59767-5

For Judy, Todd, Katrina, Victoria and John

TABLE OF CONTENTS

PREFACE

CHAPTER

SELECTED REFERENCES

PREFACE

Essential College Concepts: A Post-Collegiate Review of Ideas, Phrases and Quotations that You Should Have Learned in College, but Probably Didn't is a compendium of concepts, phrases and quotations assembled from a wide variety of, mostly, Western sources. It embodies the rich originality and "intertexuality" of our cultural heritage and seeks to liberate ideas from their specialized niches by demystifying and democratizing them and incorporating them into the public domain of our common cultural vocabulary.

The purpose of *Essential College Concepts* is to provide a personal, compact, interdisciplinary overview, in time and place, of a "common body of knowledge" that can be used as (1) a post-collegiate review of the Western humanities, particularly for those who were educated in technology and other STEM disciplines, but also as (2) a college-preparatory guide for advanced secondary students and, more generally, as (3) a means for broadening, extending and updating one's general education.

Essential College Concepts is organized by subject area into chapters (American History, Anthropology, etc.). Within each chapter, (1) the Concepts and Phrases section is followed by (2) a selection of Quotations relevant to that topic and (3) a Details section in which a subset of selected concepts is discussed in extended detail. Each concept is identified by its source(s), many of which can be traced to (4) the Selected References in the back of the book, or, by using online and other search methods, to the original authors, texts and related sources. The cross-references are meant to show the interrelationship (or "intertextuality") between concepts and are presented as optional aids to those readers who are interested in obtaining further information about a particular concept.

Because the definitions for many of the concepts are brief and impressionistic, and because individual concepts are grouped in alphabetical order, rather than thematic order, readers are asked to view each concept as an interrelated picture element, or pixel, and to scan, assemble and blend them into their own portrait of the subject matter, much like a pointillist painting.

Readers are also encouraged to view *Essential College Concepts*, as well as their own education, as a work in progress, as a shared, communal database of ideas, and to submit their own favorite concepts and quotations for future editions of *Essential College Concepts*.

Please read, enjoy and share.

William W. Tilden
Kensington, California

1. AMERICAN HISTORY

CONCEPTS AND PHRASES:

Abolitionism: a reform movement of the 1830s to the 1860s that advocated the immediate and uncompensated emancipation of all African-American slaves, rather than their gradual or compensated emancipation or colonization to Africa. Its newspaper, *The Liberator*, with a circulation of 3,000, had a greater impact in creating fear and paranoia in Southern slaveholders than in changing Northern public opinion. See Antinominan personality in Concepts and 13. American Slavery and 24. American Civil War in Details and Henry Mayer in Selected References.

Absence of feudalism and hereditary stratifications: a social condition in the British North American colonies during the 17th and 18th Centuries that has been cited as a major reason for the relative absence of class conflict and political radicalism in America history. See Primogeniture and entail in Concepts, 4. Consensus Schools of American Historiography in Details and Louis Hartz in Selected references.

Abundance of land and natural resources: a geographical determinate that has exercised a profound influence over the development of American character traits and institutions. See People of plenty in Concepts and 2. American Cultural Traits, 8. Geographical Determinism and 11. Frederick Jackson Turner/Frontier Thesis in Details and David Potter and Fredrick Jackson Turner in Selected References.

Acquisitive mentality versus **civic responsibility**: the conflict in American cultural values between private gain and public good, between economic individualism and social responsibility; a fundamental conundrum of American democracy. John Kenneth Galbraith. See Individualism, Positive central state versus laissez-fair individualism and Rugged individualism in Concepts and 3. Alexis de Tocqueville in Details.

Agrarian/yeoman ideal: the cultural symbol of the virtuous, self-sufficient, independent yeoman farmer; the family farmer in a classless, homogenous society. According to Thomas Jefferson, those who till the soil are the "chosen people of god"; Jefferson, Henry Nash Smith, Frederick Jackson Turner; see Homestead Act in Concepts and 11. Frederick Jackson Turner/Frontier Thesis in Details; versus **agrarian capitalism**: an economic system of commercial and, later, corporate farming that uses wage labor to produce cash crops for regional, national and world markets and is subject to international capital, credit, labor and market forces. Richard Hofstadter, Henry Nash Smith.

Agricultural Revolution: the transformation of American agriculture during the 19th Century as a result of the inventions of the cotton gin, steam boat, mechanical reaper and thresher and the refrigerated railroad car, as well as the growth of urban markets and the development of regional and national transportation networks of rivers, roads, canals and railroads. It permitted the large-scale, commercial production of cash crops and animal products for national and international markets and accelerated the shift away from subsistence farming. See Refrigerated railroad car and Transportation Revolution in Concepts.

Alcoholic republic: a term applied to American society in the early 19th Century in which the average person consumed the equivalent of 7 gallons of pure alcohol every year, three times the average today. W.J. Rorabaugh, Sarah Tracy and Caroline Acker. See Anti-Saloon League, Prohibition and Temperance Movement in Concepts.

American exceptionalism: the belief that the United States is historically unique, a model community, a "city upon a hill"; that Americans are God's chosen people, with a special mission to bring liberty, democracy and capitalism to the rest of the world. See John Winthrop, J. Hector St. John de Crèvecoeur, Alexis de Tocqueville, John L. O'Sullivan Abraham and Lincoln in Quotations and 6. American Exceptionalism in Details.

American family: "a training in detachment." William Bridges, Erik Erikson, John Gillis, Geoffrey Gorer, Ann Hulbert, Margaret Mead, William Tilden. See Henry Adams in Quotations.

American foreign policy: a set of strategies, policies and actions that shape and define the United States' relationships with other countries. Historically, it reflected the tension between two contradictory sets of values, realism and idealism, that is, between national self-interest, including economic and military intervention, on the one hand, and democratic ideals and the principle of self-determination, on the other. American foreign policy has also been constrained by, and flowed against, a strong counter-current of isolationism. George Kennan. See Dollar Diplomacy, Neo-Conservatism, Our detached and distant situation and Self-determination in Concepts and 22. Mexican-American War and 31. Cold War in Details.

American landscape/ecological history: Michael Conzen, William Cronon, Henry Nash Smith, Ted Steinberg, John Stilgoe, Frederick Jackson Turner.

American primitive: D. H. Lawrence's term for the cultural archetype of the strong, silent, frontier hero. See Leatherstocking Tales in Concepts.

Anti-intellectualism: an enduring tradition in American cultural and political history in which segments of society distrust and dismiss intellectuals, experts, journalists, academicians and the educated classes as elitists and reject scientific evidence that contradicts common sense or received religious truths. Karen Armstrong, Daniel Bell, Richard Hofstadter, Kevin Phillips, Frederick Jackson Turner.

Antinomian personality: a term applied to those who believe that, because they are among the "elect" (i.e., chosen or saved by God) or follow a higher law, they are not bound by human laws or traditional moral constraints; a form of spiritual anarchism. The abolitionist William Lloyd Garrison, for example, described himself as "a minority of one with God"; to Paul Tillich, "love is the ultimate law." Anne Hutchinson, Henry David Thoreau, Bob Dylan. See 10. Puritanism in Details, Antinomianism and Higher law in Philosophy/Religion Concepts and Perry Miller and Stow Persons in Selected References.

Anti-Saloon League: the political arm of the temperance movement (*q.v.* in Concepts).

Apocalyptic tradition: see Millennialism in Philosophy/Religion. Karen Armstrong, Perry Miller.

Asymmetrical warfare: guerrilla warfare waged by local, poorly equipped, informally organized, but highly motivated, insurgents against well-equipped, high-tech military forces. It was characteristic of the American War of Independence, the Philippine-American war, the Vietnam war and the Afghanistan and Iraq wars.

Babbitt: Sinclair Lewis's satirical novel, published in 1922, about a good-natured small-businessman who tries, but fails, to escape the materialism, complacency, conformity, boosterism and philistinism of American middle class culture; also, the cultural archetype that embodies those qualities.

Better and wiser sort: the propertied elite, who, according to the precepts of 18th Century republicanism, should govern the country; versus the **"middling"** and **"meaner"** sorts. See Class structure in colonial America in Concepts.

Bible Belt: geographical areas that are associated with Christian fundamentalism and, not infrequently, Scotch-Irish/Ulster-Scotch culture in the United States (*q.v.* in Concepts).

Bill of Rights: the first Ten Amendments to the Constitution of the United States, which guarantee freedom of religion, speech and press; the right to assembly peacefully and to bear arms; protection from unreasonable searches and seizures, double jeopardy and self-incrimination, and the right to due process and a speedy and public trial by an impartial jury.

Bison: a national cultural icon. By 1882, the original North American herd of over twenty-five million was reduced to 5,000 by buffalo hunters, who killed them for their hides, and, not incidentally, removed the primary source of food, fuel and shelter for the Plains Indians. The bison serves as a symbol of the wanton destruction of natural resources. Ted Steinberg. See Conservation movement and Environmental/Green movement in Concepts.

Bitch Goddess Success: William James's term for the national obsession with wealth and material success. See 2. American Cultural Traits and Values in Details.

Born equal: a major precept of American political and cultural ideology, which is based on Locke's concept of the mind at birth as a *tabula rasa*, or blank tablet. It is reflected in the Declaration of Independence's self-evident truth that "all men are created equal." The term was first used by Alexis de Tocqueville. See *Tabula rasa* in Concepts.

Boston Brahmins: 19th Century New England patrician families of inherited wealth, such as the Cabots and the Lodges, who served as cultural models of discreet, upper class "old money," as opposed to the vulgar, ostentatious display of vastly greater wealth by successive generations of the "nouveau riche." Oliver Wendell Holmes, Henry Adams. See Kevin Phillips in Selected References.

Bread-and-butter trade unionism: the philosophy of Samuel Gompers, the president of the American Federation of Labor, and other labor leaders of the late 19th and early 20th Centuries who sought higher wages, fewer hours and better working conditions for workers, rather than broader, more inclusive social-justice reforms. See Labor movement in Concepts.

British political model: a political system that is characterized by parliamentary democracy, compromise, toleration of dissent, loyal opposition and public spiritedness, but also, at one time, by imperialism, bigotry, provincialism and class privilege.

Broker state: a political system in which the national government serves as a mediator or power broker between competing special interest groups, such as organized labor and big business. The interests of the public at large, consumers, the marginalized and the un-enfranchised are, generally, not addressed in this model. John Chamberlain. See Countervailing powers in Concepts for examples of competing interest groups.

John Brown: an abolitionist who, at Harper's Ferry, Virginia in 1859, sought to seize a federal armory, incite a slave rebellion and wage guerrilla warfare against slaveholders. Although his project failed and he was hung, the raid caused panic and paranoia among Southern slave-holders, who believed that it was the result of a "Black Republican" party plot. Brown became a martyr to many who opposed slavery and shifted public opinion in the North against slavery. David S. Reynolds. See Slave revolts in Concepts.

Brown versus Board of Education (1954): a landmark Supreme Court decision that partially overturned Jim Crow laws established in the South after Reconstruction to enforce racial segregation. It declared that "separate but equal" educational facilities were inherently unequal, and was one of the pivotal events leading to the civil rights/black freedom movement of the 1960s. Taylor Branch. See Jim Crow laws in Concepts and 32. Civil Rights/Black Freedom Movement in Details.

Burned-over District: the metaphorical name given to a geographical area in western New York in which religious revivals and the Second Great Awakening took place during the 1820s to the 1840s, and from which many social reform movements rose, including abolitionism and women's rights. The term refers to the emotional and social fervor left in the wake of those revivals. Charles

Finney. See Freedom's ferment and Oneida community in
Concepts and 17. Great Awakening Cycle/Revivalism in Details.

Bush Doctrine: a foreign policy that justified the use of unilateral
actions and preemptive war by the United States against
individuals and regimes that represented a potential or perceived
threat to its security; it was used as justification for the invasion of
Iraq in 2003. See Neo-Conservatism in Concepts.

Child labor laws: a series of child-protection laws that were passed
during the Progressive Era of the early 20th Century. One
prohibited children under sixteen years of age from working more
than 8 hours a day, but it was ruled unconstitutional by the U. S.
Supreme Court because it limited a child's right to sell his or her
labor.

City: see Suburbanization in Concepts and 15. Urbanization and 16.
the Anti-Urban Cultural Tradition in Details.

City upon a hill: see John Winthrop in Quotations and 6. American
Exceptionalism in Details.

Civil disobedience: acting in an illegal but non-violent manner to
achieve social change; a method of asserting a higher moral law by
submitting to the civil consequences (including arrests, fines and
jail) for violating, in a nonviolent manner, what is perceived to be
an unjust or immoral human law or a pervasive public practice,
such as a fugitive slave law or a poll tax or a racially segregated
public transportation system. Henry David Thoreau, Mahatma
Gandhi, Martin Luther King, Jr. See Natural rights in Concepts
and 32. Civil Rights/Black Freedom Movement in Details.

Civil rights movement/black freedom movement (1954-1968): see
Brown versus Board of Education and Jim Crow laws in Concepts
and 32. Civil Rights/Black Freedom Movement in Details.

Civil War: see 24. American Civil War in Details.

Class structure in colonial America: the class system in 17th and 18th
Century British colonial America, which consisted of three broad
socio-economic categories: (1) the **"better and wiser sort"** of
large landholders, merchants, professionals and Crown officials,
(2) the **"middling sort"** of small farmers, artisans, shopkeepers
and petty officials, and (3) the **"meaner sort"** of laborers, servants,
sailors and drifters. Clinton Rossiter. See 20. Class Structure and
22. Social Mobility in Sociology Details.

Cold War: see the 31. Cold War in Details.

Communist Party: a political party established in the United States in 1919 that sought to achieve, through revolutionary struggle, a workers' socialist state. It played an active role in the 1930s and 1940s in establishing industrial unions and in opposing racism. Because of its radicalism and close association with the Soviet Union, it came under broad political and cultural attack during the Cold War of the late 1940s and 1950s. At its peak in the 1930s, the Communist Party in the U. S. had 60,000 members, but, by the 1950s, membership had declined to 10,000, of whom 1,500 were FBI informants. Michael Kazin, Ellen Schrecker. See McCarthyism and Socialist Party in Concepts and 31. Cold War in Details.

Confidence man: the cultural archetype of the con-man, swindler or trickster. Herman Melville.

Conservation movement: a series of Progressive reforms in the late 19th and early 20th Centuries that were based on two conflicting objectives: (1) the conservation of natural resources for their efficient, commercial use (such as logging and mining); versus (2) the preservation of nature from commercial development and exploitation, the protection of its beauty and spirituality and its stewardship and legacy for future generations. The conservation ethic of the Progressive Era was later embodied in the environmental movement of the late 20th and the early 21th Centuries. See Cult of nature and Environmental/Green movement in Concepts.

Conservatism: see 3. Conservatism in Political Science Details.

Cotton engine (or "gin"): the 1793 invention by Eli Whitney, which efficiently separated the seeds from the fibers of inland, short-staple cotton (which, until then, had required many hours of manual labor to remove the seeds from a single pound) and, thereby, made the cultivation of cotton enormously profitable. Whitney's invention (1) increased the demand for slave labor to cultivate the now very profitable plant; (2) drove the expansion of slavery (which, until then, had been moribund) and the cotton plantation system from the Upper South into the Lower South (including Texas) for new lands to cultivate; (3) precipitated a war with Mexico in 1846 and the expropriation of the northern half of its territory; (4) insured the economic and political ascendency of the Southern planter class ("King Cotton") and (5) laid the foundation for sectional conflict and, eventually, the American Civil War. See 23. Mexican-American War and 24. American

Civil War in Details and 10. Economic/Technological
Determinism in Economics Details.

Counterculture: the extraordinary cultural ferment of the 1960s and
1970s, which included the civil rights and anti-Vietnam War
movements, women's liberation, the sexual revolution, gay
liberation, the environmental movement, the widespread use of
recreational drugs, rock-and-roll, etc. See 34. Countercultural
Ferment of the 1960s and 1970s in Details.

Countervailing powers: a system of economic checks and balances in
which, in theory, large, competing interest groups keep any one
group from dominating the market place and public policy, e.g.,
corporations versus unions; consumers versus producers; exporters
versus importers; legacy media versus online/social media;
traditional hotel and taxicab industries versus peer-to-peer
networks. John Kenneth Galbraith.

Creel Committee on Public Information: a federal government
agency in the First World War that used censorship, propaganda,
doctored photos and exaggerated stories of German atrocities to
influence American public opinion to support the nation's
involvement in the war, which was described as a "just, holy war"
by its chairman, George Creel. Kathryn Olmstead. See Sedition
Act of 1918 in Concepts.

Cult of domesticity: the 19th Century middle-class ideal of "true
womanhood" as one who embodied purity, piety, submission and
domesticity. According to this ideal, the woman's proper sphere
was in the home, where she was expected to provide a sanctuary
for her husband and children and "fulfill the roles of a calm and
nurturing mother, a loving and faithful wife, and a passive,
delicate, and virtuous creature and to unfailingly inspire and
support [her] husband." Catherine Lavender, Barbara Welter. See
The Feminine Mystique in Concepts, Henry Adams in Quotations
and 35. Feminism in Details.

Cult of efficiency: an essential feature of 19th and 20th Century
industrial capitalism, as well as an obsessive American cultural
practice and trait, which seeks to eliminate waste, reduce costs and
maximize efficiency by streamlining and rationalizing every phase
of a work process. The practice was derived, in part, from the
relative high cost of labor in the United States in relation to the
abundance of natural resources, which was one of the driving
forces for labor-saving, technological innovations. See Desperate
haste and Scientific management in Concepts, the Protestant ethic

in Economics Concepts, 6. Freud's Anal Personality Traits in Psychology Details and 24. Information Technology/Metaphor of the Machine in Sociology Details.

Cult of nature: the 19th Century belief that nature was the locus of freedom, virtue, spirituality and sublimity. The idealization of nature may have been a cultural response to the inexorable forces of industrialization and urbanization. Charles Feidelson, R. W. B. Lewis, Leo Marx, Perry Miller, Henry Nash Smith. See Conservation movement and Environmental/Green movement in Concepts and 21. New England Transcendentalism in Details.

Cult of the strenuous life: Theodore Roosevelt.

Culture by the book: a culture of self-improvement in which, from colonial times, the rising middle class was eager to avoid giving away its humble origins by its behavior and speech patterns and, so, turned to etiquette and self-help books for advice and guidance. Since "culture," in this case, was acquired through reading, American pronunciation was based on the spelling of the written word and not by oral tradition, as was the case in England. Daniel Boorstin, H. L. Mencken.

Culture of contradictions: a culture based on conflicting ideals of individualism and conformity, political egalitarianism and economic elitism, idealism and materialism, perfectionism and skepticism, the "habit of introspection" and the "longing for community." Richard Chase, Phillip Slater, William Tilden. See 2. American Cultural Values and Traits in Details.

Culture of narcissism: a culture whose members are characterized by both self-love and self-doubt, as well as by materialism and consumerism, self-absorption, self-indulgence, hedonism, a sense of entitlement, the cultish veneration of youthfulness, an indifference to history and a fear of aging and death. Christopher Lasch, Alexis de Tocqueville.

Cycles of corruption and purification, materialism and idealism, private self-interest and public good: the cyclical nature of American political and social history. Lincoln Steffens, Arthur Schlesinger. See 36. American Generational Cycles in Details.

Democracy: the 17th and 18th Century political philosophy that all white men, including those without real, or landed, property, should be entitled to vote and hold political office, which was a radical, leveling concept at the time. Universal white male suffrage was not achieved in the United States until the 1820s with the elimination of property qualifications and the rise of Jacksonian democracy and political equality was not achieved for women or African-Americans until the 20th Century; versus **republicanism**: the political philosophy that guided the American Revolution and the drafting of the U. S. Constitution, which held that only the "better and wiser sort" (or, "the rich and well born" according to Alexander Hamilton and the Federalists), that is, white men who owned real property and, thus, had a "stake in society," should be able to vote and hold political office; implicit in the concept was the fear of mob rule by the "meaner sort." See Franchise and Stake-in-society in Concepts. Clinton Rossiter.

Democracy of cupidity versus **democracy of fraternity**: two contrasting versions of democracy: (1) the former embodies the economic individualism that prevailed in the United States after the American Revolution of 1776, while (2) the latter exalts the communal cooperation and class solidarity that is associated with the French Revolution of 1789. Richard Hofstadter. See Individualism in Concepts and John Winthrop in Quotations.

Democratic imperialism: see Dollar Diplomacy, Manifest Destiny and Neo-Conservatism in Concepts and 6. American Exceptionalism in Details. Walter La Feber, Ernest May, Albert Weinberg.

Desperate haste: Henry David Thoreau's term for his countrymen's obsessive concern with time, speed and efficiency; one of America's cardinal cultural traits. James Gleick, William Tilden. See Cult of efficiency and Scientific management in Concepts and 24. Information Technology/Metaphor of the Machine in Sociology Details.

Dollar Diplomacy: the term coined by Theodore Roosevelt to describe the use of economic, diplomatic and military power to promote American business interests abroad; a foreign policy dominated by the search for, and protection of, overseas markets for American businesses; a form of economic imperialism. Charles Beard, Gabriel Kolko, Walter La Feber, William Appleman Williams.

Double consciousness: see W. E. B. Du Bois in Quotations. Du Bois, Ralph Waldo Emerson.

Double potentiality: the paradoxical coexistence within a cultural value system of radical, even anarchic, individualism in a mass society dominated by Lockean conformity. See Antinomian personality, Individualism, McCarthyism, Red Scare, Salem Witch Trials and Sedition Acts of 1798 and 1918 in Concepts and 3.

Alexis de Tocqueville, 4. Consensus and 5. Conflict Schools of Historiography and 31. Cold War in Details. Marvin Meyers, William Tilden.

Dred Scott (1857): the decision by the U. S. Supreme Court that voided the Missouri Compromise of 1820. It ruled that a person being held as a slave while residing in a free state or the federal territories could not be freed by that state or the U. S. Congress because it would deprive the slave owner of his personal property. The decision enraged those opposed to the expansion of slavery into the western territories (i.e., those that had not yet been incorporated into the Union as states) and accelerated the movement toward civil war. See Free Soil Party in Concepts.

Dual/shared sovereignty: a political system in which sovereignty is shared, to varying degrees, by a central authority and regional authorities. It reflects the tension between centralization and decentralization and the balance of political power between the center and the periphery. In the 18th Century, North American colonial legislatures considered themselves to be coordinate and coequal with British Parliament, united by a common sovereign, with the exclusive right to levy taxes. Similarly, in the first half of the 19th Century, Southern states considered themselves to be sovereign entities within a federated system with the right to withdraw or secede from the United States. In both cases, the issues of shared sovereignty were resolved only by war, specifically, the American War of Independence (1775-1783) and the American Civil War (1860-1865). See Balanced government and the separation and division of powers in Political Science Concepts.

Economic elitism versus **political egalitarianism**: two conflicting and contradictory currents in American political and social thought: (1) the former accepts the concentration of wealth and plutocracy, while (2) the latter celebrates equality and individual opportunity; the Hamiltonian versus Jeffersonian traditions. Vernon Louis Parrington, Fredrick Jackson Turner. See Plutocracy in Concepts; Thomas Jefferson, James Madison, John Jay, Alexis de Tocqueville and Louis Brandeis in Quotations and 25. Social Darwinism in Details.

Economic inequality/concentration of wealth: the redistribution of wealth upwards. In the United States the top 1% of households accounts for over 30% of all income and holds 40% of all assets.

There is greater inequality in the United States than in almost any other democracy in the developed world. Jacob Hacker and Paul Pierson, Paul Krugman, Kevin Phillips, Thomas Piketty, Joseph Stiglitz. See Great Gatsby curve, Plutocracy and Social Mobility in Concepts.

Economic take-off: in the stages-of-economic-growth model, the point at which a partially-developed agrarian nation, through investments in its social infrastructure (i.e., its educational, transportation, communication, legal and financial systems) and capital accumulation, reaches a critical mass and begins to achieve significant and sustained growth and, eventually, economic maturity. In the United States, it is thought that economic take-off began in the second and third quarters of the 19th Century (that is, between 1825 and 1875). W. W. Rostow. See 20. American System in Details and 21. Development Economics in Economics Details.

End of ideology: the thesis of some Consensus school historians that, in the middle of the Twentieth Century, after two world wars and the defeat of totalitarianism, political ideologies had become irrelevant and exhausted, and that future public policy would be guided, instead, by pragmatic and technocratic issues. The idea resurfaced in Francis Fukuyama's 1989 essay, "The End of History" (*q.v.* in Historiography Concepts). Daniel Bell. See 4. Consensus Schools of American Historiography in Details and Convergence theory in Economics Concepts.

Enlightenment: the 18th Century philosophy, world view and "climate of opinion" that celebrated human reason, science, progress, social improvement, religious toleration, natural rights and political liberty. Its outlook was optimistic, secular and humanistic. God was reasonable and benevolent and governed the universe through natural laws, which were discovered by human reason and science, and did not intervene in nature or human affairs. Carl Becker. See Projects for the improvement of mankind in Concepts and 27. 18th Century Enlightenment/Age of Reason in Philosophy/Religion Details.

Environmental/Green movement: a grassroots social movement and ethic, beginning with the publication of Rachael Carson's *Silent Spring* in 1962, whose purpose is to protect and restore the natural environment from overdevelopment, deforestation, pollution and global warming and to use renewable energy to achieve a sustainable level of resource management and consumption. It incorporates elements of the Biblical ideal of stewardship, the Native-American reverence for wildlife, the American cult of nature (Charles Feidelson, R.W.B. Lewis, Henry Nash Smith), the New England Transcendentalist belief in the immanence of the divinity in nature and the conservation movement of the Progressive Era. Henry David Thoreau, John Muir and Theodore Roosevelt were early prophets and proponents of the conservation ethic. See Cult of nature and Conservation movement in Concepts and 21. New England Transcendentalism in Details.

Equal rights for all and special privileges for none: the slogan and stated objective of Jacksonian democracy of the 1820s and 1830s. The phrase originated with Thomas Jefferson. See 22. Jacksonian Democracy in Details.

Evangelicalism: see 17. Great Awakening Cycle/Revivalism in Details and Evangelicalism in Philosophy/Religion.

Expectant capitalists: those workers and entrepreneurs who believe in social mobility and the ethic of the "self-made man" and aspire to the American Dream of material success. Bray Hammond. See Horatio Alger mystique, Self-made man and Social mobility in Concepts and Entrepreneur in Economics Concepts.

Federal Highway Act (1956): one of the largest public works projects in the history of the United States. It (1) created a network of 40,000 miles of freeways and expressways, (2) fostered the growth of the automotive, tourist, travel and trucking industries and (3) accelerated the movement toward suburbanization, traffic congestion, pollution and the greater consumption of oil. See Suburbanization in Concepts and 20. American System in Details.

The Federalist **Papers**: a collection of 85 essays written by James Madison, Alexander Hamilton and John Jay in 1787-1788 to promote the ratification of the United States Constitution. According to *Federalist No. 10*, written by Madison, political divisions and "factions" (i.e., political parties) are caused by the unequal distribution of property which, in turn, is derived from the diversity of human "faculties." Thus, it acknowledged the economic and class basis of politics and ran counter to the philosophy stated in the Declaration of Independence that all men are created equal. See James Madison in Quotations and Benjamin Franklin in Economics Quotations.

The Feminine Mystique (1963): Betty Friedan's study of angst ("the problem that has no name") among post-World War II, middle-class housewives who longed for personal fulfillment outside the home. The "mystique" referred to the ideal of the Happy Housewife Heroine, which equated womanhood with housekeeping, childrearing and the avoidance of spinsterhood. The book did not address the needs of working class women who, at that time, constituted approximately one-third of the workforce and earned half of what men earned, but it helped to precipitate the second wave of feminism in the 1960s, which led to the third wave of feminism, which did address those needs, particularly those of women of color. Robert Self. See Cult of Domesticity in Concepts and 35. Feminism in Details.

Feminism: see 35. Feminism in Details.

Fire bell in the night: Thomas Jefferson's prophetic term for the explosive issue of the expansion of slavery into the western territories, which erupted during the Missouri Compromise debates of 1820. The issue was like a "fire bell in the night [which] awakened and filled me with terror. I considered it at once as the knell of the Union." The issue of slavery in the territories was not settled until forty-five years later after a long and bloody Civil War. See 24. American Civil War in Details.

Franchise: the right to vote. In the British North American colonies in the 17th and 18th Centuries, the franchise was extended only to white males who owned property and met specific religious criteria. In the United States, (1) universal white male suffrage was not achieved until the abolition of property qualifications in the early 19th Century during the era of Jacksonian democracy; (2) *de jure* (according to the law) but not *de facto* (according to actual practice) universal male suffrage was achieved after the Civil War by the 15th Amendment in 1870, but was nullified for most African-Americans in many states by poll taxes, intimidation, terrorism and other extra-legal means; (3) white female suffrage was achieved nationally during the Progressive Era with the adoption of the 19th Amendment in 1920; (4) the *de facto* right to vote was not achieved for all African-Americans until after the passage of the Voting Rights Act of 1965, and, (5) because they were subject to the military draft at the time, the right to vote was granted to those who were 18 years of age and older by the 26th Amendment in 1971.

Freedman's Bureau: a federal agency that (1) provided relief for freed slaves after the Civil War, (2) helped reunite the families of former slaves and (3), in cooperation with the American Missionary

Association, established a series of African-American schools and colleges in the South.

Freedom's ferment: an umbrella term applied to the extraordinarily rich and diverse religious, social and cultural reform movements that sprang up in the 1820s through the 1840s, including millennialism, revivalism, abolitionism, women's rights, peace, temperance, religious and utopian socialist communities, free public schools, prison reform, mesmerism, perfectionism, New England Transcendentalism and Mormonism. The ferment was an expression of resurgent cultural nationalism and was partially inspired by the social and religious fervor that had followed a series of revivals led by Charles Finney called the Second Great Awakening. Alice Felt Tyler. See Burned-over District, Oneida community and Utopian communities in Concepts and 17. Great Awakening Cycle/Revivalism and 21. New England Transcendentalism in Details.

Free public/common school movement: the movement in the 19th Century for universal, nonsectarian public education, in which children from nearly all ethnic, religious, and class backgrounds (except African-Americans) were educated together. Tax-supported public schools were seen as critical for the development of an educated, morally disciplined citizenry in a self-governing democracy and as means of providing equal opportunity for all. Horace Mann.

Free Soil Party: a political party of the late 1840s and early 1850s that opposed the extension of the plantation/slave-labor system into the western territories (i.e., those that had not yet been incorporated into the Union as states) and whose slogan was "free soil, free speech, free labor and free men." It served as a precursor to the Republican party and demonstrated the enduring power of the yeoman ideal of the small, independent family farmer. Eric Foner.

French and Indian War (1754-1763): the armed conflict between the British, the British North-American colonials and their Native-American allies, on one side, against the French and their Native-American allies, on the other, for control of the northern and central part of the North American continent. To pay for the enormous national debt resulting from the French and Indian War (also known as the Seven Years' War), the British Parliament enacted a series of relatively modest taxes on its British North American colonies, including the Stamp Act, which led to fierce colonial resistance, war and, ultimately, independence from the mother country. Francis Parkman, Edmund and Helen Morgan. See 18. American Revolution in Details.

Frontier thesis: that the American frontier promoted democracy and social equality and forged distinctive American character traits, such as individualism, optimism, materialism and practicality. Fredrick Jackson Turner, Walter Prescott Webb. See People of plenty in Concepts and 11. Frederick Jackson Turner/Frontier Thesis and 12. Counterarguments in Details.

Fugitive Slave Act (1850): a federal (i.e., national) law that upheld the rights of private property over those of personal liberty by requiring law enforcement officials everywhere, including those in states in which slavery had been abolished, to arrest anyone suspected of being a runaway slave and return that person, without trial, to his or her "master." The law provoked widespread resistance and civil disobedience in the North, the migration of free blacks and fugitives to Canada and the writing of *Uncle Tom's Cabin* by Harriet Beecher Stowe.

Gays in American history: Barry Adam, David Carter, Nicholas Edsall, Lillian Faderman and Stuart Timmons, Jonathan Katz, Norman O. Self. See Stonewall Riots in Concepts.

Geographical determinism: a school of thought that asserts that climate, natural resources and geography are the foundations of a natural economy, which, in turn, shapes and determines a culture. See 8. Geographical Determinism in Details.

G. I. Bill of Rights: legislation that provided low-cost mortgages and educational assistance to World War II veterans. It allowed over eight million veterans to attend college or receive vocational training, which promoted social mobility, democratized what had been an upper-class privilege and, in general, elevated and enriched the culture.

Gilded Age (1865-1900): Mark Twain's term for the post-Civil War period, which was characterized by political corruption, economic inequality, urban poverty and the accumulation and display of great wealth.

Gospel of Wealth (1889): the title of an essay by the steel magnate Andrew Carnegie in which he advanced his philosophy that it is the responsibility of men of wealth to find socially useful purposes for their riches. Carnegie (1) established a series public libraries throughout the country; (2) condemned the selfishness of millionaires who amassed great fortunes and lived ostentatiously and (3) favored high estate and progressive income taxes. In his words, "he who dies rich, dies disgraced." When asked why he didn't use part of his fortune to ameliorate the lives of his workers and their families, he responded that increased wages would only be "frittered away" on better food and clothing. See Homestead strike in Concepts.

Great Awakening cycle/revivalism: see 17. Great Awakening Cycle/Revivalism in Details.

Great Gatsby curve: a graph that depicts the declining social mobility and increasing income inequality in the United States compared to that of other developed countries. Alan Krueger, Miles Corak. See Economic inequality/concentration of wealth and Social mobility in Concepts.

Great Migration: the internal migration of six million African-Americans from the rural South to the Northern industrial cities between 1915 and 1970, which laid the foundation for the civil rights/black freedom movement in the North. Ira Berlin, Isabel Wilkerson. See 32. Civil Rights/Black Freedom Movement in Details.

Habit of introspection versus **longing for community**: two contradictory but commonly held American cultural traits, which is the inherent conflict between individualism and the need for community. Norman Holmes Pearson, Phillip Slater, William Tilden, Alexis de Tocqueville. See Individualism and Pursuit of loneliness in Concepts and 3. Alexis de Tocqueville in Details.

Headright system: the 17th Century practice of granting 50 acres of land to anyone who would pay for the transportation of a laborer or an indentured servant to the British colonies. It laid the foundation for class antagonism between wealthy landowners and landless servants, since there was little social mobility for the latter. See Indentured servants and Social mobility in Concepts.

Hideous and desolate wilderness (". . . full of wilde beasts and wilde men"): William Bradford's description of his first impression of New England, as recorded in his Journal (1620-1635). It served as a counter-image to America as garden of the world. See Cult of nature in Concepts and 6. American Exceptionalism in Details.

Holy Commonwealth: the New England Puritans' term for their Massachusetts Bay Colony, which was to be as a "Citty upon a Hill," a holy city of God on earth. Perry Miller, Stow Persons,

Herbert Schneider. See John Winthrop in Quotations and 6. American Exceptionalism and 10. Puritanism in Details.

Homestead Act (1862): federal legislation that, eventually, provided for the distribution of 270 million acres of federal lands (which constituted more than 10% of the land area of the United States), in 160-acre, quarter-square-mile sections to 1.6 million homesteaders at no cost to them in return for their improving the land. It upheld the yeoman ideal of the small, independent family farmer, although it was predicated on the removal of the original Native-American inhabitants and the expropriation of their lands. See Indian Removal and Northwest Ordinance in Concepts.

Homestead Strike (1892): a labor strike in which steel workers fought a pitched battle in Homestead, Pennsylvania against Pinkerton agents hired by the Carnegie Steel Company and in which at least five were killed and dozens were wounded. The union called the strike after the chairman of the company, Henry Frick, demanded a 22% wage reduction from the workers and attempted to break the union. See *Gospel of Wealth* in Concepts.

Horatio Alger mystique: the cultural archetype of the self-made man; the "rags to riches" theme of a person of humble origins who, through self-improvement, hard work and good moral character, becomes wealthy and successful. The myth is named after the Harvard educated author of a series of popular dime novels of the 19th Century, such as *Ragged Dick* (1868), whose characters rise from poverty and obscurity because of their luck, pluck, bravery and honesty, as much as their hard work, and, more importantly, because of the pivotal assistance of an older, wealthy patron. See the Self-made man/rags-to-riches and Social mobility in Concepts.

House Committee on Un-American Activities: a congressional committee of the 1940s and 1950s that was dedicated to rooting out disloyalty and internal communist subversion in the United States. See McCarthyism, Paranoid style in American politics and Red Scare/Palmer Raids in Concepts and 31. Cold War in Details.

How the Other Half Lives (1890): the title of a book by Jacob Riis that described life in the New York tenements in the 1880s.

Ideal of popular literacy and a learned clergy: the cultural standard of common literacy and a college-educated clergy, which was derived from the Protestant emphasis on written scripture as a means to personal salvation. In the British North-American colonies, 130 of the Puritan immigrants in the Great Migration of the 1630s were graduates of Cambridge University, and the ideal led to the founding of common schools and colonial colleges such as Harvard, Yale and Princeton. Clinton Rossiter. See Free public/common school movement in Concepts and 10. Puritanism in Details.

Immigration: see 14. Immigration in Details.

Indentured servants: those who contracted to work without wages, usually for four to seven years, in return for transportation to America and food and clothing while indentured. Outside of New England, at least half of English immigrants to the British colonies were indentured servants. It is estimated that less than 5% of indentured servants rose to the middle class in the colonial era. Clinton Rossiter, Abbott Smith. See Headright system in Concepts.

Indian Removal/Trail of Tears: the forced removal and migration in the 1830s of 20,000 to 60,000 Native Americans of five tribes (Cherokee, Chickasaw, Choctaw, Creek and Seminole) from the Southeastern United States to Oklahoma in order to open their tribal lands for land speculation, cotton cultivation and the plantation system. It is estimated that 8,000 to 16,000 Native Americans died during the removal. John Ehle, Wilbur Jacobs.

Individualism: an American cultural value and trait. It is associated with self-reliance, social and geographical mobility, the ideal of the self-made man and the distrust of collective action. The term was coined by Alexis de Tocqueville in his *Democracy in America* (1835-40), which he defined as the "feeling which deposes each citizen to isolate himself from the mass of his fellows and withdraw. . . . . He gladly leaves the greater society to look for itself." See Antinomian personality, Double potentiality, Pursuit of loneliness and Rugged individualism in Concepts and 3. Alexis de Tocqueville, 11. Frederick Jackson Turner/Frontier Thesis and 21. New England Transcendentalism in Details and Narcissism of small differences in Psychology Concepts. For economic individualism, see 3. Conservatism: Laissez-faire/Economic Individualism in Political Science Details and 3. Adam Smith/Classical/Free Market Economics in Economics Details.

Industrial Revolution: see 8. Industrial Revolution in Economics Details. Samuel Hays, Robert Wiebe.

Interstate Commerce Act (1887): legislation that established a federal commission to regulate railroads and replace their monopolistic rate-setting practices with ones that were "reasonable and just." It was one of the first federal (i.e. national) laws to regulate a private industry and represented a major departure from the laissez-faire philosophy of the time. See 4. Public Regulation Quandary in Economics Details.

Irish potato famine (1845-52): the death by starvation of at least one million Irish and the emigration of another one million, many to the United States, as a result of a potato blight. During the famine, Ireland was producing and exporting, by its absentee landlords, more than enough grain crops to feed its starving population.

Irrepressible conflict: the thesis that the Civil War was inevitable and could not have been avoided. See 24. American Civil War in Details.

Jacksonian democracy: a political movement of the 1830s and 1840s that was based on universal white male suffrage. The era was characterized by (1) greater participation by the common man (i.e., the property-less white male) in the political process; (2) the rhetorical theme of the moral restoration of the simple virtues of an agrarian republic; (3) entrepreneurial reforms against established elites ("equal rights for all and special privileges for none") and (4) the removal of Native Americans, territorial expansion and war with Mexico. See 22. Jacksonian Democracy in Details.

Japanese-American internment: the incarceration of 110,000 Japanese-Americans, including women and children, in relocation camps during World War II, based on the fear, with no evidence, that they would be disloyal and perform acts of sabotage. The United States government formally apologized to Japanese-Americans in 1988 for its "race prejudice and war hysteria" and offered reparations to the survivors.

Jeffersonian democracy: in general, the term applied to the principles and policies of the Democratic-Republican party of Thomas Jefferson, which governed from 1800 to 1824, and which was opposed by Alexander Hamilton and the Federalists. It stood for (1) a simple, agrarian republic, with civic virtue and the yeoman farmer as its cornerstones, as well as (2) the Bill of Rights and limited government, and opposed (3) a strong central government, urbanization and merchant and manufacturing elites. The term also refers to an idealized form of representative government that was to be led by a natural aristocracy of education and talent rather than by an artificial aristocracy of wealth and birth.

Jim Crow laws: a series of laws established in the South after Reconstruction (1865-1877) to enforce racial segregation and "separate but equal" facilities in public schools, public transportation, hotels, restaurants, restrooms, drinking fountains, etc. Many of these laws were not abolished until the civil rights/black freedom movement of the 1950s and 1960s. See *Brown versus Board of Education* and *Plessy versus Ferguson* in Concepts and 32. Civil Rights/Black Freedom Movement in Details.

Just and equal laws: see Mayflower Compact in Concepts.

Keayne, Robert: a prominent 17th Century Boston businessman who was fined 200 pounds in 1637 for overcharging his customers and excessive profiteering. His case illustrates the strict regulation of economic activity, including fee and price controls, imposed by local authorities in colonial America. See John Winthrop in Quotations.

King Phillip's War (1675-78): an armed conflict waged by Native-Americans against New England colonists, in which half the towns of New England were attacked, twelve were completely destroyed and the equivalent of 8% of the adult white male population was killed. The war was started by a pan-Indian alliance led by the sachem Metacomet, known as King Philip, because of the mistreatment of Native-Americans and the loss of their lands to white colonists. 5,000 Native Americans, or 25% of their population, were killed and 1,000, including women and children, were sold into slavery. Nathaniel Philbrick.

Know-Nothings: members of an anti-Catholic, anti-immigrant political party of the 1850s. It is now a generic term for nativism and xenophobia. John Higham.

Labor movement: the movement to organize and represent workers collectively by labor unions, which bargain on their behalf with employers to obtain better working conditions, higher pay and better benefits. Traditionally, a union job was a means of advancement into the middle class, with a living wage, health care insurance and a pension. At the height of union membership in the 1950s, 35% of private sector employees were represented by unions. Currently, less than 12% of the American workforce is organized and represented collectively. Historically, trade unionism was been less successful in the United States than in

Europe because of (1) the ideology of economic individualism, self-help and social mobility; the distrust of collective action; the ideal of the self-made man and the view of some workers of themselves as "expectant capitalists"; (2) religious, class, racial and ethnic divisions in the workforce (skilled versus unskilled, white versus black, native versus immigrant, Protestant versus Catholic) and (3) the rigorous legislative and judicial defense of "due process" and the sanctity of private property and the implacable hostility of laissez-faire capitalism and the pro-business state. Lizabeth Cohen, Alan Dawley, Bray Hammond, Michael Kazin, Bruce Laurie, David Montgomery, Sean Wilentz. See Noble and Holy Order of the Knights of Labor and Wobblies in Concepts; 26. Reform Darwinism in Details; Globalization and Offshore outsourcing in Economic Concepts and 26. Cultural hegemony in Sociology Concepts.

Laissez-faire capitalism: see 3. Adam Smith/Classical/Free Market Economics in Economics Details.

Leatherstocking Tales (1823-1841): a series of novels by James Fennimore Cooper which portrayed its hero, Natty Bumppo, as a mythic frontiersman, a child of nature. It served as the prototype of the American Western hero in popular culture. Richard Chase, D. H. Lawrence, R. W. B. Lewis, Henry Nash Smith.

Levittowns: post-World War II, mass-produced, suburban housing tracts and towns in New York, Pennsylvania and New Jersey. With their white picket fences and modern kitchen appliances, they served as cultural emblems of the suburbanization and middle-class prosperity of post-World War II America. See Federal Highway Act and Suburbanization in Concepts and 25. Urbanization in Details.

Lincoln, Abraham (1809-1865): the 16th President of the United States, who has been portrayed as (1) an archetypal backwoodsman, rail-splitter and self-educated country lawyer; (2) a successful corporate railroad lawyer, consummate politician and coalition builder, and (3) the national savior who led the country through a bloody civil war, preserved the Union and emancipated four million Americans from slavery. Lincoln was elected in 1860 on a platform that promised to preserve the Union and not to interfere with slavery where it then existed. Until Sherman's federal troops captured Atlanta in September 1864, Lincoln was not expected to be elected to a second term. His Gettysburg Address has been described as a semi-sacred text, along with the

Declaration of Independence and the Constitution. David Donald, Eric Foner, Doris Kearns Goodwin, James M. McPherson, Allan Nevins, Benjamin P. Thomas. See the 24. American Civil War in Details.

Log cabin: a powerful cultural and political symbol of a candidate's humble origins, which became important with the rise of the "common man" in politics and the distrust of political elites during the Jacksonian Era of the 1820s and 1830s; Daniel Webster is said to have regretted not having been born in one. See 22. Jacksonian Democracy in Details.

Lost world of Thomas Jefferson: the thesis that much of history is irretrievably lost, including that of well-documented historical figures such as Thomas Jefferson. Daniel Boorstin.

Loving versus Virginia (1967): a landmark decision by the Supreme Court that overturned laws in the United States that prohibited interracial marriage.

Ludlow Massacre (1914): an event in which the Colorado National Guard attacked a tent city of striking mine workers and their families, killing 19 to 25 people, including 2 women and 11 children. In the ensuing battle over the next ten days, an additional 50 to 174 miners, militia and camp guards were killed. It was the most violent labor conflict in American history.

Lyceum movement: a loose network of local associations in the 19th Century that offered moral, cultural and intellectual self-improvement to adults by sponsoring classes, lectures, discussions, debates, dramatic performances and musical entertainment. The lecture circuit featured figures such as Ralph Waldo Emerson, Henry David Thoreau, Oliver Wendell Holmes, Henry Ward Beecher and Horace Greeley and, later, Susan B. Anthony, Elizabeth Cady Stanton and Mark Twain. See Self-improvement in Concepts.

Lynchings: extrajudicial executions by groups or mobs. Between 1880 and 1968, approximately 4,000 African-Americans were murdered by hanging, shooting or being burned alive for violating Southern mores, some as insignificant as accidently touching a white woman. The objective was to enforce a code of white supremacy and terrorize African-Americans into submitting to a rigid caste system. Lynchings were often communal events, which were attended by large groups of people and accompanied by a festive, carnival-like atmosphere. Crystal Feimster, Eric Foner, Ida

B. Wells. See 32. Civil Rights/Black Freedom Movement in Details.

Machine in the garden: a common theme in early 19th Century American Romantic literature and art in which the image of a steam locomotive, for example, or another industrial object, rudely interrupting the bucolic tranquility of the countryside, served as a metaphor for the unwelcome intrusion of industrialism and urbanization into nature. R. W. B. Lewis, Leo Marx, Henry Nash Smith. See Cult of nature in Concepts and 16. Anti-Urban Cultural Tradition in Details.

Madisonian pluralism: the coexistence of diverse and competing political, economic, cultural and religious groups in society, each with the freedom to contribute to the marketplace of ideas, which prevents the monopoly of any one point of view; it is a philosophy that is derived from *The Federalist No. 10*, in which James Madison proposed that it is better to have many competing factions in order to prevent any one faction from dominating the political system; versus **tyranny of the majority/Lockean conformity**: coercive conformity and the regimentation of morality; see McCarthyism, Paranoid style in American history, Red Scare, Salem witch trials and Sedition Acts in Concepts and 3. Alexis de Tocqueville, 4. Consensus Schools of Historiography and 31. Cold War in Details; versus **elite pluralism**, in which economic, political, social and cultural influence is wielded asymmetrically by a few powerful groups. Stuart Hall, Joseph Stiglitz. See Cultural hegemony in Sociology Concepts and 15. Elites/ Oligarchies in Sociology Details.

Malefactors of great wealth: Theodore Roosevelt's term for the socially irresponsible rich. See *Gospel of Wealth*, Plutocracy and Robber baron thesis in Concepts.

Manifest Destiny: the 19th Century belief that it was America's divine mission to populate the North American continent, "which Providence has given us for the development of the great experiment of liberty and federated self-government entrusted to us" (John l. O'Sullivan); the slogan was used as justification for American westward territorial expansion in the 1840s and thereafter. Anders Stephanson, Albert Weinberg. See John L. O'Sullivan in Quotations; 6. American Exceptionalism and 23. Mexican-American War in Details, and *Lebensraum* in Political Science Concepts.

Marbury versus Madison (1803): the Supreme Court decision that established the principle of judicial review; that is, that the United States Supreme Court can rule whether an executive or legislative action is unconstitutional and, thus, void. See Separation of Powers in Political Science Concepts.

Marshall Plan: a program in which the United States provided $12 billion in aid to Europe for its reconstruction after World War II, partially in order to undercut the influence of the Soviet Union and prevent the spread of communism.

Mass production: the production of large quantities of standardized goods at relatively cheaper unit prices, based on the total rationalization of the production process, i.e., the specialization and division of labor, the standardization and interchangeability of parts, the moving assembly line, economies of scale and the application of scientific management principles and techniques. Industrialization and mass production, beginning in the 19th Century, made consumer goods more affordable to a larger number of people, created a mass consumer market and led to a rising standard of living and an expanding middle class. See Cult of efficiency and Scientific management in Concepts and 8. Industrial Revolution in Economics Details.

Mayflower Compact: the governing document and social compact of the Plymouth Colony, which was signed in 1620 by the adult men (both "Saints" and "Strangers," that is, Separatists and Non-Separatists) onboard the *Mayflower*. The signers pledged to "covenant and combine ourselves together into a civil body politic . . . to enact, constitute, and frame such just and equal laws . . . for the general good of the colony." It established the principles of self-government, the right to choose one's leaders and majority rule in the British North American colonies. See Pilgrims in Concepts.

McCarthyism: the term applied to the political and cultural atmosphere of the 1950s in which anti-communist paranoia, hysteria and witch hunting led many political leftists and dissidents, including those in government, entertainment and academia, to be investigated, blacklisted and terminated from their employment, often based on little or no evidence, for their alleged disloyalty, subversion and/or participation in an international communist conspiracy. See Paranoid style in American politics in Concepts and 31. Cold War in Details.

Melting pot: a popular metaphor for the assimilation and homogenization of immigrant groups in the United States, notwithstanding the class, racial and ethnic prejudice and exclusionary barriers that were directed against them. An alternative metaphor of the **"salad bowl"** more accurately represents the diversity, multiculturalism and unique contributions of ethnic groups. See 14. Immigration in Details.

Metaphor of the machine: see Machine in the garden in Concepts and 24. Information Technology/Metaphor of the Machine in Sociology Details. Henry Adams, Jacques Ellul, James Gleick, Leo Marx, Lewis Mumford.

Mexican-American War (1846-1848): see 23. Mexican-American War in Details.

Middlebrow: Van Wyck Brooks' pejorative term for popular, middle-class culture. See Popular culture in Concepts and High-, middle- and low-brow in Art Concepts.

Middle Passage: the transportation, under horrific conditions, of approximately 12 million enslaved West Africans to North and South America from the 17th through the 19th centuries, of whom an estimated 1.5 million (or 12.5%) died on the voyage. Approximately 400,000 enslaved Africans were shipped to the British North-American continental colonies that later became the United States. Ira Berlin, John Hope Franklin, Greg Grandin. See 13. American Slavery in Details.

Military-industrial-university-media complex: the central thesis of a school of thought that political and economic power in the United States is exercised in concert by an interlocking elite of political, corporate, military, academic and media leaders, who share a common world view and move easily between institutions. The complex originated in the massive public military expenditures and research and development projects during World War II and the Cold War of the 1950s and 1960s. President Dwight Eisenhower first identified the complex and named its first two components. Jane Mayer, C. Wright Mills. See Permanent warfare economy/military Keynesianism in Concepts and 15. Elites/Oligarchies in Sociology Details.

Monroe Doctrine: a pillar of American foreign policy since it was promulgated in 1823. It declared that any attempt by a European power to interfere in the affairs of any country in the Western Hemisphere would be considered an act of aggression against the United States. In effect, it defined the United States' sphere of influence as the Western Hemisphere and restricted the right of self-determination of other countries while paying homage to it.

Moral crusade/moral restoration theme: a common characteristic of middle-class reform movements of the 19th and 20th centuries, including abolitionism, Jacksonian Democracy and Progressivism, which sought to endow their social-political movements with a moral purpose and restore the imagined traditional values and virtues of an earlier era. David Donald, Richard Hofstadter, Marvin Meyers, George Mowry. See Abolitionism, Prohibition, Temperance and War on Drugs in Concepts and 22. Jacksonian Democracy and 29. Progressivism in Details.

Moral uplift: the term applied to late 19th and early 20th Century middle-class efforts to end poverty by educating and reforming the moral character of the "deserving poor" by exhorting them to abstain from drinking alcohol, practice self-discipline, develop a work ethic and practice good hygiene. See Self-improvement in Concepts.

Moving assembly line: a major component of the mass production process, which was first used in slaughterhouses in the mid-19th Century and applied by Henry Ford to the production of automobiles in 1913. See Mass production in Concepts and Industrialization in Economics.

Muckrakers: Theodore Roosevelt's pejorative term, borrowed from John Bunyan's *Pilgrim's Progress*, for reform journalists of the Progressive Era. Their articles in popular magazines such as *McClure's*, *Collier's* and *Munsey's* were exhaustively researched and exposed a variety of social ills, including (1) political corruption in cities, the United States Senate and trusts such as Standard Oil and the Central Pacific Railroad; (2) child labor abuses; (3) life in the slums; (4) unsafe and unsanitary working conditions in the meat packing and other industries, and (5) dangerous and unsafe foods and patent medicines. Reform journalists had a profound impact on the national conscience and inspired the passage of many Progressive reforms. See 29. Progressivism in Details.

Mugwumps: Republican middle-class patrician reformers who opposed political corruption in their own party by voting for the Democratic Presidential candidate in 1884 and, later, initiated and supported Progressive reforms. Generally, the term applies to a high-minded reformer who places principle over patronage and political allegiance.

National gun culture: a culture in which the firearm is an icon, a cultural symbol, an expression of national identity and an emblem of manhood and personal freedom, as well as an implement of violence and death. Only 15% of families in colonial America owned firearms, and half of those were in disrepair. It was not until the Colt revolver replaced the knife in the years before and since the Civil War that the gun culture was established and the homicide rate rose dramatically. Today there are approximately 300 million firearms in the United States and an annual death rate by firearms of approximately 30,000. It has been estimated that more Americans have died from guns in the last 45 years than in all the wars since the American Revolution. Michael Bellesiles.

Nationalism: the identification with, and sense of belonging to, a particular nation or group; a shared sense of national identity; also, the aggressive promotion of the interests of one nation at the expense of others. See 19. Origins of American Nationalism in Details.

Native-American Shoah (from the Hebrew word for "catastrophe," the term originally used to describe the genocide of six million Jews during the Second World War): the catastrophic reduction in the population of indigenous people in North and South America by 40 to 100 million people (or 90% of the pre-Columbian population) within 130 years of European colonization by diseases, warfare, slavery, brutality and overwork. In New England, the plagues of 1614-1620 along the Atlantic coast killed tens of thousands of Native-Americans and led to the abandonment of hundreds of villages, which permitted the English colonization of the coastal areas (Governor Bradford attributed the plagues to "the good hand of God," which "favored our beginnings" by "sweeping away great multitudes of the natives . . . that he might make room for us"). Woodrow Borah, Sherburne Cook, William Cronin, William Denevan, F. H. Dobyns, Elizabeth Fenn, Wilbur Jacobs, Charles Mann, Nathaniel Philbrick, Russell Thornton.

Nativism/xenophobia: anti-immigrant and anti-Catholic prejudice. John Higham. See Know Nothings in Concepts.

Natural aristocracy of education and talent versus **artificial aristocracy of birth and wealth**: Thomas Jefferson's distinction between an educated elite, or meritocracy, and an elite based on birth and wealth. See Plutocracy in Concepts and Technocracy in Political Science Concepts.

Natural laws: the universal laws of nature discovered through human reason and science, which provide the basis for the social compact and natural rights. Thomas Aquinas, John Locke, Isaac Newton. See Enlightenment in Concepts.

Natural rights: universal rights based on natural laws, which exist prior to, and independent of, the state's authority to grant them, such as the right of self-government. Thomas Jefferson, John Locke, Thomas Paine, Jean Jacques Rousseau. See 27. 18th Century Enlightenment in Philosophy/Religion Details.

Neo-Conservatism: a political movement and school of thought that began in the latter third of the 20th Century. It was composed of "defense intellectuals" who opposed détente with the Soviet Union, supported the Vietnam War and endorsed the preemptive invasion of Iraq in 2003. Its organization, the Project for the New American Century, advocated American military intervention to "challenge regimes hostile to our interests" and to promote "political and economic freedom abroad." It represented a combination of preemptive militarism and Wilsonian idealism and has been described as seeking to "spread democracy by the sword" and, not incidentally, to obtain oil and extend American influence in the Middle East. See Bush Doctrine in Concepts and 6. American Exceptionalism in Details and 3. Conservatism in Political Science Details.

New Deal (1933-45): the name given to the relief, recovery and reform programs of the Franklin Roosevelt administration during the Great Depression. See 30. New Deal in Details.

New England: a term that was first used in 1616 by Captain John Smith and now applies to a region that consists of the states of Connecticut, Maine, Massachusetts, New Hampshire, Rhode Island and Vermont. The region was initially settled by dissenting Protestants, such as Pilgrims, Puritans and Presbyterians, and the primary basis of its economy was the family farm, as well as fishing, shipping and commerce. In contrast, the coastal regions of Virginia and other Southern states were generally settled by members of the established Church of England, and its economy was based on commercial cash crops such as tobacco, rice, indigo and cotton, which were cultivated on large plantations or estates and employed hired, indentured and slave labor.

New England town meeting: an early and enduring American form of direct democracy in which town members meet periodically to discuss local issues and vote on legislative, administrative and budgetary matters. Frank Bryan. See Greek democracy in Political Science Concepts.

New England Transcendentalism: a literary and philosophical movement during the first half of the 19th Century that celebrated individualism ("enjoy an original relation with the universe"), self-reliance ('trust thyself') and the sublimity and immanence of the divinity in nature. Ralph Waldo Emerson, Margaret Fuller, Henry David Thoreau; Perry Miller. See 21. New England Transcendentalism in Details.

Niagara Movement: a civil rights organization founded in 1905 in Fort Erie, Ontario, near Niagara Falls, by W. E. B. Du Bois and others who sought to end racial segregation. It led to the creation of the National Association for the Advancement of Colored People in 1910 and laid the foundation for the civil rights/black freedom movement of the 1950s and 1960s. See 32. Civil Rights/Black Freedom Movement in Details.

Nineteenth Amendment (1920): an amendment to the U. S. Constitution that extended the right to vote to women. See 35. Feminism in Details.

Noble and Holy Order of the Knights of Labor (founded in 1869): a large, inclusive union for all workers, including African-Americans and women; versus **American Federation of Labor** (1881), a federation of craft unions of skilled workers, mostly white men, organized exclusively by craft, e.g., bricklayers, carpenters, cigar-makers, teamsters; versus **Congress of Industrial Organizations** (1936), a federation of industrial unions that was organized by industry, e.g., auto workers, mine workers, steel workers, and was less exclusionary of African-Americans and women than the AFL. See Labor movement and Wobblies in Concepts.

Noble savage myth: the cultural stereotype of the indigenous, hunter-gatherer as nature's nobleman; the belief that people in a state of nature are essentially good and possess a natural, innate moral sense; James Fenimore Cooper, John Dryden, Jean Jacques Rousseau; versus **the Hobbesian thesis**: that people in a state of nature are in a state of "perpetual war of every man against his neighbor" and lead a life that is "solitary, poor, nasty, brutish and short"; Thomas Hobbes, Francis Parkman, Steven Pinker. See 12. Violence and Human Nature (the Hobbes-Rousseau Dichotomy) in Anthropology Details.

Nonconformists: Puritans (Congregationalists and Presbyterians), Separatists, Baptists, Quakers and other dissenters who did not follow the practices of the established Church of England. See 10. Puritanism in Details.

Northern industrial wage slavery: the term used by John C. Calhoun in his argument in defense of Southern chattel slavery, in which he argued for the superiority of slavery over the wage labor system of industrial capitalism, since the former provided food, clothing, housing, medical care and old age relief to the slave family, while the latter only provided a subsistence wage to the worker.

Observations Concerning the Increase of Mankind (1755): Benjamin's Franklin's demographic study on the exponential population growth of the British North American colonies. His essay influenced Thomas Malthus' *An Essay on the Principle of Population* in 1798, which, in turn, influenced Charles Darwin's theory of evolution. Overpopulation and zero-population growth is discussed in Economics Concepts.

Oneida community: a utopian community of Perfectionists, which was founded in 1848 by John Humphrey Noyes in upstate New York. It was based on the principles of gender equality, shared labor and child-rearing, mutual criticism and "complex marriage," in which each woman was the wife of every man and vice versa. Alice Felt Tyler. See Freedom's ferment and Utopian communities in Concepts.

The Other America (1962): the title of Michael Harrington's study on poverty in the United States, which influenced President Lyndon Johnson's War on Poverty. Currently, approximately 15% of Americans (or 45 million people) live in a state of poverty. See *How the Other Half Lives* in Concepts and Culture of Poverty in Sociology.

Our detached and distant situation: George Washington's term for the United States' unique geographical location, which, throughout American history, has fostered a sense of isolation and moral superiority to Old World-style intrigue and warfare. See 6. American Exceptionalism and 8. Geographical Determinism in Details.

Paradox of want in the midst of plenty: the continuing existence of poverty and inequality in a land of extraordinary abundance. Henry George, Michael Harrington, David Potter. See Economic inequality/concentration of wealth, *The Other America*, People of Plenty and Social mobility in Concepts.

Paranoid style in American politics: a common theme, a style of thought and a major psychological undercurrent in the American political tradition. Historically, it was expressed in (1) colonial resistance to Parliamentary taxation after the French and Indian War (1754-1763) to pay off the enormous British war debt, which led to the American Revolution; (2) the antebellum South's fear of a "Black Republican" party plot to incite slave rebellions and abolish slavery; (3) the post-Civil War South's fear of African-Americans' social and political power; (4) the Populist's belief that economic depressions were caused by an international conspiracy of bankers and Jews; (5) the popular belief that munitions-makers started the First World War; (6) the fear and paranoia of an internal Communist conspiracy and domestic subversion during the McCarthy era and the Cold War of the 1950s and 1960s and (7) the Islamophobia that followed the September 11, 2001 attacks on the World Trade Center and the Pentagon. Daniel Bell, Richard Hofstadter, Kathryn Olmstead, William Tilden. See McCarthyism, Red Scare, Salem Witch Trials and Sedition Acts of 1798 and 1918 in Concepts and Litigious paranoia in Psychology Concepts.

Partus sequitur ventrem ("that which is brought forth follows the womb"): the legal doctrine that, in contrast to the practice in English common law, the children of a slave mother and a white father in the United States must take the legal status of the mother not the father, which condemned the children of such unions, and their descendants, to a lifetime of involuntary servitude.

Peculiar institution: a euphemism for slavery that was used by Southern apologists, since the word "slavery' was often banned from public discourse. Kenneth Stampp. See 13. American Slavery in Details.

Penny press: the term applied to mass circulation newspapers that were introduced in the 1830s and were addressed to urban, working class audiences and supported by advertising rather than by subscription. Paul Starr.

People of plenty: David Potter's term for a culture based on material abundance and rich natural resources (which he called "physical potentialities"). Potter's thesis is an extension of Fredrick Jackson Turner's frontier thesis that westward expansion and the promise of "free land" symbolized unlimited opportunity and fostered the development of such American cultural traits as individualism, practicality, optimism, a belief in the equality of opportunity, geographical mobility, social fluidity, prodigality and wastefulness and, because of the relative scarcity and high cost of labor (in relation to the abundance of nature resources), labor-saving technological innovations. See 2. American Cultural Values and Traits and 11. Fredrick Jackson Turner/Frontier Thesis in Details. Potter's thesis runs counter to the intractable fact of poverty in the United States and the paradox of want in the midst of plenty. See Economic inequality/concentration of wealth, Paradox of want in the midst of plenty, *The Other America* and Social mobility in Concepts and 5. Conflict Schools of American Historiography in Details.

Permanent warfare economy/military Keynesianism: the theory that (1) the economic recovery from the Great Depression in the United States was caused by the massive federal military expenditures of World War II, beginning with the Lend Lease program in 1941, and (2) the economic prosperity and technological innovations in the decades following World War II, including the Cold War *mentalité* supporting foreign military interventions, were driven by massive public expenditures on defense industries, the space race, regional wars and the military-industrial-university-media complex. Norman Chomsky, Michael Kidron, C. Wright Mills, Rebecca Thorpe. See the Military-industrial-university-media complex in Concepts and the Rise and fall of great powers: the 16th Century Spanish paradigm in Historiography Concepts.

Philippine-American War (1899-1902): the guerrilla war for Philippine independence in which approximately 4,200 U. S. soldiers and 34,000 to 220,000 Filipinos died. It was characterized by the forced removal of civilians to "protection zones," atrocities, torture and the "water cure," and served as the prototype for asymmetrical warfare (*q.v.* in Concepts), including that of the Vietnam War.

Physiocrats: 18th-Century French economic theorists who held that land and agriculture were the sole sources of a nation's wealth. See Thomas Jefferson in Quotations.

Pilgrims: Brownists/Separatists who founded the Plymouth Colony in 1620 (as distinct from the vastly larger and wealthier group of Puritans who founded Massachusetts Bay Colony to the north in Boston in 1630-40 and formally remained as members of the Church of England, but sought to reform it from within of its "papist' influences). Of 102 "saints" and "strangers" (i.e., Separatists and Non-Separatists) who landed in Plymouth in 1620, only 50 survived the first year, and those only because of the kindness of local Native-Americans. The Pilgrims have been portrayed as a hapless, godly little community, a commonwealth of believers, and have played an iconic role in America's founding mythology. Plymouth Colony was later absorbed into the larger Massachusetts Bay Colony. Nathaniel Philbrick. See King Phillip's War and Mayflower Compact in Concepts.

Plaine style: a style of writing and speaking adopted by Puritans and Quakers that was simple, direct and unadorned; the term was also applied to their mode of dress, style of life and general aesthetic.

Plantation system: an economic system based on large, landed estates that used indentured or slave labor to produce cash crops such as tobacco, rice, sugar and cotton. The Northern opposition to the expansion of slavery into the western territories was based as much on the opposition to the plantation/slave-labor system and the support for the yeoman ideal of the small, family freehold system as it was on the opposition to the moral evil of slavery itself. See Agrarian/yeoman ideal and Free Soil in Concepts and 24. American Civil War in Details.

Planter class: generally, a socio-economic group composed of those who owned a plantation and 20 or more slaves. On the eve of the Civil War, approximately 50,000, or a little less than $2/10^{th}$ of 1 percent of the white population, owned 20 or more slaves, yet this class dominated the country's political economy and controlled many of its opinion- and decision-making institutions. See 13. American Slavery and 24. American Civil War in Details and Cultural hegemony in Sociology Concepts.

Plessy versus Ferguson (1896): the Supreme Court decision that upheld the constitutionality of "separate but equal" racial segregation in public places. It was not overturned until *Brown versus Board of Education* in 1954 and the Civil Rights Act of 1964. See *Brown versus Board of Education* and Jim Crow laws in Concepts and 32. Civil Rights/Black Freedom Movement in Details.

Plutocracy: a form of government in which power is held by the wealthy, both (1) directly through their influence in the government (by campaign contributions to candidates and causes [primarily through super PACs], lobbying, providing jobs to former government officials, and serving as members of Congress, ambassadors and other government officials) and (2) indirectly through their influence in the media and opinion-, policy- and decision-making institutions, such as think tanks, journals, academic programs, fellowships and advocacy and "grass-roots" organizations, the funding for which is channeled through private, tax-exempt political foundations. According to John Jay, the first Chief Justice of the Supreme Court, "the people who own the country ought to govern it." Currently, nearly half the members of congress are millionaires. With the Supreme Court decision in *Citizens United* in 2010 and the advent of super PACs (political action committees), the top 100 super PAC donors accounted for more than 60% of the $349 million raised in the 2012 election. The condition reflects the contradiction in American values between the ideal of social and political equality and the reality of economic and political inequality. David Brock, Jane Mayer, Kevin Phillips. See Economic inequality/concentration of wealth in Concepts and Donor class, Patronage system and Super PACs in Political Science Concepts and Louis Brandeis in Political Science Quotations.

Popular culture: folk, popular and mass cultures, which are often described in terms of their opposition to elite or high culture ("high brow," "middle brow" and "low brow" are derived from the pseudo-scientific study of phrenology in 19th Century). Historically, popular culture has been expressed through such varied media as almanacs, sermons, agricultural fairs, husking bees, country music, the penny press, minstrel shows, carnivals, vaudeville, ragtime, jazz, nickelodeons, movies, radio, television, magazines, popular music, rock and roll, rap and hip-hop, breakdancing, celebrity journalism, tabloids, electronic social media, etc. Herbert Gans, Clifford Geertz, John Kouwenhoven, Dwight Macdonald, Bernard Rosenberg and Daniel Manning White, Jane and Michael Stern, Alexis de Tocqueville, James Twitchell.

Populism (1890s): an agrarian political movement that grew out of the economic depression of the 1890s and was led by Midwestern wheat and Southern cotton farmers. Although it was viewed at the time as an expression of agrarian radicalism and dismissed by its opponents as "hayseed socialism," the People's Party advocated many political, economic and social reforms (including a graduated income tax, the right of workers to organize and bargain collectively and an eight-hour day) that were later adopted by Progressivism and the New Deal. "Populist" is now a generic term that is used to describe a popular or radical leader of the political left or right who speaks, in some contexts demagogically, against elites and on behalf of ordinary people. Lawrence Goodwyn, John Hicks, Richard Hofstadter, Michael Kazin. See 28. Populism in Details.

Positive central state: the central feature of political philosophies that support a strong, national government to promote social and economic progress, provide for the national defense, insure the common welfare and redress social injustice. It was a central component of Progressivism (1890-1920), and New Deal and post-New Deal liberalism (1933-1968). Alexander Hamilton, Herbert Croly, Lester Ward; Theodore Roosevelt, Woodrow Wilson, Franklin D. Roosevelt, Harry Truman, John F. Kennedy, Lyndon B. Johnson; see 20. American System, 26. Reform Darwinism, 28. Populism, 29. Progressivism and 30. New Deal in Details; versus **laissez-faire individualism**: an economic and political philosophy that advocates minimum governmental regulation and taxation and enshrines political liberty and economic individualism as the basis of economic progress. William Graham Sumner, Herbert Hoover, Ayn Rand, Barry Goldwater, Ronald Reagan. See Rugged individualism in Concepts; 25. Social Darwinism in Details; 3. Adam Smith/Classical/Free Market Economics in Economics Details; Libertarianism in Political Science Concepts and 3. Conservatism in Political Science Details.

Possession by right of first occupancy versus **the Biblical injunction to subdue and till the earth**: the former is a property right established in English common law; the latter was used to rebut the common law doctrine and justify the expropriation of Native-American lands by European-Americans, since Native-Americans, generally, were nomadic hunter-gatherers who did not farm or "subdue the earth." Possession by right of first occupancy was later re-asserted by European-Americans against other European-Americans as the basis for preemption, or "squatters' rights," in the settlement of the American West. William Cronon.

Post-Enlightenment: a term applied to the 20th and 21th Centuries, a period that is said to be characterized by the erosion of the Enlightenment values of reason, order, optimism, secularism and faith in science, human progress and social improvement. The *zeitgeist* is thought to be the result of 20th Century world wars, mass movements, totalitarianism, genocide, the threat of nuclear annihilation and the rise of religious fundamentalism. See Neo-Orthodoxy in Philosophy/Religion, 4. Sigmund Freud in

Psychology Details and 16. Mass Society and 17. Erich Fromm in Sociology Details.

Post-industrialism: the term applied to the national economy of the late 20th and early 21th Centuries, which is characterized by the shift from manufacturing to service- and knowledge-based industries, and is accompanied by the loss of well-paid unionized jobs, offshore outsourcing of industries and decreased opportunities for workers to advance into the middle class. Daniel Bell, Paul Romer.

Pragmatic versus **utopian liberalism**: two separate strands of American progressivism: (1) **pragmatic reformers** are described as practical, realistic and, if necessary, willing to compromise and accept limited, incremental reforms, while (2) **utopian reformers** are characterized as idealistic and uncompromising and seek to achieve broader, more inclusive social reforms. The former accepts a half-loaf of reform, while the latter demands the whole loaf. The two traditions are somewhat analogous to Max Weber's **ethics of responsibility** versus the **ethics of ultimate ends**. The categories are relative and time-bound since reforms which are termed "utopian" in one generation (e.g., the abolition of slavery, the 8-hour day, child labor laws, the right of women to vote, social security, medical insurance) are often taken for granted in the next. The division between pragmatic realists and ideological purists is also found among political conservatives. Daniel Aaron, Michael Kazin, Christopher Lasch, Vernon Louis Parrington, Arthur Schlesinger, Max Weber.

Preemptive war: the use of military force by one nation against another nation that is perceived to be a potential or perceived threat to it. The doctrine was used by the United States to justify its invasion of Iraq in 2003. See Bush Doctrine and Neo-Conservatism.

Primogeniture and entail: the exclusive right of the eldest son to inherit his family's estate in tact; a method for perpetuating a landed aristocracy. The practice was largely abolished in the United States by the late 18th and early 19th Centuries. See Absence of feudalism and hereditary stratifications in Concepts.

Progressivism (1900-1920): a middle-class reform movement that implemented a wide range of social and political reforms, including anti-trust legislation, women's suffrage, child labor laws, workplace safety regulations, pure food and drug laws, prohibition of the sale of alcohol, the national regulation of banking and

interstate commerce and the conservation of natural resources. See
29. Progressivism in Details and 5. Progressivism/Liberalism in
Political Science Details.

Prohibition (1920-1933): a "noble experiment" (according to Herbert
Hoover) in moral and social engineering that was authorized by the
18th Amendment to the U. S. Constitution and later repealed by the
21th Amendment. It prohibited the "manufacture, sale, or
transportation [but not consumption] of intoxicating liquors" and
was accompanied by social resistance, the breakdown of traditional
moral standards, political corruption, organized crime and the
wholesale evasion of the law. Frederick Lewis Allen, William
Leuchtenburg, Lisa McGirr, James Timberlake, Sarah Tracy and
Caroline Acker. See Alcoholic republic, Temperance movement
and War on drugs in Concepts and 29. Progressivism in Details.

Projects for the improvement of mankind: Benjamin Franklin's term
for projects that contribute to human progress and social
improvement. After retiring at the age of 42 from a successful
career as a printer, writer and publisher, Franklin devoted the rest
of his life to public service, scientific studies and "projects for the
improvement of mankind." These included the inventions of the
lighting rod, an improved stove, bifocals and swim fins;
demographic and time-and-motion studies; a subscription library;
fire insurance and participation in the drafting of the Declaration of
Independence and the U. S. Constitution. Franklin embodies the
18th Century Enlightenment ideals of human reason, science,
progress and social improvement.

Prostitution: the profession of an estimated 5% to 10% of the women
in American cities in the late 19th Century. It was largely
criminalized between 1910-1915 through the efforts of the
Women's Christian Temperance Union. Ruth Rosen.

Providential conception of American history: the belief that
American history has been guided by God. George Bancroft. See
6. American Exceptionalism in Details.

Public rights: those that are asserted in opposition to private property
rights, as when, for example, in 1739, Ben Franklin and his
neighbors petitioned the Pennsylvania Assembly to prohibit a
Philadelphia tannery from dumping its wastes in public spaces.

Puritanism: an Anglo-American form of Calvinism. Non-separating
Congregationalists and Presbyterians were nonconformists who
sought to reform the Church of England from within and purge it
of its "papist" influences. 20,000 Puritans founded Massachusetts

Bay Colony in the Great Migration from 1630 to 1640. See New England in Concepts and 10. Puritanism in Details.

Pursuit of loneliness/bowling alone: a metaphor for the lack of sense of community, civic engagement and political involvement in American society. Alexis Tocqueville; Norman Holmes Pearson, Robert Putnam, Philip Slater, William Tilden. See Habit of Introspection and Individualism in Concepts and 3. Alexis de Tocqueville in Details.

Quiet desperation: Henry David Thoreau's term for his countrymen's "desperate haste" in their obsessive pursuit of material success. See 2. American Cultural Values and Traits and 3. Alexis de Tocqueville in Details and 16. Mass Society and 17. Erich Fromm in Sociology Details.

Racism: the personal, institutional and, often, legally-sanctioned prejudice by one race or ethnic group against another. Historically, in the United States, it was manifested in chattel slavery, the forced removal of Native-Americans to reservations, violence, exclusion, racial segregation, xenophobia, deportations, job discrimination, lynchings, disenfranchisement, anti-Semitism, internment and ethnic profiling.

Railroad land grants: approximately 175 million acres of federal and state public lands, which represented a land area greater than 8% of the lower continental United States, that were given to private railroad companies by federal and state governments in the 19th Century to spur economic development and build the physical infrastructure for an integrated national economy. The practice contradicted the laissez-faire ideology of classical economics and was accompanied by widespread corruption, mismanagement and inefficiency (much of the original tracks and road beds were so poorly constructed that they had to be rebuilt), as well as financial speculation, panics and, eventually, the bankruptcy of many railroads. Richard White. See Transportation Revolution in Concepts and 20. American System in Details.

Red Scare/Palmer Raids (1919-1920): a series of police raids, arrests and mass deportations that were a manifestation of the nativism and anti-radical hysteria that erupted after the First World War. The climate of fear was a response to (1) a series of post-war labor strikes, (2) anarchist and socialist agitation, (3) the dread of a spreading Bolshevik Revolution, and (4) a series of bombs directed at prominent business and political leaders, including U. S. Attorney General Mitchell Palmer. Between 3,000 to 10,000 leftists were arrested, often without due process, and over 500 were deported. The Red Scare served as a precedent for the Second Red Scare of the McCarthy era in the 1950s. Murray B. Levin. See McCarthyism and Paranoid style in American politics in Concepts and 31. Cold War in Details.

Reform Darwinism: a series of late 19th and early 20th Century counter-theories to Social Darwinism. They proposed that (1) group-level selection, social cooperation and altruism are as important in human evolution as competition and economic individualism, and (2) "genetic" (i.e., biological) evolution has been replaced by "telic" (i.e., social and purposeful) evolution, in which humans can collectively plan and control their own destinies, reform society and end social injustices through collective action and the positive liberal state. Eric Goldman, Richard Hofstadter. See 25. Social Darwinism and 26. Reform Darwinism in Details.

Refrigerated railroad car: introduced in 1880, it permitted the nationalization of the meat-packing industry in the Midwest and the year-round shipments of fruits and vegetables from Florida and the West Coast to the rest of the country, which spurred economic development in those areas.

Religious toleration: the peaceful coexistence of people with different religious beliefs. The Protestant Reformation's emphasis on written scripture as a means to personal salvation and the absence of the absolute doctrinal authority of the Roman Catholic Church led to an endless series of Protestant fissions and schisms, many over minor doctrinal issues, and the proliferation of many denominations and sects. The multiplicity of Protestant denominations led, eventually, to coexistence, religious toleration and, finally, the separation of church and state. The process was summarized in Voltaire's observation that "if there were only one religion in England there would be danger of despotism, if there were two, they would cut each other's throats, but there are thirty, and they live in peace and happiness." See Soul libertie in Concepts and Secularism in Philosophy/Religion Concepts.

Right of self-determination: a fundamental principle of American foreign policy, which is enshrined in the Monroe Doctrine, Open Door Notes, Wilson's Fourteen Points, and the Truman, Nixon and Bush Doctrines. Ironically, the principle has been used by the

United States to justify its military intervention and covert action in other countries. George Kennan. See Monroe Doctrine in Concepts.

Robber baron thesis: that capitalists are river-boat gamblers, speculators, pirates and predators, rather than heroes, producers, the "fittest" or the elect; Matthew Josephson, Thorstein Veblen; versus the **entrepreneurial thesis**: that entrepreneurs are the driving force for technological innovation and economic progress; Joseph Schumpeter. See 15. Joseph Schumpeter/Creative Destruction in Economics Details.

Rugged individualism: the term coined by Herbert Hoover to contrast the American tradition of self-reliance with the "European philosophy" of paternalism and state socialism. Hoover used the concept to justify his laissez-faire economic policies and to deny direct federal assistance to those who were devastated by the Great Depression.

Salem witch trials (1692-93): an episode of mass hysteria in colonial New England in which 20 women and men were hanged or pressed to death for witchcraft. Additionally, according to a contemporary account, more than 150 were imprisoned, another 200 were accused and fifty confessed to witchcraft but were not executed. The convictions were based on **spectral evidence** in which witnesses for the prosecution testified that the devil appeared to them as an apparition in the image of the accused, based on the assumption that the devil could not have done so without the permission or cooperation of the accused. The witch trials have been used as a historical metaphor to describe the public paranoia and hysteria during the Red Scare of 1919-1920 and the McCarthy era of the 1950s. See Paranoid style in American politics.

Salutary neglect: Edmund Burke's term for England's relatively benign administration of its North American colonies, a policy that was reinforced by the difficulty in traveling and communicating across 3,000 miles of Atlantic Ocean. It facilitated colonial self-government and, later, the movement for independence from the mother country. See 8. Geographical Determinism in Details.

Scarcity of labor and abundance of land/natural resources: one of the causal factors in the impetus for technological innovation in the United States, particularly for labor-saving devices. See Cult of efficiency and Scientific management in Concepts and 11. Frederick Jackson Turner/Frontier Thesis in Details.

Science of human relationships: see Franklin Roosevelt in Quotations.

Scientific management: the cult of efficiency, which originated in Benjamin Franklin's time-and-motion studies on street cleaning and stockade building in the 18th Century and F. W. Taylor's industrial studies in the early 20th Century. Its objectives were, and are, to increase productivity, reduce costs and maximize efficiency by rationalizing the production process and standardizing the most minute sub-divisions of the workflow. Using his stopwatch, Taylor sought to eliminate waste and improve productivity by systematically breaking down each industrial task into its individual components. He taught a Dutchman named Schmidt, for example, how to shovel 47 tons of pig iron a day instead of 12 ½ tons by carefully specifying size of the shovel, the weight of the scoop, the arc of the swing, etc. (Schmidt's thoughts on the subject, apparently, were never recorded). Franklin's and Taylor's principles are now enshrined in nearly every industry, and their influence can be seen today at any fast food restaurant, discount store or warehouse distribution center. Daniel Bell, Samuel Haber, William Tilden. See Protestant ethic and Specialization and division of labor in Economics Concepts, 6. Freud's Anal Personality Traits in Psychology Details and 24. Information Technology/Metaphor of the Machine in Sociology Details.

Scopes Trial (1925): a celebrated trial in which a high school science teacher was convicted of teaching Darwin's theory of evolution, which was a violation of Tennessee law. His conviction was overturned on a technicality, and fundamentalists/creationists were ridiculed and went into a period of cultural retreat until the latter part of the 20th Century.

Scotch-Irish/Ulster Scots: Anglo-Scotch Presbyterians who migrated to North America in the 18th Century from the borderlands of northern England, southern Scotland and northern Ireland. ("Scotch Irish," "Ulster Irish" and "Ulster Scots" are approximately equivalent terms and should not to be confused with Irish Catholics, who migrated to the United States from Ireland after the Great Potato Famine of the 1840s and 1850s.) The English-Scottish borderlands were inhabited by a warrior culture, and the Protestant "Scotch-Irish" who migrated to North America tended to settle in the backcountry. They were clannish, quarrelsome, fiercely proud and independent, and were known for their lack of deference to authority, suspicion of strangers and contempt for book learning. In America, they served as the archetypal frontiersmen (including Davy Crockett and Andrew Jackson) and settled in Western Pennsylvania, Appalachia and, later, the Ozarks, Oklahoma and the Central Valley of California. They were stereotyped as poor whites and hillbillies, and, in popular culture, were associated with the Bible Belt, moonshine, evangelicalism and country-and-western music. David Hackett Fischer.

Second American Revolution: Charles Beard's term for the American Civil War, which, according to him, represented the triumph of Northern industrial capitalism over Southern agrarian feudalism. See 24. American Civil War in Details.

Sectionalism: regionalism; the tensions arising from the conflicting economic and political interests of the Northeast, South, Midwest and West. See 24. American Civil War in Details.

Sedition Act (1798): legislation that made it a federal crime to criticize the President of the United States. Congressmen, citizens and journalists were fined and imprisoned for up to 18 months, one for calling President John Adams an "ass" and another for calling him a "gross hypocrite."

Sedition Act (1918): legislation that deemed disloyal and permitted the arrest for up to ten years of anyone who publically criticized the government or dissented from the war effort during the First World War. See Creel Committee in Concepts.

Self-improvement: an American cultural value and trait, which was enabled by John Locke's concept of the mind at birth as a *tabula rasa*, or blank tablet, and sanctified by the work ethic, social mobility and the American creed of equal opportunity for all. Horatio Alger, Jr., Frederick Douglass, Benjamin Franklin, Booker T. Washington. See Horatio Alger mystique, Self-made man, Table of virtues and *Tabula rasa* in Concepts and 2. American Cultural Values and Traits in Details.

Self-made man/rags-to-riches: a common theme in popular culture, which is personified by the cultural archetype of the person of humble origins who, through self-improvement, hard work and good moral character, becomes wealthy and successful. It is represented in Benjamin Franklin's *Autobiography*, Frederick Douglass' "Self-Made Men," the dime novels of Horatio Alger, Jr. and Andrew Carnegie's *Gospel of Wealth*. See Horatio Alger mystique, Social mobility and Table of virtues in Concepts.

Seneca Falls Convention (1848): the formal beginning of the women's rights movement, which included the declaration that "all men and women are created equal." See 35. Feminism in Details.

Sexuality/history of in America: J. D'Emilio and E.B. Freedman, Jonathan Katz, Ruth Rosen.

Shaker folk art: vernacular art, usually furniture and other household objects, which are characterized by their functionality, harmony, purity and simplicity. See Vernacular tradition in Concepts.

Sherman Antitrust Act (1890): landmark legislation that outlawed monopolies and other combinations that reduced competition and restrained trade. It was a major departure from the prevailing laissez faire ideology of the time. See Trust busting versus regulated monopolies/oligopolies in Concepts and 3. Adam Smith/Classical/Free Market Economics and Public Regulations Quandary in Economics Details.

Silent Spring (1962): the book by Rachael Carson that described the effects of pesticides on wildlife and launched the Environmental/Green movement (*q.v.* in Concepts).

Sir Walter Scott's Disease: Mark Twain's term for the Southern antebellum cult of chivalry and its exaggerated sense of pride and honor, which, in his view, was responsible for the American Civil War. See 24. American Civil War in Details.

Skyscraper: a term that was originally applied to tall sailing ships. One of the first terrestrial skyscrapers to use a steel frame was the 10-story Home Insurance Building in Chicago, which was built in 1885. The invention of the Otis "safety elevator" in 1852 was a prerequisite for the development of the skyscraper.

Slave revolts: armed uprisings by slaves. There were at least 250 documented cases of slave insurrections in the United States, including the German Coast/Orleans Territory slave rebellion of 1811 and those by Gabriel Prosser in Virginia in 1800, Denmark Vesey in Charleston, South Carolina in 1822 and Nat Turner in Southampton County, Virginia, in 1831. Hebert Aptheker, Edward Baptist, John Hope Franklin.

Slavery: see 13. American Slavery Details.

Sober pursuits of honest industry: the phrase used by Andrew Jackson to differentiate legitimate businesses from, and cast opprobrium on, banks and financial speculators.

Social Darwinism: a social-economic theory and world view popular in the late 19th and early 20th Centuries that was loosely based on Charles Darwin's theory of evolution, the struggle for existence and the survival of the fittest. According to the tenets of Social Darwinism, the richest are the fittest, and philanthropy and social reforms are futile since they interfere with natural laws and permit the poor and "unfit" to reproduce, thus, impeding human progress. Hebert Spencer, William Graham Sumner. See Reform Darwinism in Concepts and 25. Social Darwinism and 26. Countervailing Theories/Reform Darwinism in Details.

Social Gospel: a late 19th and early 20th-Century religious-based social justice movement that advocated the application of Christian ideals to social issues, such as poverty and extremes of wealth. It provided the religious justification for Progressive reforms. Washington Gladden, Walter Rauschenbusch. See 26. Reform Darwinism in Details.

Socialist Party: a political party established in 1901 that advocated public ownership of the means of production, the eight-hour day and old-age pensions. The Socialist Party under Eugene V. Debs won 900,000 votes in 1912 but declined because of its opposition to World War I and the division in its ranks over the Russian Revolution. The relative failure of socialism in the United States has been attributed to: (1) the nation's relative material abundance, which was associated in the popular mind with the success of capitalism ("too much roast beef and apple pie"); (2) the ideology of economic individualism, self-help and social mobility; the distrust of collective action; the ideal of the self-made man and the view by some workers of themselves as "expectant capitalists"; (3) the absence of feudalism and hereditary distinctions and stratifications in colonial America, which led to the relative absence of class conflict and social radicalism compared to Europe; (4) the fact that the two-party political system tends to dampen social, class and ideological divisions and (5) the implacable opposition of the country's dominant economic, legal, political and media institutions. Lizabeth Cohen, Louis Hartz, Richard Hofstadter, Michael Kazin. See 4. Consensus and 5. Conflict Schools of American Historiography in Details.

Social mobility: the upward and downward movement of individuals, families and groups from one socioeconomic stratum to another. In the United States it is estimated that (1) less than 5% of indentured servants rose to the middle class in the colonial era, according to Clinton Rossiter and Abbott Smith; (2) 60-70% of the business elite in 19th Century were from the upper or upper-middle classes (C. Wright Mills in Richard Hofstadter); (3) currently, only

8% of the men born to families in the lower fifth of income rise to the top fifth in income. Jacob Hacker and Paul Pierson, Paul Krugman, Kevin Phillips, Thomas Piketty, Gary Solon and David Zimmerman, Joseph Stiglitz. See Economic inequality/ concentration of wealth and Great Gatsby curve in Concepts.

Soul libertie: liberty of conscience; freedom of religion and thought; the doctrine that the government should have no role in regulating religious thought or practice, which was a radical and heretical idea in the 17th Century when it was advanced by Roger Williams and others. Roger Williams; John M. Barry. See Religious toleration in Concepts and Secularism in Philosophy/Religion Concepts.

Southern apologists/fire-eaters: a term applied to those in the ante-bellum period who defended human slavery as a positive good and, eventually, advocated secession of the Southern slave states from the United States. See 24. American Civil War in Details.

Spoils system/rotation in office ("to the victor belong the spoils"): the system implemented during the Jacksonian Era, which was viewed at the time as a democratic reform, to remove entrenched office-holders from government jobs and install political loyalists from the victorious party. The practice was continued by both political parties until it was partially eliminated on the federal level by the Pendleton Civil Service Reform Act of 1883, which established a merit-based civil service system. See Patronage system in Political Science Concepts.

Stake-in-society: a 17th and 18th century political doctrine in which ownership of "real" (i.e., landed) property provided "sufficient evidence of permanent common interest with and attachment to the community," and, thus, conferred the right to vote and hold political office. It was the basis for excluding property-less white males from voting until the 1820s and the rise of Jacksonian democracy. John Locke. See Franchise in Concepts.

Stamp Act Crisis (1765): the angry and sustained response by British North American colonials to legislation by the British Parliament that levied a "stamp tax" on legal documents and newspapers in the colonies to raise revenue to reduce the enormous war debt incurred from the French and Indian War. The Stamp Act was seen by the colonials as "taxation without representation" and a violation of their rights as Englishmen. It precipitated massive colonial resistance and a chain of events that led, ten years later, to the American Revolution and independence from Great Britain. Edmund and Helen Morgan. See Dual/shared sovereignty and

French and Indian War in Concepts and 18. American Revolution in Details.

Standardization and interchangeability of parts: a key feature of the mass production process. The technique was first used by Eli Whitney in the production of 10,000 muskets under a 1798 contract with the United States government. It replaced unique, handcrafted products that were produced individually from start to finish by skilled craftsmen with ones assembled from standardized, interchangeable parts produced in batches by semi- and unskilled laborers. See Division of labor in Economics.

State sovereignty: the keystone of a political theory that the United States is a confederation of sovereign states, each of which has the right to nullify federal (i.e., national) legislation and secede from the United States if it chooses. The theory was challenged and rendered void by a long and bloody Civil War. See Dual/shared sovereignty in Concepts and 24. American Civil War in Details.

Status anxieties/displaced social groups: the anxieties associated with a decline in social status by one group relative to other groups. Historically, status anxieties have been identified as a causal factor in, and the dynamic basis of, both reform and reactionary movements. For example, the Progressive movement in the early 20th Century was thought to be driven, in part, by middle-class reformers whose traditional, individualist values were threatened by large-scale organizations such as trusts, labor unions and urban immigrant political machines. More recently, a decline in the status of white, native-born, blue-collar male workers (relative to immigrants, women, minorities, white collar workers, public employees, the college-educated, etc.) is thought to have been a critical factor in working class resistance to social reform movements in the latter half of the 20th Century. Daniel Bell, David Donald, Richard Hofstadter, George Mowry. See 28. Populism and 29. Progressivism in Details.

Stonewall Riots (1969): a milestone in the gay liberation movement, which was precipitated by the spontaneous resistance to a routine (at the time) police raid on a gay bar in New York City. It galvanized the gay-lesbian community and encouraged it to abandon a subculture of secrecy and shame; to resist the cultural oppression, homophobia and opprobrium of mainstream society and to develop a sense of self-pride and communal solidarity. It is analogous to Rosa Parks refusing to give up her seat on a segregated bus in Montgomery, Alabama in 1955, which ignited the civil rights/black freedom movement of the 1960s. David Carter, Robert Self. See 34. Countercultural Ferment of the 1960s and 1970s in Details.

Strict constructionism: a school of jurisprudence that advocates a narrow, literal interpretation of the United States Constitution. "Originalism" is an extreme version of strict constructionism that seeks to follow the original intent and meaning of the "Founding Fathers," who drafted the Constitution in 1787; versus **broad constructionism**, in which the Constitution is viewed as an organic document that has evolved to address the changing circumstances that have occurred since the 18th Century.

Suburbanization: the growth of satellite communities adjacent to central urban areas as a result of (1) improvements in transportation, particularly rail transit systems, highways and expressways, (2) the attraction of open spaces, (3) federal mortgage subsidies for single family homes and (4) the wish to escape urban congestion and crime. Kenneth Jackson, John Stilgoe. See Federal Highway Act and Levittowns in Concepts and 15. Urbanization in Details.

Symbolic groups: those that are identified by their social and ideological significance as much as by their economic and class interests, although some control the opinion- and decision-making institutions of society. Examples include antebellum Southern plantation owners, post-Civil War captains of industry, Wall Street financiers, Main Street businessmen, family farmers, ethnic groups, young urban professionals, college students, blue-collar workers, retired persons, military veterans, religious groups, sports celebrities, NRA members, soccer moms, GLBTs, etc. See identity politics in Political Science Concepts. Daniel Bell.

Table of virtues: Benjamin Franklin's daily journal of 13 virtues, which were arranged in a matrix, or grid, with the virtues arranged in horizontal rows and the days of the week arranged in vertical columns. The intersecting cell of each virtue was marked with "a little black spot" for each day it was not observed. The virtues included temperance, silence, order, resolution, frugality ("waste nothing"), industry ("lose no time"), sincerity, justice, moderation, cleanliness ("tolerate no uncleanliness"), tranquility, chastity and humility ("imitate Jesus and Socrates"). Franklin confessed that "I was surpris'd to find myself so much fuller of faults than I had imagined." His hyper-rational method for self-improvement served as the cultural prototype of the self-made man and anticipated modern cognitive behavioral psychology, which attempts to change behavioral patterns through daily practice and to reduce positive behavior to a habit. See Self-improvement in Concepts, 2. American Cultural Values and Traits in Details, Protestant ethic and the rise of capitalism in Economic Concepts and 6. Freud's Anal Personality Traits in Psychology Details.

Tabula rasa: John Locke's concept of the mind at birth as a blank tablet, from which follows the self-evident truth that all men are created equal and that there is no innate human depravity nor original sin. It laid the intellectual foundation for the 17th and 18th Century Enlightenment's concepts of natural rights, representative democracy and social improvement (through, for example, universal public education). Its inherent environmentalism ran counter to the tenets of Calvinism and Puritanism, as well as, later, to structuralism and sociobiology.

Temperance movement: a 19th Century moral reform movement that linked the consumption of alcohol to social evils such as crime, poverty, prostitution and domestic violence. It culminated in the ratification of the 18th Amendment to the Constitution in 1919, which initiated the Prohibition Era, which lasted until the amendment was repealed in 1933. Lisa McGirr, James Timberlake, Sarah Tracy and Caroline Acker. See Alcoholic republic, Moral crusade/moral restoration theme and Prohibition in Concepts.

Third American Revolution: a term applied to the New Deal (1933-1945), which was said to have established a welfare state on capitalistic foundations and modified laissez-faire economics with Keynesian economics. See 30. New Deal in Details and 16. Keynesian Economics in Economics Details.

Thirteenth Amendment (1865): an amendment to the U. S. Constitution that abolished slavery in the United States and liberated four million human beings and their descendants from a lifetime of involuntary servitude.

Tradition of the new: an American cultural tradition and trait. Harold Rosenberg's term was originally applied to the inexorable trend in modern art in which the "advance guard" is perpetually driven to differentiate itself from mainstream and commercial art. See Culture of narcissism in Concepts; J. Hector St. John de Crèvecoeur in Quotations and 2. American Cultural Values and Traits and 11. Frontier Thesis in Details.

Transplanted European institutions: institutions that are derived from English common law and English and European traditions of religion, education and representative government. They provided the critical, formative influence on American institutions, character traits and historical development, according to one school of thought; versus **Frederick Jackson Turner's frontier thesis** that the frontier was the primary force that shaped the American character. Louis Wright. See 12. Counterarguments to the Frederick Jackson Turner/Frontier Thesis in Details.

Transportation Revolution: an umbrella term encompassing the invention of the steam boat and the development of canals and railroad networks in the 19th Century, which provided the nexus by which a sense of sectional and national identity was achieved. It laid the physical infrastructure for national economic development and provided the means by which American producers could sell their products in regional, national and world markets. See Railroad land grants and the Federal Highway Act in Concepts and 20. American System in Details.

Trust busting versus **regulated monopolies/oligopolies**: two early 20[th-]Century responses, other than laissez-faire, to the problem of large-scale economic organizations, such as trusts, monopolies and oligopolies, which eliminated meaningful competition. Woodrow Wilson's New Freedom program proposed that the national government dismantle the trusts ("trust busting") and restore and regulate competition among small business units. Theodore Roosevelt's New Nationalism, on the other hand, accepted the inevitability of large-scale combinations but sought to have the national government regulate them in the public interest. See 3. Adam Smith/Classical/Free Market Economics and 4. Public Regulation Quandary in Economics Details.

Tweedledum and Tweedledee: William Allen White's pejorative term, derived from Lewis Carroll's *Through the Looking Glass*, to denote the lack of substantive differences between Theodore Roosevelt's and Woodrow Wilson's Progressive reform programs. Thereafter, the term has been used to indicate the lack of significant differences between the two major political parties or their candidates.

Tyranny of opinion/tyranny of the majority: coercive conformity and the regimentation of morality; versus Madisonian pluralism (*q.v.* in Concepts). See McCarthyism, Paranoid style in American politics, Red Scare, Salem Witch Trials and Sedition Acts in

Concepts and 3. Alexis de Tocqueville and 4. Consensus and 5. Conflict Schools of Historiography in Details.

Ugly American: the stereotype of the boorish American traveler who is indifferent to the language, standards and values of other cultures. William Lederer and Eugene Burdick.

Un-American: a pejorative term used as early as the 1820s by politicians to describe their opponents. It served as a hackneyed, but often potent, form of character assassination.

Uncle Tom's Cabin (1854): a novel by Harriet Beecher Stowe that portrayed to white readers and audiences the humanity and suffering of African-American slaves. Stowe was said to have been told by President Lincoln, "so, you're the little woman who wrote the book that started this great war."

Unsafe at Any Speed (1965): the title of a book by Ralph Nader about car safety problems that led to the expansion of product liability laws and the resurgence of the consumer protection movement.

Utilitarian ethic: the philosophy of the greatest good for the greatest number; also, the American cultural trait of pragmatism and practicality. John Stuart Mill, Vernon Louis Parrington. See Frederick Jackson Turner in Quotations, 11. Frederick Jackson Turner/Frontier Thesis and 27. Pragmatism/Radical Empiricism in Details.

Utopian communities: a wide range of ideal, or "utopian," communities that were established in the North and Midwest in the first half of the 19th Century in response to the rise of industrial capitalism and economic individualism and in the aftermath of a wave of religious revivals known as the Second Great Awakening. Many were based on the principles of cooperative labor, egalitarianism, socialism, religious communism and artistic or spiritual development. They included those at Amana, Brook Farm, Fruitlands, Hancock, Hopedale, New Harmony, New Lebanon and Oneida. Charles Nordoff, Alice Tyler. See Burned-over District, Freedom's ferment and Oneida community in Concepts.

Vernacular tradition: one in which utilitarian art objects are celebrated for their clean, graceful simplicity, economy of line, functional nature and utilitarian purpose. The American vernacular tradition is represented by such iconic cultural symbols as Shaker furniture, the Pennsylvania/Kentucky long rifle, the Colt revolver, the steam boat, the clipper ship, the skyscraper, the automobile, freeways/expressways ("America's pyramids"), and the soup can. John Kouwenhoven. See Popular culture and Shaker folk art in Concepts and Folk art in Art.

Vietnam War: see 31. Cold War and 33. Vietnam War in Details.

Vox populi, vox dei ("the voice of the people [is] the voice of god"): an aphorism attributed to Alcuin, an 8th Century English abbot, the full quotation of which was: "And do not listen to those who keep saying, 'the voice of the people is the voice of God,' because the tumult of the crowd is always close to madness." See Democracy in Concepts and 6. American Exceptionalism in Details.

War as an antidote to materialism: Theodore Roosevelt's rationale for supporting the United States' entry into the First World War.

War as the nemesis of reform: Richard Hofstadter's thesis that the United States' participation in the First World War led to the death of Progressivism and a reaction against the moral idealism that had been used to justify it. The thesis was also applied to the Vietnam War of the 1960s and 1970s and its effects on Lyndon Johnson's War on Poverty and post-World War II liberalism. William Jennings Bryan, Richard Hofstadter.

War on drugs: federal and state programs that were launched in the 1970s by President Richard Nixon to criminally prohibit the production, distribution and consumption of psychoactive drugs. Approximately 1.5 million Americans are arrested every year for drug offenses, half of whom are for marijuana. Approximately 20% of state prisoners and 50% of federal prisoners are serving time for drug offenses. The federal government spends $15 to $20 billion a year on criminal drug enforcement, far more than it does on educational and treatment programs for substance abuse. Sarah Tracy and Caroline Acker. See Moral crusade/moral restoration theme and Prohibition in Concepts.

Waving the bloody shirt: a political term that was derived from an incident in which the bloody nightshirt of an Ohio carpetbagger that was, supposedly, waved on the floor of House of Representatives by a congressman in 1871 to condemn the atrocities of the Klu Klux Klan against freed slaves and their white, Republican supporters. (A carpetbagger was a Northerner who traveled to the South after the Civil War to aid newly emancipated African-Americans and/or to seek financial gain.) The term now refers to any method used by politicians to inflame their supporters and slander their opponents. Joseph McCarthy used it in 1950 when he waved a list, but never revealed the names, of 205 supposedly known Communists working for the U. S. State Department. Eric Foner.

Wealth and democracy: see Economic elitism versus political democracy, Economic inequality/concentration of wealth, Plutocracy, Robber Baron thesis, Social Darwinism and Social mobility in Concepts; Thomas Jefferson, John Jay, Alexis de Tocqueville and Louis Brandeis in Quotations; Donor class, Patronage system and Super PACs in Political Science Concepts; 20. Class Structure in Sociology Details and Lewis Lapham and Kevin Phillips in Selected References.

Wealth as a badge of social superiority and/or a sign of God's grace: see 25. Social Darwinism in Details and Cultural hegemony in Sociology Concepts.

Wise and frugal government: one of the objectives and virtues of an agrarian republic, according to Thomas Jefferson.

Wobblies: members of the Industrial Workers of the World, an industrial union that was formed in 1905 by socialists, anarchists and trade unionists, and reached its peak membership in the early 1920s with 40,000 members. The IWW attempted to provide one big union for all workers, including women, immigrants and African-Americans (in contrast to the American Federation of Labor, which, generally, was restricted to white male craft workers). It sought to foster a sense of solidarity among workers in the revolutionary struggle to overthrow the capitalist class and establish a workers' democracy. The IWW used strikes and boycotts and opposed the United States' participation in the First World War. Its leaders were Eugene V. Debs, "Mother" Mary Jones, "Big Bill" Haywood and Joe Hill, and its members included miners, dockworkers, lumberjacks, textile workers and migrant farmworkers. At times, IWW members were beaten, arrested, imprisoned and, in several cases, murdered by vigilantes, with the support of local authorities. Peter Cole, Michael Kazin. See Labor movement in Concepts.

Wounded Knee Massacre (1890): an event in which the U. S. 7th Cavalry opened fire on an encampment of Lakota/Sioux in South Dakota, killing 150 to 300 men, women and children.

Yankee: a word derived from the Dutch *Jan* for John or Johnny.

Yellow journalism: the use of sensational war-mongering to sell
     newspapers and, later, to raise television and cable news ratings.
     The technique was used successfully in the Mexican-American
     War of 1846, the Spanish American War of 1898, World War I in
     1917 and the invasion of Iraq in 2003.

QUOTATIONS:

- *For we must consider that we shall be as a city upon a hill, the eyes of all people are upon us; so that if we shall deal falsely with our god in this work we have undertaken . . . we shall be made a story and a byword through the world.* -- John Winthrop.

- *We must entertain each other in brotherly affection, we must be willing to abridge ourselves of our superfluities for the supply of others' necessities. We must uphold a familiar commerce together in all meekness, gentleness, patience and liberality. We must delight in each other, make others' conditions our own, rejoice together, mourn together, labor, and suffer together, always having before our eyes our commission and community in the work, our community as members of the same body.* -- Winthrop.

- *What, then, is the American, this new man?* -- J. Hector St. John de Crèvecoeur.

- *The Revolution was effected before the war commenced. The Revolution was in the minds and hearts of the people.* -- John Adams.

- *I am not a Virginian but an American.* -- Patrick Henry.

- *The cause of America is in a great measure the cause of all mankind.* -- Thomas Paine.

- *Those who labor in the earth are the chosen people of God.* -- Thomas Jefferson.

- *Equal rights for all, special privileges for none.* – Jefferson.

- *I hope we shall crush . . . in its birth the aristocracy of our moneyed corporations, which dare already to challenge our government to a trial of strength and bid defiance to the laws of our country.* – Jefferson.

- *Indeed, I tremble for my country when I reflect that God is just; that his justice cannot sleep forever.* -- Jefferson.

- *The most common and durable source of factions has been the various and unequal distribution of property. Those who hold and those who are without property have ever formed distinct interests in society.* -- James Madison, *Federalist No. 10.*

- *The people who own the country ought to govern it.* -- John Jay.

- *I think I can see the whole destiny of America contained in the first Puritan who landed on those shores.* -- Alexis de Tocqueville.

- [Americans] *are forever varying, altering, and restoring secondary matters; but they carefully abstain from touching what is fundamental. They love change, but they dread revolutions.* -- Tocqueville.

- [Americans] *live in a state of perpetual self-adoration.* -- Tocqueville.

- *The manufacturing aristocracy which is growing up under our eyes is one of the harshest that ever existed in the world; but at the same time it is one of the most confined and least dangerous. Nevertheless, the friends of democracy should keep their eyes anxiously fixed in this direction; for if ever a permanent inequality of conditions and aristocracy again penetrates into the world, it may be predicted that this is the gate by which they will enter.* -- Tocqueville.

- *Our manifest destiny is to overspread the continent allotted by Providence for the free development of our yearly multiplying millions.* -- John L. O'Sullivan.

- [Americans are God's] *almost chosen people.* -- Abraham Lincoln.

- *Fellow citizens, we cannot escape history.* -- Lincoln.

- *With malice toward none, with charity for all.* -- Lincoln.

- *Do I contradict myself?*
  Very well, then, I contradict myself.
  (I am large - I contain multitudes.) -- Walt Whitman.

- *The American woman at her best* -- *like most other women* --
  exerted great charm on the man, but not the charm of a primitive
  type. . . . When closely watched, she seemed [to be] *making a*
  violent effort to follow the man, who had turned his mind and hand
  to mechanics. The typical American male had his hand on a lever
  and his eye on a curve in his road; his living depended on keeping
  up an average speed of forty miles an hour, tending always to
  become sixty, eighty, or a hundred, and he could not admit emotions
  or anxieties or subconscious distractions, more than he could admit
  whiskey or drugs, without breaking his neck. . . . He must leave
  her, even though his wife, to find her own way, and all the world saw
  her trying to find her way by imitating him. . . . She must, like the
  man, marry machinery. -- Henry Adams.

- *We can have democracy in this country, or we can have great*
  wealth concentrated in the hands of a few, but we can't have both.
  - Louis Brandeis.

- *That coarseness and strength combined with acuteness and*
  inquisitiveness; that practical, inventive turn of mind, quick to find
  expedients; that masterful grasp of material things, lacking in
  artistic but powerful to effect great ends; that restless, nervous
  energy; that dominant individualism, working for good and for
  evil, and withal that buoyancy and exuberance which comes with
  freedom -- *these are the traits of the frontier.* -- Frederick
  Jackson Turner.

- [Double consciousness is the] *sense of always looking at one's self*
  through the eyes of others, of measuring one's soul by the tape of a
  world that looks on in amused contempt and pity. One ever feels
  his two-ness -- *an American, a Negro; two warring souls, two*
  thoughts, two unreconciled strivings; two warring ideals in one
  dark body, whose dogged strength alone keeps it from being torn
  asunder. -- W. E. B. Du Bois.

- *Today, we are faced with the preeminent fact that, if civilization is*
  to survive, we must cultivate the science of human relationships –

the ability of all peoples, of all kinds, to live together and work together, in the same world, at peace. – Franklin Roosevelt.

AMERICAN HISTORY DETAILS: (1) Major Themes in American History, (2) American Cultural Values and Traits, (3) Alexis de Tocqueville, (4) Consensus Schools of American Historiography, (5) Conflict Schools of American Historiography, (6) American Exceptionalism, (7) Counterarguments to American Exceptionalism, (8) Geographical Determinism, (9) Colonial Gender Ratios, (10) Puritanism, (11) Frederick Jackson Turner/Frontier Thesis, (12) Counterarguments to the Frontier Thesis, (13) American Slavery, (14) Immigration, (15) Urbanization, (16) Anti-Urban Cultural Tradition, (17) Great Awakening Cycle/Revivalism, (18) American Revolution/War of Independence, (19) Origins of American Nationalism, (20) American System/American Way, (21) New England Transcendentalism, (22) Jacksonian Democracy, (23) Mexican-American War, (24) American Civil War, (25) Social Darwinism, (26) Countervailing Theories/Reform Darwinism, (27) Pragmatism/Radical Empiricism, (28) Populism, (29) Progressivism, (30) New Deal, (31) Cold War, (32) Civil Rights/Black Freedom Movement, (33) Vietnam War, (34) Countercultural Ferment of the 1960s and 1970s, (35) Feminism and (36) American Generational Cycles.

1. **Major Themes in American History**: Natural Geography, Native-Americans, European Discovery and Exploration, Colonial Era, Puritanism, 18th-Century Enlightenment, French and Indian War, War of Independence, United States Constitution, Early Nationalism, Jacksonian Democracy, Romanticism, Social Ferment of 1830s-40s (temperance, anti-slavery, women's rights, public schools, utopian communities), Mexican-American War, Slavery, American Civil War, Industrialization, Immigration, Urbanization, Realism/Naturalism, Social Darwinism, Populism, Progressivism, World War I, Cultural Homogenization of the 1920s (movies, radio, automobiles, mass advertising), Great Depression, New Deal, World War II, Cold War, McCarthyism, Suburbanization, Affluence and Consumption, Civil Rights/Black Freedom Movement, Vietnam War, Counterculture, Sexual Revolution, Women's Liberation, Environmentalism, Nixon-

Reagan-Bush Counter-Revolution, Evangelical Politics, War on Terrorism and Great Recession.

2. **American Cultural Values and Traits**: egalitarianism ("born equal"; "equal rights for all, special privileges for none"), individualism, self-reliance, optimism, work ethic, self-improvement, competition, achievement, success ethic, materialism, acquisitiveness, abundance/prosperity ("the people of plenty"), prodigality/wastefulness, social mobility, geographical mobility, utilitarianism/pragmatism, lack of ideology, lack of historical consciousness, anti-intellectualism, political mediocrity (Alexis de Tocqueville), provincialism, indifference to art, quantitative cast of thought, litigiousness, monomania, public moralism, personal privacy and freedom, religious toleration, cultural pluralism, nationalism/patriotism, dissent, civil disobedience, public-spiritedness, voluntary associationalism, philanthropy/humanitarianism, social improvement, faith in science, technology and progress, narcissism/self-indulgence, violence, paranoia, racism, sexism, nativism, militarism and imperialism. Daniel Bell, Daniel Boorstin, James Bryce, Erik Erikson, Benjamin Franklin, Geoffrey Gorer, Richard Hofstadter, D. H. Lawrence, Margaret Mead, Vernon Louis Parrington, George Pierson, David Potter, David Reisman, Arthur Schlesinger, Sr., William Tilden, Alexis de Tocqueville, Frederick Jackson Turner.

3. **Alexis de Tocqueville** (1805-1859) was a French political thinker, social scientist and observer of American customs and institutions. In his *Democracy in America* (1835-40), he identified a range of American character traits and values, including (1) the principle of equality ("born equal"); (2) "individualism" (the term was coined by de Tocqueville, which he defined as the "feeling which deposes each citizen to isolate himself from the mass of his fellows and withdraw. . . . . He gladly leaves the greater society to look for itself"); (3) the tyranny of the majority (coercive conformity and the regimentation of morality); (4) materialism and money-making (the "monotonous" love of wealth); (5) egoism and economic self-interest; (6) the aristocracy of manufacturers; (7) political mediocrity; (8) liberty of the press; (9) public-spiritedness; (10) respect for the law, morality and religion; (11) the relatively higher social status of American women ("I have nowhere seen woman occupying a loftier position. . . . Her mind is just as fitted as that

of man to discover the plain truth, and her heart as firm to embrace it"); (12) voluntary associationalism; (13) national vanity and "perpetual self-adoration" and (14) the legal recognition and moral acceptance of human slavery (the "spectacle of man's degradation by man"). See Tocqueville in Quotations.

4. **Consensus Schools of American Historiography** propose that, although political conflicts often preempt the foreground (with passionate rhetoric and political melodrama), there is usually an unspoken, underlying political consensus in the United States that limits the range of social discourse at any given time. The culture of consensus is derived from (1) a shared core of common values (a belief in democracy, majority rule, freedom of expression, capitalism, equal opportunity, social mobility), which is also known as the Lockean consensus ("we are all Republicans; we are all Federalists" -- Thomas Jefferson); (2) the absence of feudalism and hereditary stratifications in colonial America, which resulted in the relative lack of class conflict and social radicalism in American history (Louis Hartz); (3) the abundance of land and scarcity of labor, which fostered social fluidity, geographical mobility and labor-saving technological innovations (Fredrick Jackson Turner); (4) the Anglo-Saxon spirit of compromise and accommodation (Herbert Baxter Adams, Francis Parkman); (5) Madisonian pluralism (*q.v.* in Concepts); (6) the philosophy of Scottish common sense realism, American pragmatism/ instrumentalism and the lack of ideology (Daniel Bell, Daniel Boorstin, John Dewey, Richard Hofstadter, Turner); (7) the two-party political system, which dampened sectional, class and ideological divisions (Bell, Hofstadter); (8) a federated system of government that is based on checks and balances and the separation and division of powers (see Balanced government in Political Science); (9) the tradition of English common law with its principle of *stare decisis* ("let the precedent stand"); (10) the sense of a shared history and national identity and the importance of tradition and continuity; (11) the fact that social and political reforms have often followed a dialectical pattern of prolonged resistance to changes in the status quo, followed by brief periods of incremental reforms, followed by the acceptance of those reforms and, finally, a new consensus, which a later backlash and period of counter-reform cannot completely reverse. Daniel Bell, Daniel Boorstin, James

MacGregor Burns Louis Hartz, Richard Hofstader, Alexis de Tocqueville, Frederick Jackson Turner.

5.   **Conflict Schools of American Historiography** focus on the economic, sectional, racial, gender, class, ethnic, religious and cultural conflicts and divisions that have characterized American history. These historians explore the issues of (1) the historically marginalized and oppressed (e.g., Native-Americans, African-Americans, women, the working class, immigrants, the poor); (2) slavery, racism, religious bigotry, xenophobia, sexism, poverty, war and imperialism; (3) class divisions and economic inequality; (4) rural-urban political and social divisions; (5) agrarian radicalism; (6) labor activism and class warfare; (7) cultural hegemony (see 25. Social Darwinism in Details), and (8) the control of political institutions and the media by the wealthy class and corporate interests. Charles Beard, Carl Becker, Eugene Genovese, Lynn Hunt, Gabriel Kolko, Christopher Lasch, Michael A. Lebowitz, Jesse Lemisch, Jane Mayer, C. Wright Mills, Vernon Louis Parrington, Arthur Schlesinger, Jr., Stephan Thernstrom. See Culture wars in Sociology Concepts.

6.   **American Exceptionalism** is the belief that the United States is historically unique, a model community, a "city upon a hill"; that Americans are God's chosen people, with a special mission to bring liberty, democracy and capitalism to the rest of the world. The doctrine is associated with a complex of ideas, values and beliefs that are derived from a number of sources, including:

1)   The Puritans' view of their Massachusetts Bay community as the New Jerusalem, a "holy commonwealth" in the wilderness, with a covenant with God, and of history as the unfolding of the divine plan. Perry Miller, Stow Persons, Herbert Schneider.

2)   The 18th and 19th Century view of America as a *tabula rasa*, or blank tablet; of the West as a symbol of the Edenic myth, of America as the garden of the world ("in the beginning, all the world was America" -- John Locke; "what, then, is the American, this new man?" -- J. Hector St. John de Crèvecoeur). R. W. B. Lewis, John Locke, Henry Nash Smith.

3)   The absence of feudal traditions and hereditary stratifications. Louis Hartz.

4) The germ theory of liberty, i.e., that the Anglo-Saxon traditions of liberty, common law and self-government were born in the Teutonic forests of pre-history. Tacitus; Herbert Baxter Adams, Oliver Wendell Holmes, Jr., Francis Parkman, Theodore Roosevelt.

5) The Declaration of Independence, the American Revolution and the triumph of the Enlightenment principles of natural rights, government by the consent of the governed and the belief that all men are created equal, which served as a model for the world.

6) The abundance of fertile land and rich natural resources, which created a land of unprecedented material abundance and prosperity ("the people of plenty"). David Potter, John Galbraith.

7) The Protestant work ethic. Max Weber.

8) The belief in economic opportunity and social mobility ("the American Dream"). See Horatio Alger mystique and Self-made man/rags-to-riches in Concepts.

9) The providential conception of American history and the doctrine of Manifest Destiny. John Winthrop, George Bancroft, John O'Sullivan.

10) Scientific discoveries and technological innovations (the "tradition of the new"), which placed the United States on the leading edge of material progress.

11) Democratic imperialism and "spreading democracy by the sword." See Dollar Diplomacy and Neo-conservatism in Concepts.

12) The triumph of capitalism and the end of history: in his 1989 essay, "The End of History," Francis Fukuyama argued that, with the end of the Cold War and the triumph of capitalism, history had reached "the end point of mankind's ideological evolution and the universalization of Western liberal democracy [which is] the final form of human government."

13) Christian millennialism and evangelicalism ("I trust God speaks through me" -- George W. Bush).

7. **Counterarguments to American Exceptionalism** assert that American exceptionalism is a dangerous myth that betrays an arrogant sense of superiority; that it is narcissistic, racist and ethnocentric, and that it portrays a provincial world view that the United States is above international law and exempt from the

cycles of human history. Morris Berman, Pat Buchanan, Niall Ferguson, Greg Grandin, Herbert London, Michael Parenti, Donald Pease, Fareed Zakaria.

The somber realities of American history provide a counter-narrative to the idea of American exceptionalism. These include:

1) The dispossession and internment of the continent's original human inhabitants and the expropriation of their lands.
2) Chattel slavery for millions of human beings.
3) Racial segregation and ethnic and religious discrimination.
4) Brutally competitive laissez-faire capitalism.
5) The exploitation and degradation of the natural environment.
6) Economic imperialism and unilateral military interventions in sovereign countries.
7) Social dysfunctionality: compared to the developed countries in Western Europe, the United States has higher rates of poverty, income inequality, homicide and incarceration, and lower rates of public expenditures for education, health care and pensions.
8) The decline of American empire and the loss of global hegemony, which was caused by (a) the concentration of wealth and the decline of the middle class; (b) globalization, the overseas outsourcing of jobs and the loss of the United States' industrial base; (c) the degradation of its social infrastructure, including public education; (d) the country's enormous national debt and (e) the rise of China as an economic superpower.
9) The loss of moral authority from the nation's support of authoritarian governments, preemptive war, rendition, torture, the suspension of habeas corpus and the collateral killing of civilians in regional wars in Southeast Asia and the Middle East.

8. **Geographical Determinism** is a school of thought that asserts that climate, natural resources and geography are the basis of a natural economy, which, in turn, shapes and determines a culture. For example, in the British North American colonies, which later became the United States: (1) the abundance of fertile land and rich natural resources enabled geographical mobility, social fluidity and a culture of material abundance (David Potter); (2) 3,000 miles of the Atlantic Ocean between the mother country and her North

American colonies fostered a sense of "salutary neglect," which permitted colonial self-government and led, eventually, to independence from Great Britain; (3) "our detached and distant situation" (George Washington), with oceans on two borders and neighbors who were relatively weak militarily, fostered a sense of isolation and moral superiority to Old World-style intrigue and warfare, and delayed the need for a large, standing army; (4) glacial soil in New England made slavery less profitable there, which preserved the family farm from large-scale, landed estates and enabled the resistance to the plantation/slave labor system. James Truslow Adams, David Potter, Clinton Rossiter, Frederick Jackson Turner. See 11. Frederick Jackson Turner/Frontier Thesis in Details, 4. Geographical Determinism in Historiography Details and 10. Economic/Technological Determinism in Economics Details.

9. **Colonial Gender Ratios** suggest that the relative scarcity of Euro-American women in the British North American colonies (with a ratio of two white women to three white men) resulted in their relatively elevated legal and social status, as well as their idealization and romanticization; yet Euro-American women were not so scarce that inter-marriage between Euro-American men and Native-American or African-American women became socially or legally acceptable (as it did in the French and Spanish colonies). Herbert Moller.

10. **Puritanism** was an Anglo-American version of Calvinism, which sought to purify and restore the primitive simplicity of the established Church of England by purging it of its "papist" (i.e., Catholic and High Anglican) influences. 20,000 Puritans from eastern and southern England (primarily Norfolk, Suffolk, Essex and Kent counties) immigrated to the Massachusetts Bay Colony in the Great Migration from 1630 to 1640. Puritans used a congregational form of church government in which each congregation was autonomous and free to choose its own minister. The Puritans of New England thought of themselves as a "holy commonwealth," God's chosen people, a "city upon a hill," a government of Christ-in-exile in the New World and a covenanted community of the elect (in which God and the elect were bound to each other by a series of covenants, or contracts).

Puritan theology was based on a belief in original sin, predestination and justification by faith (i.e., salvation and redemption from sin by God's grace alone, rather than through leading a sanctified life or performing good works). It focused on the centrality of the religious conversion experience in which election by divine grace was accompanied by spiritual regeneration and psychic rebirth. The conversion experience was intensely personal, during which the individual was visited by God or Jesus, forgiven for his or her sins, infused with the Holy Spirit, spiritually "re-born" and promised eternal life. For first-generation Puritans, the conversion experience, once it was publically professed and examined, became the means by which "visible saints," or the "elect," were distinguished from the unregenerate and were admitted into the community of the "elect," with the right of male members to vote and hold public office (Puritan theocracy has been described as a "democracy of the elect"). Karen Armstrong, William James, Stow Persons, Kevin Phillips. See 17. Great Awakening Cycle/Revivalism in Details and Evangelicalism and Religious conversion experience in Philosophy/Religion Concepts.

The Protestant emphasis on written scripture established a cultural standard of common literacy and the ideal of a learned clergy (130 of the 20,000 Puritan immigrants in the Great Migration were Cambridge University graduates), which, in turn, led to the founding of common schools and colonial colleges, such as Harvard, Yale, Princeton and Dartmouth. Among Protestants, differing interpretations of scripture led to theological disputes, schisms and the multiplicity of sects, which, in turn, led to religious coexistence and, eventually, religious toleration, as each church or sect lost its monopoly of theological, political and social power. David Hackett Fischer, Perry Miller, Stow Persons, Clinton Rossiter, Herbert Schneider, Max Weber. See Voltaire's quotation in Religious toleration in Concepts and 18. Protestant Reformation in Philosophy/Religion Details.

11. **Frederick Jackson Turner** (1861-1932)/**Frontier Thesis** proposed that: (1) the westward expansion by Euro-Americans across the North American "frontier" (which he defined as the borderland or zone between settled, farmed areas and unsettled areas of nomadic, Native-American hunter-gatherers) promoted democracy and social equality among Euro-Americans and forged

American character traits such as individualism, optimism, materialism, practicality and "that restless, nervous energy"; (2) the relative scarcity of labor and the abundance of land and natural resources among Euro-Americans fostered geographical mobility, relative social fluidity and labor-saving technological innovations and (3) the frontier served as a safety value for social discontent among Euro-Americans. The frontier thesis has been described as a form of ethnocentrism and geographical determinism, as well as a semi-scientific restatement of the agrarian ideal of the West as a symbol of the Edenic myth, of America as the garden of the world (Henry Nash Smith), of America as a process of "perennial rebirth." Recently, New Western historians have focused on the cultural diversity and the critical role played by women and minorities in Western development, as well as on the nomadic hunter-gatherers and sedentary, agricultural Native-Americans whom the Euro-Americans displaced. The end of the frontier and abundant natural resources has symbolized and foreshadowed the eventual exhaustion of those resources on a global scale and the end of unlimited material abundance. Frederick Jackson Turner; Daniel Boorstin, Elizabeth Fenn, Christopher Lasch, R. W. B. Lewis, Henry Nash Smith, Ted Steinberg, Walter Prescott Webb.

12. **Counterarguments to the Frontier Thesis** emphasize (1) ethnocentrism of its assumptions; (2) the paramount importance of transplanted European institutions to Euro-American historical development (the novelty and insecurity of the wilderness predisposed settlers to cling to familiar institutions); (3) the barriers to social mobility and commercial agriculture/ agrarian capitalism (which required capital, credit, technical knowledge and the sale of cash crops on volatile national and world markets); (4) the perception of the city as the locus of social mobility and economic opportunity; (5) the fact that many more farmers moved to the city than workers moved to the farm and (6) the observation that Western expansion was characterized by speculation, greed, the dispossession of its original Native-American inhabitants, diseases, ethnic oppression and genocide, and ecological devastation. William Cronon, Elizabeth Fenn, Peggy Pascoe, Nathaniel Philbrick, Earl Pomeroy, Richard White, Donald Worster, Louis Wright. See Native-American Shoah in Concepts.

13. **American Slavery** has been called America's "original sin." Chattel slavery is the ownership of one human being by another; a "slave" is the legal, personal property of its owner/master for the slave's lifetime and the lifetimes of his or her descendants. Approximately 12 million West Africans were kidnapped and shipped to the Americas as slaves (see Middle Passage in Concepts), of whom approximately 400,000 landed in what is now the United States, beginning in 1619 and ending in 1865. African-American slaves were used primarily to work on commercial cash crops that required intensive manual labor, such as tobacco, rice, indigo and cotton.

Slavery may have been economically moribund by the end of the 18th Century, but, with the invention of the cotton engine (or "gin") by Eli Whitney in 1793, the cultivation of inland, short-staple cotton became enormously profitable, which led to the resurgence and expansion of slavery and cotton culture into the Deep South, the economic and political ascendency of "King Cotton" and, ultimately, the Civil War. On the eve of the Civil War in 1860, there were four million African-American slaves in the United States, who constituted 12% of the population and whose total value as property was worth more than the total value of all the capital invested in banks, factories and railroads (Eric Foner, Greg Gandin). These human beings were owned by less than 400,000 slave-holders, or less than 1.5% of the white population. Approximately 50,000 slaveholders, or a little less than 2/10th of 1 percent of the white population, owned 20 or more slaves, yet this planter class dominated the country's political economy and controlled many of its opinion- and decision-making institutions.

Slavery was justified as a "positive good" by Southern apologists on various historical, scriptural and pseudo-scientific grounds (Biblical precedent, Greek democracy, tropical heat, racial inferiority, etc.), all of which contradicted the American creed that "all men are created equal." Other cultures and other historical eras have legally recognized slavery, but, in most of those cases, a slave's condition was viewed as an accident of circumstance (from war, capture, kidnapping, etc.) and not as the result of the slave's inherent inferiority. In the United States, on the other hand, slavery was confined to one race, which allowed it to be rationalized and justified on the grounds of the inherent superiority of the white race and the inherent inferiority of the black race, which created a legacy of racism and white supremacy in the North and South for more than a century after slavery itself had been abolished.

Historians have argued over the profitability of slavery and whether or not it would have died out gradually on its own accord without a civil war (Albert Beveridge thought it would have died out; Iran Berlin, Stanley Engerman, Robert Fogel and David Reynolds argued that it would not; see 24. American Civil War in Details). After a long and bloody Civil War, in which 625,000 Americans died, slavery was formally abolished by the passage of the 13th Amendment in 1865, but white supremacy, Jim Crow segregation, sharecropper peonage/serfdom, violence, terrorism, lynching and disenfranchisement continued until the latter half of the 20th Century, and racism, discrimination, stereotyping and racial-profiling continue today. In 2008 and 2009, the United States Congress formerly apologized for the "fundamental injustice, cruelty, brutality and inhumanity of slavery," but did not provide reparations to its descendants. Herbert Aptheker, Ira Berlin, John Blassingame, Frederick Douglass, Stanley Elkins, Robert Fogel and Stanley Engerman, John Hope Franklin, Eugene Genovese, Herbert Gutman, Steven Hahn, Winthrop Jordan, Lawrence W. Levine, David S. Reynolds, Kenneth Stampp, Frank Tannebaum.

14. **Immigration** is the keystone of the nation's historical development and cultural identity. The New World in general, and the United States in particular, is a nation of immigrants. Historically, the successive waves of immigrants into what is now the continental United States consisted of Paleo-Indians from eastern Siberia, Spanish, French, English, Dutch, West Africans, Scotch-Irish/Ulster-Scots, Germans, Irish, Chinese, Japanese, Central Europeans, Italians, Mexicans, Puerto Ricans, Filipinos, Southeast Asians, Latin Americans and Indians from southern Asia.

In the colonial North America that later became the United States, approximately 400,000 to one million Europeans immigrated during the 17th and 18th Centuries, half of whom, outside of New England, were indentured servants. In addition, approximately

400,000 West African slaves were forcibly imported into what is now the United States between 1619 and 1865. Benjamin Franklin opposed German immigration because he felt that they could not be assimilated. By 1765, the white population was 2,200,000, which consisted of approximately 70% English, 15% Scots and Scotch-Irish/Ulster-Scots, 10% German and Dutch, and 5% Irish. In 1790, African Americans numbered about 760,000, or 19% of the population of 4 million people. From 1836 to 1914, thirty million Europeans migrated to the United States, initially from Ireland and Germany and, later, from Southern and Eastern Europe.

Since the early 20th Century, the **"melting pot"** (a term was taken from the title of an 1908 play by Israel Zangwill) has served as a popular metaphor for the cultural assimilation and homogenization of immigrant groups in America, notwithstanding the class, racial and ethnic prejudice and exclusionary barriers which were directed against them. The counter-metaphor of the **"salad bowl"** more accurately recognizes the diversity, multiculturalism and unique contributions of various ethnic groups. June Granatir Alexander, Roger Daniels, Oscar Handlin, Tamara Hareven, Clinton Rossiter, Carl Wittke, Virginia Yans-McLaughlin.

15. **Urbanization** is the process by which cities are founded and grow as a result of their strategic location, internal growth, migration from farms and villages and immigration from other countries. Historically, the city has served as a cultural symbol, the locus of economic opportunity and the center of art and culture. It is characterized by variety and diversity, cultural innovation, social mobility, extremes of wealth, "desperate haste" (Henry David Thoreau), impersonality, anonymity, moral relativity and the loss of traditional values (Carl Degler). It is also associated with regional economic and cultural hegemony, immigration, ethnic enclaves, assimilation, entrepreneurship, political machines, poverty, crime, gangs, tenements, skyscrapers, traffic congestion, public transportation, professional and cultural elites, philanthropy, museums, theaters, restaurants, sports teams and urban parks and green belts. See 10. The Rise of Urban Civilizations in Anthropology and Behavioral/Population Sink in Psychology Concepts.

The U. S. Census Bureau defines "urban" as an area having a population of 2,500 or more. In 1765, Philadelphia had a population of 30,000, New York 18,000 and Boston 15,000. By 1860, on the eve of the Civil War, less than 20% of the population lived in "urban" areas of 2,500 or more. By 1900, 40% of Americans lived in "urban" areas, and three cities had populations of one million or more (New York, Chicago and Philadelphia). Today, approximately 80% of Americans live in "urban" areas. Gunther Barth, Michael Conzen, Carl Degler, Paul Kramer and Frederick Holborn, Richard Lehan, Clinton Rossiter, David Schuyler, John Stilgoe, Stephan Thernstrom, Richard Wade.

16. **Anti-Urban Cultural Tradition** reflects the cultural ambivalence and tension between nature and civilization, the country and the city, the pastoral and the commercial, which was expressed in the works of Albert Bierstadt, Thomas Cole, James Fenimore Cooper, Ralph Waldo Emerson, Nathaniel Hawthorne, Ernest Hemingway, Thomas Jefferson, Herman Melville, Henry David Thoreau and Mark Twain. In this tradition, the city represents (1) the unwelcome intrusion of commerce and industry into the tranquility and spirituality of nature and the countryside; (2) the displacement of the independent yeoman/family farmer, who serves as the bulwark of the virtuous, classless, homogenous republic; (3) the center of regional, national and international hegemony; (4) materialism, financial speculation, extremes of wealth, political corruption, crime, ugliness, squalor, debauchery ("the mobs of great cities [are as] sores on the strength of the human body" -- Thomas Jefferson); (5) the end of the frontier (Fredrick Jackson Turner); (6) the despoliation of the natural environment, and (7) the post-apocalyptic urban wasteland (Mike Davis). Thomas Jefferson; Mike Davis, Leo Marx, Perry Miller, Lewis Mumford, Vernon Louis Parrington, Henry Nash Smith, Frederick Jackson Turner, Morton White.

17. **Great Awakening Cycle/Revivalism** reflects the waxing and waning of religious enthusiasm in American history and is associated with Christian evangelicalism, fundamentalism and Pentecostalism. Summer tent revivals were common in rural America and were usually conducted by itinerant preachers. The core of the revival was the immediate, personal and intensely emotional experience of being possessed by the Holy Spirit,

accepting Jesus as one's personal savior and being freed from the threat of eternal damnation. The experience was often an ecstatic one, which was accompanied by cries, shrieks, swooning and convulsions. Since religious emotionalism and "New Light" theology tended to be socially disruptive and relatively democratic, it was often opposed by the traditional, established, "Old Light," mainstream churches.

There have been four major religious revival periods in American history: (1) the **First Great Awakening**, in the 1730s and 1740s, was associated with George Whitefield and Jonathan Edwards; (2) the **Second Great Awakening**, from 1800 to 1840, was associated with Charles Finney, the "Burned-over District" in upstate New York and "freedom's ferment" (Alice Felt Tyler), which resulted in a series of social reforms in the 1830s and 1840s, including women's rights, temperance and abolitionism; (3) the **Third Great Awakening**, from 1880 to 1900, was associated with the Social Gospel movement and Progressive Era reforms, and (4) the **Fourth Great Awakening**, in the latter half of the 20th Century, is associated with the Billy Graham crusades of the 1950s and 1960s, the Jesus countercultural movement of the 1960s and 1970s, television evangelism, the reaction against sexual permissiveness, homosexuality and abortion and the introduction of religious issues into the political sphere. Sidney Ahlstrom, Thomas Kidd, William McLoughlin.

18. **American Revolution/War of Independence** (1775-1783) developed in the aftermath of the French and Indian War (1754-1763), which had been fought by British and British-American colonial troops and their Native-American allies against the French and their Native-American allies for control of the northern and central part of the North American continent. The French and Indian War lasted nine years and created an enormous war debt. To pay for that debt and to provide for the military defense of the colonies, the British Parliament enacted (and, subsequently and partially, rescinded) a series of relatively modest taxes on its North American colonies (the "stamp tax" on newspapers and legal documents, for example, was lower than similar duties imposed in the mother country). Over the thirteen years between the end of the French and Indian War and the beginning of the War of Independence, successive Parliamentary revenue proposals ignited

increasingly fierce colonial resistance which, in turn, led to increasingly oppressive and coercive responses from the mother country, which ended, ultimately, in military occupation by the British, armed rebellion by the thirteen colonies, a declaration of independence, war, and, with critical financial and military assistance from France, victory and independence for the American colonies.

Generally, there are two schools of historiographical interpretation on the causes of the Revolution: (1) the **ideological/constitutional schools**, which focus on the colonials' defense of their natural rights as Englishmen and the underlying constitutional issues (loyalty to a common sovereign versus the supremacy of Parliament; the "dual sovereignty" of Parliament and the British colonial assemblies; internal versus external taxation; virtual representation, etc.), which was summarized in the slogan, "no taxation without representation" (at one point during the Stamp Act crisis of 1765, the British Minister, George Grenville proposed that the colonial assemblies tax themselves rather than have the Parliament do so, but the colonial assemblies did not respond to the proposal); and (2) the **economic schools** of interpretation, which focus on the material self-interests of the British-American colonials, including the collateral economic effects from Parliamentary taxation and legislation on colonial land speculators and smugglers, restrictions on domestic industries, the impact of the scarcity of specie and the lack of paper money on upper-class colonial debtors and the exclusion of colonial middlemen from the tea trade.

Approximately one-third of the British-American colonials supported independence from England, one-third remained loyal to the Crown (including Benjamin Franklin's son William, who moved to England after the war and never talked to his father again), and one-third were neutral or indifferent. Although there were social and economic divisions and some radical, democratic elements in the independence movement, the American Revolution has generally been viewed as a middle-class revolution, with the educated and propertied classes leading the movement for independence and relatively little immediate or direct social transformation resulting from it (other than the confiscation of Loyalists' properties and the opening of the western territories for settlement). However, the triumph of the Enlightenment principles of natural rights and government by the consent of the governed and the belief that all men are created equal served as a model for the world (including the French Revolution of 1789) and laid the foundation for universal white male suffrage, which was achieved in the 1810s through the 1830s, the abolition of slavery after the American Civil War, and, eventually, suffrage for women and African-Americans in the 20th Century.

19. **The Origins of American Nationalism:** prior to the development of a shared sense of national identity, Americans identified themselves as members of their colony and, later, their state, that is, as Virginians or Pennsylvanians, rather than as citizens of the United States. Milestones in the development of a national consciousness and a shared sense of national identity were: (1) the colonial postal system; (2) the war against the French from 1754 to 1763; (3) the inter-colonial Committees of Correspondence and the united resistance to acts of Parliament; (4) the War of Independence, including the winter of 1777-78 at Valley Forge; (5) the adoption of the United States Constitution and the creation of a national government; (6) Parson Weems' biography of Washington in 1800; (7) Andrew Jackson's victory at the Battle of New Orleans in 1815; (8) the publication of Noah Webster's American dictionary in 1828; (9) the American literary renaissance of the 1820s-1850s (William Cullen Bryant, James Fenimore Cooper, Ralph Waldo Emerson, Nathaniel Hawthorne, Washington Irving, Henry Wadsworth Longfellow, Herman Melville, Edgar Allan Poe, Henry David Thoreau, Walt Whitman); (10) the development of regional transportation networks of roads, canals and railroads; (11) the development of the electrical telegraph in the 1840s; (12) mass circulation newspapers (the penny press) and, ironically, (13) the American Civil War itself.

20. **American System/American Way** was a national economic program that was proposed in the late 18th and early 19th Century by Alexander Hamilton, Tench Coxe, Henry Carey and Henry Clay. It called for (1) a strong national government; (2) a planned national economy; (3) domestic manufacturing for a domestic market; (4) a high tariff to protect domestic industries from foreign competition and generate revenue; (5) a national bank; (6) a uniform currency; (7) "internal improvements" at federal expense

for (a) physical infrastructure (roads, canals, etc.) to facilitate intra-
and inter-sectional trade, and (b) the "moral, political and
intellectual improvement" of its citizens (Henry Clay) and (8) the
distribution of the proceeds from sale of public lands to the states
to pay for those "internal improvements."

The American System contradicted the basic tenets of laissez-faire
capitalism and was never implemented in a single, systematic
manner. However, over the years, many of its components were
implemented, although intermittently and on a piecemeal basis.
These included (1) the imposition of a high protective tariff before
and after the Civil War to protect American industries from foreign
competition; (2) the granting of massive federal subsidies to the
railroads in the 19th Century and the highway and airline industries
in the 20th Century; (3) the granting of federal lands to the states to
raise funds to establish and endow "land-grant" colleges for
teaching agriculture, science, military science and engineering and
the "intellectual improvement" of their citizens and (4) the
establishment of the Federal Reserve System in 1913, which
provides a uniform national currency and serves as the nation's
central bank.

21. **New England Transcendentalism** was a literary and
    philosophical movement of the second quarter of 19th Century that
    served as the quintessential expression American Romanticism. It
    has been viewed as a reaction against both the original sin and
    religious orthodoxy of Puritanism/Calvinism, on the one hand, and
    the scientific rationalism of the 18th Century Enlightenment, on the
    other. Transcendentalism celebrated (1) individualism ("enjoy an
    original relation with the universe"; "the infinitude of the private
    man"); (2) self-reliance ("trust thyself"); (3) the immanence of the
    divinity (or Over-Soul) in all life; (4) the beauty and sublimity of
    nature; (5) the moral law of compensation; (6) "double
    consciousness," i.e., the reflective self (in the world of ideas) over
    the actual self (in the here and now) and understanding over
    reason; (7) antinomianism, civil disobedience, and the imperatives
    of a higher law and (8) a life of spiritual simplicity and integrity
    ("simplify, simplify"; "to live deliberately"; "the mass of men lead
    lives of quiet desperation" and "desperate haste"; "to be awake is
    to be alive"; "I was determined to know beans"). Bronson Alcott,
    Emily Dickinson, Ralph Waldo Emerson, Margaret Fuller, Herman

Melville, Henry David Thoreau, Jones Very and Walt Whitman
were notable exponents of New England Transcendentalism.

22. **Jacksonian Democracy** (1828-1840s) was both the cause and
consequence of the extension of universal white male suffrage (by
the elimination of property qualifications) in the 1810s through
1830s. Andrew Jackson ("Old Hickory") was portrayed as the
hero of the common man, a child of nature, the hero of the Battle
of New Orleans and a self-made man, as well as an entrepreneurial
capitalist and planter/slave-holder, who owned 150 slaves. The era
of Jacksonian democracy was characterized by (1) greater
participation by the common man (i.e., the property-less white
male) in the political process; (2) rhetorical allegiance to the theme
of the moral restoration of the simple virtues of an agrarian
republic; (3) entrepreneurial reforms against established elites
("equal rights for all and special privileges for none"), including
the war against the Second National Bank, which was portrayed as
a symbol of elitism and privilege; (4) mass politics and the spoils
system ("rotation in office"); (5) the forced removal of 20,000 to
60,000 Native Americans and the expropriation of their tribal lands
in the southeastern United States for the expansion of cotton
plantation/slave-labor system and (6) an aggressive policy of
Manifest Destiny, which resulted in war with Mexico and the
annexation of the northern half of its territory. Richard Hofstadter,
Jon Meacham, Marvin Meyers, Robert Remini, Arthur Schlesinger,
Jr., John William Ward, Sean Wilentz.

23. **Mexican-American War** (1846-1848) was precipitated by
President Polk's stationing American troops on Mexican soil on
the north bank of the Rio Grande River instead of the more
northerly Nueces River, with the intention of provoking Mexico
into war with the United States in order to annex not only Texas,
but also New Mexico and Alta California. It represents an early
example of American military conquest and territorial expansion,
which was justified by the doctrine of Manifest Destiny and driven
by Southern slaveholders' need for new lands on which to cultivate
cotton. The war was opposed by many Northerners and anti-
slavery advocates: Henry David Thoreau went to jail rather than
pay taxes to support the war; Ulysses Grant called the Mexican
War "one of the most unjust ever waged by a stronger against a
weaker nation." It laid the foundation for a decade of sectional

tensions, which led, eventually, to the American Civil War. The Treaty of Guadalupe Hidalgo, which ended the war, forced Mexico to cede what is now California, Nevada, Utah, New Mexico, and most of Arizona and Colorado, which, including Texas, constituted over half of Mexico's territory, to the United States for $18 million. Many slaveholders in Congress advocated the annexation of all of Mexico and Cuba as well. Amy Greenberg, Robert Johannsen, Ramón Edwardo Ruiz.

24. **American Civil War** (1861-1865) was the bloodiest war in American history. Its causes have been debated extensively, some of which are thought to have been: (1) the expansion of slavery into the western territories (i.e., those that had not yet been incorporated into the Union as states) and the fear by the North and Midwest that the Southern plantation/slave-labor system would displace the freehold family farm; (2) the Southern belief that the United States was a confederation of sovereign states and secession from the United States was legal; (3) the Northern desire to preserve the Union from Southern secession; (4) the conviction by many of the moral evil of slavery and its contradiction of the national creed that "all men are created equal"; (5) sectional and economic divisions (Northern industrialists and Midwestern family farmers versus Southern planters/slaveholders; industrial capitalism versus agrarian feudalism; Charles Beard); (6) "Sir Walter Scott's disease" (the cult of Southern chivalry, with its exaggerated sense of pride, honor and manhood and its tradition of dueling to settle disputes; Mark Twain, Amy Greenberg); (7) Southern nationalism, arrogance and intransigence, which was derived from "King Cotton's" economic and political ascendency (cotton accounted for nearly 60% of all American exports in 1860, and the dollar value of humans held in bondage was $3 billion, which was more than the total value of all the capital invested in banks, factories and railroads; Edward Baptist, Eric Foner, Greg Gandin); (8) the fear, hysteria and paranoia in the South over the threat of slave insurrections and the conviction that John Brown's Harper's Ferry raid was a "Black Republican" party plot and that all Northerners were abolitionists; (9) the election of Abraham Lincoln (who promised not to interfere with slavery where it then existed), which was the immediate cause of the secession of the Upper South; (10) the firing on the federal Fort Sumter in Charleston Harbor, South Carolina, by Confederate forces. The

Civil War was the deadliest war in American history, with at least 625,000 deaths, or approximately 30% of young Southern white males and 10% of Northern white males (John Huddleston).

As noted elsewhere, historians have argued over the profitability of slavery and whether or not it would have died out gradually on its own accord without a civil war. Some historians (Iran Berlin, Stanley Engerman, Robert Fogel and David Reynolds) assert that it would not have died out on its own, since, between 1850 and 1860, cotton production doubled and the value of a field-slave doubled to $2,500. Historians have also debated whether or not the Civil War was inevitable ("the irrepressible conflict"), and, if so, at what point it became so (see Broken symmetry in Science Concepts). Lincoln was elected on his promise to prevent the expansion of slavery into the Western territories and to preserve the Union, but as the war itself progressed and the bloodshed and slaughter increased, the objective of the war shifted from preserving the Union to ending slavery, and the moral justification of the war shifted to the expiation of the nation's historical sin of slavery. After the end of the war and the ratification of the 13th Amendment in 1865, four million human beings were legally freed from chattel slavery and a lifetime of involuntary servitude for themselves and their descendants.

25. **Social Darwinism** was a social-economic theory and world view popular in the late 19th and early 20th Centuries that was loosely based on Charles Darwin's theory of evolution, the struggle for existence (Robert Malthus), natural selection (Darwin and Alfred Russel Wallace) and survival of the fittest (Herbert Spencer). According to the tenets of Social Darwinism, humanitarianism, social justice and, even, philanthropy were futile since they interfered with the natural laws of brutal competition and would permit the poor and "unfit" to reproduce, thus, impeding human progress (William Graham Sumer). The theory was predicated on a Hobbesian view of nature as brutal and ruthless ("red in tooth and claw") and represented a synthesis of Calvinism (predestination, the inevitability of suffering, the fit are the elect) and classical laissez-faire capitalism (economic scarcity, the struggle for existence, self-seeking individualism, competition and "antagonistic cooperation"). Social Darwinism was, and is, used to justify political and economic domination by the wealthy (the

richest are the fittest), the sanctity of private property, anti-labor legislation, resistance to social reforms and support for militarism and imperialism (might makes right). See Eric Goldman and Richard Hofstadter in Selected References.

26. **Countervailing Theories/Reform Darwinism** assert that (1) Social Darwinism conflates "fitness" with excellence, and biological evolution with social progress; (2) the wealthy are unfit and predatory (Thorstein Veblen; Matthew Josephson); (3) rampant acquisitiveness, materialism and extremes of wealth are un-Christian (the Social Gospel movement); (4) group-level selection, social cooperation and altruism are as important in human evolution as competition (Edward Bellamy, Henry George, Walter Rauschenbusch; see Group-level selection in Anthropology) and (5) "genetic" (i.e., biological) evolution is blind and wasteful and has been replaced by "telic" (i.e., purposeful) social evolution, in which humans can collectively plan and control their own destinies, reform society and end social injustice through collective action and the positive liberal state (Herbert Croly, Theodore Roosevelt, Lester Ward).

For cultural materialists, Social Darwinism represents a classical example of the class basis of ideas, of the cultural hegemony of the dominant class in which the ideology, or self-validating values, of the capitalist elite (in this case the success ethic and the Horatio Alger paradigm of the self-made man) are infused throughout society, creating in the general population a misplaced validation of their own subordinate status and a belief in the fairness of "moral capitalism" and the probability of their own upward mobility as "expectant capitalists" (to use Lizabeth Cohen's and Bray Hammond's terms). Antonio Gramsci, Raymond Williams. See Cultural Hegemony in Sociology Concepts.

27. **Pragmatism/Radical Empiricism** is a philosophy that was developed in the United States in the late 19th and early 20th Centuries by John Dewey, William James and Charles Peirce. It contradicted the determinism of Social Darwinism, provided renewed philosophical support for democracy, pluralism and progress and served as the intellectual foundation for 20th Century reform movements. Historically, the discovery of radioactivity and Einstein's theories of relativity destroyed the Newtonian "block

universe" of an enclosed, monistic, cosmic machine. Pragmatism offered, instead, an open-ended universe of individual freedom and choice, novelty, variety, flux, spontaneity, chance and indeterminacy, and stressed the boundless, creative potential of the individual; truth was perceived as a process not an essence; knowledge was acquired through action and learning by doing, not through spectatorship or the passive receipt of knowledge. See Richard Hofstadter in Selected References.

28. **Populism** (1890s) was an agrarian movement for economic, political and social reforms that laid the foundation for later Progressive and New Deal reforms. It was viewed at the time as an expression of agrarian radicalism and was dismissed by its opponents as "hayseed socialism." The People's Party was formed in 1891 in response to the economic depression and the distress of Midwestern wheat and Southern cotton farmers. It advocated a wide spectrum of reforms, including: (1) an inflationary currency ("free silver"); (2) government ownership of the railroad, telegraph and telephone industries; (3) a graduated income tax; (4) the right of workers to organize and bargain collectively; (5) an eight-hour day; (6) the initiative, referendum and recall; (7) the direct election of U. S. senators (who, at the time, were elected by the state legislatures) and (8) postal savings banks. Many of their reforms were later adopted during the Progressive Era and the New Deal.

The Populist movement also contained elements of paranoia, anti-Semitism (including the belief that financial speculation and economic depressions were caused by an international cabal of Jews and bankers), white supremacy and rural antipathy to the cities and urban immigrants. The People's Party was a third-party movement whose agenda was co-opted by the Democratic Party and William Jennings Bryan in the election of 1896 over the single issue of "free silver' (the "cowbird" of the reform movement), which was thought to provide an inflationary solution to the deflationary gold standard and a means of getting the country out of a severe economic depression. "Populist" is now a generic term that is used to describe a popular or radical leader of the political left or right who speaks, in some contexts demagogically, against elites and on behalf of ordinary people. Lawrence Goodwyn, John Hicks, Richard Hofstadter, Michael Kazin.

29. **Progressivism** (1900-1920) was a political and social movement, primarily, of middle-class reformers who sought to purify government and big business of corruption and restore individualist values and opportunity in the face of large-scale organizations such as trusts, unions and urban immigrant political machines. Progressivism has been viewed as a moral crusade ("a carnival of purity," "the American people beating a carpet") that was driven by the status anxieties of a displaced social elite (patrician and middle-class reformers versus immigrants, laborers, plutocrats and robber barons), as well as a response to the objective evils of industrialization. Progressivism was deeply influenced by reform journalism ("muckraking"), Populist reform proposals, Reform Darwinism, philosophical pragmatism, the Social Gospel movement and the principles of scientific management. It implemented (1) limited trust-busting (with Theodore Roosevelt's approach of regulating big businesses and oligopolies in the public interest, generally, prevailing over Woodrow Wilson's approach of breaking up the trusts and regulating competition among smaller units); (2) child labor laws; (3) women's suffrage; (4) prohibition of alcohol; (5) civil service reform; (6) the initiative, referendum and recall; (7) the direct election of U. S. senators; (8) pure food and drug laws; (9) workplace safety regulations; (10) federal regulation of national banking and interstate commerce and (11) the conservation of natural resources. John Morton Blum, Eric Goldman, Alonzo Hamby, Samuel Hays, Richard Hofstadter, William Leuchtenburg, Arthur Link, George Mowry, Robert Wiebe.

30. **New Deal** (1933-45) is the name given to the relief, recovery and reform programs of the Franklin Roosevelt administration during the Great Depression. It has been characterized as pragmatic rather than ideological (in which reform was a technical, not a moral, issue) and experimental, improvisational and remedial. It re-affirmed the role of the positive, progressive national government and modified the, primarily, laissez-faire economy by subjecting it to regulation by the national ("federal") government, which had the effect of imposing a welfare state on capitalistic foundations, as one historian described it. The New Deal coalition consisted of a range of social, economic and political interest groups (progressive Wall Street financiers, Main Street businessmen, organized labor, urban political machines, large agricultural producers, tenant

farmers, Southern white segregationists, African-Americans) in which the national government was viewed as a broker in mediating competing interests and needs. In retrospect, the New Deal served as a holding action against the Great Depression until the massive government expenditures of Lend Lease and World War II brought the economy out of the Depression. See Permanent warfare economy/military Keynesianism in Concepts and 16. John Maynard Keynes/Keynesian Economics in Economics Details.

The New Deal implemented a wide range of programs for reform, economic stimulus and recovery, including (1) federal relief and public works projects; (2) the minimum wage and fair labor standards; (3) social security; (4) the right of workers to organize and bargain collectively; (5) the regulation of the banking, securities, public utilities and transportation industries; (6) federal insurance for savings deposits; (7) homeowners' loans; (8) agricultural assistance; (9) public hydroelectric power projects; (10) rural electrification programs; (11) conservation programs and (12) publically supported arts, music, theater and writers projects. James MacGregor Burns, Lizabeth Cohen, Eric Goldman, David M. Kennedy, William Leuchtenburg, Arthur Schlesinger, Jr., Howard Zinn.

31. **Cold War** is the term used to describe the military, diplomatic, economic and ideological struggle between the United States and its allies against the Soviet Union and its allies for the period from 1945 to 1991. The era was marked by the Soviet Union's hegemony in Central and Eastern Europe, the Berlin Blockade of 1948-49, the Korean War of 1950-54, the Soviet suppression of the Hungarian Revolution of 1956, the Vietnam War of 1959-1975, the construction of the Berlin Wall by East Germany in 1961, the invasion of Cuba by agents of the United States in 1961 at the Bay of Pigs, the Cuban missile crisis in 1962, the invasion of Czechoslovakia by the Warsaw Pact in 1968 and the Soviet invasion and occupation of Afghanistan in 1979. It was followed by a general period of détente and relatively peaceful coexistence marked by the rapprochement between the United States and China in the 1970s and 1980s, and ended with the collapse of the Soviet Union in 1991.

The Cold War took place in a bipolar world of two nuclear
superpowers and their allies and was shadowed by the specter of
thermonuclear war and the mutually assured destruction of
civilization (the "balance of terror"). Both blocs competed for the
support of "Third World" developing countries and aggressively
intervened in their domestic affairs to gain their loyalty and
massively subsidized their ruling, often repressive, regimes to
insure it. The Cold War was characterized by (1) the Soviet
Union's post-World War II occupation of Central and Eastern
European countries (creating an "Iron Curtain") and the brutal,
totalitarian suppression of liberty and dissent in communist
countries; (2) the United States' support of pro-Western
authoritarian governments, brutal military dictatorships, CIA-
backed coups of socialist governments in Guatemala, Iran and
Chile and assassination attempts in Cuba, Africa and elsewhere;
(3) horrifically expensive military economies in both countries,
which were based on massive public expenditures for weapons and
a missile race; (4) espionage and counter-espionage; (5) the
internal suppression of dissent; (6) proxy wars and (7) anti-colonial
wars of national liberation, insurgency and counter-insurgency.
The United States' policy was one of containment, that is, to use
military and non-military means to contain Soviet influence and
stop the spread of communism. The total military expenditures for
the Cold War by the United States is estimated to have been $8
trillion. See Permanent warfare economy/military Keynesianism
in Concepts and the Rise and fall of great powers: the 16th Century
Spanish paradigm in Historiography Concepts.

Domestically, the Cold War *mentalité* pervaded every aspect of
American culture and politics during the 1950s and 1960s. It was
based on a Manichean world view of absolute good versus absolute
evil, of democratic freedom versus godless communism. The anti-
communist paranoia and witch hunts of the 1950s (McCarthyism/
the Second Red Scare) presumed the existence of a communist
conspiracy, directed from abroad, to subvert American democratic
institutions and impose a communist dictatorship on the United
States. American civil liberties were restricted and liberal dissent
was deemed unpatriotic and "un-American" (the civil rights
movement, for example, was viewed as a communist plot by J.
Edgar Hoover, the Director of the FBI). Methods of political
repression included loyalty oaths, blacklists, firings, censorship,

book purges, domestic spying on dissidents, red-baiting, character assassinations and guilt by association. Daniel Bell, John Lewis Gaddis, Jonathan Haslam, Richard Hofstadter, Gabriel Kolko, Walter LaFeber, Melvyn Leffler, Robert McMahon, Kathryn Olmstead, Raymond Pearson, Geoffrey Roberts, Herbert Swope, William Appleman Williams.

32. **Civil Rights/Black Freedom Movement** (1954-1968) was the movement to end racial segregation, disenfranchisement and discrimination against African Americans. This phase of the movement was initiated by the landmark Supreme Court decision, *Brown versus Board of Education of Topeka Kansas* in 1954, which partially overturned Jim Crow laws established in the South after Reconstruction to enforce racial segregation. The decision declared that "separate but equal" public educational facilities were inherently unequal. It was one of the pivotal events leading to the civil rights movement and marked a turning point in black civil rights by shifting the struggle from gradualism and legalism to large and sustained campaigns of mass civil resistance and non-violent protest.

Significant events in the civil rights/black freedom movement included (1) the refusal of Rosa Parks to sit at the back of a public bus in Montgomery, Alabama in 1955, which precipitated a successful bus boycott; (2) the brutal murder of 14-year old Emmitt Till in Mississippi in 1955, which portrayed to Northern audiences the brutality of Southern white supremacy; (3) the desegregation of Little Rock Central High School in 1957, under the protection of federal troops; (4) the Greensboro, North Carolina lunch counter sit-ins by students in 1960 and other sit-ins of public and commercial facilities; (5) freedom rides through the South; (6) voter registration drives; (7) marches and boycotts, including the March on Washington in 1963.

These campaigns met with massive white resistance in the South, which were punctuated by beatings of civil rights demonstrators by law enforcement officials and civilians and by assassinations, including the assassination of Dr. Martin Luther King, Jr., in 1968. This phase of the civil rights movement culminated in the passage of the Civil Rights Act of 1964, the Voting Rights Act of 1965 and the Fair Housing Act of 1968, which prohibited discrimination in employment practices, ended segregation in schools, the workplace and in public accommodations, protected voting rights and banned discrimination in the sale or rental of housing. The idealism and activism that motivated the civil rights movement flowed into the anti-Vietnam War movement and was a major catalyst for the countercultural ferment of the 1960s and 1970s (*qq. v.* in Details). Taylor Branch.

33. **Vietnam War** (1959-1975) has been viewed as (1) a war for Vietnam's national independence from French and, later, American colonialists, (2) Vietnam's civil war, (3) a response by the United States to the invasion of South Vietnam by North Vietnam and/or (4) an episode in the Cold War by the United States against the spread of international communism. The Vietnam War served as an example of modern asymmetrical warfare (of insurgency and counter-insurgency), which devolved into a war of attrition and a quagmire in the jungles of Southeast Asia. It was characterized by the massive use of fire-power and carpet bombings, including the use of napalm and the herbicide Agent Orange. During the conflict, the U. S. dropped more than 7 million tons of bombs on Vietnam, Laos and Cambodia, which was more than twice the tonnage dropped on all of the European and Asian theaters during World War II. In effect, it became necessary to destroy the country in order to save it from communism. 57,592 Americans and between 1.5 and 2.5 million Vietnamese died during the war (the latter represented 21% to 36% of Vietnam's population of seven million). Agent Orange alone is thought to have killed or maimed 400,000 and caused 150,000 to 500,000 birth defects. Domestically, military conscription and resistance to the war shaped, defined, polarized and radicalized a generation of young Americans.

34. **Countercultural Ferment of the 1960s and 1970s** represented the nation's Second "Freedom's Ferment" (the first occurred in the 1830s-1840s [*q.v.* in Concepts]) and consisted of overlapping political and cultural currents. These included:
    1) The civil rights/black freedom movement.
    2) The anti-Vietnam War movement.
    3) The women's liberation movement, which was associated with
       (a) the first commercial oral contraceptive, Enovid, in 1960;
       (b) Betty Friedan's *The Feminine Mystique* in 1963 and (c) the

Supreme Court decision *Roe v. Wade* in 1973, which legalized abortion. See 35. Feminism in Details.

4) The sexual revolution, which resulted in more permissive and tolerant sexual mores. It was associated with women's liberation, the birth control pill, *Playboy*, mini-skirts and topless swimsuits, free love, etc.
5) Rock-and-roll music, with its open and sexually suggestive lyrics and cross-racial identifications.
6) Casual, recreational drug use.
7) The environmental/green movement.
8) The gay liberation movement.
9) Seniors' rights.
10) Disability rights.
11) The consumer protection movement.
12) Christian evangelicalism, which was fed by both (a) the "Jesus Freaks," a subset of the counterculture's search for spiritual meaning and contempt for consumerism and materialism; as well as, ironically, (b) a religious and traditionalist backlash against the counterculture's political and cultural radicalism, especially its opposition to the Vietnam war, its use of drugs and its sexual permissiveness.
13) A legacy of participatory democracy, grassroots activism and a belief in the power of collective action.

The youthful, counterculture revolt of the 1960s and 1970s was driven by (1) college student activists and post-World War II baby boomers; (2) John F. Kennedy-inspired idealism; (3) reaction against the conformity, consumerism and materialism of the "Silent Generation" of the 1950s and the Cold War culture of apathy and anti-communist paranoia; (4) parental permissiveness ("Spock latitudinarianism"); (5) middle-class prosperity and upward mobility of the 1950s and 1960s; (6) visceral reaction to television news images of Southern segregationists and their brutal repression of African-American civil rights, as well as those of military and civilian casualties in an extended and unpopular war in Southeast Asia and (7) opposition to conscription, the military-industrial-university complex and the Vietnam war. Terry Anderson, Theodore Roszak, Robert Self.

35. **Feminism** is an umbrella term applied to a series of political, social and cultural movements and ideologies whose objectives

were, and are, to (1) obtain and protect equal rights for women, including the right to vote; (2) establish and insure women's legal and economic independence (including the right to own property, enter into contracts and work outside the home); (3) allow women to control their own reproductive health as a means of emancipation and self-determination; (4) end patriarchy and male dominance; (5) redefine gender roles; (6) end workplace discrimination and unequal pay; (7) establish child care and parental leave; (8) share child-rearing and domestic tasks with their domestic partners and (9) end sexual objectification, sexual harassment and domestic violence.

Historically, in the United States, feminism has been expressed in three main waves of activism (although Hilary Hallett and others have viewed it as "one continuous wave of feminism [which] has emphasized different elements at different times"):

1) **The first wave** began with the Seneca Falls Women's Rights Convention in 1848, which stated in its Declaration of Independence that "all men and women are created equally." The movement was led by women such as Elizabeth Cady Stanton, Susan B. Anthony and Lucretia Mott, the latter two of whom had participated in the abolitionist movement and were guided by the Quaker belief in the equality of the sexes. The struggle for the rights of women to vote and to live and work independently of men (including the right to hold property and enter into contracts) characterized the women's rights movement in the 19th and early 20th Centuries and culminated in the passage of Nineteenth Amendment in 1920, which granted women the right to vote. Women suffragettes, under the leadership of Jane Addams, Margaret Sanger and others, fought for a variety of other social issues as well, including peace, temperance, the right to birth control and the struggle against racism and poverty.

2) **The second wave** of feminism in the 1960s and 1970s, which was known as the women's liberation movement, was precipitated by the publication of Betty Friedan's *Feminine Mystique* in 1963, a study of enforced domesticity and angst ("the problem that has no name") among post-World War II, middle-class housewives, who longed for personal fulfillment outside the home. It is associated with (a) women working outside the home during and after World War II and the

increasing enrollment of women in college; (b) the sexual revolution of the 1960s, which was enabled by the birth control pill in 1960, *Roe v Wade* in 1973, which legalized abortion, and more permissive and tolerant sexual mores and the erosion of double sexual standards; (c) the reaction against male patriarchy, particularly, in the leadership of the civil rights and anti-Vietnam War movements of the 1960s, as well as in the academic, business and professional worlds. It is also associated with (d) Title VII of the Civil Rights Act of 1964, which prohibited employer discrimination on the basis of race, color, religion, sex or national origin; (e) local, consciousness-raising affinity groups; (f) studies of female sexuality (Masters and Johnson; *Our Bodies Ourselves*); (g) the founding of the National Organization of Women in 1966; (h) the drive to ratify the Equal Rights Amendment and (i) Title IX of the 1972 Education Amendments, which sought to end gender discrimination in higher education, including access to athletic programs, and led to the development of women's studies programs in colleges and universities. The women's liberation movement led to greater legal and social equality and economic independence for women, with large numbers entering careers and professions formerly reserved for men, including those in academia, medicine, law and politics.

3) **The third wave** of feminism developed in the 1990s in response to the criticism that the second wave was overly influenced by the values and perspectives of middle class white women. It focused, instead, on the special needs of working class women, women of color and women in the post-colonial, developing world. Third wave feminism is also associated with "focusing on women's empowerment rather than their victimization and as taking pleasure in fashion, romance, and sex" (Hallett).

Since then, feminism has diverged into a series of multiple and, sometimes, overlapping and contradictory streams, including: (1) feminist theory (on gender inequality, power structures, patriarchy, stereotyping, objectification); (2) feminist literary criticism (*q.v.* in Literary Concepts); (3) radical/Marxist feminism, which asserts that the oppression of women is caused by hierarchical, male-dominated capitalism; (4) post-essential feminism, which asserts that gender roles are social constructed rather than biologically

determined or derived from an essential, universal female identity;
(5) anti-pornography and anti-prostitution feminism, which is
opposed by (6) sex-positive and sex-worker feminism; (7) lipstick
feminism, which seeks to reclaim the traditional symbols of
femininity such as make-up and sexually suggestive clothing to
provide valid, empowering choices; (8) separatist feminism; (9)
eco-feminism and (10) post-feminism. Nina Bayn, Nancy Cott,
Barbara Epstein, Eleanor Flexner, Linda Gordon, Hilary Hallett,
Julie Jeffrey, Alice Kessler-Harris, Judith Newton, William
O'Neill, Daniel Rivers, Ruth Rosen, Anne Scott, Robert Self, Kish
Sklar, Christine Stansell, Rosemarie Tong, Alice Felt Tyler.

36. **American Generational Cycles** is a paradigm, based on Karl
Mannheim's theory of generations, which was developed and
applied by William Strauss and Neil Howe, that shows that
American history has followed a generational pattern of social
change that repeats itself in the following cycle:
1) The **idealist generation**, which is educated, inner-directed,
spiritual, visionary and narcissistic; it is represented by writers,
teachers and preachers.
2) The **reactive generation**, which is cynical, risk-taking,
alienated, pragmatic, liberty-seeking and focused on survival;
it is represented by entrepreneurs, generals, industrialists and
salesmen.
3) The **civic generation**, which is outer-directed, heroic,
achieving, organizational, community-minded and technology-
driven; it is represented by scientists, statesmen, economists,
diplomats and builders.
4) The **adaptive generation**, which is conformist, risk-averse,
consensual, sensitive and focused on social justice issues; it is
represented by artists, lawyers, therapists and legislators.

Strauss and Howe have identified and categorized the following
generations in American history:

Puritan (born 1584-1614)	Idealist
Cavalier (b. 1615-1647)	Reactive
Glorious (b. 1648-1673)	Civic
Enlightenment (b. 1674-1700)	Adaptive
Great Awakening (b. 1701-1723)	Idealist
Liberty (b. 1724-1741)	Reactive
Republican (b. 1742-1766)	Civic

Compromise (b. 1767-1791)	Adaptive
Transcendental (b. 1792-1821)	Idealist
Gilded (born 1822-1842)	Reactive
Progressive (b. 1843-1859)	Adaptive
Missionary (b. 1860-1882)	Idealist
Lost (b. 1883-1900)	Reactive
GI (b. 1901-1924)	Civic
Silent (b. 1925-1942)	Adaptive
Boom (b. 1943-1960)	Idealist
Generation X (b. 1961-1981)	Reactive
Millennial (b. 1982-2004)	Civic

See Theory of Generations in Historiography and Sociology Concepts.

2. ANTHROPOLOGY

CONCEPTS AND PHRASES:

Adaptation: the evolutionary process by which an organism adjusts to the imperatives and constraints of its environment, or a trait that enhances that adjustment, the success of which is measured by its "fitness," that is, its enhanced ability to survive and pass along its genes. For example, humans who migrated to the northern latitudes where there is less sunlight developed paler skin, which allowed more sunlight to be absorbed by the body, which enabled those individuals with the trait to synthesize vitamin D (which is needed for the absorption of calcium) from less sunlight. Marvin Harris. See 2. Natural Selection in Details.

African exodus: the migration, approximately 60,000 years ago, of a small band of anatomically modern humans, perhaps as few as 150 to 1,000 individuals, who crossed the Red Sea from East Africa, and colonized the rest of the world. They served as the founding population from whom all non-Africans are descended. Luigi and Francesco Cavalli-Sforza, Steve Olson, Spencer Wells. See 6. Out-of-Africa Hypothesis in Details.

Aggression as innate versus **aggression as socially conditioned**: see 12. Violence and Human Nature (the Hobbes-Rousseau Dichotomy) in Details.

Agricultural/Neolithic revolution: the domestication of plants and animals, beginning approximately 11,000 years ago in the Middle East, which laid the foundation for the rise of civilization. See 9. Agricultural/Neolithic revolution in Details.

Altriciality: infant helplessness. In humans, the prolonged period of infant helplessness is thought to be a causal factor in pair-bonding, the sexual division of labor and the rise of culture. Herbert Spencer. See Obstetrical dilemma, Pair-bonding and the Sexual contract in Concepts and 4. Bipedalism in Details.

Anatomically modern humans: *Homo sapiens sapiens*, who evolved in Africa approximately 200,000 years ago. See 3. Hominin Family Tree in Details.

Animism: the belief that all entities and objects in nature have a soul or spiritual essence.

Anterior insula: that part of the primate brain in which perceived unfairness elicits a strong emotional reaction, which suggests that the sense of fairness is innate in humans.

Anthropocene epoch: the informal name given to the era in which we are now living, which began with the Industrial Revolution around 1750 CE and marks the momentous impact of human activity on the natural environment, including mass extinctions, deforestation, pollution and global warming, the latter derived, primarily, from the burning of fossil fuels. Some argue that the impact of humans on the environment began 11,500 years ago with the introduction of agriculture, or even 45,000 years ago with the beginning of the mass extinctions of mega-fauna by modern humans. Paul Cruzen.

Arboreal: living in trees; the primary mode of living for our pre-bipedal ancestors.

Bipedalism: walking upright on two legs, which is one of the distinguishing features of the human species. Since bipedalism preceded encephalization (that is, walking upright preceded the development of a large hominin brain), it is hypothesized that walking upright freed the hands to make tools and weapons and carry food back to a base camp, which facilitated the development of fine motor skills, cooperative hunting, group living and the rise of social intelligence. See Mankind/hand, Obstetrical dilemma and Pair-bonding in Concepts and 4. Bipedalism and 5. Social Brain Hypothesis in Details.

Blombos Cave: the site of the earliest evidence of modern human symbolic behavior, dating from approximately 75,000 to 100,000 years ago and located on the coast of South Africa. Symbolic behavior was represented in shell beads, engraved cross-hatched patterns on ocher and an ocher tool kit that may have been used for body decoration. See Symbolic behavior in Concepts.

Body ornamentation: a form of symbolic behavior in which body paint, tattoos, feathers, beads, shells and other forms of jewelry are used to express one's individuality as well as one's affiliation with a particular social group. See Symbolic behavior in Concepts.

Carrying capacity: the maximum number of a given species that can be sustained in a given habitat.

Catastrophic/mega-droughts: long periods of severely restricted rainfall, which are thought to be a contributing factor in the collapse of some societies and civilizations, including that of the Mayans in Mesoamerica by the year 1000 CE and the Anasazi in what is now the Southwestern United States around 1300 CE. Jared Diamond.

Cave paintings: wall painting at Chauvet, Altamira and Lascaux in southwest Europe, which date from approximately 35,000 to 18,000 years ago. They consist of stylized horses, aurochs, bison and reindeer and represent some of the earliest surviving examples of humanity's aesthetic sense and symbolic consciousness. See Susanne Langer in Quotations.

Clade: a group that shares the same ancestor.

Clan: an extended kinship group.

Concealed ovulation/hidden estrus: an evolutionary adaptation in human females that fostered pair-bonding, continuous sexual relationships, kinship recognition, food-sharing and shared child-rearing. By mating with a particular woman repeatedly throughout her menstrual cycle rather than mating with multiple women during the times when they may or may not be fertile, a male increases the chances of producing a child and passing along his genes. It also reinforces the emotional bonds between the couple and increases the parental investment in the child. See Sexual contract in Concepts.

Control of fire: a development that is thought to have occurred approximately 800,000 years ago, or earlier. Fire provided warmth, a sense of community and protection from predators. It also enabled the exploitation of additional food sources by providing for the cooking of tough, fibrous foods, which resulted in the evolution of smaller jaws and teeth from eating softer foods.

Cosmologies: culturally bound theories or myths that seek to explain the origin of the universe.

Cultural diffusion/adaptation: the transfer of cultural practices and techniques, such as farming, from one group to another, usually through direct contact, imitation, intermarriage, trade or common media; versus **colonization/physical displacement**, in which one cultural group physically colonizes a territory and displaces an earlier group.

Cultural relativity: the belief that each culture is unique, is guided by his own values, ideals, imperatives and constraints and should be understood in its own terms; versus **ethnocentrism**: judging other cultures by the value-system of one's own culture. Ruth Benedict, Franz Boas, Bronislaw Malinowski, Margaret Mead, Max Weber. See Ethnocentrism and Variety/plasticity of human cultures in Concepts and Max Weber in Quotations.

Culture: a set of learned behaviors, values, beliefs, ideals, customs, symbols, language and traditions that are shared by a particular group.

Defensive aggression: the forceful and, often, exaggerated response to perceived threats against one's group or home territory. It is associated with the male hormone testosterone and the maternal hormone oxytocin. See Nesting instinct, Oxytocin, Territoriality and Testosterone in Concepts and 12. Violence and Human Nature in Details.

Displays: stereotypical, often unconscious, behaviors that are expressed in greetings, courtship rituals, competition, challenges, domination, erudition and submission. See Sexual/courtship displays in Concepts.

Division of labor: a pattern of behavior that is characteristic of many hunter-gatherer societies in which men hunted and waged war and women gathered and raised children. The division may be derived from the biological, reproductive and nurturing imperatives and capacities of women, the prolonged period of helplessness of human infants and the moderate physical dimorphism of men relative to women. See Altriciality, Nesting instinct, Oxytocin and Testosterone in Concepts.

Dominance/status hierarchies: the predominant form of social organization in many animal species, which is said to promote order and stability, if not equity and justice, within the group. See Class and Class signifiers/class imagery in Sociology Concepts and 20. Class Structure in Sociology Details.

Dunbar's number: the thesis that the maximum effective size of stable, cohesive social groups is 150 individuals (with a range of 100 to 250), which is the typical size of hunting-gathering clans, military companies and other traditional social groups. It is said to be the maximum number of people with whom a single individual can maintain personal, face-to-face relationships, which is cognitively limited by the size of the neo-cortex. Thus, large, modern, complex, hierarchical organizations and nation-states are constrained by this tribal and cognitive parameter. Robin Dunbar, Malcolm Gladwell. See Tribalism in Concepts and 5. Social Brain Hypothesis in Details).

Enculturation: the process by which an individual learns and absorbs the language, values, norms and practices of the culture in which it is living.

Endogamy versus **exogamy**: marrying inside, versus outside, one's religious, ethnic or social group, class or clan.

Ethnocentrism: judging other cultures by the value-system of one's own culture; viewing the behavior and values of other cultures as inferior; versus **cultural relativity** and **xenocentrism** (*qq.v.* in Concepts).

Ethnography: the direct, empirical study of a cultural group.

Ethnology: the comparative study of multiple cultural groups.

Ethology: the study of animal behavior.

Facial differentiation: an adaptation that may have evolved as a result of human bipedalism, an upright posture and the loss of an acute sense of smell, which was a consequence of the loss of quadrupedal locomotion and the elevation of the nose above the ground. Facial differentiation allowed bipedal humans to recognize and visually identify each other as individuals, in the absence of olfactory signals. Sigmund Freud. See Pheromones in Concepts.

Feast-famine cycles: alternating periods of abundance and scarcity, which are thought to have influenced the evolution of the body's ability to regulate, store and metabolize body fat. A "fat switch," or, more specifically, a genetic mutation, has been identified which encodes an enzyme that directs the body to store calories, particularly those from fructose, as fat rather than burn them as energy. Unfortunately, the gene cannot be turned off in the face of modern, super-caloric abundance and sedentary life-styles. James Neel, Richard J. Johnson and Peter Andrews.

Fertility cults: religious sects whose beliefs, rituals and practices involved physical and symbolical re-enactments of sexual and reproductive behaviors, which were used to maintain and celebrate fertility.

Fight-or-flight versus **tend-and-befriend strategies**: in humans, the fight response to a frightful or stressful situation, which is often manifested in anger, aggression or argument, as opposed to the flight response, which is expressed in avoidance, social withdrawal or substance abuse. Tend-and-befriend strategies, on the other hand, involve affiliation, social bonding and mutual defense and are more typically a female's response to stress than a male's.

Fitness: the degree of adaptation by an organism to its environment, which is defined in the teleological calculus of sociobiology as surviving and passing along its genes, that is, as maximizing its reproductive success. See Adaptation, Sexual/courtship displays and Sexual selection in Concepts and 2. Natural Section in Details.

Folklore: myths, legends, folktales and ballads.

Founder's effect: the reduction in genetic diversity that occurs when a small, colonizing population breaks off from a larger population and forms a new colony in a new geographical area. The genetic variants, or mutations, carried by the founding members of the new colony occur at a relatively higher frequency within the smaller, isolated population than the larger population from which it sprang. In this context, an unusual physical trait or genetic variant is more easily reinforced and spread throughout the smaller population of the new colony than it would be in a larger, more diverse, parent population, where it is relatively less common and, perhaps, would eventually die out. See Genetic drift in Concepts.

Founding myths/myths of origin: those that are used to explain the origin and justify the legitimacy and sacredness of the existing social order. Mircea Eliade.

FOXP2: a gene that is associated with the development of speech and language.

Gender dimorphism: the average difference in body size between males and females of the same species. Extreme male-female dimorphism (i.e., large males and small females, which is characteristic, for example, of gorillas) is correlated with competition among males for, and monopoly of, females, which results in polygyny, or harems. Humans are moderately dimorphic, with males being on average 5% to 20% larger than females, which is associated with pair-bonding, mild polygyny and relative gender equality.

Genetic drift: random genetic changes, which have a greater impact on smaller populations. See Founder's effect.

Genotype: the inherited genetic instructions of an individual or group; versus **phenotype**: the physical traits or observable characteristics of an individual or group; i.e., the outward physical manifestation of the genotype. See 8. Human Genes and DNA in Science Details.

Gracile versus *robustus*: slender versus robust body types; the former are thought to be better adapted to hot, tropical climates, while the latter are thought to retain body heat more efficiently and, thus, are more suited to colder climates. Marvin Harris.

Grandmother hypothesis: that the survival of a group is enhanced by the survival of its post-reproductive women, who care for its young and transmit cultural knowledge across multiple generations. K. Hawkes. See Group-level selection in Concepts.

Grave goods: those possessions that are thought to be necessary for the journey to, and residence in, an afterlife. They define the status of the buried individual and presume the existence of an afterlife at the same level of social stratification.

Grooming: among primates, a method of signifying status, promoting social bonding and diffusing group tension.

Group-level selection: a means of social evolution in which the advantage of natural selection is conferred on the group rather than the individual. Altruism, cooperation and self-sacrificing behavior by individual members within the group reinforce the group's cohesion and solidarity, provide an advantage to the group in trade and war with other groups and increase the chances that the genes of at least some of its members will be successfully transmitted to future generations, even at the cost of the sacrificial behavior of certain individual members (by, for example, fighting or dying to protect the group); see Kinship selection; versus **individual selection**, in which selfishness, competition and egoism confer an evolutionary advantage on a particular individual by enhancing that individual's chances of surviving, reproducing and passing along its genes within the group but, perhaps, at the expense of the group's chances of survival and, thus, the individual's. See 25. Social Darwinism in American History Details.

Group size as modulated by predation versus resource competition: the calibrated trade-off between (1) the benefits provided to a larger group by the increased protection against predators versus (2) the cost of increased competition among individual members within the larger group for limited resources. Among primates, group size is thought to be positively correlated with brain size and one of the driving factors in social intelligence. See 5. Social Intelligence/Social Brain Hypothesis in Details.

Holocene interglacial: the geological epoch in which we are now living, which began at the end of the last ice age, approximately 12,000 years ago. It partially overlaps the informally termed Anthropocene epoch (*q.v.* in Concepts), which began with the Industrial Revolution in 1750 CE and marks the significant impact of human activity on the natural environment, including extinctions, deforestation, pollution and global warming.

Hunting hypothesis: that the hunting and killing of animals, particularly large game animals, over long distances, was the driving force of human evolution. Hunting was associated with (1) bipedalism (which freed the hands to make and carry tools and weapons to and from a base camp); (2) endurance running (which was enabled by the development of long legs, the loss of fur and an increase in the number of sweat glands) and (3) overhand throwing skills, which led to the successful use of projectiles to hunt prey (projectile predation). These physical adaptations allowed hominins to (4) hunt large game over long distances (persistence hunting) and (5) shift to a high caloric meat diet, which spurred brain growth, and led to more complex forms of social relationships. These included (6) the sexual division of labor (in which men hunted and women gathered food plants and tended to children in a base camp); (7) male coalitions and cooperative hunting; (8) reciprocal altruism (food sharing) and (9) pair-bonding and parental investment. William Calvin, Joseph Ferraro, Helen Fisher, Neil Roach. See Killer ape hypothesis, Male coalitional violence, Projectile predation and Sexual Contract in Concepts.

Hunting-gathering/foraging: the preeminent, pre-agrarian mode of subsistence, which lasted until the beginning of the Neolithic Revolution and the invention and spread of agriculture approximately 11,000 years ago, and which continues today in some remote areas of the world. Most hunting bands consist of 10 to 50 individuals and are relatively egalitarian. Recent empirical studies have shown than many contemporary hunter-gatherer societies spend far less time acquiring food and shelter than humans in modern societies and, thus, have been described as the "original affluent societies." Richard Borshay Lee and Marshall Sahlins. See Tribalism in Concepts.

Ice Ages: see 8. Ice Ages in Details.

Incest taboo: the prohibition, universal in nearly all cultures, of marriage and sexual relations between various degrees of blood relatives. Since the deleterious effects of inbreeding and the survival advantage of exogamy (i.e., marriage outside the kinship group) are not immediately self-evident to the human agents themselves, the mechanism by which this occurs is still a mystery.

Killer ape hypothesis: that war and aggression, as well as persistent carnivory (i.e., hunting, killing and eating animals), was a major factor in human evolution. Robert Ardrey, Raymond Dart. See Hunting hypothesis in Concepts and 12. Violence and Human Nature in Details.

Kinship group: a band or clan whose members are related by blood or marriage; the basic social unit of pre-industrial societies.

Kinship selection: group selection applied at the extended family level. It involves unconscious strategies that encourage the survival and reproductive success of the extended family, even at the expense of its individual members, by facilitating altruism, cooperation and self-sacrificing behavior among close relatives, which increases the likelihood of an individual's passing along at least some of his or her genes. See Group-level selection in Concepts.

Lateralization: the specialization of functions in the left and right hemispheres of the brain. There is some evidence of left-brain specialization in pre-modern hominins, which would indicate, possibly, the existence of elementary language skills.

Long distance/endurance running: a survival advantage for hominins, which was made possible by bipedalism, the loss of body hair and the more efficient use of sweat glands. It enabled bipedal hominins to travel more efficiently to and from base camp and to engage in long-range/persistence hunting. See Hunting hypothesis in Concepts.

Luxury/prestige goods: objects that are used for status and display; they represent the material expression of social differentiation and stratification. See Symbolic behavior in Concepts.

Male coalitional violence: the hypothesis that, throughout human history, war and aggression have been associated with young males organized into bands of various forms (foraging and raiding groups, clans, Hoplites, Marine platoons, football teams, fraternities, street gangs, terrorist cells, etc.) that compete against other male bands for resources, mates, spoils, defense of territory, revenge, etc. Bands are characterized by the symbols and rituals of identification and bonding, which intensify the solidarity of the in-group and dehumanize the out-group. Christian Mesquida and Neil Wiener, Malcolm Potts and Thomas Haden. See Narcissism of small differences and Tribalism in Concepts and 12. Violence and Human Nature in Details.

Mate copying: the attraction of females for males who already have female mates.

Matrilineal/patrilineal descent: a social grouping in which kinship is traced through the mother's or father's lineage.

Matrilocal/patrilocal/neo-local residence: a residential pattern in which a couple, or pair-bond, tends to live with or near, respectively, (1) the female's family, or (2) the male's family or (3) at a new location. In many cultures it is common for the female rather than the male to leave her natal family and live with or near the male's family, since this allows blood brothers to remain together and more easily define and defend their territory and results in wider genetic diversity for women. Recent studies of contemporary hunter-gatherer groups suggest that neo-locality is the prevalent kinship pattern, since only 10% of the members of the studied groups were closely related by blood.

Midden: an ancient refuse heap or waste dump.

Mirror neurons: those brains cells that are activated both when an animal performs an action and, more importantly, when that animal observes another animal performing a similar action. The mirroring in the mind (i.e., the firing of the corresponding neurons in the brain of the animal observing the other's action) is thought to be the psychological mechanism underlying such behaviors as inferring intention, imitation and empathy and is one of the bases for the theory of mind (*q.v.* in Psychology Concepts).

Modes of subsistence: hunting-gathering/foraging, pastoralism, agriculture and commerce. Adam Smith.

Monogamy: marriage between two individuals; versus **polygamy**: marriage between more than two individuals, which may consist of **polyandry** (marriage between one female and multiple males) or **polygyny** (marriage between one male and multiple females).

Moralizing gods hypothesis: that the development of powerful, all-seeing, punitive, moralizing deities who (1) could see inside a person's mind, (2) encouraged prosocial behavior, (3) punished selfishness and cruelty and (4) demanded rituals and costly displays of devotion was the result of a shift from nomadic, hunter-gathering societies to large-scale, agricultural settlements, which needed such supernatural agents to enforce social cooperation and a sense of solidarity among large groups of people. Although religious beliefs and sacred rituals reinforced in-group trust and solidarity, they also promoted mistrust and conflict with outgroups and provided the moral imperatives to kill and die for a cause. Scott Atran, Jeremy Ginges, Ara Norenzayan.

Morgan, Lewis Henry: a 19th-Century American anthropologist who studied the Iroquois of North America and established the now discredited paradigm of linear, technology-based anthropology, which categorized and ranked cultural evolution through the stages of (1) Lower Savagery (eating fruits and roots), (2) Middle Savagery (the use of fire), (3) Upper Savagery (the invention of the bow and arrow), (4) Lower Barbarism (horticulture and the invention of pottery), (5) Middle Barbarism (the domestication of plants and animals), (6) Upper Barbarism (the use of bronze and iron and the invention of the wheel) and (7) Civilization. Morgan's studies on kinship and property and the relationship between social structure and material culture and technological evolution influenced Karl Marx and Frederick Engels. See Cultural relativity in Concepts.

Mutation: a random, permanent, inheritable change or variant in a gene or sequence of DNA. See Genes and DNA in Science Details.

Narcissism of small differences: the urge to exaggerate minor differences between similar individuals or groups in order to preserve a sense of uniqueness, separation and otherness. Freud used the term to suggest that human aggression is innate. The concept is often applied to groups with adjoining territories who are constantly at war with each other, such as the Protestants and Catholics in Northern Ireland, the Palestinians and Israelis in the West Bank, and the Crips and the Bloods in East Los Angeles. The sense of uniqueness and superiority, and the feelings of antipathy directed at those who are virtually similar, may be derived from the fact that the "other" is unconsciously perceived as a sexual or resource competitor. Sigmund Freud; Ernest Crawley,

Glen Gabbard. See Male coalition violence, Territoriality and
Tribalism in Concepts.

Natal group: the group into which one is born.

Native-American Shoah (from the Hebrew word for "catastrophe,"
the term used to describe the genocide of six million Jews during
the Second World War): the catastrophic reduction in the
population of indigenous people in North and South America by 40
to 100 million people (or 90% of the pre-Columbian population)
within 130 years of European colonization by diseases, warfare,
slavery, brutality and overwork. Woodrow Borah, Sherburne
Cook, William Cronin, William Denevan, F. H. Dobyns, Wilbur
Jacobs, Charles Mann, Nathaniel Philbrick, Russell Thornton.

Natural selection: see 2. Natural Selection in Details.

Neanderthals: archaic, collateral relatives of modern humans who
shared a common ancestor but were not directly related.
Neanderthals lived approximately 300,000 years ago, were cold-
adapted to the Eurasian ice ages and died out approximately 30,000
years ago. There is evidence of some interbreeding between them
and modern humans in Eurasia, which resulted in modern non-
Africans inheriting 1% to 3% of their DNA from Neanderthals.
Neanderthals became extinct at about the same time as
anatomically modern humans colonized Eurasia because they (1)
were less efficient in competing for the same resources, or (2)
didn't reproduce as efficiently and/or (3) were exterminated by
modern humans.

Neoteny: the retention of infant physical features, such as large eyes or
soft skin, into adulthood. The trait may confer an advantage to
young members of those species, such as humans, who are
dependent on caregivers for prolonged periods. Stephen Jay
Gould.

Nesting instinct: a behavioral pattern that is associated with the
maternal hormone oxytocin. It is expressed in such traits as
parental nurturing, trust, pair-bonding, cooperation and altruism,
but also in exaggerated, defensive aggression directed against
outsiders who threaten the group and its territory. Carsten De
Dreu. See Defensive aggression, Oxytocin, Territoriality and
Tribalism in Concepts and 12. Violence and Human Nature in
Details.

Noble savage myth: the cultural stereotype of the indigenous hunter-
gatherer as nature's nobleman; the belief that people in a state of
nature are essentially good and possess a natural, innate moral

sense; see Jean-Jacques Rousseau in Quotations; versus **Thomas Hobbes' thesis** that people in a state of nature are in a state of perpetual "war of all against all," in which "the life of man [is] solitary, poor, nasty, brutish and short." See 12. Violence and Human Nature (the Hobbes-Rousseau Dichotomy) in Details.

Obstetrical dilemma: an evolutionary problem that is derived from the fact that walking upright on two legs (i.e., bipedalism) results in a narrower birth canal for the mother at the same time that a larger brain requires a larger cranium for the fetus. The dilemma of moving a larger cranium through a narrower birth canal was resolved by delivering the human fetus at an earlier stage in its physical development. This has resulted in a prolonged period of infant helplessness and dependency on its parents, which is thought to be a causal factor in pair-bonding, the sexual division of labor and the rise of culture. Herbert Spencer. See Altriciality and Pair-bonding in Concepts and 4. Bipedalism and 5. Social Intelligence in Details.

Omnivory: the ability to eat a wide variety of plant and animal foods, a hominin trait that is associated with superior intelligence and the ability to exploit a wide range of habitats.

Oral tradition: in non-literate societies (i.e., those without a written language), the primary method for transmitting knowledge and cultural traditions from generation to generation, using stories, speeches, songs, poems and folktales.

Oxytocin: a maternal hormone, which is expressed in such behavioral traits as parental nurturing, trust, pair-bonding, cooperation and altruism, but also in exaggerated, defensive aggression directed against outsiders who threaten the group and its territory; it tends to promote the solidarity of the in-group and dehumanize the out-group. Carsten De Dreu. See Nesting Instinct and Territoriality in Concepts.

Out-of-Africa hypothesis: the universally accepted theory that the evolution to anatomically modern humans occurred in Africa about 200,000 years ago, and that, approximately 60,000 years ago, a small band of modern humans migrated from East Africa across the straits of the Red Sea and colonized the rest of the world, serving as the progenitors from whom all modern non-Africans are descended. See 6. Out-of-Africa Hypothesis in Details.

Pair-bonding: a distinctively human behavioral pattern, which is contrasted with the promiscuous behavior of other primates and is thought to be derived from concealed ovulation and the prolongation of infant helplessness. Pair-bonding is a relationship between two people in which food and child-rearing are shared in exchange for a continuous sexual relationship. Because fathers could more easily recognize their children and pair-bonds could more easily recognize each other's relatives, it permitted kinship recognition within and among neighboring bands whose brothers and sisters and sons and daughters had intermarried. Thus, it fostered social cohesion and inter-group cooperation and facilitated the coalescing of bands into tribes. See Concealed ovulation, Obstetrical dilemma and Sexual contract in Concepts.

Patriarchy (Greek for "rule of the father"): a social system of male privilege and female subordination in which nearly all economic and legal power is held by men. Since most hunter-gatherer societies were relatively egalitarian, patriarchy may have begun with the invention of agriculture and the development of permanent human settlements. It also may be associated with the male hormone testosterone (which is linked to aggression and dominance), gender dimorphism, the sexual division of labor, patrilocality and male coalitional violence (*qq.v.* in Concepts).

Pheromones: chemical scents that are used to identify and convey information among members of the same species. They are used to mark territory, establish dominance, signal a predator or indicate sexual availability. With the advent of bipedalism and an upright posture, humans lost some, but not all, of their ability to detect smells, some of which are now communicated on a subliminal level. See Facial differentiation in Concepts.

Population bottleneck: the hypothesis that the extraordinary genetic homogeneity and relative lack of genetic diversity among all modern humans today is result of the near extinction of the human race, which may have taken place during a long volcanic winter following the catastrophic eruption of Mt. Toba, a super volcano in Sumatra, approximately 70,000 years ago. The event may have left a very small group of human survivors, perhaps fewer than 20,000, from whom all humans living today are descended. Stanley Ambrose, Ann Gibbons, Henry Harpending, Michael Rampino, Stephen Self.

Potlatch: status-related gift-giving and redistributive feasts, which were practiced by certain indigenous cultures in which status was achieved or affirmed by periodically giving away one's wealth. Philanthropy is a modern analogue and exhibits a similar status-related component. Ruth Benedict, William Tilden.

Potsherd/sherd: a fragment of pottery; "shard' usually refers to a glass fragment but can also refer to a fragment of pottery.

Pre-Clovis: the term applied to Paleo-Indian cultures pre-dating 13,000 years ago, whose ancestors may have crossed the land bridge from Siberia to Beringia as early as 23,000 year ago, settled there for approximately 8,000 years (the Beringia incubator or standstill hypothesis) and, approximately 14,500 years ago, used an ice-free corridor through the Laurentide ice sheet or along the Pacific coast to settle the American continents. "Clovis" is the name given to a culture dating to approximately 13,000 years ago whose members were once thought to be the original, founding population that colonized North and South America from northeast Asia; it is associated with a distinctive fluted projectile point and the extinction of North American mega-fauna.

Projectile predation: the use of wood, bone and stone projectiles to hunt and kill game. It has been hypothesized that Achuelian hand axes were used by Homo erectus approximately 1.5 million years ago as missiles, or "killer frisbees," to hunt, stun and kill prey, and that wooden throwing spears were used for hunting beginning approximately 300,000 years ago. See Hunting hypothesis in Concepts.

Prosocial behavior: behavior that is intended to benefit others. It may be motivated by empathy, altruism or anticipated reciprocity and may be associated with parental nurturing, trust, social cooperation and the maternal hormone oxytocin. Patricia Churchland, Philip Kitsch, Donald Pfaff, Frans de Waal. See Group level selection, Kinship selection, Mirror Neurons, Oxytocin and Theory of mind in Concepts and Social Intelligence/Social Brain Hypothesis in Details.

Proto-Indo-European language: the prototype of all modern Indo-European languages, which, according to recent studies, was spread either by (1) Middle Eastern farmers approximately 8,000 years ago or (2) nomadic Kurgan/Yamnayan pastoralists/warriors from the steppes north of the Black Sea approximately 4,500 years ago.

Reciprocal altruism: a form of cooperative social behavior that involves helping others with the expectation that others will help you; it is a factor in social evolution and group-level selection (*q.v.* in Concepts).

Rites of intensification: ceremonies and rituals that are used to instill a sense of group solidarity, often in anticipation of, or in response to, a war or crisis.

Rites of passage: cultural and religious ceremonies and rituals that formally recognize the transitions in the physical state and social status of an individual as she or he passes through the various stages of life, including birth, childhood, puberty, initiation into adulthood, marriage, child bearing and death.

Rump presentation: an appeasement or submission signal used by subordinate members of some primate groups to dominant members to deflect attention, diffuse tension, invite intercourse or avoid being attacked.

Savannah hypothesis: that a cooler, drier climate, which began, perhaps, 2.5 million years ago, led to a reduction in the African rain forest and fostered the evolution of human bipedal locomotion over the newly opened grasslands. Bipedalism freed the hands to make and carry tools, weapons and food from and to a base camp, which, in turn, led to social complexity, social intelligence (encephalization) and human culture; Thure Cerling, Raymond Dart; see 4. Bipedalism in Details. This hypothesis has been challenged by the **turnover-pulse hypothesis**, which proposes that, because (1) very early bipedal hominins lived in woodlands, not dry, open grasslands, and (2) new species of hominins also appeared during wet, humid periods that punctuated the drier periods, hominin evolution was driven by the need to adapt to the challenges of dramatic climate changes and the arrival and disappearance of food sources. Richard Potts, Elizabeth Vrba.

Science schmaltz: Steven Pinker's term for scientific studies that eulogize peaceful tribes, altruistic apes, neuroplasticity, epigenetics, group selection, mirror neurons "and other distortions of science for dubious moral uplift." See 12. Violence and Human Nature in Details.

Sexual contract: an arrangement in which food, particularly meat, was provided by the male to the female and her children in return for a continuous sexual relationship. Because bipedalism and an upright posture led to the prolongation of infant helplessness, it was necessary for women to remain near the base camp to raise their children while men hunted. This division of labor was reinforced by pair-bonding, in which food and child-rearing were shared in exchange for a continuous sexual relationship, and in which sex was used to reward, satisfy and bind the pair-bond. Helen Fisher. See Concealed ovulation/hidden estrus and Pair-Bonding in Concepts.

Sexual/courtship displays and rituals: behaviors, symbols and rituals in various animal species, including humans, which (1) announce sexual availability, (2) provide a means for demonstrating fitness, (3) facilitate sexual selection and choice among potential mates and (4) offer an invitation for sexual intercourse and/or pair-bonding. Examples include colorful plumage and ornamentation; coquettish behavior; singing, dancing and drinking; building a nest (or renting an apartment); displaying physical prowess (through combat, sports, jogging or working out); threatening or fighting rivals; the conspicuous display of status symbols (weapons, clothing, jewelry, etc.); grooming; perfume and other odor signals; body language, including lordosis (or arching of the back in human females, through the use of high heel shoes); self-mimicry and the use of sexual symbols and analogues (red lipstick for the labia; a purse for the vagina, and guns, pens and automobiles for the phallus); humor; erudition; kindness, generosity and altruism. Jared Diamond, Marvin Harris, Desmond Morris.

Sexual selection: generally, the process of choosing a mate based on certain physical traits and behavioral patterns. In humans, the principle of similarity (also known as assortative mating) is often operative, i.e., that like tend to select like, but the opposite is not uncommon. Human males are said to prefer youth and physical attractiveness in potential mates, while females prefer wealth, status and kindness in potential mates.

Shaman: a spiritual or holy person, who may possess a gift for healing.

Shame versus **guilt cultures**: the former are associated with sanctions that involve public embarrassment, humiliation and dishonor from violating public norms, while the latter are associated with private remorse resulting from self-directed blame and violations of internalized moral standards. Shame cultures are said to be characterized by outer-directed behavior and personality types, while guilt cultures are manifestations of inner-directed behavior and personality types. Ruth Benedict, David Reisman.

Social brain hypothesis: that cognitive evolution and the expansion of the hominin brain was driven by the social challenges and complexities of living in groups. These challenges involved cooperative hunting, food sharing, mutual grooming, reciprocal altruism, coalitional politics, balance of power, alliances, etc. Robin Dunbar, Nicholas Humphrey, Richard Leakey. See Toolmaker hypothesis in Concepts and 4. Bipedalism and 5. Social Intelligence/Social Brain Hypothesis in Details.

Sociobiology: a school of scientific thought that maintains that individual and social behavior is largely inherited, that is, that it is the product of genes and natural selection. Inherited behaviors include those associated with gender, aggression, territoriality, mating, reciprocal altruism, social cooperation, intelligence, anxiety/stress-response, introversion, etc. Sociobiology has been criticized as a form of biological determinism and has been challenged by studies that demonstrate a reciprocal relationship between nature and nurture, biology and the environment. Steven Pinker, Edward O. Wilson. See Variety/plasticity of human cultures in Concepts, the Nature-nurture continuum in Science Concepts and 10. Epigenetics/Gene Expression and 11. Adaptive/Developmental Plasticity in Science Details.

Spoken language: one of the distinguishing features of anatomically and behaviorally modern humans. The origin of human speech has not been determined, but it may be derived from mother-infant interactions, cooperative hunting, communal singing and chanting, and/or the development of social cognition and the complexities of living in large groups; it is also associated with variants involving the "speech gene" FOXP2.

Stone-knapping: a method for making stone tools from flint, chert, obsidian and other rocks by striking and pressure flaking. Stone and wooden tools were the primary technology of hominins from the Paleolithic Era, which began approximately 3.3 million years ago, to the beginning of the Bronze Age 5,300 years ago.

Stratigraphic model: a conceptual, hierarchical paradigm with biology at its base and successive economic, social, psychological and cultural layers; versus **webs of significance**: a conceptual model in which all domains are inter-linked without vertical ranking. Clifford Geertz.

Structuralism: a school of thought that maintains that societies are governed by underlying, often unconscious, structures that guide social behavior, such as kinship patterns, rituals, myths and *a priori* rules of grammar. Noam Chomsky, Jonathan Culler, Claude Lévi-Strauss, Ferdinand de Saussure. See 2. Structuralism and 4. Post-structuralism in Literary Concepts Details.

Symbolic behavior: a quintessential feature of anatomically and behaviorally modern humans. Beginning approximately 100,000 years ago, symbolic behavior was expressed in body coloring and ornamentation, tattoos, jewelry, carvings and, later, Venus figurines, cave paintings, grave goods, religious structures and other trans-utilitarian art objects. See Blombos Cave, Body ornamentation, Cave paintings, Upper Paleolithic cultural revolution and Venus/goddess figurines in Concepts and Susanne Langer in Quotations.

Syncretism: the blending of two or more religious beliefs or cultural traditions.

Taboo: a culturally imposed prohibition, such as a food or incest taboo (*q.v.* in Concepts).

Territoriality: (1) a sense of spatial possession, occupation and/or ownership; (2) a specific, bounded geographical area, with the right to occupy, mate, hunt and forage, which an animal may defend against other animals of the same species; (3) an area or home range in which an animal lives and travels, which may contain a nest, a den or a base, a mating site and a range of food resources, and the boundaries of which are marked by scenting, displays and aggression. Geographical surface areas and spatial references are cognitively mapped by "place cells" in the mammalian brain, which indicate location, direction, grid and boundaries. Competition for resources and the conquest and defense of territories are thought to be one of the major causes of inter-group aggression and warfare among humans. Social groups, including tribes, nation-states and street gangs, are said to be imprisoned by their sense of territoriality. Desmond Morris. See Defensive aggression, Male coalitional violence, Narcissism of small differences and Nesting instinct in Concepts and 12. Violence and Human Nature in Details.

Testosterone: a male hormone that is associated with sexual expression, aggression, competition, dominance, status, power and patriarchy. A recent study has shown that, in the last 80,000 years, humans have evolved, through cultural selection, to produce less testosterone (as evidenced by smaller brow ridges and other facial traits), which has promoted social cooperation. Robert Cieri, James Dabbs. See Male coalition violence, Nesting instinct and Oxytocin in Concepts and 12. Violence and Human Nature in Details.

Tool-maker hypothesis: that the challenges and complexities of making stone tools was the driving force in the expansion (encephalization) of the hominin brain, since it required abstract thinking, planning, patience, self-control and developing if-then-logic processes and mental templates of the final product. Although the "man the tool-maker" hypothesis has been displaced by the **social brain hypothesis** (*q.v.* in Concepts), recent empirical studies involving neurological imaging/brain scans of stone knapping by modern archeologists, using magnetic resonance imaging and diffusion tensor imaging (DTI), have shown that the seemingly simple task of making tools from formless pieces of rock requires complex and sophisticated cognitive skills, which are recorded in heightened neural activity in the right inferior frontal gyrus of the prefrontal cortex. Although these empirical studies do not address the question of cause and effect (did the social brain lead to more sophisticated tool making, or vice versa?), they do suggest a meeting point between the two schools, since both sets of mental processes involve learning and teaching complex processes that may have involved linguistic as well as social and manual skills. Kenneth Oakley, Dietrich Stout. See 10. Economic/Technological Determinism and 11. Counterarguments to Economic/Technological Determinism In Economics Details.

Totemism: the veneration of an animal or plant as the symbolic or spiritual ancestor or emblem of a group, clan or tribe. The modern use of an animal or plant (e.g., an eagle, bear, lion, dove, lily, rose or maple leaf) as an emblem to represent a kingdom, dynasty, nation-state, corporation, school or sports team is a vestige of this tribal expression.

Trading networks: a medium for economic exchange, cross-cultural contact and cultural diffusion. Long distance trading routes provided the means to exchange materials such as shells, beads, flint, obsidian, fish and furs, and, later, metals, grain, olive oil, wine, cedar, dye, fish sauce, spices, slaves, pottery, jewelry, textiles, drinking vessels, etc.

Tribalism: the shared culture, sense of unity, common identity and loyalty among members of a tribal group. Hunter-gatherer tribes are usually described as open, cooperative and egalitarian, but are also associated with ethnocentrism, xenophobia, territoriality and inter-tribal violence. See Defensive aggression, Male coalitional violence, Narcissism of small differences, Nesting instinct, and

Territoriality in Concepts and 12. Violence and Human Nature in Details.

Upper Paleolithic cultural revolution: the hypothesis that modern symbolic human behavior rose approximately 40,000 years ago, which was expressed in figurative art, musical instruments and body ornamentation and sophisticated blade, needle and fish-hook technologies. Modern cognitive and symbolic behavior is also represented in earlier artifacts discovered in caves and rock shelters along the South African coast that date from approximately 75,000 to 100,000 years ago; Jared Diamond; see Blombos cave in Concepts and Susanne Langer in Quotations. This hypothesis has been challenged by the **cultural continuity hypothesis**, which maintains that early anatomically modern humans (beginning approximately 200,000 years ago) were as cognitively advanced as those today and that behavioral modernity was the result of "behavioral variability" in response to differing environmental conditions and the gradual accumulation of knowledge, skills and culture, which occurred over tens of thousands of years. Dorion Sagan, John Shea, John Skoyles.

Urban civilizations: those that rose independently, beginning approximately 5,000 years ago, in the Tigris-Euphrates, Nile, Indus and Yellow-Yangtze river valleys and later in Mesoamerica and the Andes Highlands. They are associated with (1) the consolidation of regional networks of farming villages; (2) large-scale ceremonial centers and temples; (3) long distance trading networks; (4) central granaries; (5) irrigation systems; (6) centralization of political authority; (7) professional military warfare; (8) social stratification (kings, nobles, priests, warriors, scribes, merchants, craftsmen, peasants, slaves); (9) craft specialization and (10) writing/notational systems. See 10. Rise of Urban Civilizations in Details.

Variety/plasticity of human cultures: the wide range of cultural practices and behaviors in pre-literate societies, which anthropologists have documented and which attest to the adaptability and diversity of human cultures, as opposed to linear, monistic theories of biological or material determinism. Ruth Benedict, Franz Boas, Margaret Mead. See Cultural relativity in Concepts and Max Weber in Quotations.

Venus/goddess figurines: Upper (i.e., Later) Paleolithic female figurines, dating from approximately 35,000 to 20,000 years ago, which were created from ivory, bone, stone and fired clay. They were stylized, exaggerated and, often, steatopygous (i.e., having fatty buttocks and thighs) and may have represented fertility goddesses, amulets, sex objects or other forms of wish fulfillment for plentitude in times of scarcity or companionship in times of solitude.

Violence and human nature: see Thomas Hobbes and Jean-Jacques Rousseau in Quotations and 12. Violence and Human Nature (the Hobbes-Rousseau Dichotomy) in Details. Human aggression has been classified as: (1) instrumental (i.e., motivated by plunder, sexual and territorial conquest), (2) revengeful, (3) status-driven (dominance, recognition, elimination of rivals) and (4) religious/ideological.

QUOTATIONS:

- [People in a state of nature are in a state of] *war of all against all, [in which there is] continual fear and danger of violent death, and the life of man* [is] *solitary, poor, nasty, brutish, and short.* -- Thomas Hobbes.

- [People in a state of nature] *must have been the happiest and most durable epoch. . . . . The example of savages, almost all of whom have been found in this state, seems to confirm that the human race had been made to remain in it always; that this state is the veritable youth of the world; and that all the subsequent progress has been in appearance so many steps toward the perfection of the individual, and in fact toward the decay of the species.* – Jean-Jacques Rousseau.

- *"Culture" is a finite segment of the meaningless infinity of the world process, a segment on which human beings confer meaning and significance. . . . The transcendental presupposition of every cultural science lies not in our finding a certain culture or any "culture" in general to be valuable but rather in the fact that we are cultural beings, endowed with the capacity and the will to take a deliberate attitude toward the world and to lend it significance.* -- Max Weber.

- *There is no absolutely "objective" scientific analysis of culture . . . . All knowledge of cultural reality . . . is always knowledge from particular points of view.* – Weber.

- *The power of understanding symbols, i.e. of regarding everything about a sense-datum as irrelevant except a certain form that it embodies, is the most characteristic mental trait of mankind. It issues in an unconscious, spontaneous process of abstraction, which goes on all the time in the human mind: a process of recognizing the concept in any configuration given to experience, and forming a conception accordingly.* -- Susanne Langer.

ANTHROPOLOGY DETAILS: (1) Anthropology, (2)
Natural Selection, (3) Hominin Family Tree, (4) Bipedalism, (5) Social
Intelligence/Social Brain Hypothesis, (6) Out-of-Africa Hypothesis,
(7) Paleogenetics/Archaeogenetics, (8) Ice Ages, (9)
Neolithic/Agricultural Revolution, (10) Rise of Urban Civilizations,
(11) Other Significant Cultural Events in Prehistory and (12) Violence
and Human Nature (the Hobbes-Rousseau Dichotomy).

1. **Anthropology** is the study of humans, primarily those in pre-
    literate and pre-industrial societies, as well as their hominin
    ancestors. It uses empirical methods to study the particular
    characteristics of specific cultures and, by using cross-cultural
    comparisons, to identify specific cultural determinates, as well as
    the universals in human nature that are common across all cultures.

2. **Natural Selection** is the mechanism by which evolution occurs,
    according to the Darwinian-Mendelian evolutionary paradigm,
    which is based on the following precepts: (1) organisms compete
    for limited natural resources, which results in a "struggle for
    existence" (Thomas Malthus); (2) individual variants in physical
    traits arise from random, inheritable, genetic mutations (Gregor
    Mendel), which results in (3) the "natural selection" of those traits
    that are best adapted to the environment (Charles Darwin, Alfred
    Russel Wallace, Edward Wilson), and, thus, are more likely to be
    passed along through the genes, which results in (4) the "survival
    of the fittest" (Herbert Spencer).

    The Darwinian-Mendelian evolutionary model is a pillar of
    modern science and has been reinforced by theories of group-level
    selection and social evolution, as well as by recent discoveries in
    epigenetics, or gene expression, and the interaction between genes
    and the environment. See Adaptation, Fitness, Group-level
    selection and Sociobiology in Concepts; 25. Social Darwinism and
    26. Reform Darwinism in American History Details, and 10.
    Epigenetics/Gene Expression and 11. Adaptive/Developmental
    Plasticity in Science Details.

3. **Hominin Family Tree** [simplified and approximate]:
    1) Sahelanthropus tchadensis (Toumaï): 7 million years ago.
    2) Orrorin tugenensis: 6 million years ago.

3) Ardipithecus ramidus: 4.4 million years ago.
4) Australopithecus afarensis: 3.5 million years ago.
5) Homo habilis: 2.8 million years ago.
6) Homo erectus: 1.9 million years ago.
7) Homo heidelbergensis/archaic Homo sapiens: 600,000 years ago.
8) Homo neanderthalensis (a bilateral cousin): 300,000 years ago.
9) Homo sapiens (anatomically modern humans): 200,00 years ago.

4. **Bipedalism** (i.e., walking upright on two legs) is one of the distinguishing features of hominins. The evolutionary adaptation may have been caused the shrinking of the African rain forest and the spread of the open grasslands and/or the rapid climatic fluctuations which began approximately 2.5 million years ago (see Savannah hypothesis versus turnover-pulse hypothesis in Concepts). Walking upright freed the hands to make and carry tools, weapons and food from and to a base camp. However, an upright posture also resulted in a smaller birth canal, which, in turn, required that the human fetus be delivered at an earlier stage in its physical development. This led to the prolongation of human infancy and an extended period of infant helplessness and child care (compared to other primates), which, in turn, led to the sexual division of labor in which men hunted and women stayed near base camp and raised the relatively helpless children. This division of labor was associated with pair-bonding, in which continuous sexual relationships were exchanged for food-sharing and shared child-rearing. William Calvin, Raymond Dart, Brian Fagan, Helen Fisher, Marvin Harris, Nicholas Humphrey, Richard Leaky, Herbert Spencer. See Pair-bonding and Sexual contract in Concepts.

5. **Social Intelligence/Social Brain Hypothesis** is the theory that hominin encephalization (i.e., increased brain size) and cognitive evolution was less the cause of improved technology (tool-making) than the effect of increased social intelligence, which was driven by the challenges and complexities of living in groups. These challenges involved social learning (the transmission of cultural skills and information), cooperative hunting, food sharing, mutual grooming, reciprocal altruism, coalitional politics, alliances, balances of power, etc. Thus, cognitive evolution is correlated

with social complexity and the challenges of living in groups, including balancing competition and cooperation within the group, rather than with technological innovations involved in tool-making and manipulating the material environment (which remained stable and unchanging over tens of thousands of years). The social brain and cultural intelligence hypotheses have been supported by recent primate studies that correlate the size of social networks with the size of the prefrontal cortex and areas of the brain involved in sociality. Richard Byrne, Robin Dunbar, Nicolas Humphrey, Carl van Schaik, Andrew Whiten. See Tool-maker hypothesis in Concepts and Social cognition/social intelligence in Psychology Concepts.

6.   **Out-of-Africa Hypothesis** is the theory that the evolution to anatomically modern humans occurred in Africa about 200,000 years ago. Approximately 60,00 years ago a small band of modern humans, possibly as few as 150 to 1,000, migrated from East Africa across the straits of the Red Sea and colonized the rest of the world, serving as the progenitors from whom all modern non-Africans are descended. The out-of-Africa hypothesis stands in opposition to the now discredited multiregional model (Milford Wolpoff), in which modern humans evolved independently from Homo erectus in multiple regions of the world. The African exodus model is now almost universally accepted, although with some interbreeding that occurred between modern humans and hominins outside of Africa. Modern non-Africans, for example, share 1% to 3% of their DNA with Neanderthals, and some South Asian groups share an additional small percentage of their genes with Denisovans, a now extinct species of hominins. Luigi Cavalli-Sforza, Steve Olson, Spencer Wells.

Recent genetic evidence suggests that the small founding population of human colonists, after they left East Africa by crossing the Red Sea, may have migrated in two waves along two routes: (1) approximately 55,000 years ago, one group moved eastward along the southern coastline of Arabia, Pakistan and India to Southeast Asia (with some interbreeding with Denisovans) and Melanesia and Australia; (2) approximately 45,000 years ago a second group moved north from the Middle East into central Asia and then split into two groups, with one group migrating westward to colonize Europe and the other eastward to colonize Asia and, about 14,000 years ago, crossing the Beringia land bridge to populate the Americas.

7. **Paleogenetics/Archaeogenetics** is a field of study that uses DNA and genetic variants to identify hominin remains and trace prehistoric migrations of haplogroups (i.e., those related by unique patterns of genetic variants). Most genes are shuffled and mixed in kaleidoscopic fashion from generation to generation through sexual reproduction, but the mutations, or genetic variants, which occur on the Y chromosome (which is passed down from father to son) and the non-coding mitochondrial DNA, or mtDNA (which lies outside the cell nucleus and which is inherited only through the mother), are generally passed down intact from generation to generation. Thus, they serve as genetic markers, or signatures, which provide a method for tracing lines of descent and constructing genetic trees linking individuals to groups (haplogroups) and groups to related groups. Because variants occur at a given rate, geneticists can map the progression of mutations on the Y chromosome and the mtDNA and identify and determine when and where variant haplogroups rose and separated from the parent population and trace their subsequent movements. Luigi Cavalli-Sforza, Steve Olson, Colin Renfrew, Brian Sykes, Spencer Wells. See Genes and DNA in Science Details.

8. **Ice Ages** provided the context in which modern human hunter-gatherers survived and subsisted in Eurasia until the continental glaciers retreated approximately 12,000 years ago. During the Last Glacial Maximum (approximately 25,000 years ago) the European hunter-gatherer populations retreated into three refugia: (1) Iberia, (2) the Balkans and (3) the Ukraine. As the glaciers retreated, these hunter-gatherers re-colonized, Western Europe from Iberia, Central Europe from the Balkans, and Eastern Europe from the Ukraine. William Calvin.

9. **Neolithic ("New Stone Age")/Agricultural Revolution** is defined as the domestication of plants and animals, which occurred independently in several places, beginning around 11,000 years ago. In contrast to the gathering and cultivation of wild plants, which occurred earlier, the domestication of plants and animals is defined as the deliberate selection and cultivation of specific traits, such as those in cereal grains that allowed the seeds to remain on

the stem for easier harvesting rather than falling to the ground as they did with wild plants. This process occurred in (1) the Fertile Crescent and Anatolia (i.e., the upper Tigris-Euphrates river valleys in what is now Iraq and Syria, as well as in Lebanon, Israel, Jordan and Turkey), (2) China, (3) India, (4) Mesoamerica and (5) the Andes Highlands. The type, timing and sequence of each domestication event was a function of latitude, chance (the availability of native founder crops, the domesticability of local animals, etc.) and other geographical determinants.

Horticulture initially supplemented rather than supplanted hunting and gathering. The first villages predated sustained agriculture and were based on a hunting-gathering mode of subsistence. Farming villages were permanent, self-sufficient settlements with little social differentiation (Barry Cunliffe). The high caloric diet of cereal grains increased birth rates (by reducing the interval between births), which more than offset the increased mortality rates (from poor communal sanitation, unclean water and animal and crowd diseases), and led to rapid population growth and migration along fertile river valleys and coastlines. Food surpluses laid the foundation for the rise of city-states and urban civilizations, which were associated with regional networks of farming villages, centrally located granaries, irrigation systems, trading networks, ceremonial centers and religious monuments, craft specialization, political centralization, social stratification and organized warfare. Barry Cunliffe, Jared Diamond. See 10. The Rise of Urban Civilizations in Details.

In Southwest Asia, the domestication of plants and animals originated in the Fertile Crescent and Anatolia approximately 11,500 years ago and was introduced into Europe via the Balkans approximately 8,000 years ago. One wave of Neolithic farmers may have traveled by sea from along the Mediterranean coast and another wave is thought to have colonized Central Europe through the Danube river corridor. The latter culture is identified by its distinctive linear patterned pottery and its rectangular houses (Linear Pottery culture, or LBK). Migration is thought to have consisted of small groups of farmers settling in empty or low density areas in fertile river valleys, along lakes and the coast, which led to rapid population growth and the co-existence, adaptation, resistance or displacement of the original hunter-gatherers. See Cultural diffusion/adaptation versus colonization/displacement in Concepts.

10. **The Rise of Urban Civilizations** was enabled and constrained by the Neolithic/Agricultural Revolution's food surpluses and higher birth rates. These led to increased population densities and increased competition for limited resources, especially in those areas which were enclosed or circumscribed by geographical conditions (Robert Carniero), which resulted in wars with neighboring groups for resources and, thus, selective cultural pressures for centralization of political authority, the rise of the state and the professionalization of the military.

Beginning approximately 5,000 years ago, early urban civilizations rose in the Tigris-Euphrates, Nile, Indus and Yellow-Yangtze river valleys, and, later, Mesoamerica and the Andes Highlands. These were characterized by:

1) Political centralization, with a central, often hereditary, ruler, a state bureaucracy and a professional army, and urban control over regional trading centers and networks of agricultural villages.
2) Social stratification of hereditary elites, warrior and priestly classes, professional scribes and bureaucrats, merchants, craft workers, peasants/farmers, laborers and slaves.
3) Craft specialization, including metal working and jewelry and pottery making.
4) Large-scale public works projects, including fortifications, irrigation systems (Karl Wittfogel) and religious structures and temple systems, which involved organizing and controlling large groups of people.
5) Long-distance trading routes, in which raw materials were exchanged for craft work and prestige goods.
6) Wars of conquest, as well as defensive wars.
7) Taxation of the agricultural classes and the extraction of tribute from subjugated provinces.
8) Notational/writing systems.

According to Sigmund Diamond, Europe's many mountains ranges and rivers fostered the development of small, competing, independent city-states and, initially, militated against the rise of large, absolutist empires and despotisms.

11.   **Other Significant Cultural Events in Prehistory** (i.e., predating written language):
1) Proto Indo-European language, which rose either in (a) Western Turkey/Anatolian and was spread by Middle Eastern farmers beginning approximately 8,000 years ago, or (b) the steppes north of the Black Sea and was spread by nomadic Kurgan/Yamnayan pastoralists/warriors approximately 4,500 years ago.
2) The Bronze Age, which began in 3,300 BCE.
3) The phonetic alphabet, which was invented in 1,800 BCE by Phoenician/Semitic workers in Egypt who simplified and democratized the hieroglyphics of the scribes/priests.
4) The Iron Age, which began in 1,100 BCE.

12.   **Violence and Human Nature (the Hobbes-Rousseau Dichotomy)** is a subject about which there are, generally, two schools of thought:
1) **Thomas Hobbes' thesis that human aggression is innate** is advanced, in various forms, by Hobbes, Robert Ardrey, Raymond Dart, Norbert Elias, Sigmund Freud, Lawrence Keeley, Konrad Lorenz, Christian Mesquida and Neil Wiener, Desmond Morris, Robert Muchembled, Steven Pinker, Malcolm Potts and Thomas Haden. It supported by the following arguments and studies:
   a) To Thomas Hobbes (1588-1679), people in a state of nature are in a state of perpetual "war of all against all," in which there is "continual fear and danger of violent death, and the life of man [is] solitary, poor, nasty, brutish and short." Because of this, people voluntarily give up their natural rights and enter into a social contract to establish a civil society, ceding those natural rights to the leviathan state under an absolute monarchy as a necessary condition to prevent violence and anarchy and protect themselves from their own natural depravity.
   b) To Sigmund Freud (1856-1939), human aggression (the death instinct) is innate, and civilization represents the repression of primitive sexual and aggressive impulses, which is necessary for life in an orderly society. Recent studies in neuroscience have confirmed that violence originates in the ancient circuitry of the subcortical brain (particularly, the amygdala and the

hypothalamus) or, in Freudian terms, the id, which is triggered by perceived threats to the self, family, tribe, status, territory, etc., which the pre-frontal cortex (in Freudian terms, the ego) struggles to control. R. Douglas Fields.

c) Sociobiology has sought to demonstrate that aggression and territoriality are largely inherited behaviors. The male hormone testosterone, for example, is associated with sex, aggression, warfare, competition, dominance, status, patriarchy, power and hierarchy (James Dabbs). The maternal hormone oxytocin is expressed in such traits as maternalism, trust, social bonding, cooperation and altruism, but also in ethnocentrism and defensive aggression, which is directed, often forcefully and in an exaggerated fashion, against outsiders who threaten the group or the home territory. Carsten De Dreu.

d) Recent anthropological and historical research suggests that violence and warfare have been endemic throughout human history and pre-history: homicide rates among hunter-gatherer societies were 15% compared to 3% to 5% in societies in which the state has a monopoly of power, and even the "gentle" tribal groups such as the Inuit and !Kung had murder rates comparable to those of modern inner cities.

e) Malcolm Potts and Thomas Haden and Christian Mesquida and Neil Weiner have shown that male coalitional violence (*q.v.* in Concepts) has prevailed throughout human history, and that war and aggression are associated with young males organized into bands of various forms that compete against other male bands for resources, mates, spoils, defense of territory, revenge, etc.

f) Steven Pinker and Robert Muchembled assert that violence and anarchy were endemic in hunter-gatherer societies, but that the "chronic raiding and feuding that characterized life in a state of nature" has declined over the last 5,000 years. They provide evidence to support Hobbes' thesis that a strong central state has minimized interpersonal aggression, and show, counter-intuitively, that violence in modern times, despite massive technological warfare, has actually decreased significantly because of (i) the rise of the modern state, (ii) the rule of law, (iii) the influence of social norms proscribing violence, (iv) the role of trade and cooperation, (v) the increased status and empowerment of women and (vi) improved education and prosperity.

2) **Jean-Jacques Rousseau's thesis that human aggression is socially conditioned** is advanced, in various forms, by Rousseau, Ruth Benedict, Franz Boas, Carol and Melvin Ember, Douglas Fry and Patrick Soderberg, Debra Martin, Margaret Mead, Amy Nivette, Robbins Schug and Fran de Waal. It is supported by the following arguments and studies:

   a) Jean-Jacques Rousseau (1712-1778) proposed that the hunter-gatherers are nature's noblemen; that people in a state of nature are essentially good and possesses a natural, innate moral sense, which the institutions of civilization have repressed and corrupted with private property, crime, war, exploitation, inequality and decadence.

   b) Classical anthropologists such as Franz Boas, Ruth Benedict, and Margaret Mead have documented a wide range of cultural practices and behaviors in pre-literate societies that attest to the variety, plasticity, adaptability and diversity of human societies, and highlighted peaceful cultures such as the !Kung, Inuit and Arapesh of New Guinea ("both men and women are natural maternal, gentle, responsive and unaggressive").

   c) Recent scholarship by Carol and Melvin Ember, Amy Nivette, Debra Martin and Robbins Schug has shown a wide variability in homicide rates among pre-literate groups, with a wide disparity between those who live in small bands and those who live in small agricultural villages, with food-producers generating higher rates of violence than foragers.

   d) Douglas Fry and Patrick Soderberg's study of 21 mobile foraging-band societies has shown that lethal aggression within these societies is infrequent and arises from personal disputes (interfamilial disputes, competition over a mate, etc.) among individuals rather than from organized warfare or coalitional aggression against other groups. This is because: (i) the size of mobile foraging groups is too small to support warfare; (ii) the composition of groups fluctuates, and kinship and social networks between groups militates against intergroup hostility; (iii) groups are egalitarian, with no one person having the authority to order others to go to war; (iv) foraging areas are wide and population densities are low, which makes defense of territories difficult; (v) surplus or prestige goods (which might serve as the impetus for warfare) are rare, and (vi) "conflicts within and between groups are easily handled by separation and other conflict-resolution mechanisms."

e) Those who study the social behavior of animals, particularly primates, such as Frans de Waal, have shown the importance of cooperation, food sharing, altruism and conflict resolution among those animals. Bonobo chimpanzees, for example, are matriarchal, use sex to diffuse social tensions and exhibit low levels of aggression.

3. ART

CONCEPTS AND PHRASES:

Aesthetics: the study and appreciation of art and beauty.

Anti-art: art that presents itself as opposed to traditional, commercial and elitist art. See Dada, Commodification and Fluxus in Concepts.

Apollonian: art that embodies reason, order, restraint and rationality; versus **Dionysian**: art that celebrates the imagination, emotions and madness. Friedrich Nietzsche. See 12. 18th Century Neoclassicism and 13. Romanticism in Details.

Arabesque: a decorative style of Islamic art that is characterized by intricate, rhythmic and geometric patterns, scrolling, intertwined foliage, etc. It reflects Islam's opposition to the representation of humans and animals.

Aristotle's *Poetics*: see 4. Aristotle in Details.

Ars est celare artem ("it is true art to conceal art"): a phrase attributed to the Roman poet Ovid.

Art as bourgeois neurosis: the proposition that art reflects the social repression and cultural hegemony of the dominant class; also, that the neurosis of the individual artist, and the creative process itself, is derived from a quid pro quo of sacrificial pain and suffering. Herbert Marcuse, Karl Marx, Friedrich Nietzsche, Lionel Trilling, Edmund Wilson.

Art as divine madness: Plato's proposition that beauty and poetry "come from madness, when it is given as a gift of the god."

Art as the imitation and perfection of nature: see Seneca in Quotations and 4. Aristotle in Details.

Art as play: that art represents instinctual liberation, the recovery of childhood and the pure love and joy of beauty. Norman O. Brown, Herbert Marcuse.

Art as sublimated sexual energy: that art is derived from instinctual repression, sublimation, substitute gratification and wish fulfillment. Norman O. Brown, Sigmund Freud, Herbert Marcuse.

Art Deco (approximately 1920s and 1930s): an architectural movement and artistic style that was decorative and eclectic; evoked stylized glamour and modernism and utilized Babylonian, Egyptian and Aztec motifs. It was characterized by streamlined shapes, zigzag geometrical patterns, chevrons and sunbursts and aluminum and stainless steel materials. The Chrysler Building in Manhattan is an example of Art Deco architecture.

Art for art's sake (Aestheticism): the doctrine that each work of art provides its own unique, autonomous, intrinsic truth and aesthetic pleasure without reference to any external, didactic, utilitarian or social-political purpose. According to Walter Benjamin, industrialization and the mechanical reproduction of art democratized cultural consumption, which generated an elitist reaction of cultural mystification and ritualization of art-for-art's-sake. Aubrey Beardsley, Edgar Allan Poe, Dante Gabriel Rossetti, James McNeill Whistler, Oscar Wilde; Harold Bloom, Walter Pater, Edmund Wilson. See Autotelic and Formalism in Concepts, Poe in Quotations and Formalism and Symbolism in Literary Concepts.

Art Nouveau (1890-1915): an artistic movement whose works were characterized by natural forms, curved lines and rhythmic plant and floral patterns. It was associated with the Arts and Crafts and *Japonisme* movements and is represented in the works of Aubrey Beardsley, Antoni Gaudi, Gustav Klimt and Charles Tiffany.

Aura: the unique, magical, elusive presence of an original work of art; the "here and now of the artwork; its unique existence in a particular place," which represents its "creativity and genius, eternal value and mystery," according to Walter Benjamin. Although, to Benjamin, the aura decays when it is mechanically reproduced, reproduction serves to liberate the work from "high art" ritualism and fetishism and make it available to a wider audience.

Autotelic: the proposition that each work of art tells its own truth in its own terms without reference to the biographical details of its creator or its cultural and historical context; a tenet of New Criticism and Formalism (*qq.v.* in Literary Concepts). It is presented in opposition to utilitarian, ideological and didactic art.

See Art for art's sake and Formalism in Concepts and Edgar Allan
Poe in Quotations.

Avant-garde: innovative, experimental, "edge" art in the "advance
guard" of culture, which is said to be the essence of modernism.
Although it seeks to differentiate itself from mainstream and
commercial art, such art is often absorbed and commodified in ever
shorter cycles by the very culture industry it seeks to escape.
Clement Greenberg, Harold Rosenberg. See Tradition of the new
in Concepts.

Barbizon school (1830-1870): a group of painters who sought to
portray the gentle, simple dignity of life in the countryside, of
people working in the fields and of nature in the open air. It is
represented in the works of Jean-Baptiste-Camille Corot, Gustave
Courbet and Jean-Francois Millet.

Bauhaus: an architectural movement of the 1920s founded by Walter
Gropius and associated with the International Style (*q.v.* in
Concepts). It stressed the importance of art and design in daily
life, the harmony of form and function, the lack of ornamentation
and the reconciliation of traditional craftsmanship with mass
production and industrial technology.

CAD: computer-aided design.

Cage's *4'33"* ("Four minutes, thirty-three seconds"): a composition in
which the performers do not play their instruments and only
incidental background sounds are heard; an example of conceptual
and (non-)performance art (*qq.v.* in Concepts). John Cage. See
Federico Fellini in Quotations.

Cairn: a pile of stones that serves as a monument or landmark.

Calligraphy: the art of hand lettering.

Camera lucida/camera obscura: optical devices that project an image
onto a flat surface. David Hockney suggests that Caravaggio, Jan
Van Eyck, Hans Holbein, Diego Velasquez, Jan Vermeer and
others used lens and other optical devices to project images of their
subjects onto canvas, which could then be outlined in more detail
and depth than those drawn in freehand.

Cathedral: the central church, or bishop's "throne," of the diocese,
which was adapted from the Roman basilica. It consists of a
central nave with columns and aisles on either side, a transept set
perpendicular to the main axis, behind which is a choir and, often,
a semi-circular or vaulted apse.

Cave paintings: wall painting at Chauvet, Altamira and Lascaux in southwest Europe, which date from approximately 35,000 to 18,000 years ago. They depict stylized horses, aurochs, bison and reindeer and represent some of the earliest surviving examples of humanity's aesthetic sense and symbolic consciousness. See Susanne Langer in Quotations.

Centering: the positioning of a lump of clay on a spinning potter's wheel.

CGI: computer-generated imagery; the use of three-dimensional computer graphics to create a virtual world of static or moving images, such as those in films, cartoons, video games, simulators, etc. See *In silico*, Photoshop and Special effects in Concepts.

Chiaroscuro ("light-dark"): a painting technique that uses contrasts between light and dark to achieve a sense of three-dimensional volume. It was used by Caravaggio, Francisco Goya, Leonardo da Vinci, Rembrandt, Diego Velazquez, Jan Vermeer and others. See Tenebrism in Concepts.

Collage: an assemblage of paper, cloth, photos, news clippings or other miscellaneous ephemera that are pasted on a flat, two-dimensional surface.

Commodification: the transformation of ideas, human beings, works of art, sexual relationships, nature, animals, etc. into products with assigned economic values that can be bought and sold in the marketplace. Karl Marx, Friedrich Engels.

Conceptual art: art that is experienced intellectually as an idea or a concept rather than aesthetically as an object. It has been viewed as a reaction to the formalism and commodification of art. Examples include Christo's Paris traffic jam, John Cage's *4'33"*, Robert Rauschenberg's erasure of a drawing by Willem De Kooning, and a blank space in a newspaper in which readers were invited to fill in their own art work. See Fluxus and Performance Art in Concepts.

Constructivism: a movement in post-World War I Bolshevik Russia that rejected autonomous, autotelic art in favor of art with a social purpose, that is, art in the service of the Revolution, in which the role of the artist was to participate in public life and the struggle for social justice. Constructivism celebrated technology and the machine aesthetic, was characterized by a jagged, angular industrial style and was expressed through media such as graphic design, posters and photomontages.

Dada (1915-1924): an art movement that was irreverent, satirical, experimental and absurdist. It sought to deflate the pomposity of formal, traditional, commercial art by embracing the irrational, using, for example, nonsense verse, automatic drawing and noise music, and treating ordinary objects, such as a urinal (in Marcel Duchamp's *Fountain*), as "art." It represents an early example of "anti-art." Salvador Dali, Duchamp and Man Ray. See Anti-art and Fluxus in Concepts and 20. Surrealism in Details.

Daguerreotypy: the first successful photographic process, which was developed by Joseph Niépce and Louis Daguerre in France and introduced in 1839.

Decorative arts: functional art objects such as those in ceramics, mosaics, glassware, jewelry, weaponry, furniture, textiles, etc.

Draftsmanship: the technical accuracy and craftsmanship of an artist's drawings.

E*n plein air* ("in open air"): painting outdoors in the natural light of the open air. The style was facilitated by the development in the mid-19th Century of portable easels and manufactured paint sold in tubes. It is represented in the works of painters such as John Constable, Winslow Homer, Claude Monet, Camille Pissarro and Auguste Renoir.

Everyman is an artist: a proposition suggested by Brian Keeble.

Fauvism: the term applied to a group of early 20th Century post-impressionists, including Henri Matisse and André Derain, who called themselves *les Fauves*, or "the wild beasts," and were known for their use of intense colors and imaginative patterns.

Fluxus ("to flow"): an anti-art movement of the 1960s and 1970s that has been described as Neo-Dadaism. Experimental, communitarian and anti-commercial, it created pieces from every-day "found objects" and staged unique, playful, do-it-yourself inter-media events, performances, happenings and "scores" involving scripted and unscripted interactions with the audience based the expectation of randomness and indeterminacy. John Cage, George Maciunas, Yoko Ono. See Dada, Conceptual art and Performance art in Concepts.

Folk art: art that is produced by traditional communities using local materials. It reflects shared communal values and tends to be functional, utilitarian and decorative rather than purely aesthetic.

Examples include traditional costumes, folk dances, music, baskets, rugs, quilts, chests and furniture. See Popular culture in Concepts.

Foreshortening: a pictorial technique that creates the illusion of depth on a flat, two-dimensional surface by shortening the distance along the line of sight relative to its dimensions across the line of sight. See Perspective in Concepts.

Formalism: a school of thought that proposes that the aesthetic value of a work is determined by its form (that is, its shape, line, color, etc.) rather than by its content or context. It focuses on the aesthetic experience of the autonomous, thing-in-itself, the pure, abstract form. Clement Greenberg. See Art for art's sake in Concepts.

Form follows function: a principle usually applied to architecture, but also to folk and vernacular art, in which the form or shape of an object is determined by its utility and function. Louis Henri Sullivan; John Kouwenhoven. See Vernacular art in Concepts.

Frescoes: wall paintings made on fresh plaster. Masterpieces in the medium were created by Fra Angelico, Sandro Botticelli, Giotto, Fernando Leal, Michelangelo, Raphael, Diego Rivera and others.

Genre painting: a style of painting associated with the 17th Century Dutch school, which portrayed ordinary people engaged in everyday activities, such as a peasant marriage feast, communal ice skating, a tavern scene or a domestic kitchen. The genre is represented in the works of Pieter Brueghel the Elder, Pieter de Hooch, Jan Steen and Jan Vermeer.

Gothic: see 7. Gothic in Details.

Greek temple: a rectangular wooden or stone structure that served as the dwelling place of a god, since it housed the statue of the deity. It was constructed in the post and lintel style of vertical posts or columns supporting horizontal beams. Columns with capitals of Doric, Ionian or Corinthian design were arranged in colonnades around an inner room (*cella*), which housed the statue. These columns supported a horizontal entablature of a cornice, frieze and architrave, which in turn, along one axis, supported a low pitched, triangular gable, or pediment. The structure was often painted in bright red, blue and white colors.

High-, middle- and low-brow: a method of classifying art using categories that are derived from the 19th Century pseudo-science of phrenology and reflects the class conflict of the original culture war. The tripartite schema provides a means for high/elitist culture to differentiate itself from middle and mass or popular culture. "Middle brow" is associated with bourgeois mediocrity and pretention and, in some critical circles, ranks lower in authenticity than unpretentious, low-brow schlock. Van Wyck Brooks, Clement Greenberg, Russell Lynes, Dwight Macdonald, Bernard Rosenberg and David Manning White, Susan Sontag, James Twitchell, Virginia Woolf. See Kitsch/Schlock/Camp, Folk art, Mass culture and Popular culture in Concepts.

Horizon line: the apparent line in a painting or photograph that separates the earth or the sea from the sky; the line to which all points on a picture plane converge.

Horror vacui ("fear of empty space"): filling all available space in a painting.

Icon: a sacred image or representation, which, itself, was often worshiped.

Iconoclast: originally, one who destroyed religious icons and sacred images in order to prevent their veneration, based on the Biblical injunction against worshiping "graven images." The term now refers to one who attacks conventional beliefs and institutions. Those who venerate such religious images are called **iconophiles**.

Iconography: the study of religious and cultural images and symbolic representations.

Idealization: the representation of the human form or nature in an idealized fashion without flaws or imperfections; a characteristic of classical Greek art.

Illuminated manuscripts: handwritten manuscripts decorated with elaborate and colorful rubrics, illustrations, marginalia and lettering, often in gold leaf. They were produced primarily in monasteries but also, later, in commercial scriptoria during the 1200s through the 1400s. See Codex and Printing press in Literary Concepts.

Illusion: a simulation of reality; a fundamental characteristic of art. See The Real Thing in Concepts; Seneca, Pablo Picasso and Susanne Langer in Quotations and 4. Aristotle in Details.

In silico ("in silicon"): a work that is produced by a computer. See CGI, Photoshop and Special effects in Concepts.

Intaglio: an object in which an image is incised, carved or engraved into the surface; versus **cameo**, in which the image is raised in relief above the surface.

International Style: (1920s-1960s): a style of architecture that was associated with the Modernist movement and Le Corbusier, Walter Gropius, Ludwig Mies van der Rohe and Richard Neutra. It stressed simplicity ("less is more"), functionality, lack of ornamentation and the use of glass and steel to highlight the transparency (or "honest expression") of the structure. It's rectangular, box-like "machine aesthetic," in which buildings were seen as "machines for living," was criticized for being ugly, monotonous, sterile and inhuman. The International Style was superseded in the 1970s by the Postmodern and Hi-tech architectural styles. See 25. Postmoderism in Details.

Kinetic art: art that contains moving parts and depends on motion for its aesthetic effect.

Kitsch: a shallow, gaudy, sentimental, pretentious work, such as Cecil B. DeMille's *The Ten Commandments* or paintings by Walter Keene or Thomas Kinkade; versus **schlock**: a cheap, shallow, unpretentious work, such as *The National Lampoon's Animal House,* the *Jerry Springer Show* or any tabloid reality show; versus **camp**: a deliberately ostentatious, exaggerated and affected work, often from an ironic or satirical point of view, such as *Hairspray*, pieces by Andy Warhol or performances by Liberace and Bette Midler. Susan Sontag.

Landscape painting: a genre that depicts natural scenery, often pastoral and idealized, and attempts to evoke the beauty, spirituality and power of nature. Western examples are provided by Paul Cezanne, John Constable, the Hudson River school, Claude Lorrain, Claude Monet and J. M. W. Turner. See Pastoral in Concepts and Marshall McLuhan in Quotations.

Lithography: a method of printing, often in color, using a stone or flat metal plate; the color prints of Currier and Ives are famous examples.

Machine in the garden: a common theme in early 19th Century American Romantic literature and art in which the image of a steam locomotive, for example, or another industrial object rudely interrupting the bucolic tranquility of the countryside served as a metaphor for the unwelcome intrusion of industrialism and urbanization into nature. Henry Adams, R. W. B. Lewis, Leo Marx, William Morris, Lewis Mumford, John Ruskin, Henry Nash Smith. See Marshall McLuhan in Quotations, 13. Romanticism in Details and 16. Anti-Urban Cultural Tradition in American History Details.

Marxist criticism: a school of criticism in which art is viewed as conditioned or determined by the social and economic context in which it is produced. It focuses on the alienation of the artist and the appropriation or commodification of art by the dominant class. See Commodification in Concepts, Cultural hegemony in Sociology Concepts and 9. Cultural Materialism in Sociology Details.

Mass culture: an (often) pejorative term applied to modern popular culture, which is criticized for its mediocrity, philistinism and pandering to the lowest common denominator. Theodor Adorno, Clement Greenberg, Dwight Macdonald, Bernard Rosenberg and David Manning White, Lionel Trilling, James Twitchell, Gore Vidal, Edmund Wilson. See High-brow, middle-brow, low-brow and Popular culture in Concepts and 16. Mass Society in Sociology Details.

Masterpiece: originally, a work produced by a journeyman to qualify for advancement to a master craftsman in his guild, such as a gold cup or salt cellar for a goldsmith's guild; now, an outstanding work of an artist or writer. See Guild system in Economics.

Minimalism: "less is more"; an art movement in which objects are reduced to their essences; the aesthetic of absence. Ludwig Mies van der Rohe. See 23. Minimalism in Details.

Montage: a compressed film narrative created by editing and special effects, in which short, rapid cuts and overlaid images suggest the condensed passage of time; for example, a close-up of a racing locomotive or a newspaper headline coming off the press. See Photomontage in Concepts.

Mosaics: small pieces of colored glass, tile or stone that are attached to a flat surface to form images and scenes; a medium which was commonly used in Roman, Christian and Islamic art.

Museum (Greek for "house of the Muses"): an institution housing a collection of artistic, cultural, historical and/or scientific objects. See Greek temple in Concepts.

Nature assemblages/collages: arrangements of natural objects such as driftwood or stones in aesthetic, non-functional and, often, ephemeral constructions. Andy Goldsworthy.

Non-representational art: that which is abstract or nonfigurative. According to Theodor Adorno and Frederic Jameson, non-representational art reflects the abstract nature of social relationships in an impersonal, industrialized society. Abstract art is represented in Cubism and Abstract Expressionism (*qq.v.* in Details) and the works of Josef Albers, Paul Cezanne, Helen Frankenthaler, Lee Krasner, Agnes Martin, Joan Mitchell, Piet Mondrian, Mark Rothko, Albert Pinkham Ryder, James McNeill Whistler and others.

Objet d'art: a physical object with an aesthetic function or appeal, such as a carving, a piece of jewelry, a gold salt cellar or a urinal (Duchamp's *Fountain*). The term is also applied pejoratively to ersatz art objects that are used as "props" in interior design. See Vernacular art in Concepts.

Oil-based paint: a slow-drying, linseed-oil based medium, which, by the 1500s, largely replaced quick-drying, egg-based tempera. It was recently disclosed that Picasso used commercial house paint for many of his canvases, which suggests that the medium is not as important as the form or the message.

Pastiche: a medley of musical, literary or cinematic fragments cobbled together in imitation of one or more original works.

Pastoral: a genre in literature, poetry, music and art that depicts the idealized country life of the shepherd or herdsman. The genre includes works by Ludwig van Beethoven, Thomas Cole, Claude Debussy, Giorgione, Claude Lorrain, Nicolas Poussin and Antoine Watteau.

Patronage: the traditional method for commissioning works of art and providing financial support to artists and musicians, which was used by princes, nobles, aristocrats and churchmen and, later, by the merchant bourgeoisie, until it was supplanted by the consumer art market and public-supported museums, theaters and concert halls.

Performance art: a form of live or action art that consists of unique and non-repeated events, sometimes scripted and sometimes not, in which the artist performs before an audience, who may or may not be involved in the performance. Performance art includes "happenings" and spontaneous street theater, as well as performances by individual artists. In Marina Abramovic's "The Artist is Present," the artist sits silently in the Museum of Modern Art while spectators take turns sitting opposite her. See Conceptual art and Fluxus in Concepts.

Perspective: a technique for creating the illusion of depth on a flat, two-dimensional surface by reducing the size of objects as they recede in the distance, using one or more vanishing points to create the illusion of depth. Filippo Brunelleschi was one of the first to use the technique in the early 1400s. See Foreshortening in Concepts.

Photomontage: a photographic collage or composite made by cutting and joining a number of photos; also, a film montage.

Photoshop: the use of computer software to digitally manipulate, enhance or re-construct a photographic image from one or more images. See CGI, *In silico* and Special effects in Concepts.

Poetry of imperfection: Simon Schama's term for Rembrandt's realistic but warm and sympathetic treatment of his subjects, as opposed to the idealized beauty of classical art. See Idealization in Concepts.

Pointillisme: an impressionistic style of painting that uses small dots and brush strokes to create an optically blended image; a similar effect is achieved by the grid of pixels in digital photography and television and computer monitors. The technique was used by Camille Pissarro, Georges Seurat and Paul Signac.

Popular culture: one that is often described in terms of opposition by elite or high culture. Historically, popular culture has been expressed through such varied media as almanacs, sermons, agricultural fairs, husking bees, country music, barn dances, tent revivals, the penny press, minstrel shows, carnivals, vaudeville, ragtime, jazz, nickelodeons, movies, radio, television, magazines, popular music, rock and roll, rap and hip-hop, breakdancing, celebrity journalism, tabloids and electronic social media. Herbert Gans, Clifford Geertz, John Kouwenhoven, Dwight Macdonald, Bernard Rosenberg and David White, Jane and Michael Stern, James Twitchell. See Folk culture, High-brow/low-brow and Mass Culture in Concepts and 25. Postmodernism in Details.

Prairie style (1900-1920): a Midwestern school of architecture associated with Frank Lloyd Wright, whose buildings are notable for their flat, horizontal, functional lines and project simplicity, integrity and harmony with their environment and celebrate the organic unity of man and nature, function and form.

Precisionism (1916-1931): an American art movement that portrayed industrial objects and landscapes, such as factories and bridges, as well as commercial products, such as matchboxes and watches, with an abstract, hyper-photographic realism. The movement was foreshadowed in the still-lifes of William Harnett and John Peto and is represented in the works of George Ault, Stuart Davis, Charles Demuth, Edward Hopper, Gerald Murphy, Georgia O'Keefe and Charles Sheeler.

Program music: music that suggests a story or narrative through imaginative images, references and correlatives to the world outside the music; versus **absolute music**: nonrepresentational music that is enjoyed as pure sound and form without explicit meaning.. Hector Berlioz.

*Q**uattrocento*** and ***Cinquecento***: the contemporary terms for the Italian Renaissance of the 15th and 16th centuries. The term "Renaissance" was not used until 1855. See 8. Renaissance in Details

The **Real Thing**: a short story by Henry James, Jr. in which the author suggests that the artistic illusion is often more authentic than the reality itself. In the story, an artist's professional models portray an older patrician couple in genteel poverty with greater verisimilitude than the actual patrician couple themselves, who are self-conscious about being painted. A similar principle is suggested in physics in which the very act of observing affects the object being observed. See Heisenberg's principle of uncertainty in Science Concepts.

Red-figure style: a style of ancient Grecian pottery that portrayed light reddish orange figures on a black background, which was developed in Athens around 520 BCE and largely replaced the **black-figure style** of black figures on a reddish orange background developed earlier in Corinth.

Renaissance ("rebirth"): the cultural, literary and scientific flowering that occurred in Europe during the 1400s and the 1500s. It was driven by the revival of interest in classical antiquity and served as a bridge between the Middle Ages and the beginning of the modern era. The term was first used in 1855. See 8. Renaissance in Details.

Romanesque/Norman style (900s to the 1100s): a style of architecture that featured massive walls, rounded arches and vaulted ceilings, and was superseded by the spires, pointed arches, glass windows and flying buttresses of the more graceful and soaring Gothic style. See 6. Romanesque/Norman in Details.

Rubric: a common feature of medieval illuminated manuscripts (*q.v.* in Concepts) in which a word or section of text is written in red ink to highlight it or provide commentary.

Salons: the drawing rooms of upper-class female patrons, initially in Italy and France in the 17th and 18th Centuries, in which writers, artists and intellectuals of both sexes gathered in the afternoon for conversation, reasoned debate and, of course, refreshments.

S'fumato ("in the manner of smoke"): an artistic technique that is used to shade and soften scenes and borders. It was used by Leonardo da Vinci in his *Mona Lisa*.

Shaker art: vernacular art, usually furniture and other household objects, that is characterized by its functionality, harmony, purity and simplicity. See Vernacular tradition in Concepts.

Simulacrum: a likeness or imitation of reality; for example, Disneyland's Main Street or Las Vegas's Venetian canals. See CGI and Special effects in Concepts.

Socialist realism: the official art of Stalinist Russia, which depicted the heroic struggles of the working class. The term should not be confused with Social Realism, which is described in 21. Social Realism in Details.

Special effects: mechanical, visual and digital techniques, including those derived from computer-generated imagery and graphics (CGI), to create a virtual world of simulated images. See CGI, *In silico* and Photoshop in Concepts.

Stele: a vertical stone slab or pillar with inscriptions or designs that serves as a monument or marker.

Structuralism: a school of thought that asserts that a work of art can only be known as it is mediated by, or filtered through, structures, which are defined as the underlying, often unconscious, mental processes and socialized preconceptions that a viewer brings to a work. See 2. Structuralism in Literary Concepts Details.

Sturm und Drang ("storm and drive" or "storm and stress"): a late 18th Century German proto-Romantic movement that was characterized by its intense expressions of individuality, subjectivity and emotion, in contrast to the prevailing rationalism of the time.

Ludwig van Beethoven, Johann Wolfgang Goethe, Johann Gottfried Herder and Friedrich Schiller. See 13. Romanticism in Details.

Stylized: a slightly contrived, unreal or artificial effect, rather than a natural, literal or realistic one.

Symbolic consciousness: the ability to symbolize, to see one thing in terms of another, to invest meaning in the world, which represents "the most characteristic mental trait of mankind," according to Susanne Langer (*q.v.* in Quotations).

Tenebrism: a style of painting that uses extreme contrasts between light and dark (with darkness dominating) to achieve a dramatic effect; an extreme form of *chiaroscuro* (*q.v.* in Concepts). The technique was used by Caravaggio, Georges de La Tour, and José Ribera.

Terra cotta ("baked earth"): clay-based earthenware, which is used in pottery, pipes, sculpture, figurines, facades, etc.

Tracery: elaborate and intricately interlaced patterns, which are found in Islamic architecture, as well as in the stonework supporting Gothic arched windows.

Tradition of the new: Harold Rosenberg's term for the inexorable trend in modern art in which the "advance guard" is perpetually driven to differentiate itself from mainstream and commercial art. See Avant-garde in Concepts.

Triptych: a painting in three sections or on three hinged panels, which was popular in the Middle Ages.

Tromp-l'oeil ("deceive the eye"): an optical illusion in which a three-dimensional object appears to emerge out of a flat, two-dimensional surface or frame. The technique was used by Salvador Dali, Jan van Eyck, William Harnett, René Magritte, John Peto and others.

Universal in the particular: one of the effects of a work of art, which is to reveal a universal truth or an insight through the particularities of the work itself. See Aristotle, Pablo Picasso and Susanne Langer in Quotations.

*V*anitas: the use of symbols such as a skull, flowers, fruit or a hourglass to remind the viewer of the transience of life and the inevitability of death.

Venus/goddess figurines: Upper (i.e., Later) Paleolithic female figurines, dating from approximately 35,000 to 18,000 years ago, which were carved from ivory, bone and stone or created from fired clay. The figurines were stylized, exaggerated and, often, steatopygous (i.e., having fatty buttocks and thighs) and may have represented fertility goddesses, sex objects, amulets or other forms of wish fulfillment for plentitude in times of scarcity, or companionship in times of solitude. They represent some of the earliest expressions of humanity's aesthetic sense and symbolic mode of consciousness. See Susanne Langer in Quotations.

Vernacular tradition: one in which utilitarian art objects are celebrated for their clean, graceful simplicity, economy of line, functional nature and utilitarian purpose. The American vernacular tradition is represented by such iconic cultural symbols as Shaker furniture, the Pennsylvania/Kentucky long rifle, Colt revolver, steam boat, clipper ship, skyscraper, automobile, freeways/expressways ("America's pyramids") and the soup can. John Kouwenhoven.

QUOTATIONS:

- [A poem is] *a light and winged holy thing.* -- Socrates.

- *The aim of art is to represent not the outward appearances of things, but their inward significance.* -- Aristotle.

- *Poetry is finer and more philosophical than history, for poetry expresses the universal, and history only the particular.* -- Aristotle.

- *It is art to conceal art.* – Ovid.

- *All art is but imitation of nature.* -- Seneca.

- *We have taken it into our heads . . . to write a poem simply for the poem's sake. . . . Would we but permit ourselves to look into our own souls we should immediately there discover that under the sun there neither exists nor can exist any work more thoroughly dignified, more supremely noble, than this very poem, this poem per se, this poem which is a poem and nothing more, this poem written solely for the poem's sake.* -- Edgar Allan Poe.

- *I have created the creative.* -- Herman Melville.

- *All art constantly aspires towards the condition of music.* -- Walter Pater.

- *Life imitates Art far more than Art imitates Life.* – Oscar Wilde.

- *Form ever follows function.* -- Louis Henri Sullivan.

- *Art is limitation; the essence of every picture is the frame.* -- G. K. Chesterton.

- *Art is a lie which makes us realize truth.* -- Pablo Picasso.

- *Less is more.* -- Ludwig Mies van der Rohe.

- *For it is ultimately the function of art, in imposing a credible order upon ordinary reality, and thereby eliciting some perception of an order in reality, to bring us to a condition of serenity, stillness, and reconciliation.* -- T. S. Eliot.

- *Art, I suppose, is only for beginners.* -- Aldous Huxley.

- *The power of understanding symbols, i.e. of regarding everything about a sense-datum as irrelevant except a certain form that it embodies, is the most characteristic mental trait of mankind. It issues in an unconscious, spontaneous process of abstraction, which goes on all the time in the human mind: a process of recognizing the concept in any configuration given to experience, and forming a conception accordingly.* -- Susanne Langer.

- *The real is what resists symbolization absolutely.* -- Jacques Lacan.

- *The tradition of the new.* -- Harold Rosenberg.

- *The machine turned Nature into an art form.* -- Marshall McLuhan.

- *Any man worthy to be called an artist should swear one oath: Dedication to silence!* -- Federico Fellini in *8½*.

- *At some point in life, the world's beauty becomes enough. You don't need to photograph, paint, or even remember it. It is enough.* -- Toni Morrison.

- *Interpretation is the revenge of the intellect upon art.* -- Susan Sontag.

- *The mill doesn't make the water run.* -- David Goines.

ART DETAILS: (1) Western Artistic Styles and Movements, (2) Egyptian Art, (3) Archaic, Classical and Hellenistic Greek Art, (4) Aristotle, (5) Roman Art, (6) Romanesque/Norman Art, (7) Gothic Art, (8) Renaissance, (9) Mannerism, (10) Baroque Art, (11) Rococo/Later Baroque Art, (12) 18th Century Neoclassicism, (13) Romanticism, (14)

Realism, (15) Impressionism, (16) Naturalism, (17) Post-Impressionism, (18) Cubism, (19) Expressionism, (20) Surrealism, (21) Social Realism, (22) Abstract Expressionism, (23) Minimalism, (24) Pop Art and (25) Postmodernism.

1. **Western Artistic Styles and Movements:** Egyptian (3150-332 BCE), Archaic Greek (600-480 BCE), Classical Greek (480-323 BCE), Hellenistic Greek (323-168 BCE), Roman (168 BCE-400 CE), Byzantine (400 CE-1450), Romanesque/Norman (late 900s-1100s), Gothic (1100s-1300s), Renaissance (1400s-1500s), Mannerism (1520-1600), Baroque (1600-1700), Rococo (1700s), Neo-Classicism (1750-1815), Romanticism (1800-1850), Pre-Raphaelite (1860s), Realism (1850-1900), Impressionism (1860-1900), Arts and Crafts (1860-1910), Naturalism (1880-1910), Art Nouveau (1890-1915), Post-Impressionism (1880-1900), Expressionism (1880-1930s), Beaux Arts/Neo-Classicalism (1890-1920s), Fauvism (1905-1908), Ash Can School (1908-1930s), Cubism (1907-1920s), Dadaism (1917-1920s), Surrealism (1920s-1930s), Constructivism (1920s), Precisionism (1920s-1930s), Art Deco (1920-1940), Bauhaus (1919-1930), International Style (1920s-1970s), Social Realism (1920s-1930s), Abstract Expressionism (1940-1950s), Pop Art (1950s-1960s), Minimalism (1960s), Postmodernism (1970 -   ).

2. **Egyptian Art** (3150-332 BCE) was guided by the belief that the purpose of visual representation was to preserve the soul of the represented object in the afterlife. Thus, objects were drawn from the perspective in which they could be seen most clearly and completely, with each part of the object viewed from its most characteristic angle, which was often in profile and, thus, resulted in a flat, stylized projection of the subject without any spatial depth (E. H. Gombrich). Because art served a religious purpose as well as to reinforce the stability and harmony of the existing social order, art standards were rigid and unchanging over thousands of years. Egyptian art is represented in wall paintings, statues, tombs, temples, obelisks and the pyramids.

3. **Archaic, Classical and Hellenistic Greek Art** (600-168 BCE) was characterized by its simplicity and harmony and its idealization of nature and the human form. The representation of the human form progressed from rigid poses to relaxed, natural

poses to virtuoso displays. Greek art is represented in marble and bronze sculpture (*kouroi*, or nude male youths, and draped or nude gods and goddesses); temples (Doric, Ionic, and Corinthian column and capital styles, with elaborately sculpted friezes and brightly painted colors); pottery (amphora, kraters, hydriai, jugs and cups), seals and coins. The black-figure style of pottery (of black figures on a light reddish orange background) was largely superseded in the 6th Century BCE by the red-figure style (of light reddish orange figures on black backgrounds).

4. **Aristotle** (384–322 BCE) defined art as the imitation (*mimesis*) and perfection of nature. In *Poetics*, he proposed that the purpose of drama is to purify and cleanse the emotions (*catharsis*). He identified the essential elements of drama as (1) character (*ethos*), (2) plot (*mythos*), (3) dialogue or speech (*lexis*), (4) spectacle (*opsis*), (5) the hero's miscalculation or tragic flaw (*hamartia*), (6) the reversal of fortune (*peripeteia*) and (7) the hero's tragic revelation or realization (*anagnorisis*) of the true nature of things.

5. **Roman Art** (168 BCE-400 CE) was practical, utilitarian and deeply influenced by its Greek antecedents. It was represented in civil engineering and public architecture (vaulted arches, roads, amphitheaters, aqueducts, public baths, basilicas [royal halls] and triumphal columns); mosaics; wall and panel paintings; portraits; and still-lifes and busts of emperors, who were portrayed with matter-of-fact realism.

6. **Romanesque/Norman Art** (late 900s-1100s) was an architectural style that was characterized by its massive, fortress-like towers and churches, with thick walls, ribbed vaults and rounded windows and arches. According to E. H. Gombrich, the style represented "the [Christian] Church militant" against the forces of barbarism and paganism.

7. **Gothic Art** (1100s-1300s) was a medieval architectural movement and artistic style that originated in France and spread throughout the rest of western Europe. Originally, "Gothic" was a pejorative term applied later by Renaissance Italians in the 1530s to the "barbarian" style from north of the Alps for the period between the end of the Classical period (marked by the sack of Rome in 410 by the Germanic hordes, or "Goths") and the beginning of the Italian

Renaissance. Gothic art represented the "triumphant" expression of Christian faith (Gombrich), whose purpose was to tell a sacred story with simple piety and faith ("painting can do for the illiterate what writing does for those who can read," according to Pope Gregory). Gothic cathedrals featured flying buttresses to support higher open walls, pointed arches, tracery and stained glass windows, all of which created the effect of soaring lightness and weightlessness. Gothic art was also represented in sculpture, frescos, altar pieces and illuminated manuscripts.

8. **Renaissance** (1400s to 1500s) was a period of cultural rebirth that emerged from the "Middle" or "Dark Ages" (approximately 400 to 1300) that had followed the collapse of the Roman Empire. The period has been described as an age in which the medieval veil of "faith, illusion and childish prepossession" was removed from the eyes of human consciousness (Jacob Burckhardt). It was inspired by the rediscovery of classical antiquity, including ancient Greek and Latin texts, and was characterized by a renewed interest in classical learning, humanism ("man is the measure of all things"), the flowering of arts (including the use of oil painting and the discovery of linear perspective), vernacular literature and scientific curiosity. The Renaissance served as a bridge between the Middle Ages and the modern era. The contemporary Italian terms for the Italian Renaissance of the 15th and 16th centuries were *Quattrocento* and *Cinquecento*. The term **"renaissance"** is derived from the Italian *rinascere*, "to be reborn," and was first used in 1855. Renaissance art is represented in the works of Sandro Botticelli, Pieter Brueghel, Filippo Brunelleschi, Donatello, Albrecht Durer, Jan Van Eyck, Lorenzo Ghiberti, Giotto, Leonardo da Vinci, Andrea Mantegna, Masaccio, Michelangelo, Raphael and Titian.

Historically, the Renaissance was associated with (1) the revival of trade and commerce after the Black Death of the 1340s and 1350s; (2) the exodus of Greek scholars to Western Europe from Constantinople after its fall to the Ottoman Turks in 1453; (3) the rise of the Italian city-states and the merchant republics such as Venice and Florence and the patronage of the arts by their banking and merchant families (such as the Medici); (4) the discovery and exploration of the New World; (5) the invention of the printing press using moveable metal type in the 1440s and the spread of the printed word; (6) the Protestant Reformation, which began in 1517; (7) the Roman Catholic Counterreformation and (8) the publication of Copernicus's *On the Revolutions of the Heavenly Spheres* in 1543, which marked the beginning of the scientific revolution and laid the foundation for the 17th Century and 18th Century Enlightenment.

9. **Mannerism** (1520-1600) was an artistic style and movement that was characterized by its cool elegance, witty and affected manners, displays of virtuosity and its exquisite attention to detail, as well as by its elongated forms, stylized poses, garish colors, distorted perspectives and dramatic movements. The term is derived from *maniera*, or "stylishness." Mannerist style is represented in the works of Benvenuto Cellini, El Greco, Parmigianino and Tintoretto.

10. **Baroque Art** (1600-1700) was an artistic style and movement that was encouraged and supported by the Roman Catholic Church in reaction to the austerity and asceticism of the Protestant Reformation during what was known as the Counter-Reformation. According to the Catholic Church, the purpose of art was to communicate religious and mythological truths to the faithful in a dramatic and emotional way and to glorify the triumphant power of the Church and the monarchy. Baroque art was characterized by its exuberance, emotional intensity, dramatic effect, luxury, sensuousness and grandeur, and its abundance of detail, including rich draperies, living flesh, fluffy clouds and pink-cheeked cherubs. The term is derived from the Spanish term for "rough or imperfect pearl." The style is represented in the works of Gian Lorenzo Bernini, Caravaggio, Peter Paul Rubens and Diego Velazquez.

11. **Rococo/Late Baroque Art** (1700s) was a style that has been described as delicate, playful, witty, elegant, florid, frivolous and affected. It evoked pale colors, asymmetrical designs and curves, leisurely aristocratic lifestyles and sexually suggestive themes. "Rococo" refers to the fancy pebbles and shells used in ornamental gardens. The style is represented in the works of Francois Boucher, Jean-Honoré Fragonard, Giovanni Tiepolo and Antoine Watteau.

12. **18th Century Neoclassicism** embodied the Enlightenment ideals of reason, order, harmony, balance and restraint. It drew on Greek and Roman classicism and Renaissance humanism, and reflected the Apollonian spirit of the head (reason) over the heart (emotion). Neoclassicism is represented in the works of Jean-Baptiste-Camille Corot, Jacques-Louis David, Thomas Gainsborough, Jean-Antoine Houdon, Joshua Reynolds and Christopher Wren. See 27. 18th Century Enlightenment/Age of Reason in Philosophy/Religion Details for a list of writers and philosophers of the 18th Century Enlightenment.

13. **Romanticism** (1780-1850) was a reaction against the cool, scientific rationalism of the 18th Century Enlightenment. It celebrated the primacy of feelings, the extremes of emotions (*Sturm und Drang*), the value of intuition, originality and the imagination, and the subjective experience of the individual. Romantics stressed the heroic nature of the individual genius, revered the beauty, sublimity and spirituality of nature and abhorred the evils of industrialism and urbanization and their incursion into nature. Romantic values are represented in the works of Washington Allston, Albert Bierstadt, William Blake, Frederic Church, Thomas Cole, John Constable, Francisco Goya and J. M. W. Turner. See 28. Romanticism in Philosophy/Religion Details for a list of Romantic writers and poets.

14. **Realism** (1850-1900) sought to portray everyday life accurately and objectively. It is represented in the works of Gustave Courbet, Thomas Eakins, Winslow Homer and Jean-Francois Millet.

15. **Impressionism** (1860-1900) was characterized by its fascination with natural light, "open air," ocular vision and color. It sought to capture the immediate, fleeting, visual impressions of, mostly, outdoor scenes. It has been viewed, in part, as a response to the invention of photography and the advent of photographic realism. The style is represented in the works of Mary Cassatt, Edgar Degas, Edouard Manet, Claude Monet, Camille Pissarro, Pierre Auguste Renoir and Alfred Sisley. See *En plein air* and *Pointillisme* in Concepts.

16. **Naturalism** (1880-1910) sought to record everyday life realistically, scientifically and objectively. It was influenced by

Darwin's theory of evolution (the struggle for existence and the survival of the fittest) and focused on the darker, more sordid aspects of nature and urban and industrial realities, which were portrayed in materialistic and deterministic terms. Naturalism is reflected in the works of Thomas Eakins and Winslow Homer and in the writings of Stephen Crane, Theodore Dreiser, Frank Norris and Emile Zola.

17. **Post-Impressionism** (1886-1905) was a reaction against the passive naturalism of Impressionism. Paul Cezanne sought to convey, through art, the sense of order, form, solidity and depth in nature; Paul Gaugin sought to portray the intensity and primitive simplicity of children of nature, and Vincent Van Gogh used art to express his emotions and inner feelings. These three approaches laid the foundations for, respectively, Cubism, Primitivism and Expressionism.

18. **Cubism** (1907-1920) sought to deconstruct and reconstruct (in the mind's eye) their subjects by flattening them on two-dimensional surfaces and showing them without depth or perspective from multiple points of view simultaneously. It explored the relationship between geometrical forms, space and movement and was influenced by Cezanne, African folk art, jazz and motion pictures. The movement is represented in the works of Georges Braque, Juan Gris, Fernand Léger and Pablo Picasso.

19. **Expressionism** (1900-1930) sought to express the artist's innermost feelings and personal visions, often with passionate colors and in an exaggerated and distorted fashion. The movement is represented in the works of Vincent Van Gogh, Ernst Ludwig Kirchner, Oskar Kokoschka and Edvard Munch.

20. **Surrealism** (1920s) sought to visually convey the dreamlike qualities of the irrational and the unconscious. It is represented in the works of Salvador Dali, Marcel Duchamp, Max Ernst, Arshile Gorky, Frida Kahlo, Joan Miro and Georgia O'Keefe.

21. **Social Realism** (1930s) provided unvarnished but sympathetic portraits of common people, urban poverty, racial injustice and the hardships of everyday, working class life. Social Realism should not be confused with the Socialist realism of Stalinist Russia (*q.v.*

in Concepts). The movement is represented in the works of
Thomas Hart Benton, Edward Hopper, Dorothea Lange, Jack
Levine, Reginald Marsh, José Clemente Orozco, Diego Rivera,
Ben Shahn, David Siqueiros and Grant Wood.

22. **Abstract Expressionism** (post-World War II) consisted of both
non-representational "action paintings," as well as tranquil
paintings of abstract images and color fields. The former were
perceived as events, as ends in themselves, in which the canvas
became "an arena in which to act." They were characterized by
rapid and forceful brushstrokes, wielded with an emotional
intensity to express the creativity of the artist's unconscious mind.
The latter consisted of more abstract, reflective images and blocks
of color. Willem de Kooning, Richard Diebenkorn, Helen
Frankenthaler, Lee Krasner, Joan Mitchell, Robert Motherwell,
Barnett Newman, Jackson Pollock, Mark Rothko and Cy Twombly
are representative artists of the movement.

23. **Minimalism** (mostly, the 1960s-1980s) sought to strip away the
non-essential elements of their subjects and expose their essence.
It was guided by (1) Mies van der Rohe's philosophy that "less is
more"; (2) the aesthetic of absence and (3) the Japanese tradition of
simplicity and essentiality and its concept of *Ma*, or empty space.
Minimalism is represented in the works of Josef Albers, John
Cage, Donald Judd, Agnes Martin, Piet Mondrian, Barnett
Newman, Ad Reinhardt and Frank Stella.

24. **Pop Art** (1950s-1960s) was characterized by its iconic and ironic
treatment of commercial, mass-produced objects and images of
popular culture, including those in advertising, mass entertainment,
retail sales and comic books. Pop art has been viewed as a reaction
against Abstract Expressionism and the esoteric elitism of modern
art. It viewed common, commercial objects and images from a
classical, artistic perspective, thereby endowing 20th Century
global consumer capitalism with its own timeless, ironic
iconography. The movement is represented in the works of David
Hockney, Jasper Johns, Roy Lichtenstein, Claes Oldenburg, Robert
Rauschenberg, Wayne Thiebaud and Andy Warhol.

25. **Postmodernism** (1970 -   ) is a fluid term, a vernacular style and
a cultural philosophy. As a **vernacular style**, postmodernism

projects a tone that is cool, skeptical, ironic, eclectic, whimsical, self-mocking and blasé. It focuses on surfaces; celebrates the fragmentation, trivialization and commercialization of culture and blurs the distinction between high art and consumer/commercial art (Todd Gitlin). According to Frederic Jameson, postmodernism is an expression of late/high consumption capitalism and commodity fetishism, which is distinguished by its ceaseless transformation of style, its connoisseurship of surface and its emphasis on packaging and reproducibility. Postmodernism embodies the truth that art has become commodified (*q.v.* in Concepts). Examples of postmodernism include Pop art, Las Vegas, Disneyland, shopping malls, office buildings with bright colors and Chippendale scrolls and non-orthogonal lines (i.e., not intersecting at right angles), and the performances of Madonna and Lady Gaga.

As a **cultural philosophy**, postmodernism presents itself as opposing or superseding "modernity." Modernity is identified with faith in technology, objective knowledge, scientific truth, rationality, functionality, hierarchy, authority and power. In its place, postmodernism offers an alternative set of concepts and constructs: (1) the denial of absolute truth and the belief that knowledge and reality are socially constructed; (2) the collapse of cultural hierarchies, the rejection of monolithic power structures and their replacement by pluralities of power; (3) the commodification of knowledge; (4) the end of history; (5) skepticism of grand themes, orthodoxies, canons and meta-narratives; (6) randomness and indeterminacy; (7) self-referentiality and intertextuality; (8) irony (and post-irony); (9) the simulacra of electronic media; (10) language as oppression; (11) less is bore; (12) the theater of the absurd and (13) the literature of silence. For a criticism of Postmodernism's moral relativity, see Alan Sokal in Sociology Quotations.

Postmodernism should not be confused with **post-structuralism**, although both share a common conceptual framework of indeterminacy and the belief that there is no objective truth, that reality is socially constructed, and that social dynamics and power hierarchies play a critical role in conceptual relationships. Post-structuralism is a critical literary theory, while postmodernism is broader, more inclusive cultural term and vernacular style that incorporates the insights of post-structuralism and other schools of critical thought. See 4. Post-structuralism in Literary Concepts Details.

4. ECONOMICS

CONCEPTS AND PHRASES:

Advertising: an in dustry whose objectives are to create a demand, project a life style, enhance good will and, not least, sell the products and services of its clients. See Overproduction and Product differentiation in Concepts.

Agribusiness: large-scale, capital-intensive corporate farming, which uses wage labor, produces cash crops for national and world markets and is subject to international capital, credit, labor and market forces; versus subsistence and family farming. See Agrarian/yeoman ideal in American History Concepts.

American System/American Way: see 7. American System in Details.

Amortization: the retirement or elimination of a debt by making fixed payments in regular installments over a fixed period of time; also the reduction in the accounting value of an asset in fixed amounts over a fixed period of time, such as depreciation. See Depreciation in Concepts.

Ananke: economic necessity.

Apprenticeship system: once, a common method for learning a trade in which a young man contracted, usually for seven years, to exchange his labor for food, lodging and training. It usually involved living in the master craftsman's household and, afterwards, becoming a journeyman (literally, a "day worker") and, eventually, a master craftsman. See Guild system in Concepts.

Asymmetric information: insider information; the seller knows the automobile is a lemon, or the stock is over-valued, but the buyer does not.

Barter economy: a system in which goods and services are exchanged directly between traders without an intermediate medium of exchange, such as money. See Medium of exchange in Concepts.

Behavioral economics: a field of study that focuses on the non-rational factors involved in economic decision-making, such as impulsiveness, risk/loss avoidance, non-reciprocal altruism, rules of thumb, herd behavior, and what Keynes called "animal spirits." See 23. Behavioral Economics in Details.

Bipolar economy: an hour-glass economy, with a shrinking middle-class and a growing disparity between the rich and the poor; also, the manic upswings and the depressive downswings of the business cycle. See Dual economy and Hourglass economy in Concepts.

Bounded rationality: the proposition that rational decision-making is limited, or bounded, by uncertainty, ignorance, irrationality, practicality, rules of thumb, competing interests, and self-limiting or "satisficing" (i.e., good enough) choices. It challenges the classical model of the rational economic decision-maker (*homo economicus*). Herbert Simon. See 23. Behavioral Economics and 24. Neuro-Economics in Details.

Bourgeoisie: approximately, the middle class. The term is derived from the French term for "walled market town," since, historically, it was associated with the rise of chartered medieval towns, whose citizens ("burghers") enjoyed more privileges than the serfs, who lived in villages and were subject to more restrictive feudal regulations. The interests of town merchants and craftsmen sometimes clashed with those of the feudal, landed aristocracy and, thus, the urban middle class served as a historical force for political liberalization until the Industrial Revolution of the 19th Century. At that time, the term shifted to industrialists and financiers, who, in Marxist theory, were the capitalist ruling class, that is, the social class who owned the means of production and exploited the working class. Marxists differentiate between the *haute bourgeoisie* of financiers and industrialists and the *petite bourgeoisie* of professionals, white-collar workers, shopkeepers and small business owners. Today the term *bourgeois* is commonly applied to a wide range of socio-economic groups including the nouveau riche, the upper-middle class, the middle class and the lower-middle class. At various times, it has also been used pejoratively to refer to those who are materialistic, conventional and conformist and who strive for social advancement and the conspicuous display of wealth, learning and culture. See 20. Class Structure and 21. Social Classes in the United States in Sociology Details.

Break-even point: the point at which the accumulated income generated from an investment or a project equals its original cost. See Payback period in Concepts.

Buddhist economics: an ethic that seeks to mitigate the despoliation of the natural environment, redress the imbalance between the city and the country and provide an alternative model to the cash nexus of impersonal market forces and the systematic cultivation of consumption and greed ("more, further, richer, quicker"). See Moral capitalism and Overproduction in Concepts and 22. E. F. Schumacher/Small-is-Beautiful Economics in Details.

Business cycle: capitalism's inherent cycle of expansion and contraction, boom and bust. Joseph Schumpeter suggested that the typical business cycle lasts from 7 to 11 years and has four stages: (1) expansion, (2) crisis (with a stock market crash and numerous bankruptcies), (3) recession and (4) recovery. See Creative destruction, Manic capitalism, Overproduction and Panics, depressions and recessions in Concepts.

Business model: a long range plan that defines an enterprise's *raison d'être*, that is, it's objectives, financial plans and strategies for making a profit.

Buyers' market: a condition in which the supply of a product exceeds its demand, which tends to depress its price; versus **sellers' market**, in which the demand for a product exceeds its supply, which tends to drive up its price.

Buyer's remorse: post-purchase regret.

Capital (derived from Latin for "head" of cattle or livestock): generally, tangible assets, such as cash, stocks, promissory notes, supplies, tools, equipment, machinery, buildings, furniture and factories, as well as intangible assets such as patents and copyrights, that are used to produce goods and services. It is one of the four factors of production (the others are natural resources, labor and technology). The term also refers to accumulated or surplus wealth.

Capitalism: an economic system based on the private ownership of the means of production with the objective of making a profit. Historically, it was associated with commerce and trade, medieval towns, the rise of the urban bourgeoisie, the Protestant ethic, mass production and the Industrial Revolution. See Mass production, Protestant ethic and the rise of capitalism in Concepts and 3. Adam Smith/Classical/Free Market Economics and 8. Industrial Revolution in Details.

Cartel: an international syndicate of sellers and/or buyers that is organized to divide markets among themselves, fix prices and limit supply, e.g., those for oil, diamonds, precious metals and maple syrup.

Cash nexus: the approximate term used by Karl Marx to describe the system of social relationships that prevails in modern, market-driven economies. These relationships are characterized by anonymous, impersonal market forces, economic individualism, "naked self-interest" and personal profit over social responsibility, which replaced the tight-knit communities, social networks and ethical norms (of fairness and mutuality) of traditional societies. Marx, E. P. Thompson. See Commodification in Concepts, Karl Marx in Quotations and 11. Ferdinand Tönnies/*Gemeinschaft* in Sociology Details.

Central economic planning: the centralized planning and control of economic activity, including resource allocation, interest, wages, prices, etc. The degree of control ranges from (1) the **command economy** of North Korea, to (2) the **mixed command/state capitalism** of Russia and China, in which the government controls the economy and serves as a single, huge corporation, to (3) the **democratic socialism** of modern European welfare states, in which the national government controls key industries, to (4) the **state monopoly capitalism** of Japan and South Korea, in which networks of large, private corporations (*keiretsu* and *chaebol*) work in partnership with governmental ministries to coordinate national economic planning to (5) the **mixed/managed economy** of Keynesian economics in the United States. Central economic planning stands in opposition to **laissez-faire economic systems**, in which there is little or no governmental regulation, taxation or oversight of business activities. See Laissez-faire economics, Market economy versus planned economy, State capitalism and State monopoly capitalism in Concepts and 3. Adam Smith/Classical/Free Market Economics, 7. American System, 16. Keynesian Economics and 20. Neoclassical Synthesis in Details.

Class: a set of hierarchical categories that are used to define social stratification. They are based on socio-economic criteria, usually wealth and income, but also on hereditary rank, relationship to the means of production (David Ricardo, Karl Marx) and education, status, prestige and power (Max Weber). See Class in Sociology Concepts and 14. Max Weber, 20. Class Structure and 21. Social Classes in Sociology Details.

Class basis of ideas: the doctrine that ideas are conditioned or determined by the social and economic environment in which they arise; also, that ideology reflects the economic interests of the dominant class. See Cultural hegemony in Concepts and 10. Economic/Technological Determinism in Details.

Class conflict/class warfare: see Benjamin Franklin, James Harrington, Thomas Jefferson, Abraham Lincoln, James Madison, Karl Marx and Jean-Jacques Rousseau in Quotations and 9. Karl Marx/Dialectical Materialism in Details.

Classless society: the purported goal of communism, which is partially based on Marx's reading of anthropologist Lewis Henry Morgan's studies on egalitarian hunter-gatherer societies such as the Iroquois of North America. See Morgan, Lewis Henry in Anthropology Concepts.

Commodification: the transformation of ideas, human beings, works of art, sexual relationships, nature, animals, etc. into products with assigned economic values that can be bought and sold in the marketplace. Karl Marx. See Cash nexus, Consumer culture and Fetishism of commodities in Concepts.

Comparative advantage: a fundamental tenet of free trade and classical economics. See in 5. David Ricardo/Law of Comparative Advantage in Details.

Compensation ratios: the ratio of the compensation paid to corporate executives relative to the median pay of their workers. Currently, major corporate chief executive officers receive, on average, more than 300 times the average pay of their workers.

Competition versus **monopoly/oligopoly**: the basic conundrum of classical, free market economics, which is that, although competition (the rivalry among a large number of producers to sell the most goods and services at the highest profit) is the *sine qua non* of the free market system, because of economies of scale and other factors, competition often leads to the concentration and consolidation of a large number of small producers into a small number of large producers or one large producer (that is, oligopoly or monopoly), which reduces competition, distorts market forces and contradicts the free market model. See Economies of scale,

Monopolies/oligopolies and Trust busting in Concepts and 3.
Adam Smith/Classical/Free Market Economics in Details.

Conspicuous consumption/conspicuous waste: a characteristic of the
"pecuniary" or wealthy classes, according to Thorstein Veblen.
See Consumer culture and Fetishism of commodities in Concepts
and 13. Thorstein Veblen in Details.

Consumer culture: one in which individuals are preoccupied with the
acquisition of material goods and services and the enhancement of
personal beauty, youth and status. The concept is reflected in
Alexis Tocqueville's materialism, Karl Marx's fetishism of
commodities, Thorstein Veblen's conspicuous consumption/
conspicuous waste and Christopher Lasch's culture of narcissism.
Modern consumerism is associated with the Industrial Revolution,
a rising middle class, status symbols, advertising and globalization,
and is accompanied by threats to the sustainability of the natural
environment. See Commodification, Conspicuous consumption,
Fetishism of commodities, Institutional prodigality and Mass
Production in Concepts and Culture of narcissism in Sociology
Concepts.

Consumer protection movement: a reform movement whose
objectives are to insure the safety of food, medicine, automobiles,
toys and other consumer products. Milestones in the movement
include the enactment of the Pure Food and Drug Law in 1906, the
establishment of Food and the Drug Administration in 1927, the
founding of the Consumers Union in 1936 and the publication of
Ralph Nader's book, *Unsafe at Any Speed*, in 1965, which led to
the expansion of product liability laws and the resurgence of the
consumer protection movement.

Convergence theory: that, because of technological developments,
capitalism and socialism have merged and been superseded by the
new technocratic, bureaucratic state. Daniel Bell, John Kenneth
Galbraith, Clark Kerr, Max Weber. See Technocracy in Concepts.

Corporate welfare state: a government that provides subsidies, price
supports, loan guarantees, tax breaks, contracts and preferential
treatment to corporations and big businesses.

Corporation: a legal entity with privileges and liabilities that are
distinct from those of its owners and employees. It is the dominant
social institution of modern, capitalistic societies. Joel Bakan,
Adolph Berle and Gardiner Means, Martin Sklar. See Thomas
Jefferson and John Marshall in Quotations.

Cost-benefit analyses: methodologies that examine the ratio of expected costs of a project to its expected benefits over a range of probabilities. Opportunity costs (i.e., those benefits that are foregone by undertaking one project rather than alternative ones) are also factored into the analysis.

Cottage industries: those in which products, such as cloth, pins, nails and clothing, were produced in the individual homes and workshops of workers and their families. The system was largely replaced in the 19th Century by the centralized factory system. See Factory system in Concepts.

Countervailing powers: in theory, a system of economic checks and balances in which large, competing economic interest groups keep any one group from dominating public policy, e.g., corporations versus unions; consumers versus producers; exporters versus importers; legacy media versus online/social media; traditional hotel and taxicab industries versus peer-to-peer networks. John Kenneth Galbraith.

Counting house: the room or office in which a firm's financial transactions were recorded and sales and profits were tallied; an emblematic feature of 18th and 19th Century merchant capitalism.

Creative destruction: the ceaseless process of disruption and transformation, which is the central feature of capitalism, according to Joseph Schumpeter and Karl Marx. "The new consumers' goods, the new methods of production or transportation, the new markets, the new forms of industrial organization . . . incessantly revolutionize the economic structure *from within*, incessantly destroying the old one, incessantly creating a new one" (Schumpeter). The bourgeoisie "cannot exist without constantly revolutionizing the instruments of production" (Marx). See Manic capitalism in Concepts, Karl Marx in Quotations and 15. Schumpeter/Creative Destruction in Details.

Crony capitalism: a system of informal, personal relationships, friendships and family and collegiate ties within a group of businesses and between those businesses and governmental officials for the purpose of mutual financial gain. It is characterized by nepotism, favoritism, collusion, corruption and the distortion of free market competition. Its effects are mitigated by transparency, full disclosure, regulatory oversight, professional accounting and auditing standards and practices, and criminal sanctions against bribery, corruption and insider trading.

De-industrialization: the decline in manufacturing industries and the shift to service, financial and information industries. Daniel Bell, Paul Romer. See Post-industrial economies in Concepts.

Democratic socialism: a system that combines political democracy with centralized economic planning and the national ownership of the means of production.

Dependency ratio: the ratio of age-dependents (i.e., those under the age 15 and over the age of 64) to the working population.

Dependency theory: that developing countries cannot control their economic destinies because of the dominance of advanced industrial economies. Andre Gunder Frank. See 21. Development Economics in Details.

Depreciation: the expired utility, or usefulness, of an asset; the incremental reduction in the value of an asset, or, more accurately, the allocation of its net cost, over its useful life. For example, a truck with a ten-year useful life, would be depreciated, using the straight-line method, by 10% of its original cost (less its expected salvage value) each year. For a business, annual depreciation is recorded as a tax deductible business expense, and, for this example, by the end of the tenth year, the asset would have a book value equal to its salvage value. See Amortization in Concepts.

Deregulation: the removal of governmental regulations and oversight of an economic activity or industry such as the stock market or the banking, trucking, communications and airlines industries. See Reaganomics in Concepts.

Development economics: a branch of economics that offers theories and strategies for promoting economic growth in underdeveloped countries. See 21. in Details.

Dictatorship of the bourgeoisie: see 9. Karl Marx/Dialectical Materialism in Details.

Dictatorship of the proletariat: in Marxist theory, the precursor to the classless, stateless, egalitarian society of pure communism.

Diseconomies of scale: the negative consequences that accompany an increase in the size or scale of a business or industry. These include higher administrative and overhead costs, reduced personal contact with customers, bureaucratic inertia, inefficiencies and the loss of entrepreneurial initiative, as well as the additional costs to society such as the loss of small businesses, traffic congestion, pollution, waste, etc. See Economies of scale in Concepts.

Disembourgeoisment: the displacement and downward mobility of individuals and families from the middle class. See Downward mobility, Economic inequality/concentration of wealth and Social mobility in Concepts.

Dismal science: David Ricardo's term for the study of economics, since it involves inequality, material scarcity and economic self-interest.

Disposable income: net household income after deducting fixed expenses such as mortgage payments, insurance, utilities, real estate taxes, etc.

Double-entry bookkeeping: a system of accounting developed in Florence and Genoa in the 14th Century, in which every financial transaction is recorded (or posted) twice, once as a debit (or left-handed) entry in one account and once as a credit (or right-handed) entry in another account, which, theoretically, by adding all the debits and credits at the end of an accounting period, will insure that all transactions have been recorded for that period. For example, the purchase of a truck is recorded as a debit in a fixed asset account and a credit in a notes payable account.

Double failure: the thesis that both the free market and socialist models have failed. See Convergence theory in Concepts.

Downward mobility: the decline of the middle class in postindustrial America. It is associated with globalization, the offshore outsourcing of jobs, economic recession, de-unionization, regressive taxation, inequality and the concentration of wealth. Jacob Hacker and Paul Pierson, Paul Krugman, Kevin Phillips, Thomas Piketty, Joseph Stiglitz. See *Disembourgeoisment*, Economic inequality/concentration of wealth, Great Gatsby curve and Social Mobility in Concepts.

Downsizing: reducing the size of a firm by "laying off" a number of its employees. The term "lay off" once suggested the temporary suspension of employment because of seasonal economic conditions, but it is now commonly used as a euphemism for permanent termination.

Dual economy: an economy with an oligopolistic core, dominated by a few large companies, and smaller, competitive, peripheral sectors. It also refers to an hour-glass or bipolar economy of affluence and subsistence. See Bipolar economy in Concepts.

Eco-feminism: a movement and school of thought which holds that the degradation of the natural environment has been caused by the patriarchal values of domination, conquest, competition and exploitation. In contrast, the matriarchal values of empathy,

compassion, cooperation and nurturing are needed to heal the
Mother Earth; Vandana Shiva. See Environmentalism/Green
movement in Concepts and 35. Feminism in American History
Details.

E-commerce: business transactions that are conducted electronically
over the Internet, as opposed to those that are conducted
personally, face-to-face, in physical, brick-and-mortar facilities.
See Weightlessness in Concepts and 24. Information
Technology/Metaphor of the Machine in Sociology Details.

Economic inequality/concentration of wealth: the redistribution of
wealth upwards. In the United States, the top 1% of households
receives over 30% of all income and holds 40% of all assets.
There is greater inequality in the United States than in any other
democracy in the developed world. According to Oxfam, eighty-
five of the world's wealthiest individuals have a combined wealth
equal to that of the bottom 50% of the world's population (that is,
3.5 billion people). Jacob Hacker and Paul Pierson, Paul
Krugman, Kevin Phillips, Thomas Piketty, Joseph Stiglitz. See
Great Gatsby curve and Social Mobility in Concepts.

Economic self-interest: the master motor of economic activity
according to classical/free market economics. See 3. Adam
Smith/Classical/Free Market Economics and 23. Behavioral
economics in Details.

Economic take-off: in the stages-of-economic-growth model, the point
at which a partially-developed agrarian nation, through
investments in its social infrastructure (i.e., its educational,
transportation, communication, legal and financial systems) and
capital accumulation, reaches a critical mass and begins to achieve
significant and sustained growth and, eventually, economic
maturity. In the United States, it is thought that economic take-off
began during the second and third quarters of the 19th Century (that
is, between 1825 and 1875). W. W. Rostow. See 21.
Development Economics in Details.

Economic/technological determinism: see 10. Economic/
Technological determinism and 11. Counterarguments in Details.

Economic trade leads to political liberalization: Bernard Bailyn's
thesis that the breakdown of Puritan orthodoxy and hegemony in
New England in the 17th and 18th Centuries was the result of
commercial contact and trade with other cultures; an argument
that was used in later historical contexts, including foreign
policies which encouraged trade and détente with hostile,

authoritarian and fundamentalist nations. Bailyn's thesis is built on the classical free market premise that economic interests generally transcend ideology and religious orthodoxy.

Economies of scale: the premise that, up to a point, bigger is better. As more units of a good are produced, the incremental unit cost of each additional unit declines since fixed costs are distributed over a large number of units. Economies of scale permit larger companies to compete unequally with smaller ones; thus, concentration and consolidation is a natural and inevitable tendency of free market capitalism. This was recognized when John D. Rockefeller's Standard Oil Trust crushed small, independent oil producers in the late 19th Century by secretly colluding with railroads for reduced transportation rates (based on volume discounts) for its oil. See Diseconomies of scale in Concepts and 3. Adam Smith/Classical/Free Market Economics in Details.

Economy (Greek for "household management"): generally, a system for the production, distribution and consumption of goods and services.

Ejidos: communally owned and worked agricultural lands in Latin America; versus *latifundia*: large-scale, privately-held, landed estates, which are often owned by absentee landlords and produce a single cash crop, such as sugar or coffee, for export.

Elasticity of supply and demand: the degree to which sellers and buyers respond to increases or decreases in the price of a product or service. For example, the demand for heating oil is much less elastic, or sensitive to price increases (since people need to heat their homes, regardless of the price) than the demand for restaurant meals (which are discretionary and can be foregone as prices increase). See Supply and demand in Concepts.

Emerging/developing economies: those countries that, through rapid economic growth, are transitioning from less developed to developed economies. These include India, Brazil, Mexico, Indonesia and Turkey. See Economic take-off in Concepts and 21. Development Economics in Details.

Enclosure: generally, the appropriation of public lands for private benefit. Specifically, it refers to the fencing and privatization of English public, or common, lands, beginning in the 16th Century, so that private landowners could raise sheep. In England, this ended the communal tradition of using open fields for grazing livestock and mowing hay. It produced a landless working class which fed the migration to the cities and provided a source of cheap labor for industrialization. See Tragedy of the commons in Concepts.

Entitlements: social programs that provide for basic human needs, such as food, health care, public education, unemployment insurance and pensions.

Entrepreneur (French for "one who undertakes"): an individual who incurs the risks and reaps the reward for organizing the factors of production, including capital and technology, to produce a product or provide a service. According to Joseph Schumpeter, the entrepreneur is the creative engine of capitalism and the dynamic agent for change and innovation.

Entrepreneurial versus **corporate capitalism**: the former is personified by the individual innovator who launches his or her own enterprise, raises capital, assumes the risk for its loss and receives the benefits of its success; versus the corporate model of the large-scale, impersonal, hierarchical, bureaucratic business organization, which grows through increasing market share, acquiring competitors, researching and developing new products and/or purchasing smaller, more innovative businesses.

Environmental accounting: see True cost accounting in Concepts.

Environmental/Green movement: a grass-roots social movement and ethic whose purpose is to protect and restore the natural environment from overdevelopment, deforestation, pollution and global warming, and to use renewable energy to achieve sustainable resource management. It embodies and extends the Biblical ideal of stewardship, the American cult of nature (Charles Feidelson, R. W. B. Lewis, Henry Nash Smith), the New England Transcendentalist belief in the immanence of the divinity in nature, and the conservation movement of the Progressive Era. Henry David Thoreau and John Muir were early prophets and proponents of the ethic. See Eco-feminism and Stewardship of natural resources in Concepts.

Equity: (1) the net dollar value of an asset, home or business; that is, its current market value minus any outstanding debts, mortgages, or other liabilities; (2) stocks and the stock market, as opposed to bonds and the debt market and (3) fairness. See Just price in Concepts and Anterior insula in Anthropology Concepts.

Ethical investing: socially responsible investing in companies that advance the common good by promoting environmental, human rights, labor and consumer standards and practices.

Ethnic family capitalism: in the United States, small proprietorships owned by first- and second-generation immigrant families, who often work long hours to achieve financial stability, material success and the "American Dream."

Expectant capitalists: those workers and entrepreneurs who believe in social mobility and the ethic of the "self-made man" and aspire to the "American Dream" of material success. Bray Hammond. See Self-made Man in Concepts and Horatio Alger mystique in American History Concepts.

Externalities: the true, hidden costs to society generated by a business or industry's operations, which, often, are not reflected the latter's reported costs or profits. These include: (1) society's investments in infrastructure (schools, roads and bridges, hospitals, police and fire services) that enable the company to do business; (2) water and air pollution (including global warming caused by burning of fossil fuels), traffic congestion and healthcare costs to employees, clients and neighbors and (3) non-reimbursed social costs for providing public education, training and, in some cases, food stamps and welfare payments to its employees. See Free-rider problem, GDP and GPI, Living wage, Subsistence wage, Tragedy of the commons, True cost/environmental/full cost accounting and Working poor in Concepts.

Fabian socialism: a political movement founded in England in the late 19th Century that seeks to achieve democratic socialism gradually through incremental reforms rather than through class conflict or violent revolution. The movement takes its name from the Roman general, Favius Maximus, who successfully fought Hannibal in a war of attrition by using delaying tactics and avoiding direct frontal assaults and pitched battles. See Democratic socialism in Concepts.

Factors of production: (1) arable land and other natural resources, such as timber, coal, oil, natural gas, etc., (2) labor, (3) capital and (4) technology, which are organized to produce a product or provide a service.

Factory system: a system for manufacturing and assembling products at a centralized location by using wage labor and a central power source. The system became common in the early 19th Century in England, Western Europe and the United States and largely replaced the domestic or putting-out system in which products were distributed as piecework and produced in the homes and workshops of the workers and their families. See 8. Industrial Revolution in Details.

Federal Reserve System: the nation's central bank, which was established in 1913 as a result of the Panic of 1907 and the near collapse of the private banking system. It serves as the nation's central bank by regulating the banking system, managing the money supply, setting interest rates, modulating swings in the business cycle and serving as the lender-of-last-resort to financial institutions in times of financial crisis. See 7. American System/American Way in Details.

Fetishism of commodities: materialism; consumerism; "things are in the saddle and ride mankind" (Ralph Waldo Emerson). Emerson, Karl Marx, Henry David Thoreau, Alexis de Tocqueville. See Commodification and Consumer culture in Concepts, Adam Smith in Quotations and Culture of narcissism and Status symbols in Sociology Concepts.

First-mover advantage: the competitive advantage enjoyed by the first individual or organization to introduce a new product or service.

Free-rider problem: a situation in which an individual or a company enjoys the benefits of a public good without contributing to its cost or maintenance (including its fair share of taxes); for example, clean air and water, transportation systems, public schools and parks, police services, emergency medical care. These include companies that pay no taxes or transfer their profits to headquarters overseas (corporate inversions) to avoid taxes. See Enclosure, Externalities and Tragedy of the Commons in Concepts.

Game theory/prisoner's dilemma: a feature of rational, decision-making models in which, in various simulation games, participants seek to maximize the rewards and minimize the costs to themselves. In most cases, participants are predisposed to cooperate with each other unless they are cheated by the other party, in which case they revert to a strategy of tit-for-tat. Versions include zero-sum and nonzero-sum outcomes. John von Neumann. See Free-rider problem in Concepts and Anterior insula in Anthropology Concepts.

GDP (Gross Domestic Product): the total value of all the goods and services produced domestically by a nation in one year; it serves as a quantitative measure of that nation's economic well-being; versus **GPI** (Genuine Progress Indicator and other quality-of-life indices), which seeks to quantitatively measure the social and environmental wellbeing of a nation and its citizens by using such criteria as education, healthcare, job security, economic equality, gender equality, political freedom and stability, crime rates, air and water pollution and resource sustainability.

Globalization: the globally integrated production and distribution of goods and services. It is associated with (1) technological improvements in global transportation and communications, including the Internet; (2) the expansion of multinational corporations; (3) the extension of international finance and the portability of capital; (4) the reduction in trade barriers (free trade); (5) the increased mobility of labor across national borders; (6) the offshore outsourcing of jobs from developed countries to less developed ones; (7) the rising middle and technocratic classes in developing countries; (8) the Westernization and growth of global consumer markets; (9) low, often, subsistence wages and dangerous working conditions in underdeveloped countries; (10) environmental degradation and resource depletion and (11) the downward pressure exerted on wage levels in developed countries. William Greider.

Great Gatsby curve: a graph that depicts the declining social mobility and increasing income inequality in the United States compared to that of other developed countries. Miles Corak, Alan Krueger. See Economic inequality/concentration of wealth and Social mobility in Concepts.

Gresham's law: that bad money drives out good; the flight of capital from nations with weak economies or unstable legal and political systems to those with strong ones, i.e., "safe havens." See 5. David Ricardo/ Law of Comparative Advantage in Details.

Guild system: local associations of craftsmen, artisans and tradesmen, which rose during the Middle Ages. Guilds were organized by craft and designed to maintain trade secrets, restrict competition, control prices and uphold labor and quality standards. Each craft maintained an apprenticeship system, judged the "masterpieces" that elevated a journeyman to a master craftsman and served as a social and fraternal organization for its members.

High-tech(nology): cutting edge, state-of-the-art technology, which includes information technology, nanotechnology, biogenetics, quantum processing, artificial intelligence, fusion, robotics, etc.

Homo economicus: the archetypal economic decision-maker of classical economics, who is presumed to be motivated by rational self-interest (that is, by reason and selfishness). See Bounded rationality and Rational expectations in Concepts and 3. Adam Smith/Classical/Free Market Economics, 23. Behavioral Economics and 24. Neuro-Economics in Details.

Hourglass economy: one that is characterized by a declining middle class, bipolar income distribution and extremes of affluence and poverty. See Bipolar economy and Economic inequality/concentration of wealth in Concepts.

Incremental cost: the additional cost incurred in making one additional unit of a product, which declines as output increases and fixed costs are spread over more units. See Economies of scale in Concepts.

Industrial capitalism: see 8. Industrial Revolution in Details.

Industrial democracy: a fluid term for socio-economic systems in which workers participate in their company's decision-making processes to various degrees, ranging from team-building, quality circles, consultation and collective bargaining to profit-sharing and representation on the board of directors to partial or full ownership and control of the company. On a macro-level, the term also refers to a political economy in which all members have equal economic and political power to influence how their society, including the workplace, is governed.

Industrial Revolution: see 8. Industrial Revolution in Details.

Inflation: an increase in prices for goods and services, which may be caused by increased costs to producers (the "cost-push") and/or increased demand from consumers (the "demand-pull").

Information Age: see 24. Information Technology/Metaphor of the Machine in Sociology Details.

Institutional investors: insurance companies, pension funds, mutual funds and private equity and hedge funds, which invest large amounts of money in stocks, bonds, currencies, businesses, emerging markets, real estate, etc.

Institutionalized prodigality: the superabundance and superfluity of modern consumer culture, which Herbert Marcuse called "production for waste." Marcuse, David Potter, William Tilden, Thorstein Veblen. See Consumer culture, Manic capitalism, Overproduction and Planned obsolescence in Concepts and 15. Herbert Marcuse and Cultural Materialism in Psychology Details.

Intellectual property rights: the legal rights to intangible assets such as inventions, software and artistic, literary and musical works.

Interdependency: a fundamental characteristic of modern industrial societies, which is the result of the specialization and division of labor and the large-scale integration and globalization of economic activities. See Globalization in Concepts and 13. Emile Durkheim/organic solidarity in Sociology Details.

Intermediate technology: in developing countries, a middle way between traditional agrarianism and full-scale industrialization. See 22. E. F. Schumacher/Small-is-Beautiful Economics in Details.

Invisible hand: a pillar of classical economic theory, which holds that individuals, in pursuing their own selfish economic interests, thereby promote the common good. See Adam Smith in Quotations and 3. Adam Smith/Classical/Free Market Economics in Details.

Just price: the concept, common in traditional, pre-industrial societies, of a fair price, in which the seller recoups the costs of his or her labor and materials plus a moderate, but not exorbitant profit, and does not raise prices in times of hardship or scarcity. The concept was superseded by the capitalist ethos of "rational self-interest" (i.e., reason and greed), in which, for example, the price of an inexpensive, life-saving drug can be raised to exorbitant levels in order to maximize the returns to its investors. Thomas Aquinas, E. P. Thompson. See Keayne, Robert and Moral capitalism in Concepts and John Winthrop in American History Quotations.

Keayne, Robert: a prominent 17th Century Boston businessman who was fined 200 pounds in 1637 for overcharging his customers and excessive profiteering. His case illustrates the strict regulation of economic activity, including fee and price controls, imposed by authorities in colonial America. Bernard Bailyn. See Just price in Concepts.

Keynesian economics: a school of economic thought that advocates a mixed economy (i.e., partially state-planned and partially market-driven) and regulated markets. See 16. Keynesian Economics in Details.

Labor-intensive industries: those that provide a comparative economic advantage to countries with a cheaper, unorganized and unprotected labor force relative to those with higher wage levels, stronger labor protections and higher safety standards. These include textiles, clothing, shoes, electronics assembly, etc. See 5. David Ricardo/Law of Comparative Advantage in Details.

Labor theory of value: that the value of a product is proportional to the amount of labor used to produce the product. Aristotle, Thomas Aquinas, John Locke, Adam Smith, David Ricardo, Karl Marx.

Laissez-faire economics (French for "let do" or "let them do as they please"): an economic system in which there is little or no governmental regulation, taxation or oversight of business activities; a basic tenet of free market economic theory. See 3. Adam Smith/Classical/Free Market Economics in Details.

Law of diminishing returns: that increased inputs lead to increased outputs, but, after a certain point, at a declining rate of output.

LDCs: less developed countries, many of which are characterized by extreme poverty, authoritarian governments, cronyism, corruption and ethnic strife.

Leading, coincident and lagging economic indicators: quantitative indices that measure, respectively, the future, current and past phases of the business cycle. The unemployment rate, for example, is usually regarded as a lagging indicator since it does not start to go down until after an economic recovery is underway.

Legacy costs: a company's or an industry's toxic waste clean-up costs, unfunded pension obligations, potential legal judgments and other costs that could be passed on to future owners or to the public.

Living wage: the hourly wage, regionally-adjusted, that is needed to provide a worker with minimum, basic needs, such as food, shelter, clothing, utilities, transportation and health care. See Social justice, Subsistence Wage and Working poor in Concepts.

Luddites: skilled English textile workers in the early 19th Century who sabotaged and destroyed the labor-saving machinery that had put them out of work. Their uprising is emblematic of the enduring conflict between the imperatives of "rational" capitalism and the immediate human needs of workers, who must work to house and feed themselves and their families. In modern "mixed" economies, unemployment insurance provides some relief from downturns in the business cycle and from structural realignments caused by technological innovations and other factors. See

Creative destruction in Concepts and 15. Joseph Schumpeter/
Creative Destruction in Details.

Lumpen proletariat (a term derived from the German word for "rag"):
the underclass, i.e., those outside the formal, legal economy. It
includes the homeless, the chronically unemployed, beggars,
prostitutes, petty criminals, addicts, drug dealers, gamblers and
bootleggers.

Macroeconomics versus **microeconomics**: see 18. Macroeconomics
and 19. Microeconomics in Details.

Managerial revolution: the separation of the professional
management of a modern corporation from its owners and
stockholders, which began in the late 19th and early 20th Centuries.
The term also refers to a society in which the ruling elite of
corporate executives and managers achieves social dominance,
political power and privilege by controlling the means of
production. Joel Bakan, Adolph Berle and Gardiner Means, James
Burnham and Martin Sklar.

Manic capitalism: the inherent tendency of capitalism, because of its
obsessive efficiencies and relatively low wages, to overproduce at
a given level of demand (which is constrained by the purchasing
power of the workers and their ability to buy the products of their
labor). This leads to a ceaseless search for new, often foreign,
markets to sell the surplus products; faster product cycles and ever
increasing rates of return. "The need of a constantly expanding
market for its products chases the bourgeoisie over the entire
surface of the globe" (Karl Marx). The term also refers to the
manic upswings and depressive downswings of the business cycle,
with its tendency toward speculation, irrational crowd behavior,
booms, bubbles and busts. William Greider. See Bipolar
economy, Business cycle, Creative destruction, Overproduction
and Panics, depressions and recessions in Concepts.

Margin: the gross profit per unit of a given product.

Marginal propensity to consume or save: the behavioral tendency by
consumers to either buy more or to save more as a result of an
increase in income. The marginal propensity to consume is higher
for those with lower incomes and the marginal propensity to save
is higher for those with higher incomes. Thus, public policies
designed to stimulate aggregate demand and consumption, such as
an increase in the minimum wage or a decrease in the sales tax, are
more effective since they are directed at those with highest

propensities to consume, i.e., those with the lowest income. Conversely, tax breaks for the wealthy, such as lower taxes for capital gains, lead to more savings (since the wealthy have a higher propensity to save) and, thus, greater investment in the economy and the stock market. See Marginal utility, Overproduction and Working poor in Concepts and 16. Keynesian Economics and 17. Supply-side Economics in Details.

Marginal utility: the incremental increase in usefulness, happiness or satisfaction from a discrete increase in income. For example, five dollars given to a homeless person provides more satisfaction or utility to that individual than the same five dollars given to a wealthy person dining in a fine restaurant.

Market economy versus **planned economy**: see Central economic planning, State capitalism and State monopoly capitalism in Concepts and 3. Adam Smith/Classical/Free Market Economics and 16. Keynesian Economics in Details.

Mass production: the production of large quantities of standardized goods at relatively cheaper unit prices based on the total rationalization of the production process, i.e., the specialization and division of labor, the standardization and interchangeability of parts, the moving assembly line, economies of scale and the application of scientific management principles and techniques. Industrialization and mass production, beginning in the early 19th Century, made consumer goods more affordable to a larger number of people, created a mass consumer market and led to a rising standard of living and an expanding middle class. See 8. Industrial Revolution in Details.

Material culture: the economic and reproductive relationships in the substructure, which, according to the tenets of cultural materialism, drive changes in the superstructure (art, ideology and religion; social, cultural, political and legal institutions). See 10. Economic/Technological Determinism in Details and 9. Cultural materialism in Sociology Details.

McJobs: unskilled, low paying, dead-end service jobs of the, so called, service proletariat; one of the consequences of the shift from an industrial-based to a service-based economy and the loss of well-paid union jobs.

Medium of exchange: a measure of value, as well as a means for exchanging unlike products and services. Media include wampum, gold, fiat money, food stamps, cigarette, virtual currency, etc.

Mercantilism: see 2. Mercantilism in Details.

Military-industrial-university-media complex: the central thesis of a school of thought that political and economic power in the United States is exercised in concert by an interlocking power elite of political, corporate, military, academic and media leaders, who share a common world view and move easily between institutions. The complex originated in the massive public military expenditures and research and development projects during World War II and the Cold War of the 1950s and 1960s. President Dwight Eisenhower first identified the complex and named its first two components. Jane Mayer, C. Wright Mills. See Permanent warfare economy and Power elite in Concepts.

Mixed economy: an economic system that contains elements of both socialism and capitalism, that is, government regulation and private ownership. See 16. Keynesian Economics in Details.

Modes of production: (1) the factors of production (land and other natural resources, labor, capital, technology) and (2) the (social) relations of production. Modes include slavery, feudalism, capitalism, socialism and communism. See 9. Karl Marx/Dialectical Materialism in Details.

Modes of subsistence: hunting-gathering/foraging, pastoralism, agriculture and commerce. Adam Smith.

Monetarism: a school of economic thought that maintains that changes in the money supply drive inflation and aggregate demand.

Monopolies/oligopolies: markets that are dominated by a single or a small number of large producers of a commodity or service, who control the market for that commodity or service and can restrict competition and charge higher prices. Oligopolies are common in oil and other natural resource industries, telecommunications, mass media, banking, air travel, beer and food-processing. Monopolies and oligopolies contradict the basic tenets of classical economics of free markets and open competition. See 3. Adam Smith/Classical/Free Market Economics and 4. Public Regulation Quandary in Details.

Moral capitalism: an idealized socio-economic system that (1) is based on fairness, ethical behavior and social justice; (2) contains mixed elements of both socialism and capitalism, i.e., government regulation and private ownership; (3) provides a fair return to the laborer for the product of his or her labor and (4) seeks to strike a balance between private selfishness and social responsibility, between economic individualism and humanitarian ideals.

Lizabeth Cohn. See Industrial democracy, Living wage, Mixed economy, Public rights, Social Justice and Stewardship of natural resources in Concepts and John Winthrop in American History Quotations.

Moving assembly line: a major component of the mass production process, which was first used in slaughterhouses in the mid-19th Century and adopted by Henry Ford for the production of automobiles in 1913. It is associated with the standardization and interchangeability of parts, the specialization and division of labor and scientific management. See Mass Production and Scientific management in Concepts.

Multinational corporations: private, for-profit institutions through which globalization is often channeled. They exhibit varying degrees of concern for the well-being of their workers and the societies in which they operate. See Globalization and Neo-colonialism in Concepts.

Multiplier effect: a basic tenet of Keynesian economic theory that the economic stimulus provided by increased governmental spending and public investment not only directly creates new jobs, but also, because of a multiplier factor, creates a ripple effect of secondary spending, which leads to increased consumption, increased production, increased employment and, eventually, to increased tax revenues. For example, a federal grant given to a city to upgrade it streets provides payments directly to the construction worker who works on the project, but also indirectly to that worker's grocer, landlord, dentist and holder of his or her automobile loan. John Maynard Keynes, Paul Samuelson. See 16. Keynesian Economics in Details.

Nation of shopkeepers: a term that originated with Adam Smith and was later appropriated by Napoleon to suggest that England's strength was based on its trade and commerce, rather than its military power.

Neoclassical synthesis: the unification of classical/free market and Keynesian economic theories; the dominant paradigm in economics today. See 20. Neoclassical Synthesis in Details.

Neo-colonialism: a term applied to multinational corporations that use underdeveloped countries as sources of cheap labor and natural resources and as markets to dump surplus goods.

Neoliberalism: a school of economic thought that advocates free trade, globalization, private enterprise, deregulated markets, privatization and property rights. See 17. Supply-side Economics in Details.

Neuro-economics: see 24. Neuro-economics in Details.

Non-renewable resources: clean air and water, arable land and fossil fuels such as oil, coal and natural gas, etc.

Offshore outsourcing: the transfer of blue- and white-collar jobs from developed countries to developing countries with lower wage rates and cheaper production costs. See Globalization in Concepts and 5. David Ricardo/Law of Comparative Advantage in Details.

Opportunity costs: the benefits foregone by choosing one investment option over others; for example, the income lost by buying a vacation home instead of investing in a retirement savings plan.

Organized labor: workers who are organized and represented by unions, which bargain collectively with employers on their behalf to obtain better working conditions and higher pay and better benefits. Currently, less than 12% of the American workforce is organized and represented collectively. Traditionally, a union job was a means of advancement into the middle class, with a living wage, health care insurance and a pension. See Globalization and Offshore outsourcing in Concepts and Labor movement in American History Concepts.

Overpopulation: one of the factors in world hunger and the loss of nonrenewable natural resources. Thomas Malthus; Harrison Brown. See World hunger/nutritional bipolarity and Zero-population growth in Concepts and 16. Robert Malthus/The Struggle for Existence in Details.

Overproduction: the fact that, as a result of technological innovations and the ever increasing efficiencies of industrial capitalism, the global production of goods tends to exceed the demand for them at a given level of income distribution and purchasing power, except in wartime. As a result, the global supply of workers far exceeds the demand for their labor. For example, it now takes approximately 30 person-hours to make one automobile, whereas it took approximately 300 hours in 1909. This has resulted in a permanently underemployed global workforce and the downward pressure on wages in advanced economies to fall to the levels of those in developing countries. The relative lack of income, or purchasing power, of workers to buy the products of their own labor leads, in turn, to additional overcapacity and overproduction.

Overproduction is one of the basic conundrums of capitalism. A more equitable distribution of income would allow more people to purchase those goods, but greater consumption creates greater strains on environmental resources. A possible solution would be to scale back global consumption at the upper extreme and find a middle way or balance to insure that all the world's citizens have a comfortable, productive, sustainable existence. William Greider, Herbert Marcuse, E. F. Schumacker. See Globalization, Institutional prodigality, Manic capitalism, Planned obsolescence, Purchasing power and Working poor in Concepts and 16. Keynesian Economics and 22. E. F. Schumacker/Small-is-Beautiful Economics in Details.

Panics, depressions and recessions: a major component of the business cycle. In the United States, they occurred in 1792, 1808, 1819, 1837-43, 1857, 1873-79, 1882-85, 1893-98, 1907, 1929-40 (Great Depression), 1948-49, 1953-54 (Post Korean War), 1957-58, 1960-61, 1973-75 (OPEC oil embargo), 1988-92 (savings and loan crisis), 2001-03 (dotcom bust) and 2008-2013 (the Great Recession, which was caused by the subprime housing bubble and the Wall Street financial crisis). See Business cycle and Creative destruction in Concepts.

Pareto Principle: the 80/20 rule; that, for example, 80% of a company's sales are made to 20% of its customers. Vilfredo Pareto.

Payback period: the length of time it takes for the income from an investment to pay back its original cost at an assumed rate of return. See Break-even point in Concepts.

Perceived value: the observation that the price of a product is often based on the customer's perceived value or appreciation of it, without reference to its original production cost. Perceived value is reflected, for example, in the price of luxury cars, jewelry, facial creams, premium wines, vintage comic books and rare postage stamps.

Perfect competition: a market in which there are a large number of sellers and buyers with perfect information and no barriers for producers to enter or exit the market. The condition is usually unstable and can result in the waste of competition in which an excessive number of suppliers produce an excessive number and variety of goods and services until the efficiencies of scale, bankruptcies and exits occur, and the large number of small producers is consolidated into a small number of large producers. See Competition versus monopoly/oligopoly and Economies of scale in Concepts and 3. Adam Smith/Classical/Free Market Economics in Details.

Permanent warfare economy/military Keynesianism: the theory that (1) the economic recovery from the Great Depression in the United States was caused by the massive military expenditures of World War II, beginning with the Lend Lease program in 1941, and (2) the economic prosperity and technological innovations in the decades following World War II, including the Cold War *mentalité* supporting foreign military interventions, were driven by massive public expenditures on defense industries, the space race, regional wars and the military-industrial-university-media complex. Norman Chomsky, Michael Kidron, C. Wright Mills, Rebecca Thorpe. See Military-industrial-university-media complex in Concepts and the Rise and fall of great powers: the 16th Century Spanish paradigm in Historiography Concepts.

Physiocrats: 18th-Century French economic theorists who held that land and agriculture were the sole sources of a nation's wealth, in contrast to mercantilism and merchant capitalism. See Yeoman/agrarian ideal in American History Concepts and Thomas Jefferson in American History Quotations.

Planned versus **free market economies**: see Central economic planning in Concepts and 3. Adam Smith/Classical/Free Market Economics and 16. Keynesian Economics in Details.

Planned obsolescence: the practice of deliberately designing products to limit their useful lives in order to increase sales of their replacements. Herbert Marcuse called it "production for waste." Marcuse, Vance Packard. See Institutionalized prodigality, Manic capitalism and Overproduction in Concepts.

Plutocracy: a form of government in which power is held by the wealthy, both (1) directly through their influence in the government (by campaign contributions to candidates and causes [primarily through super PACs], lobbying, providing jobs to former government officials, and serving as members of Congress, ambassadors and other government officials) and (2) indirectly through their influence in the media and opinion-, policy- and decision-making institutions, such as think tanks, journals, academic programs, fellowships and advocacy and "grass-roots" organizations, the funding for which is channeled through private, tax-exempt political foundations. According to John Jay, the first

Chief Justice of the Supreme Court, "the people who own the country ought to govern it." Currently, nearly half the members of congress are millionaires. With the Supreme Court decision in *Citizens United* in 2010 and the advent of super PACs (political action committees), the top 100 super PAC donors accounted for more than 60% of the $349 million raised in the 2012 election. The condition reflects the contradiction in American values between the ideal of social and political equality and the reality of economic and political inequality. David Brock, Jane Mayer, Kevin Phillips. See Economic inequality/concentration of wealth in Concepts and Donor class, Patronage system and Super PACs in Political Science Concepts and Louis Brandeis in Political Science Quotations.

Political economy: the original name given to the study of economics, which acknowledges the intimate, reciprocal relationship between economic and political power.

Post-industrial economies: those that are characterized by a decline in manufacturing industries and a rise in service- and knowledge-based industries, as well by as by the loss of well-paying union jobs, increased offshore outsourcing of work and decreased opportunities for workers to advance into the middle class. Daniel Bell, Paul Romer.

Power elite: the interlocking relationship between political, corporate, military, university and media elites. Jane Mayer, C. Wright Mills. See Military-industrial-university-media complex in Concepts and 15. Elites/Oligarchies in Sociology Details.

Pre-industrial societies: those whose economies were based on hunting and gathering, pastoralism, fishing, subsistence agriculture, resource development, household production and local and regional commerce. See 11. Ferdinand Tönnies/*Gemeinschaft* in Sociology Details.

Private equity funds: pools of private capital, the income from which is taxed at the lower rate for capital gains. Managers of these funds invest in a range of assets and instruments, and often buy distressed assets, strip them of value or restructure them, and then issue non-investment-grade debt (i.e., "junk bonds") to pay themselves and their investors back for their investments plus management fees and a profit. Private investment funds have been praised for their ability to efficiently reallocate resources and modernize marginal businesses and have been criticized for the tax advantages given to their wealthy investors, for destroying productive businesses and for encouraging highly leveraged and speculative investments.

Product differentiation: one of the objectives of advertising, which is to differentiate in the consumer's mind products that, otherwise, are virtually identical (for example, gasoline or laundry detergent) in order to avoid competition based on the lowest prices. See Perceived value in Concepts.

Profit motive: see 3. Adam Smith/Classical/Free Market Economics and 23. Behavioral Economics in Details.

Profit-sharing: the distribution of a portion of a company's profits to its employees. See Labor theory of value and Industrial democracy in Concepts.

Proletariat: originally, a Roman social class that consisted of those who owned no property; it now refers to wage laborers and the industrial working class; versus bourgeoisie, petite bourgeoisie, *salariat* and *lumpen proletariat*. See Working poor and Service proletariat in Concepts and 9. Karl Marx/Dialectical Materialism in Details.

Protectionism: the policy of protecting a nation's domestic industries from foreign competition by imposing high tariffs, quotas and other trade barriers on imported goods. It has been used as a rationale for protecting infant or inefficient industries, including agriculture, or for maintaining higher labor, wage and environmental standards or for punishing nations that do not engage in reciprocal free trade. It is contrary to the tenets of free trade and the law of comparative advantage. See 3. Adam Smith/Classical/Free Market Economics, 5. David Ricardo/Law of Comparative Advantage and 7. American System in Details.

Protestant ethic and the rise of capitalism: Max Weber's thesis that the former laid the foundation for the latter. The ethic is associated with (1) religious and economic individualism, (2) the work ethic, (3) self-reliance, (4) temperance, (5) thrift, (6) the disassociation of interest from usury, (7) capital accumulation and (8) entrepreneurial innovation. Although Weber was the first to link capitalism to Protestantism, he failed to identify the underlying psychological mechanism that links the acquisitive mentality to the rationalization process of industrialization. Max Weber; William Tilden. See Benjamin Franklin's Table of Virtues in American History Concepts, 8. Industrial Revolution and 14. Max Weber/Protestant Ethic in Economics Details and 6. Freud's Anal Personality Traits in Psychology Details.

Public goods: those goods and services that can be enjoyed by all, without exclusion, such as public schools, libraries, police and fire protection, emergency medical care, streets and sidewalks, parks and beaches, clean air and drinking water, broadcast radio and television, etc.

Public regulation quandary: see 4. Public Regulation Quandary in Details.

Public relations: the professional management of the flow of information between an individual or an organization and the public. PR firms seek to project a positive image of their clients and mitigate the effects of negative information. The service was first provided by Ivy Lee to John D. Rockefeller and was later developed in the 1920s by Edward Bernays, a nephew of Sigmund Freud. Political lobbyists for special interest groups attempt to do the same for the flow of information between their patrons, government officials and the public.

Public rights: those that are asserted in opposition to private property rights, as when, for example, in 1739, Ben Franklin and his neighbors petitioned the Pennsylvania Assembly to prohibit a Philadelphia tannery from dumping its wastes in public spaces.

Purchasing power: an individual's or a family's financial ability to buy goods and services. Low wages and income inequality constrain workers from buying products and services, which reduces the demand for them and leads to overproduction at a given level of income distribution. Conversely, greater income equality leads to greater purchasing power, greater consumption and greater prosperity. See Marginal propensity to consume or save, Overproduction and Working poor in Concepts and 16. Keynesian Economics in Details.

Quality of life indices: see GDP and GPI in Concepts.

Queuing theory: a methodology that estimates the relative costs of waiting in line for services, both to the service provider (such as a bank) and the customer. It factors in such variables as predictable versus random customer arrival rates, service rates and costs (i.e., the number of tellers on duty), speed of service, waiting costs and balking rate (i.e., when the customer becomes impatient and leaves without completing the transaction). The methodology applies to telephone queuing and online service centers, as well as to face-to-face queues.

Rational expectations: the assumption that consumers and other economic decision-makers use relevant information to adjust their decision-making, based on current events and their informed expectations of future economic conditions. Such received information (from consumer confidence indices, rising or falling interest rates, etc.) is often reflexive and can become self-fulfilling, serving to reinforce positive or negative feedback loops and leading to collective/crowd behavior (as well as, inevitably, contrarian behavior). See Bounded rationality and *Homo economicus* in Concepts and 3. Adam Smith/Classical/Free Market Economics and 23. Behavioral Economics in Details.

Reaganomics: a form of laissez-faire, supply-side economics. It is associated with deregulation, privatization and the outsourcing of public services. See Neoliberalism in Concepts and 17. Supply-side Economics in Details.

Realty: real property, i.e., land and its permanent, immovable improvements, such as buildings, machinery, dams, wells, and roads.

Redistribution of wealth: the transfer of income and wealth from one or more socio-economic groups to others, generally through taxation (including the graduated income tax and the estate and inheritance taxes), the purpose of which is to reduce income inequality and the extremes of wealth and to promote economic prosperity by increasing the purchasing power of lower income groups. The term is also used to describe the redistribution of wealth upward by tax laws that favor the rich, such as high sales taxes (which fall disproportionately on the poor) and low corporate and capital gains taxes (which disproportionately favor the rich). See Economic inequality/concentration of wealth, Marginal propensity to consume or save, Purchasing Power and Taxation in Concepts and 17. Supply-side Economics in Details.

Regressive taxation: those taxes, such as the sales tax, that fall disproportionately on lower income groups and reduce their purchasing power; versus **progressive taxation**, such as the graduated income tax, which reduces inequality and promotes economic prosperity by increasing the purchasing power of lower income groups (who have a higher propensity to consume). See Marginal propensity to consume or save, Redistribution of wealth and Taxation in Concepts.

Reification: in Marxist theory, the objectification of labor; to value the product of objectified labor over the living laborer ("the rule of the worker's product over the worker himself"); the transformation or inversion of subjects into objects and humans beings into things. See Commodification in Concepts.

Relative income hypothesis: that individuals are more concerned about their income, status and consumption relative to that of their peers than to any absolute dollar amount or standard.

***Rentier* class**: those who live off the income from investments and trust funds, including rents, stock dividends, bank and bond interest, etc.

Return on investment: the annual income generated from an investment, usually in the form of interest, dividends, rent or profit, which is expressed as a percentage of the net cost of the investment.

Risk assessment/risk management: the use of quantitative methodologies to minimize risks and maximize returns from a project or an investment. Various models factor in risks, potential losses, assumptions, probabilities and uncertainties. Risk scenarios range from projects with low potential losses but higher probabilities of occurrence to those with large potential losses but lower probabilities of occurrence. See Cost-benefit analyses in Concepts.

The Road to Serfdom: Friedrich von Hayek's influential book, published in 1944, which warned that central economic planning inevitably leads to totalitarianism and servitude. It serves as one of the pillars of libertarianism, but has been challenged by empirical studies that show that Western social-welfare states provide high levels of political freedom, social equality and quality-of-life services.

Robber baron thesis: that capitalists are river-boat gamblers, speculators, pirates and predators, rather than heroes, producers, the "fittest" or the elect; Matthew Josephson, Thorstein Veblen, Richard White; versus the **entrepreneurial thesis**: that the entrepreneur is the creative engine of capitalism and the dynamic agent of economic change and technological innovation; Joseph Schumpeter. See 15. Joseph Schumpeter/Creative Destruction in Details and 25. Social Darwinism in American History Details.

Rust Belt: geographical areas in the Northeastern and Midwestern United States whose manufacturing industries were closed or transferred to other regions or countries and whose urban centers are in economic decline. See Overproduction and Post-industrial economies in Concepts.

S*alariat*: a subset of the working class who receive salaries rather than wages for their labor, such as teachers and secretaries.

Saturated market: one in which the supply of a good or service far exceeds the demand for it. See Overproduction and Purchasing power in Concepts.

Say's law: that supply creates its own demand, e.g., more lawyers creates a demand for more legal services; a tenet of supply-side economics. Jean-Baptiste Say. See Overproduction in Concepts and 17. Supply-side Economics in Details.

Scarcity psychology: a behavioral pattern that is associated with hoarding in times of abundance as well as in times of scarcity; a paradox noted by Thomas Malthus, Sigmund Freud, Erik Erikson, David Potter and William Tilden. Retentiveness may be related to capital accumulation and the ethic of frugality. The syndrome has been interpreted by some Freudian psychologists as overcompensation for rigid or premature toilet training in childhood and the dispossession of the products of the child's labor. See Retentiveness/hoarding in Psychology Concepts and 6. Freud's Anal Personality Traits in Psychology Details.

Scientific management: the cult of efficiency, which originated in Benjamin Franklin's time-and-motion studies on street cleaning and stockade building in the 18th Century and F. W. Taylor's industrial studies in the early 20th Century. Its objectives were, and are, to increase productivity, reduce costs and maximize efficiency by rationalizing the production process and standardizing the most minute sub-divisions of the workflow. Using his stopwatch, Taylor sought to eliminate waste and improve productivity by systematically breaking down each industrial task into its individual components. He taught a Dutchman named Schmidt, for example, how to shovel 47 tons of pig iron a day instead of 12 ½ tons by carefully specifying the exact size of the shovel, the weight of the scoop, the arc of the swing, etc. (Schmidt's thoughts on the subject, apparently, were never recorded). Franklin's and Taylor's principles are now enshrined in nearly every industry, and their influence can be seen today at any fast food restaurant, discount store or warehouse distribution center. Daniel Bell, Samuel Haber, William Tilden. See Protestant ethic and Specialization and division of labor in Concepts, 6. Freud's Anal Personality Traits in Psychology Details and 24. Information Technology/Metaphor of the Machine in Sociology Details.

Self-made man: the cultural archetype of the person of humble origins who, through self-improvement, hard work and good moral character, becomes wealthy and successful. It is represented in Benjamin Franklin's *Autobiography*, Frederick Douglass' "Self-Made Men," the dime novels of Horatio Alger, Jr., and Andrew Carnegie's *Gospel of Wealth*. See Social mobility in Concepts and Horatio Alger mystique in American History Concepts.

Service proletariat: service workers in the restaurant, fast food, coffee, personal care, hospitality and other industries who work for low wages and, in some cases, tips. See Working poor in Concepts.

Sharing economy: one that consists of online, peer-to-peer exchanges of products and services, such as those in transportation, lodging, personal goods and household tasks, that are made outside traditional, brick-and-mortar businesses. The phenomenon has been praised for empowering individual entrepreneurs and providing frictionless, face-to-face exchanges and bidirectional feedback, but it has also been criticized for avoiding taxes, health and safety regulations and worker wage and workplace protections.

Small-is-beautiful economics: a school of economic thought that proposes an "intermediate technology" for underdeveloped countries between traditional agrarianism and large-scale industrialization. See 22. E. F. Schumacher in Details.

Social Darwinism: a social-economic theory and world view popular in the late 19th and early 20th Centuries that held that the richest are the fittest. It was used to justify political domination by the wealthy, laissez-faire capitalism and imperialism. Richard Hofstadter. See 25. Social Darwinism in American History Details.

Social justice: a movement that seeks to insure the rights, dignity and equality of all humans. It is grounded in religious and humanitarian values and traditions, including those of St. Thomas Aquinas, John Locke, Thomas Jefferson, liberation theology and the Social Gospel. It seeks the "equitable distribution of resources to ensure that all have full opportunities for personal and social development" (Green Party platform). Its specific objectives are to end poverty and extreme inequality, to insure human rights and equal opportunity for all and to provide public education, health care, a living wage, unemployment insurance, pensions and child-care assistance. John Rawls.

Social mobility: the upward and downward movement of individuals, families and groups from one socioeconomic stratum to another. Currently, in the United States, (1) approximately 60% of those in the upper fifth of income were born into families in the upper two fifths of income; (2) only 8% of those born in the lower fifth of income rose to the top fifth in income. Markus Jantti, Alan Krueger, Thomas Piketty, Gary Solon and David Zimmerman, Joseph Stiglitz. See *Disembourgeoisment*, Downward mobility, Economic inequality/concentration of wealth and Great Gatsby curve in Concepts.

Social overhead capital/social infrastructure: public investment in schools, universities, libraries, hospitals, legal and judicial systems, roads, bridges, canals, railroads, airports, water and sewage systems, electrical networks, telecommunications, etc. It is the foundation for the modern industrial state and a precondition for economic development, according to W. W. Rostow.

Socialism: the collective ownership of the means of production, which are regulated by the state. Socialism exists under democratic as well as authoritarian governments. See Central economic planning, Democratic socialism and *The Road of Serfdom* in Concepts.

Specialization and division of labor: the subdivision of the production process into a series of simple, repetitive tasks in which each worker contributes a small part to the final product. It is the hallmark of mass production and represents the decline of the skilled craftsman (who, heretofore, had been responsible for producing unique, handcrafted products from start to finish) and the alienation of the laborer from the product of his or her labor. It increased productivity at the expense of the mental and spiritual health of the worker, according to Henry David Thoreau and Ralph Waldo Emerson, and resulted in the "mental mutilation" of the worker, according to Adam Smith. See Standardization and interchangeability of parts in Concepts.

Stages of economic growth: see Economic take-off in Concepts and 21. Development Economics in Details. W. W. Rostow.

Standard of living: an index of material wellbeing, which is measured in both quantitative and qualitative terms. See GDP and GPI in Concepts.

Standardization and interchangeability of parts: a key feature of the mass production process, which was first used by Eli Whitney in the production of 10,000 muskets under a 1798 contract with the

United States government. The process replaced unique, handcrafted products which were produced from start to finish by skilled craftsmen with ones assembled from standardized, interchangeable parts produced in batches by semi- and unskilled laborers. See Specialization and division of labor in Concepts and 8. Industrial Revolution in Details.

State capitalism: a fluid term covering a wide range of political and economic systems, including: (1) those in which the government controls the economy and serves as a single, huge corporation, (2) those in which the state directs the economy and owns a large number of companies but also allows a range of private, for-profit enterprises and a degree of free market dynamics; (3) managed economies in which the state, large companies and unions act together to insure economic growth (see State monopoly capitalism) and (4) the Keynesian model of mixed, managed economies. See Central economic planning in Concepts.

State monopoly capitalism: "state socialism turned on its head"; a partnership between the national government and large corporations in which the government intervenes to protect the interests of big businesses, sometimes against the interests of workers, consumers and environmentalists. In Japan and South Korea, for example, networks of large, private corporations (*keiretsu* and *chaebol*) work in partnership with governmental ministries to coordinate national economic planning. Murray Rothbard.

Stewardship of natural resources: the Biblical and ethical injunction that humans are responsible for insuring that the earth and its natural resources are used and protected in a wise and sustainable manner; a cardinal principle of the conservation and environmental movements. See Environmental/Green movement, Eco-feminism, Overproduction and Tragedy of the commons in Concepts.

Subsistence wages: the minimum income needed for a worker to feed, clothe and shelter him or herself. According to Thomas Malthus, Karl Marx, David Ricardo and other economists, in the absence of other constraints, the wages of workers tend to fall to the level of bare subsistence. See Living wage, Surplus value and Working poor in Concepts and Northern industrial wage slavery in American History Concepts.

Supply and demand: a fundamental law of classical/free market economics. It describes the quantities of a product producers are willing to sell and consumers are willing to buy over a range of potential prices. A reduction in the price of a product leads to an increase in demand for it, while an increase in its price leads suppliers to produce more of it. A price equilibrium is reached when the supply equals the demand. Adam Smith. See Elasticity of supply and demand in Concepts and 3. Adam Smith/Classical/Free Market Economics in Details.

Supply-side economics: see 17. Supply-side Economics in Details.

Surplus value: the difference between the wages paid to workers and the price received for the product of their labor, from which is derived the doctrine that profits are stolen wages; versus the doctrine that profit is the premium paid to the entrepreneur/capitalist for organizing the enterprise, contributing capital and risking its loss. See Labor theory of value, Subsistence Wage and Working poor in Concepts.

Sweatshop: a term derived from the "sweater," or subcontractor, who in the 19th Century parceled out piece-work in the garment industry. Workshops were crowded and dangerous, with long hours and low pay. Currently, an alliance of students and labor unions are working to reduce the number of global sweatshops in underdeveloped countries by using public pressure on the international companies whose products are produced there to implement labor, health and safety standards.

Technocracy: (1) a form of government in which public policy and decision-making is guided by professional experts, governmental administrators, scientists, engineers and specialists and by the application of scientific methods to social issues; (2) a meritocracy and/or (3) an economy that is driven by technological innovation. Jacques Ellul, Walter Lippmann, Lester Ward, Max Weber.

Technological determinism: a school of thought that asserts that economic and technological changes in the material environment, or substructure, drive changes in the social, political, cultural, religious, ideological and legal superstructure. It is often identified with Marxism, but, although the two overlap, it has an independent history and is not necessarily driven by class dialectics. For examples and counterarguments see 10. Economic/Technological Determinism and 11. Counterarguments in Details.

Technology: the use of organized knowledge, tools, machinery, techniques and methods for practical purposes.

Too big to fail: an economic condition in which one or more large financial or insurance institutions, in a period of sharp economic decline, fails to pay its obligations to other financial institutions, which leads to a chain reaction and the catastrophic meltdown of the global financial system. With the repeal of the Glass-Steagall Act in 1999, the legal separation between commercial and investment banking was removed, which allowed banks to speculate more freely, using publically-insured savings deposits, which contributed to the sub-prime mortgage crisis and the Great Recession of 2008. The Dodd-Frank Act of 2010 seeks to reduce the risk of repeating this scenario by promoting the financial stability, establishing greater accountability and transparency and limiting speculation and "abusive" financial practices by financial institutions.

Tragedy of the commons: the thesis that individuals and companies, acting under the principle of rational, economic self-interest, monopolize, deplete and despoil shared resources, which leads to conflict, war, pollution, global warming, overfishing, deforestation, urban sprawl, traffic congestion, etc. See Enclosure, Externalities, and True-cost accounting in Concepts and 3. Adam Smith/Classical/Free Market Economics in Details.

Transfer payments: public expenditures for welfare and social security payments, business and agricultural subsidies and federal payments to state and local governments.

Trickle-down economics: a pejorative term applied to a major tenet of supply-side economics that favorable tax benefits and governmental aid to corporations, investors and the wealthy (who have a higher propensity to save) will stimulate private investment, which, in turn, will create jobs and benefit everyone in society; versus demand or consumption-side economics. See 17. Supply-side Economics in Details.

True cost/environmental/full cost accounting: accounting methods that measure the full and true social, economic and environmental costs of business entities and economic systems, including employee social costs (for public training), infrastructure, police and fire protection, waste disposal, traffic congestion, air and water pollution, global warming, deforestation and other externalities. See Externalities and GDP and GPI in Concepts.

Trust busting: intervention by the national government to restore market competition by dismantling monopolies, oligopolies and other large-scale combinations that restrain trade and distort market competition. An alternative approach is to accept the inevitability of large-scale combinations such as monopolies and oligopolies but to closely regulate them in the public interest. See 3. Adam Smith/Classical/Free Market Economics and 4. Public Regulation Quandary in Details.

Underclass: see *Lumpen proletariat* in Concepts.

Underemployment rate: that portion of the labor force that consists of discouraged job seekers who have given up looking for work, as well as involuntarily part-time workers and workers who are overqualified for the jobs they hold. See Unemployment in Concepts.

Underground economy: see Eric Schlosser in Selected References.

Unemployment: that portion of the labor force that is not currently employed but is actively looking for work. Unemployment is classified as cyclical (i.e., caused by a downturn in the business cycle), frictional (when a worker is temporarily between jobs), seasonal (when the work lasts only part of the year) and structural (in which technological changes have permanently eliminated some types of jobs and require new sets of job skills). See Underemployment rate in Concepts.

Usury: charging excessive interest or, in some cases, any interest at all, for loaning money. The practice was condemned, in varying degrees, by various religions.

Utility: usefulness or satisfaction. See Marginal utility in Concepts.

Utopian socialists: the term applied to those who, in the 19th Century, lived in small, socialist communities, held property in common and produced collectively on a small scale. It was also used pejoratively by Marx and Engels against those who believed that socialism could be achieved without class struggle or revolution. Edward Bellamy, Charles Fourier, Karl Marx, Thomas More, Robert Owen, Saint-Simon; Alice Felt Tyler. See Utopian communities in American History Concepts.

Vertical integration: the ownership by a company of its entire production and distribution chain, from the extraction of raw materials to the design, production, marketing, distribution and retail sales of its products and services. For example, (1) an oil company that owns its exploration and drilling operations, oil fields, refineries, transportation networks and retail gas stations; (2) an entertainment company that owns its television and movie production studios, television and cable channels, movie theaters, theme parks and commercial tie-in products or (3) a computer company that designs and manufactures its hardware, develops its own operating software, maintains its own network of retail stores and manages the rental and sale of its hardware, applications and content.

Viral advertising: advertising or promoting a service or product by online, "word of mouth" social networking.

Weightlessness: a condition in which physical, centralized, "brick and mortar" businesses are displaced by their virtual, decentralized, knowledge- and service-based cousins through the use of e-commerce, cloud computing, peer-to-peer networks, digital media, online "aggregation" of the news, community bulletin boards, social media, just-in-time inventories, regional distribution centers, overnight deliveries, video-conferencing, telecommuting, etc. See E-commerce and Sharing economy in Concepts and 24. Information Technology/Metaphor of the Machine in Sociology Details.

Welfare state: a government that insures the social and economic well-being of all of its citizens by providing public education, health care, a living wage, unemployment insurance, pensions, childcare, etc.; the middle way between capitalism and communism.

Westernization: the cultural adoption and absorption by traditional, pre-industrial cultures of secular, democratic, commercial, consumer values and behaviors.

Winner-take-all societies: those in which disproportionately high rewards are distributed to the very elite in the corporate, financial, legal, entertainment and sports industries; a skewed, hypercompetitive meritocracy in which the very, very few receive very, very much and the very many receive relatively little or nothing at all. Robert Frank, Jacob Hacker and Paul Pierson, Paul Krugman, Kevin Phillips, Thomas Piketty, Joseph Stiglitz. See Compensation ratios and Economic inequality/concentration of wealth in Concepts.

Working poor: those who are employed but whose incomes fall below the federal poverty line. Currently, approximately 8% to 12% of workers in the United States are defined as working poor. Jane Adams, John Kenneth Galbraith, Michael Harrington, David Shipler. See Living wage, Subsistence wage and Surplus value in Concepts.

World hunger/nutritional bipolarity: the gulf between the affluent world, with its *haute cuisine*, diet manias, obesity epidemic and junk food culture, and the impoverished world in which 800 million people are chronically undernourished and 2.5 million children die every year from the effects of malnutrition. The causes of world hunger are thought to be overpopulation, poverty, unequal access to resources, the export of cash crops and the overconsumption of resources by the affluent world (90% of all grain crops in the world, for example, is used to feed livestock). The U. S. Department of Agriculture has replaced the term "hunger" with "food insecurity," which is defined as the "limited or uncertain availability of nutritionally adequate and safe foods."

World poverty: the World Bank estimates that 1.7 billion people live in absolute poverty. According to Oxfam, eighty-five of the world's wealthiest individuals have a combined wealth equal to that of the bottom 50% of the world's population (that is, 3.5 billion people). See 6. Robert Malthus and 21. Development Economics in Details.

Zero population growth: the goal of a stable population equilibrium in which the global birth rate equals the global death rate. Its objective is ending world hunger and insuring the long term sustainability of the planet. China's one-child policy constrained its population growth by 400 million since 1979, which may have contributed to the "economic miracle" of its rapid economic progress. Paul Ehrlich.

QUOTATIONS:

- *We must be willing to abridge ourselves of our superfluities, for the supply of others' necessities.* -- John Winthrop.

- *Power follows property.* -- James Harrington.

- *All wealth is the product of labor.* -- John Locke.

- *Superfluous property is the creature of society. . . . By virtue of the first laws part of the society accumulated wealth and grew powerful, they enacted others more severe, and would protect their property at the expense of humanity. This was abusing their powers, and commencing a tyranny.* – Benjamin Franklin.

- *Every man ought to be supposed a knave, and to have no other end, in all his actions, than private interest.* -- David Hume.

- *The first man who, having fenced in a piece of land, said "This is mine," and found people naïve enough to believe him, that man was the true founder of civil society. From how many crimes, wars, and murders, from how many horrors and misfortunes might not any one have saved mankind, by pulling up the stakes.* -- Jean-Jacques Rousseau.

- *The rich only select from the heap what is most precious and agreeable. They consume little more than the poor, and in spite of their natural selfishness and rapacity, though they mean only their own conveniency, though the sole end which they propose from the labours of all the thousands whom they employ, be the gratification of their own vain and insatiable desires, they divide with the poor the produce of all their improvements. They are led by an invisible hand to make nearly the same distribution of the necessaries of life, which would have been made, had the earth been divided into equal portions among all its inhabitants, and thus without intending it, without knowing it, advance the interest of the society, and afford means to the multiplication of the species.* -- Adam Smith.

- *The age of chivalry is gone. That of sophisters, oeconomists, and calculators has succeeded; and the glory of Europe is extinguished forever.* -- Edmund Burke.

- *I hope we shall crush . . . in its birth the aristocracy of our moneyed corporations, which dare already to challenge our government to a trial of strength and bid defiance to the laws of our country.* – Thomas Jefferson.

- *The most common and durable source of factions has been the various and unequal distribution of property. Those who hold and those who are without property have ever formed distinct interests in society.* -- James Madison, *Federalist No. 10.*

- *A corporation is an artificial being, invisible, intangible, and existing only in contemplation of law. Being the mere creature of law, it possesses only those properties which the charter of its creation confers upon it, either expressly or as incidental to its very existence.* – John Marshall, *Dartmouth College v. Woodward,* 1819.

- *Things are in the saddle and ride mankind.* -- Ralph Waldo Emerson.

- *The manufacturing aristocracy which is growing up under our eyes is one of the harshest that ever existed in the world; but at the same time it is one of the most confined and least dangerous. Nevertheless, the friends of democracy should keep their eyes anxiously fixed in this direction; for if ever a permanent inequality of conditions and aristocracy again penetrates into the world, it may be predicted that this is the gate by which they will enter.* -- Alexis de Tocqueville.

- *Inventions* [such as the electric telegraph] *. . . are but an improved means to an unimproved end.* -- Henry David Thoreau.

- *Labor is the superior of capital, and deserves much higher consideration.* -- Abraham Lincoln.

- *The bourgeoisie . . . has put an end to all feudal, patriarchal, idyllic relations. It has pitilessly torn asunder the motley feudal*

*ties that bound man to his "natural superiors," and has left no
other nexus between people than naked self-interest, than callous
"cash payment." It has drowned out the most heavenly ecstasies
of religious fervor, of chivalrous enthusiasm, of philistine
sentimentalism, in the icy water of egotistical calculation. . . . It
has accomplished wonders far surpassing Egyptian pyramids,
Roman aqueducts and Gothic cathedrals; it has conducted
expeditions that put in the shade all former exoduses of nations
and crusades. [It] cannot exist without constantly revolutionizing
the instruments of production. . . . The need of a constantly
expanding market for its products chases the bourgeoisie over the
entire surface of the globe. . . . In one word, it creates a world
after its own image.* -- Karl Marx.

- *Greed is healthy.* -- Ivan Boesky.

- *Corporations are people, my friend.* – Mitt Romney.

ECONOMICS DETAILS: (1) Economics, (2) Mercantilism,
(3) Adam Smith/Classical/Free Market Economics, (4) Public
Regulation Quandary, (5) David Ricardo/Law of Comparative
Advantage, (6) Robert Malthus/The Struggle for Existence, (7)
American System/American Way, (8) Industrial Revolution, (9) Karl
Marx/Dialectical Materialism, (10) Economic/Technological
Determinism, (11) Counterarguments to Economic/Technological
Determinism, (12) Frederick Jackson Turner/End of the Frontier, (13)
Thorstein Veblen/Conspicuous Consumption and Conspicuous Waste,
(14) Max Weber/Protestant Ethic, (15) Joseph Schumpeter/Creative
Destruction, (16) Keynesian Economics, (17) Supply-side Economics,
(18) Macroeconomics, (19) Microeconomics, (20) Neoclassical
Synthesis, (21) Development Economics, (22) E. F.
Schumacher/Small-is-Beautiful Economics, (23) Behavioral
Economics and (24) Neuro-Economics.

1. **Economics** is the study of the production, distribution and
    consumption of goods and services. It has been called the "dismal
    science" by David Ricardo, since it involves inequality, material
    scarcity and economic self-interest.

2. **Mercantilism** was a 17th and 18th Century school of economic thought that advocated an active role for the state in establishing trading monopolies, exploiting its colonies for the benefit of the mother country and increasing national wealth by accumulating gold and silver; versus the **Physiocrats**, who defined national wealth in terms of land and agriculture. Graham Bannock, Robert Heilbroner.

3. **Adam Smith** (1723-1790)/**Classical/Free Market Economics** is an economic school of thought that began with the publication of Adam Smith's *Wealth of Nations* in 1776. Its basic tenets are (1) the sanctity of private property and the private ownership of the means of production; (2) the profit motive; (3) laissez-faire policies and unregulated free markets; (4) the law of supply and demand; (5) competition and (6) free trade. It assumes that individuals are motivated by rational self-interest (i.e., reason and selfishness) and that, by pursuing their own economic self-interest, they thereby promote the common good (Smith's so-called "invisible hand"). Laissez-faire (from French for "let do," or "let them do as they please") is the doctrine that a government should not interfere in the marketplace or regulate economic activity, including assisting businesses or intervening to preserve or restore competition. Adam Smith, David Ricardo; Paul Samuelson, Robert Heilbroner.

Classical, or free market, economics is based on the following assumptions: (1) markets are composed of many small buyers and sellers who (2) are rational decision-makers, (3) act in their own self-interest, (4) have equal knowledge of the market and (5) can freely enter or exit the market. Thus, (6) markets are efficient, competitive, self-regulating and in equilibrium.

Critics counter that "markets" are: (1) abstract, idealized, imperfect and amoral; (2) characterized by uncertainty, irrationality and asymmetrical knowledge and (3) often dominated by a few large buyers or sellers. See Bounded Rationality in Concepts and 23. Behavioral Economics in Details.

A major contradiction of classical economics is that its two major tenets, the **laissez-faire doctrine** and the **law of competition**, are often incompatible, since competition (through economies of scale and other factors) often leads to the consolidation of a large number of small suppliers into a small number of large ones. Thus, governmental intervention may be necessary to protect or restore market competition by regulating or dismantling monopolies, oligopolies and other large-scale organizations that restrain trade, reduce competition and distort the laws of supply and demand.

In the United States, public policy since the Progressive Era, generally, has been to accept the inevitability of large-scale organizations that dominate their markets, but to regulate them in the public interest (Theodore Roosevelt's New Nationalist approach), although with varying degrees of scrutiny and success, rather than to seek to dismantle them ("trust busting," as Woodrow Wilson's New Freedom program sought to do). To an extent, the evils and inefficiencies of large-scale monopolies and oligopolies are mitigated today by the fast pace of technological change (similar to Schumpeter's "creative destruction") and the exigencies of global competition.

4. **Public Regulation Quandary** arises from the question of who, in a regulated economy, effectively controls the regulatory machinery governing large-scale economic organizations (including trusts, monopolies, oligopolies and large corporations) and protects the public interest: (1) the elected executive, (2) the legislative body, (3) the regulatory agencies, (4) disinterested experts and public servants, (5) special interest groups, (6) the regulated industries themselves, or (7) no one? For example, after the Interstate Commerce Commission was established in 1887 to regulate railroad rates, it came under the control of the very industry it was enjoined to regulate. Today, the Securities and Exchange Commission, state public utilities commissions and many other state and federal regulatory agencies are often influenced, dominated and, even, controlled by the industries that they are charged with regulating in the public interest. Walter Lippmann and others.

5. **David Ricardo** (1772-1823)/**Law of Comparative Advantage** is a major corollary of classical economics and a keystone of free trade, which was developed in the late 18th Century and early 19th Century by Adam Smith and David Ricardo. It proposes that each nation should specialize in producing and exporting only those

products that it can produce more efficiently and cheaply (and that have the highest relative rate of return and the lowest opportunity costs) and import those that it cannot. Thus, even if a country has an absolute advantage in producing two or more products, say shoes and cell phones it should specialize in those products that provide the highest rate of return. The law of comparative advantage only works among countries that engage in reciprocal free trade with each other, that is, those that have no restrictions on exports and imports from and to each other, such as tariffs, quotas, or other trade barriers. Adam Smith, David Ricardo; Graham Bannock, Robert Heilbroner, Chris Rohmann, Paul Samuelson.

Factors that contribute to a nation's comparative advantage and economic prosperity include (1) rich natural resources (fertile soil; abundant timber, iron, copper, coal, oil and natural gas; hydroelectric power, etc.); (2) a productive labor force (that is relatively cheaper, or more skilled and educated, or that works harder or more efficiently than those of other countries); (3) access to relatively inexpensive capital; (4) entrepreneurial innovation and risk-taking; (5) cutting-edge technology (including research and development investments, administrative expertise, intellectual property protections and patent monopolies); (6) a large, domestic consumer market; (7) a large or emerging middle-class; (8) a well-developed social infrastructure (schools, universities, libraries, hospitals, roads, bridges, marketing and transportation networks); (9) a fair and independent legal system (the rule of law, an independent judiciary, effective sanctions against corruption and extralegal financial activities); (10) fair and enforced health, safety and labor standards; (11) political stability, accountability and transparency; (12) a stable and uniform currency; (13) a fair and equitable tax structure; (14) enforced accounting and auditing standards and practices and (15) an uncensored press and public media, a moral ethos and an engaged citizenry that opposes and exposes corruption, cronyism and injustice.

The concept of comparative advantage has been challenged by the recent realities of global capitalism in which nearly all the factors of production (labor, resources, currency, capital and technology) can be moved (outsourced) almost overnight from one country to another, which results in an absolute advantage to the in-sourced country, with wages falling in the outsourced country faster than they rise in the in-sourced country.

6. **Robert Malthus** (1766-1834)/**the Struggle for Existence** proposed, in his *An Essay on the Principle of Population*, published in 1798, that the competition for scarce resources inevitably leads to "the struggle for existence," and that human progress will always be inhibited by population growth, since "population, when unchecked, increases in a geometrical ratio [while] subsistence increases only in an arithmetical ratio," unless checked by famine, war, pestilence or "moral restraints." Malthus's *Essay* was influenced by Benjamin Franklin's *Observations Concerning the Increase of Mankind* (1755), and, in turn, influenced Darwin's theory of natural selection (1859). See the 5. The Darwinian-Mendelian Evolutionary Paradigm in Science Details.

7. **American System/American Way** was a national economic program that was proposed in the late 18th and early 19th Century by Alexander Hamilton, Tench Coxe, Henry Carey and Henry Clay. It called for (1) a strong national government; (2) a planned national economy; (3) domestic manufacturing for a domestic market; (4) a high tariff to protect domestic industries from foreign competition and generate revenue; (5) a national bank; (6) a uniform currency; (7) "internal improvements" at federal expense for (a) physical infrastructure (roads, canals, etc.) to facilitate intra- and inter-sectional trade and (b) the "moral, political and intellectual improvement" of its citizens (Henry Clay) and (8) the distribution of the proceeds from sale of public lands to the states to pay for those "internal improvements."

The American System contradicted the basic tenets of laissez-faire capitalism and was never implemented in a single, systematic manner. However, over the years, many of its components were implemented, although intermittently and on a piecemeal basis. These included (1) the imposition of a high protective tariff before and after the Civil War to protect American industries from foreign competition; (2) the granting of massive federal subsidies to the railroads in the 19th Century and the highway and airlines industries in the 20th Century; (3) the granting of federal lands to the states to raise funds to establish and endow "land-grant" colleges for teaching agriculture, science, military science and engineering and the "intellectual improvement" of their citizens and (4) the establishment of the Federal Reserve System in 1913, which provides a uniform national currency and serves as the nation's central bank. See Federal Reserve System in Concepts and Railroad land grants in American History Concepts.

8. **Industrial Revolution** is the name given to the historical process by which traditional, agrarian and merchant capitalist societies were transformed into capital-intensive, machine-based, manufacturing economies. Industrialization is said to have begun with the invention of an improved steam engine by James Watt in England in the 1760s. Historically, it is associated with (1) steam power; (2) textile manufacturing (particularly cotton); (3) the iron, coal and steel industries; (4) canals and railroads; (5) the standardization and interchangeability of parts; (6) the specialization and division of labor; (7) the factory system (versus the domestic or putting-out system); (8) capital accumulation; (9) corporations and large-scale organizations; (10) urbanization; (11) the mass production and distribution of goods; (12) the moving assembly line; (13) electrical power; (14) the internal combustion engine; (15) the displacement of traditional craft workers with lower-cost, often imported, unskilled labor; (16) harsh and impersonal working and living conditions for workers and (17) trade unions, strikes and class conflict. The Industrial Revolution was one of the most important events in human history since the Neolithic/Agricultural Revolution, approximately 11,000 years ago, and is coincident with, but not synonymous with, the rise of industrial capitalism in the 19th Century. Samuel Hays, Joel Mokyr, Sidney Pollard, Robert Wiebe.

9. **Karl Marx** (1818-1883)/**Dialectical Materialism** is an economic, social and political school of thought, according to which (1) societies change in dialectical stages through class conflict; (2) the modes of production consist of (a) the factors of production (land, natural resources, labor, capital, technology) and (b) the social relations of production (slavery, feudalism, capitalism, socialism and communism); (3) changes in society's economic/technological substructure drive changes in the superstructure (i.e., its art, ideology and religion; social, cultural, political and legal institutions) and (4) the dictatorship of the bourgeoisie (the

capitalist class) will inevitably be destroyed by its internal
contractions and ever greater financial crises and will be replaced
by the dictatorship of the proletariat (the working class) which will
lead, eventually, to a classless, stateless, egalitarian society of pure
communism.

Marxist theory is also associated with: (5) the labor theory of value
(*q.v.* in Concepts) and its corollary (6) surplus value (profits are
stolen wages, which are derived from expropriating the difference
between the subsistence wage cost and the market price of a
product); (7) the alienation of the laborer from the product of his or
her labor (the worker becomes an appendage of the machine); (8)
the "cash nexus" of impersonal market forces (*q.v.* in Concepts);
(9) commodity fetishism ("the rule of the worker's product over
the worker himself"); (10) the view that social existence
determines consciousness; (11) the doctrine of cultural hegemony
and false consciousness (that cultural norms and values are social
constructs that are imposed by the dominant class, but are
perceived as universally true by the general population) and (12)
the belief that religion is the opiate of the people. Karl Marx,
Friedrich Engels; Louis Althusser, Ludwig Feuerbach, Antonio
Gramsci, Raymond Williams.

10. **Economic/Technological Determinism** is a school of thought that
    asserts that economic and technological changes in the material
    environment, or substructure, drive changes in the religious,
    ideological, social, cultural and legal superstructure. It is often
    identified with Marxism, but, although the two overlap, it has an
    independent history and is not necessarily driven by class
    dialectics. James Harrington, James Madison, Karl Marx; Jared
    Diamond, Marvin Harris and others. See 4. Geographical
    Determinism in Historiography Details.

    Examples of Economic/Technological Determinism provide
    evidence of the impact of technology on human cognition and
    social structures. These include:
    1) The invention of the **printing press** in the 15th Century (a)
       enabled the printing of vernacular (i.e., non-Latin) Bibles and
       religious and secular literature, (b) democratized learning by
       encouraging literacy and facilitating the study of vernacular

languages and (c) accelerated the spread of the Protestant "heresy" in the 16th and 17th Centuries.

2) The invention of the **cotton engine (or "gin")** by Eli Whitney in 1793 made the production of inland, short-staple cotton enormously profitable because it efficiently separated the cotton fiber from the seeds (which, until then, had required many hours of manual labor to remove the seeds from a single pound of cotton). Whitney's invention (a) increased the demand for slave labor to cultivate the now very profitable plant; (b) drove the expansion of slavery (which, until then, had been moribund) and cotton production from the Upper South into the Lower South; (c) threatened the traditional family farm by the plantation/slave-labor system; (d) precipitated a war with Mexico and the expropriation of half its territory; (e) insured the economic and political ascendency of the South ("King Cotton") and (f) laid the foundation for sectional conflict, which led, eventually, to the American Civil War.

3) The discovery of **penicillin** and other drugs in the 20th Century led to a dramatic decrease in deaths from infections and diseases and a corresponding increase in the world's population. In the underdeveloped world, this placed enormous stress on colonial administrations and national governments to meet the needs of their subjects and citizens, which, in turn, led to social transformation and national independence, as well as to an increase in world-wide poverty and social turmoil.

4) The development and marketing of the **birth control pill** in the early 1960s allowed women to control whether and when to have children, which (a) fostered self-determination, (b) precipitated the feminist and sexual revolutions, (c) enabled women to move into higher education and the traditional male professions, (d) highlighted gender discrimination and (f) reinforced the demand for equal rights.

5) The development of **electronic media**, including television and the Internet, created a "global village" and facilitated the globalization of consumer capitalism, social networking, electronic publishing and the erosion of state controls. Television news, social media and mobile recording devices have provided graphic images in real time to mass audiences of civil and human rights abuses, local and regional conflicts,

grassroots movements and social trends. This has affected public opinion around the world and influenced the course of those events. See 23. Marshall McLuhan and 24. Information Technology/Metaphor of the Machine in Sociology Details.

11. **Counterarguments to Economic/Technological Determinism** assert that the material environment may condition, but does not determine, human events. Ideas and moral values are often primary, and the relationship between human consciousness and the material environment is a contingent and interactive one. Critics of economic/technological determinism make the following arguments:
   1) Human cognitive evolution was driven by the social complexities and challenges of living in groups, which involved cooperative hunting, food sharing, mutual grooming, reciprocal altruism, coalitional politics, etc., rather than by the technological innovations involved in tool-making and manipulating the material environment (which remained stable and unchanging over tens of thousands of years). See 5. Social Intelligence/Social Brain Hypothesis in Anthropology Details.
   2) Technological advances are not inevitable. Discoveries and inventions are made by autonomous individuals acting as free agents, some of whom are geniuses (e.g., Archimedes, Galileo, Johannes Gutenberg, Isaac Newton, James Watt, Edward Jenner, Thomas Edison, Alexander Fleming), many of whom are anonymous, and all of whom rely on the collective, accumulated knowledge of the past to incrementally adjust existing technologies, but all of whom provide contributions that are contingent and unique. Clifford Conner, Joel Mokyr, M. P. Squicciarini, N. Voigtlander.
   3) Humans are often authentically motivated by altruism, as well as by emotions and irrational factors, not infrequently causing them to consciously act against their own material self-interest. See 23. Behavioral Economics and 24. Neuro-Economics in Details and Anterior insula and Group-level selection in Anthropology Concepts.
   4) Religion and ideology have played a critical role in economic development and territorial expansion, as well as in magnifying human aggression, conflict and warfare. Max Weber provides an example in which a socio-religious system of values (the Protestant ethic of industry, frugality and capital

accumulation) laid the foundation for an economic system (capitalism). See 14. Max Weber/Protestant Ethic in Details, Moralizing gods hypothesis in Anthropology Concepts and 12. Violence and Human Nature in Anthropology Details.

5) Ideas, values and beliefs have an existence independent of the medium through which they are expressed and have had a profound impact on the individuals who hold them and on human history and culture. Examples include those expressed in the Bible, the Quran, St. Augustine's *City of God*, Martin Luther's *Ninety-Five Theses*, Thomas Paine's *Common Sense*, the Declaration of Independence, the Bill of Rights, Henry David Thoreau's Civil Disobedience, Harriet Beecher Stowe's *Uncle Tom's Cabin*, Karl Marx's The Communist Manifesto, D. W. Griffith's *The Birth of a Nation*, Friedrich von Hayek's *The Road to Serfdom*, Ayn Rand's *Atlas Shrugged*, Rachel Carson's *Silent Spring*, Betty Friedan's *The Feminine Mystique*, Martin Luther King, Jr.'s "I Have a Dream" speech and Alex Haley's *Roots*.

12. **Frederick Jackson Turner** (1861-1932)/**End of the Frontier** provides a metaphor and narrative for the eventual exhaustion of the earth's natural resources. Since natural resources (arable land, fossil fuels, clean air and fresh water) are finite, as they are exhausted societies are disrupted by scarcity, climate change, declining expectations, wars and economic depressions. The end of the frontier marks the symbolic and literal end of material abundance and prosperity, except for those new energy sources that can be identified and developed by new technologies. Robert Malthus, Frederick Jackson Turner, Walter Prescott Webb; Jimmy Carter, Jared Diamond, Christopher Lasch, Ted Steinberg. See Environmental/Green movement in American History Concepts and 11. Frederick Jackson Turner/Frontier Thesis in American History Details.

13. **Thorstein Veblen** (1857-1929)/**Conspicuous Consumption and Conspicuous Waste** proposed that, contrary to the tenets of Social Darwinism, wealth is not a badge of social superiority, nor proof of the elect nor an emblem of the "fittest," but rather that the leisure class is pecuniary, avaricious and predatory and is driven by invidious distinctions of conspicuous consumption and conspicuous waste. See Robber baron thesis in Concepts and 25.

Social Darwinism and 26. Countervailing Theories/Reform Darwinism in American History Details.

14. **Max Weber** (1864-1920)/**Protestant Ethic** proposed that (1) culture, religion and ideas are the driving force in society; (2) a socio-religious system of values (the Protestant ethic of industry, frugality and capital accumulation) laid the foundation for an economic system (capitalism), (3) hierarchical social stratification is based on education, status, prestige and power, as well as on class. See Scarcity psychology in Concepts, Benjamin Franklin's Table of Virtues in American History Concepts, 6. Freud's Anal Personality Traits in Psychology Details and 14. Max Weber in Sociology Details.

15. **Joseph Schumpeter** (1883-1950)/**Creative Destruction** viewed capitalism as a continuous process of "creative" destruction," which will eventually be superseded by socialism. To Schumpeter, the prime mover of capitalism was the innovating, risk-taking entrepreneur who organizes the factors of production and reaps the rewards or incurs the losses from the enterprise. His model of long term technological cycles, or waves, encompasses: (1) the Industrial Revolution (beginning in 1771), (2) the Age of Steam and Railroads (beginning in 1829), (3) the Age of Steel and Electricity (beginning in 1875), (4) the Age of Oil, Automobile and Mass Production (beginning in 1908) and (5) the Age of Information and Telecommunications (beginning in 1971). See Creative destruction in Concepts.

16. **John Maynard Keynes** (1883-1946)/**Keynesian Economics** is a school of economic thought that advocates a mixed economy (i.e., partially state-planned and partially market-driven) and regulated markets. According to Keynesian theory, the federal (national) government should intervene in the economy by using fiscal policies (public expenditures, taxation and deficit financing) and monetary policies (which modulate the money supply and interest rates) to: (1) maintain full employment; (2) even out the swings in the business cycle; (3) provide a social safety net for children, seniors, the disabled and the unemployed and (4), in times of depression and recession, stimulate investment by reducing interest rates and increasing purchasing power, using public expenditures

to increase aggregate demand and consumption. John Maynard Keynes; Robert Heilbroner, Paul Krugman, Paul Samuelson.

In Keynesian consumption-side economics, the marginal propensity to consume is higher for those with lower incomes and, conversely, the marginal propensity to save is higher for those with higher incomes. Therefore, policies that increase the relative income of poor people (through higher wages, an increased minimum wage, income tax credits, direct government payments and lower regressive sales taxes) will lead to an aggregate increase in demand, purchasing power and consumption and, thus, to an increase in the production of goods and services, which, in turn will lead to higher employment and greater over-all prosperity. See Marginal propensity to consume or save, Multiplier effect and Purchasing power in Concepts.

A major contradiction of Keynesian economics, as it is practiced, is that, although public stimulus spending, tax cuts and deficit financing by the central government are critical to bringing an economy out of a recession, the converse of balanced budgets, tax increases and deficit reductions in times of prosperity are rarely practiced, which leads to greater deficits and long-term public debt. See Permanent warfare economy/military Keynesianism in Concepts.

17. **Supply-side Economics** is a school of economic thought that maintains that supply creates its own demand; that is, by reducing taxes (particularly, on the wealthy, since they have a higher propensity to save and, thus, invest), government stimulates private investment, which leads to increased production and employment, reduced prices and increased consumption (the "trickle down" effect). It is a central feature of Reaganomics and stands in opposition to Keynesian demand/consumption-side economics, which views tax cuts for the wealthy as leading to greater income inequality, a reduction in aggregate purchasing power and an increase in speculative investments.

18. **Macroeconomics** is a branch of economics that focuses on the "sum total of economic activity," i.e., the economy as a whole, using aggregate indicators of national income, output, consumption, inflation, unemployment, savings and investment,

money supply and international trade. It is associated with Keynesian economics.

19. **Microeconomics** is a branch of economics that focuses on the economic decision-making of individual households and businesses, which affects the supply and demand for goods and services and determines prices in a competitive marketplace. It is associated with classical or market economics.

20. **Neoclassical synthesis** is a synthesis of classical and Keynesian models, of micro- and macroeconomics, and is now the dominant paradigm in mainstream economics.

21. **Development Economics** is a branch of economics that offers theories and strategies for promoting economic growth in underdeveloped countries. These theories and strategies include:
    1) The stages-of-economic-growth model (W. W. Rostow), in which traditional agrarian societies build social infrastructure (schools, roads and bridges, etc.) and accumulate capital, which leads to economic take-off and, eventually, economic maturity and a middle-class society of mass consumption.
    2) Structural changes, in which agrarian societies with surplus labor are transformed into urbanized, industrial economies.
    3) Intermediate technology (E. F. Schumacher), which offers a middle way between traditional agrarianism and full-scale industrialization. See 22. E. F. Schumacher/Small-is-Beautiful Economics in Details.
    4) Neo-colonial dependency (Andre Gunder Frank), in which Third World developing countries cannot control their economic destinies because of the dominance of advanced industrial economies.
    5) Neoliberalism, which advocates free trade, globalization, private enterprise, deregulated markets, privatization and property rights.
    6) Non-GDP indices of national well-being, such as GPI (Genuine Progress Indicator) and other quality-of-life indices, which measure the social and environmental wellbeing of a nation and its citizens, such as its education, healthcare, job security, gender equality, political freedom and stability, rule of law, equitable income distribution, crime rates, air and water cleanliness and resource sustainability.

Paul Collier, Andre Gunder Frank, Walt Whitman Rostow, Jeffery Sachs, E. F. Schumacher, Amartya Sen, Joseph Stiglitz.

22. **E. F. Schumacher** (1911-1977)/**Small-is-Beautiful Economics** is a school of economic thought that proposes an "intermediate technology," or a middle way, for undeveloped countries between traditional agrarianism and full-scale industrialization. It advocates the development of local, small-scale, labor-intensive, cooperative industries that produce for local markets and employ individual craft persons, rather than large-scale, mass production industries. It echoes Lewis Mumford's concept of a garden village, projects a Buddhist economics ethic and seeks to mitigate the despoliation of the natural environment, redress the imbalance between the city and the country and provide an alternative model to the cash nexus of impersonal market forces and the systematic cultivation of consumption and greed ("more, further, richer, quicker").

23. **Behavioral Economics** is a branch of economics, based on empirical studies, that contradicts the basic assumption of classical economics that economic man, *Homo economicus*, is motivated by rational self-interest (reason and selfishness); that is, that individuals and organizations make rational decisions to maximize benefits and minimize risks and costs to themselves. Instead, behavioral economics explores the non-rational factors in economic decision-making, such as impulsiveness, risk/loss avoidance, non-reciprocal altruism, rules of thumb, herd behavior, and what Keynes called "animal spirits." See 24. Neuro-Economics in Details and Bounded Rationality in Concepts.

24. **Neuro-Economics** is a school of economic thought that is based on empirical studies in neuroscience. These studies suggest that economic decision-making is governed by short-term, emotional factors as much as by long-term, rational ones. Neuro-economists base their conclusions on scientific research that uses functional magnetic resonance imaging (MRI) to map the conflicts within the brain between the prefrontal cortex (which manages long-term rational planning, decision-making and impulse control) and the limbic system (which is governed by short-term emotions, including the need for immediate gratification). These studies have found, for example, that happiness, as measured in the brain's

pleasure centers, is derived not from more of the same pleasure, but from new, unexpected pleasures, and that perceived unfairness elicits a strong emotional reaction in the anterior insula in both humans and their primate relatives (*q.v.* in Anthropology Concepts). Jonathan Cohen, David I. Laibson, George Loewenstein, Samuel McClure, Scott Rick.

5. HISTORIOGRAPHY

CONCEPTS AND PHRASES:

Ad fontes ("to the fountains," i.e., to the original sources): one of the first principles of historiography, which is that historical evidence should be based on original documents, manuscripts, letters, diaries, wills, eyewitness accounts and physical evidence. The principle was established by Erasmus (1466-1536) and other Renaissance scholars as a result of the renewed interest in the Greek and Latin classics. See Primary versus secondary sources in Concepts.

Agency: the capacity to make free, independent decisions and choices. See Cultural hegemony, Historical determinism and Reflexivity in Concepts.

Alternative histories: histories of what might have happened if contingencies and turning points had pivoted in other directions; the chain of events that would have occurred, for example, if Washington had not been able to withdraw his troops from Brooklyn Heights in 1776, or if the Union forces had lost the Battle of Gettysburg in 1863 or if Japan had not attacked Pearl Harbor in 1941. "The inevitability of the present violates the contingency of the past, which involves alternative choices and outcomes that would have produced alterative presents" -- Richard White. See Radical Contingency in Concepts, Richard White in Quotations and Broken symmetry in Science Concepts.

Annales School: a school of history that focuses on the social histories and cultural practices of ordinary people; including their foods, fashions and social customs. See *Longue durée* and *Mentalités* in Concepts and 6. Annales School and 7. New Social/Cultural History in Details.

Antiquarianism: the study of ancient manuscripts and artifacts; also, the tendency of some scholars to focus excessively on minor, arcane facts to the exclusion of the wider cultural context and larger historical significance.

Aristotle's four causes: in building a ship, (1) the formal cause is the design of the ship; (2) the material cause is the materials used to build it; (3) the efficient cause is the tools and workmen who actually build the ship and (4) the final cause is the intended purpose of the ship.

Assumed versus **expressed ideas of an age**: "it requires a very unusual mind to make an analysis of the obvious" -- Alfred North Whitehead. Carl Becker. See Climate of opinion, Cultural hegemony, *Mentalités* and *Zeitgeist* in Concepts.

Challenge and response: Arnold Toynbee's thesis that civilizations develop in response to challenges and decline when they fail to respond creatively to those challenges. To Jared Diamond, societies collapse when they fail to adjust to environmental crises, such as climate change. Both hypotheses are derived from the study of comparative history. Jared Diamond, Arnold Toynbee.

Climate of opinion: the *zeitgeist* or world view of a particular culture at a particular time and place. Carl Becker, Arthur Lovejoy, Alfred North Whitehead.

Cliometrics/econometrics: a branch of history that applies economic models and quantitative and statistical methodologies to the study of history, examining, for example, the profitability of slavery in the antebellum American South. Edward Baptist, Robert Fogel, Douglass North.

Cultural hegemony: a tenet of cultural materialism that, at any point in history, the dominant class's ideology or world view (e.g., patriarchy, emperor worship, slavery, feudalism, the divine right of kings, laissez-faire capitalism, Social Darwinism, dialectical materialism, the cult of personality) are social constructs that are "infused throughout society" and perceived to be universally true by the general population (including, we must assume, the appropriation of the "usable past"); Antonio Gramsci; see Usable past in Concepts and 5. Historical and Cultural Materialism in Details; versus the **post-hegemonic synthesis**, which ascribes free will, agency, autonomy and reflexivity, or self-awareness, to individuals as they make their political and cultural choices, and sees cultural hegemony in layered social structures rather than as a monolithic value system. Peter Berger and Thomas Luckmann,

Anthony Giddens, Raymond Williams. See Agency and
Reflexivity in Concepts.

Cyclical views of history: those that are based on the assumption that
history repeats itself, i.e., that there are patterns or cycles in human
history, such as the rise and fall of civilizations. Thus, according
to Thucydides, the role of the historian is to instruct posterity so
that it can recognize its own place in the historical cycle; versus
historical nominalism (*q.v.* in Concepts). Crane Brinton, Jared
Diamond, James Froude, Edward Gibbon, David Hume, Oswald
Spengler, Arnold Toynbee. See Historical nominalism and Wheel
of history in Concepts; Thucydides, Marcus Aurelius, David
Hume, Karl Marx and George Santayana in Quotations, and 2. Life
Cycle of Nations and 3. Patterns of Political-Social Revolutions in
Details.

Diachronic: studies that focus on the origins, history and development
of a subject over a period of time; versus **synchronic**: studies that
focus on the structure and functions of a subject at a given point in
time. Ferdinand de Saussure.

Dialectical materialism: a theory of history developed by Karl Marx,
according to which (1) societies change in dialectical stages
through class conflict; (2) changes in society's
economic/technological substructure drive changes in its
superstructure (art, ideology and religion; social, cultural, political
and legal institutions); (3) ideas reflect the interests, ideology and
world view of the dominant class (cultural hegemony); (4) the
dictatorship of the bourgeoisie (the capitalist class) will inevitably
be destroyed by its internal contractions and ever greater financial
crises and will be replaced by the dictatorship of the proletariat (the
working classes) which will lead, eventually, to a classless,
stateless, egalitarian society of pure communism. Marx, Friedrich
Engels; Louis Althusser, Ludwig Feurbach, Antonio Gramsci,
Raymond Williams. See Hegelian view of history in Concepts and
5. Historical and Cultural Materialism in Details.

End of history: religious, Hegelian, Marxist and other secular
versions of the end of human history. Religious versions posit the
end of the world and the destruction of the earth; secular versions
posit the end of human social evolution and the perfection of
government and society. Francis Fukuyama's 1989 essay "End of
History" is a secular version in which it is argued that, with the

end of the Cold War and the triumph of capitalism, history has reached "the end point of mankind's ideological evolution and the universalization of Western liberal democracy [which is] the final form of human government." See Dialectical materialism and Hegelian view of history in Concepts; Apocalypse, Eschatology and Millennialism in Philosophy/Religion Concepts and Perry Miller and Karen Armstrong in Selected References.

Etiology: the study of the origins and causes of historical events.

Geographical determinism: the theory that climate, natural resources and geography are the foundations of a natural economy, which, in turn, shapes the history and culture of a region. See 4. Geographical Determinism in Details and 8. Geographical Determinism in American History Details.

Great man theory of history: that certain individuals, because of their extraordinary will and character (or *charisma*, to use Max Weber's term) and/or divine assistance, have shaped the course of human history; see Histories of elites in Concepts; Thomas Carlyle, Alexis de Tocqueville and Lord Acton in Quotations and Charismatic Leader in Political Science Concepts; versus **social/economic schools of history**, which assert that history is driven by social and economic forces and contingencies; see Tocqueville in Quotations and 4. Geographical Determinism, 5. Historical and Cultural Materialism, 6. Annales School and 7. New Social/Cultural History in Details.

Hegelian view of history: that world history is the dialectical progression of humanity toward universal reason and rational self-consciousness, of the Spirit actualizing itself in the world. Marx inverted Hegel's idealism into materialism but retained the view of history as a dialectical process of thesis, antithesis and synthesis. See 12. Plato and 30. G. W. F. Hegel in Philosophy/Religion Details.

Historical determinism: theories that assert that historical events are predetermined and driven by religious or material causes. For religious forms of historical determinism, see Providential conceptions of history in Concepts; 6. American Exceptionalism and 10. Puritanism in American History Details and 16. Augustine of Hippo and 30. G. W. F. Hegel in Philosophy/Religion Details. For material forms of historical determinism, see Dialectical materialism in Concepts, 4. Geographical Determinism in Details, and 10. Economic/Technological Determinism in Economics Details. For counterarguments to religious and material determinism, see Alternative histories and Radical contingency in Concepts, Richard White in Quotations and 11. Counterarguments to Economic/Technological Determinism in Economics Details.

Historical nominalism: the thesis that every historical event is unique and unrepeatable and must be judged on its own terms; it is skeptical of grand themes and meta-narratives; versus meta-history. Wilhelm Dilthey. See Scientific history in Concepts, Leopold von Ranke in Quotations and 8. Post-structuralism in Details.

Histories of elites: schools of history that study the military, political, social and cultural leaders of a society, nation or historical era as the basis for drawing conclusions about the society, nation or era as a whole; see Great man theory of history in Concepts, Thomas Carlyle and Alexis de Tocqueville in Quotations and 15. Elites/Oligarchies in Sociology Details; versus **histories from the bottom up**, which focus on social and economic forces and the histories or ordinary people; Charles Beard, Carl Degler, Jesse Lemisch, James Harvey Robinson; see 6. Annales School and 7. New Social/Cultural History in Details.

History as philosophy teaching by example: the proposition that the purpose of history is to strip away the accidents of time and place in order to "discover the constant and universal principles of human nature"; versus historical nominalism (*q.v.* in Concepts). Dionysius of Halicarnassus, Edward Gibbon, David Hume; Carl Becker. See Thucydides, David Hume, Leopold von Ranke, George Santayana and H. Stuart Hughes in Quotations.

History as the unfolding of God's will: see Providential conceptions of history in Concepts and 6. American Exceptionalism and 10. Puritanism in American History Details.

History from inside the window: Otis Pease's description of Francis Parkman's *France and England in North America*, in which a particular frontier scene was described from the perspective of an isolated, Euro-American pioneer family inside their cabin peering out at a group of Native American raiders. Although racist and ethnocentric, in this case, it embodies the dramatic, narrative history of life on the ground as it was viewed at the time by one set of participants.

Idea of progress: the belief that human reason, science and technology will gradually improve the material and social lives of humanity. Historical progress is perceived as positive, linear (the "arrow of time"), cumulative and inevitable. The concept is associated with (1) the Christian concept of history as the unfolding of God's plan (*in statu viae*); (2) the 18th Century Enlightenment's belief in a benevolent deity, social improvement and the inevitability of human progress; (3) Darwin's theory of evolution from lower to higher life forms; (4) Hegelian and Marxist views of history as dialectically progressing toward a higher ideal or material state and (5) technological progress and the rise in living standards which accompanied the Industrial Revolution of the 19th and 20th Centuries. Carl Becker, J. B. Bury.

Infinite regression: tracing a specific historical event back through a chain of causation into the indefinite past; "the concatenation of causes stretching from the beginning of time to the end" (Bertrand Russell). For example, the Holocaust can be traced back in time to (1) the Wannsee Conference of 1942, (2) the appointment of Hitler as Chancellor and the Reichstag election of 1933, (3) Hitler's reading of Madison' Grant's *The Passing of the Great Race* in 1925, (4) Germany's humiliating defeat during the First World War, (5) Hitler's brutal, authoritarian father, (6) the German national character, (7) the long tradition of Christian anti-Semitism in Europe, including the Second Crusade through the Rhineland in the 12th Century, and, ultimately, (8) the Epistles of Paul.

Infra-history: the unrecorded history of ordinary people; a major focus of the Annales School and the New Social/Cultural History. See 6. and 7. in Details. Miguel de Unamuno.

Intellectual history: the history of ideas, as well as the thinkers who formulated and expressed them and the context in which they developed. It presumes the primacy and autonomy of ideas, which are posited to be conditioned but not determined by the material context in which they arise. Arthur Lovejoy. See 11. Counterarguments to Economic/Technological Determinism in Economics Details.

Internal biographies: those that focus on the life of the mind and the evolution of the ideas of the individual subject, and less on the outward biographical details or the historical context. Perry Miller.

Longue durée ("long duration"): the term used by the *Annalistes* to emphasize the importance of cultural continuity and long-term historical structures and trends rather than specific individuals or events or immediate causes. *Annalistes* resist periodization, and their historical time-frames are often so lengthened, and significant intervening events are often so smoothed out, that they become de-historicized and absorbed into the background. See 6. Annales School in Details.

Lost world of Thomas Jefferson: the proposition that much of the past is irretrievably lost, including even that of well documented historical figures such as Jefferson. Daniel Boorstin, Arthur Schlesinger.

*M*entalités: the term used by the *Annalistes* to describe the attitudes, collective psychology, world view and mindset of a particular culture at a particular time. See 6. Annales School in Details.

Meta-history: historiography; the philosophy of history as a discipline; also, histories with grand themes and meta-narratives (versus historical nominalism and post-structuralism). See Historical nominalism and Scientific history in Concepts and 1. Historiography and 8. Post-structuralism in Details.

Micro-history: the "search for answers to large questions in small places"; a school of history that focuses on intensive investigations and case-studies of small events, such as those involving a community, a family or a person. It stresses the free will/agency of the individual human actors rather than the determinism of economic and cultural forces. Charles Joyner. See 7. New Social/Cultural History in Details.

Models/typologies of historical change: (1) existential, (2) linear, (3) cyclical, (4) multi-linear and (5) episodic. Michael Bentley.

Narrative histories: those that involve, generally, a single, chronological story line, with extended descriptions of particular individuals and events; versus **social/analytical histories**, which focus on larger forces, groups, patterns, contexts and trends, and are more analytical and less descriptive of individual personalities and events. See Alexis de Tocqueville in Quotations.

New social/cultural history: a school of history that focuses on the history of ordinary people and their daily lives, as opposed to the history of "great men." See 6. Annales School and 7. New Social/Cultural History in Details.

Nunc pro tunc **fallacy** ("now for then"): present-mindedness; judging the past in terms of the attitudes, norms and values of the present.

Oral tradition: in non-literate societies (i.e., those without a written language), the primary method for transmitting cultural traditions and history from one generation to the next, using speeches, songs, poems and folktales. The *Iliad*, for example, was recited from memory and not written down until the 8th Century BCE, approximately 400 years after the events it celebrated. See Prehistory in Concepts.

Overdetermination: the proposition that an action or event is often determined by multiple causes, any one of which, by itself, could have caused the event. Sigmund Freud; Louis Althusser.

Periodization: the division of history into eras, periods, centuries, decades or segments, which correspond to significant events, reigns or administrations. It represents an imprecise attempt to impose a temporal or conceptual framework on the raw material of history; versus the *Longue durée* of the Annales School.

Posterity as a substitute for God and immortality: a concept of the 18th Century *philosophes,* who secularized history and placed it on a linear path of inevitable progress, scientific discovery and social improvement in order to compensate for the loss of belief in providential intervention in human history and an afterlife. Unfortunately, posterity has responded with "enormous condescension" toward the past (E. P. Thompson). Carl Becker. See Thompson in Quotations.

Post-structuralism: a school of literary thought that postulates the validity of multiple interpretations of texts, including those of history. See 8. Post-structuralism in Details.

Power of the periphery: the thesis that revolutionary changes originate on the margins, not at the core, of civilizations. Alexander Motyl.

Prehistory: pre-written history; the history of non-literate cultures, which, generally, is the province of anthropology. The study of written history has itself been described as a form of "retrospective cultural anthropology" (H. Stuart Hughes). See Oral tradition in Concepts.

Primary versus **secondary sources**: original documents, manuscripts, letters, diaries, wills, photographs, dispatches, physical evidence, eyewitness accounts and oral testimony that are directly related to historical events, etc. versus second-hand or subsequent commentaries, interpretations and analyses. See *Ad fontes* in Concepts.

Providential conceptions of history: the belief that the historical development of a particular nation, people or group is guided by God; that history is the unfolding of a divine plan. St. Augustine, George Bancroft. See 6. American Exceptionalism and 7. Puritanism in American History Details and Predestination in Philosophy/Religion Concepts.

Radical contingency: the doctrine that small, initial, random, seemingly insignificant differences and dependencies can have enormous historical consequences. For example: (1) had Cleopatra's nose been shorter, "the whole face of the world would have changed," according to Blaise Pascal (since, presumably, Mark Anthony would not have fallen in love with her, the Roman civil war would have been avoided and the Roman Republic would have survived); (2) had Corporal Hitler not moved to another spot in the trenches one morning during the First World War while his mates were eating breakfast, he would have been blow up by a stray mortar shell as they were a few minutes later (according to one report) and the Second World War and the Holocaust might never have happened; (3) had the assassination attempt on President-Elect Franklin D. Roosevelt in Miami, Florida on February 15, 1933 been successful, the Vice-President-Elect John Nance Garner, a conservative Texas Democrat, would have become President and the New Deal might never have happened. Jorge Luis Borges, Blaise Pascal, Richard White, Thornton Wilder. See Alternative histories in Concepts; Richard White in Quotations; Population Bottleneck in Anthropology Concepts and Broken symmetry, Chaos theory, Multiverse, Schrödinger's cat, Stochastic, Tychism, Uniformitarianism versus catastrophism/neo-catastrophism and Vacuum genesis in Science Concepts. For a view of history that rejects the role of historical contingencies and accidents, see E.H. Carr's *What is History?* in Selected References.

Revanchism: the desire of a defeated nation for revenge and the restoration of its lost territories through force. The rise of Nazism in Germany, for example, has been linked to its humiliation from the events that followed its defeat in the First World War. Norbert Elias.

Revisionist history: the dialectical process of thesis, antithesis and synthesis applied to historical interpretations. American Civil War historiography, for example, has gone through an infinite number of re-interpretations and cycles, which suggests that each generation uses history to project its own image onto the past, a process which is reinforced by the need of professional historians to find new ways to mine old material. See Usable past in Concepts, Voltaire and Alexis de Tocqueville in Quotations, 8. Post-structuralism in Details and David Donald in Selected References.

Rise and fall of great powers: the 16th Century Spanish paradigm: the historical analogy offered by the Spanish Hapsburg dynasty, which was the greatest military and economic power of the 16th Century as a result of the seemingly endless flow of gold and silver from its mines in the New World. However, Spain incurred huge war debts from the religious wars it waged against the Protestant Reformation, which distracted it from developing its own domestic economy and forced it, eventually, into bankruptcy, after which it went into permanent decline as a geopolitical power. The example represents either an irrelevant historical analogy or an instructive lesson on the consequences of relying on a permanent warfare economy. Paul Kennedy. See Permanent warfare economy in American History Concepts.

Scientific history: a school of history that, according to the 19th Century historian Leopold von Ranke, relies on "facts" and primary sources, and uses rigorous empirical methods "to show what actually happened," rather than provide grand themes or unifying theories. It is opposed by relativistic historians such as R. G. Collingwood, E.H. Carr, Hebert Schneider and others, who counter that historians subjectively select which facts to use: "the belief in a hard core of historical facts existing objectively and independently of the interpretation of the historian is a preposterous fallacy" -- E. H. Carr. See Historical nominalism and Meta-history in Concepts; von Ranke, E. H. Carr and Herbert Schneider in Quotations and 8. Post-structuralism in Details.

Specious present: "a pattern of thought woven instantaneously from the threads of memories, perceptions, and anticipations." Carl Becker.

Theory of generations: that a distinctive consciousness and perspective is shared by members of the same generation, or cohort, of young people reaching maturity at the same time in response to the major political, cultural and historical events of their youth, which, in turn, shapes how they respond to later events and become agents of history themselves. Karl Mannheim, Arthur M. Schlesinger, Jr., William Strauss and Neil Howe. See 36. American Generational Cycles in American History Details.

Time out of mind: from time immemorial; beyond legal memory; a de facto custom, tradition and practice, according to English common law.

Universal/world histories: general histories of mankind, as opposed to those of particular nations, regions, peoples or individuals. Examples include those by Herodotus, G. W. F. Hegel, H. G. Wells, Oswald Spengler, Arnold Toynbee and Will and Ariel Durant.

Usable past: the concept of recovering and making available to all members of society a shared sense of their past. It raises the question of "useable" by whom and for what purpose -- as a means of inclusion of formerly marginalized groups; as a patriotic narrative or as an expression of the cultural hegemony and civil religion of the dominant class? Van Wyck Brooks, John Dewey. See Cultural hegemony in Concepts.

Wheel of history: the tradition among some religions, such as Buddhism and Hinduism, of viewing history as cyclical; as eras or ages repeating themselves; versus the Western view of history as linear and progressive, or various secular and religious traditions on the end of history and the end of the world. See Cyclical views of history, End of history and Idea of progress in Concepts and Millennialism in Philosophy/Religion Concepts.

Zeitgeist: the spirit of an age; the shared intellectual, cultural, political and religious beliefs and assumptions of a particular era. See Assumed versus expressed ideas of an age, Climate of opinion and *Mentalités* in Concepts.

QUOTATIONS:

- [My history will] *be judged useful by those inquirers who desire an exact knowledge of the past as an aid to the interpretation of the future.* -- Thucydides.

- *The man of forty years, if he have a grain of sense, in view of this sameness, has seen all that has been and shall be.* – Marcus Aurelius.

- *History is only a pack of tricks we play on the dead.* -- Voltaire.

- [The purpose of history is] *to discover the constant and universal principles of human nature.* -- David Hume.

- *History . . . is indeed little more than the register of the crimes, follies, and misfortunes of mankind.* -- Edward Gibbon.

- *The history of the world is but the biography of great men.* -- Thomas Carlyle.

- *To history has been assigned the office of judging the past, of instructing the present for the benefit of future ages. To such high offices this work does not aspire: It wants only to show what actually happened.* -- Leopold von Ranke.

- *Historians who write in aristocratic ages are inclined to refer all occurrences to the particular will and character of certain individuals. . . . Historians who live in democratic ages . . . assign great general causes to all petty incidents.* -- Alexis de Tocqueville.

- *The history of all hitherto existing society is the history of class struggles.* -- Karl Marx.
-
- [History repeats itself] *the first time as tragedy, the second time as farce.* -- Marx.

- *Power tends to corrupt, and absolute power corrupts absolutely. Great men are almost always bad men.* -- Lord Acton.

- *Those who cannot remember the past are condemned to repeat it.* -- George Santayana.

- *The belief in a hard core of historical facts existing objectively and independently of the interpretation of the historian is a preposterous fallacy.* -- E. H. Carr.

- *The perspectives of history are ever shifting, for human experience . . . affords no fixed point of reference. . . . Neither the mental world nor the physical has a center and a circumference. The motion of bodies must be measured from points themselves in motion, and the meanings of events are themselves events in a constantly shifting scene. History is, therefore, a world of dark objects pretending to shine by their own reflected light.* -- Herbert W. Schneider.

- [History consists of] *case studies,* [which are] *extensions of human experience.* -- Crane Brinton, John Christopher and Robert Wolff.

- *Dates are indispensable pegs on which to hang the tapestry of history.* – E. H. Gombrich.

- *I am invisible because people simply refuse to see me.* -- Ralph Ellison.

- [History is] *retrospective cultural anthropology.* -- H. Stuart Hughes.

- *We cannot glimpse at history. We can only compare one book with another.* -- Peter Munz.

- [History seeks to redress] *the enormous condescension of posterity.* -- E. P. Thompson.

- *Every civilization is dialectically structured – that is to say, the particular factors that made its rise to power possible prove to be, in the fullness of time, the very factors that do it in.* -- Morris Berman.

- *Contingency -- the idea that what happens in the world is often a result of the unexpected combination of quite particular circumstances -- is the mark of history as a discipline. . . . To say that choices are not limitless, that we always act within constraints imposed by the past, is not the same thing a saying that there were, or are, no choices. A belief in contingency has as it corollary an obligation to imagine alternatives. . . . Considering only what happened is ahistorical, because the past once contained larger possibilities, and part of the historian's job is to make those possibilities visible; otherwise all that is left for historians to do is to explain the inevitability of the present. The inevitability of the present violates the contingency of the past, which involves alternative choices and outcomes that would have produced alternative presents.* -- Richard White.

HISTORIOGRAPHY DETAILS: (1) Historiography, (2) Life Cycle of Nations, (3) Patterns of Political-Social Revolutions, (4) Geographical Determinism, (5) Historical and Cultural Materialism, (6) Annales School, (7) New Social/Cultural History and (8) Post-structuralism.

1. **Historiography** is the study of history as a discipline; it is a form of meta-history that focuses on the methodologies of studying, interpreting and writing about the past. Historiography encompasses (1) historical events, (2) the recording and interpretation of those events and (3) the significance of those interpretations. E. H. Carr, R. G. Collingwood, James Rogers, Harvey Wish. See Historical revisionism in Concepts.

2. **Life Cycle of Nations** is James Froude's thesis that civilizations rise and fall in the following sequence: (1) a golden age of virtue and simplicity, which is followed by a period of (2) strength and power, then (3) wealth and luxury and, finally, (4) corruption and decline.

3. **Patterns of Political-Social Revolutions** is Crane Brinton's thesis that revolutions often adhere to the following paradigm: the historical stage is set with (1) the moral and financial bankruptcy of the old regime, which is accompanied by (2) the alienation of

the intellectuals and (3) the loss of nerve by the ruling class, which, with (4) the rising expectations of the lower and marginalized classes, leads to (5) a political revolution. After (6) a brief honeymoon and rule by the moderates, this is followed by (7) a *coup d' état* by radicals and extremists (i.e., the revolution overflowing its banks), (8) a reign of terror and virtue, then (9) a conservative, Thermidorean counterrevolution and the rule by a tyrant and, finally, (10) a period of repression, restoration (of the old regime) and reaction.

4. **Geographical Determinism** is a school of thought that proposes that climate, natural resources and geography are the foundations of a natural economy, which, in turn, shapes the history and culture of a region. James Truslow Adams, Jared Diamond, Marvin Harris, Johann Herder. For example:

    1) The timing and sequence of the Neolithic/Agricultural Revolution (i.e., the domestication of plants and animals), which began approximately 11,000 years ago, was a function of climate, latitude, chance and geographical determinants. See 9. Neolithic/Agricultural Revolution in Anthropology Details.

    2) Europe's mountains ranges and rivers fostered the development of small, competing, independent city-states and initially militated against the rise of large, absolutist empires and despotisms.

    3) 3,000 miles of the Atlantic Ocean between the Great Britain and her North American colonies in the 17th and 18th Centuries fostered a sense of "salutary neglect," which led eventually to American independence.

    4) The extremely profitable cultivation short-staple cotton in the American South, which quickly exhausted the soil, led to the rapid geographical expansion of the plantation/slave-labor system from the Upper South to the Lower South, the annexation of the northern half of Mexico, sectional discord and, eventually, the American Civil War.

    5) The industrial world's dependence on oil in the 20th and 21th Centuries has led to an unending series of conflicts, wars and intrigues in the Middle East, which is the source of most of the world's oil reserves.

5. **Historical and Cultural Materialism** is a synthesis of Neo-Marxist and Neo-Freudian schools of thought in which history and culture are viewed as the material expressions of productive/reproductive processes, and the non-material culture (art, ideology and religion; social, cultural, political and legal institutions) is seen as driven, conditioned or determined by the material culture of the substructure (that is, the economic/ productive and sexual/reproductive relationships). Cultural materialists focus on historical contexts, power structures, cultural hegemony (the dominant ideology or world view of the ruling elites which governs the culture and validates and re-enforces cultural practices), marginalized groups and issues of gender, sexuality, race and class. Theodor Adorno, Erich Fromm, Jürgen Habermas, Marvin Harris, Max Horkheimer, Herbert Marcuse, Felix Weil, Raymond Williams. See 10. Economic/Technological Determinism and 11. Counterarguments to Economic/ Technological Determinism in Economics Details and 9. Cultural Materialism in Sociology Details.

6. **Annales School** is a school of history that focuses on the social histories and cultural practices of ordinary people, including their foods, fashions and social customs. It (1) uses the quantitative methods of the social sciences, (2) relies on original sources, such as court records and oral histories; (3) analyzes economic, social, cultural and geographical factors to reconstruct the daily lives, the collective *mentalités*, the underlying structures and the world views that shaped those cultures; (4) studies trends over long time periods (see *Longue durée* in Concepts) and resists the periodization of history and (5) focuses on common people rather than elites or specific individuals or events. Philippe Aries, Marc Bloch, Fernand Braudel, Lucien Febvre, Michel Foucault.

7. **New Social/Cultural History** is history from the bottom up, which was deeply influenced by the French Annales School. It (1) studies the histories of ordinary people and their daily lives, as opposed to the histories of "great men" or political, diplomatic, military or constitutional history; (2) focuses on micro-historical events that illuminate the wider cultural context (the "search for answers to large questions in small places"), which involves intensive investigations and case-studies of small events such as those of a community, a family or a person; (3) employs

quantitative methods and empirical techniques from the social sciences and (4) is characterized by its analytical, inter-disciplinary, anti-elitist and socially inclusive approach. Lynn Hunt, Lawrence Stone.

8. **Post-structuralism** is a school of literary criticism that views language and meaning as fluid and unstable and allows the validity of multiple truths and alternative interpretations. Historians influenced by post-structuralism tend to be suspicious of grand themes, orthodoxies, canons and meta-narratives, and give voice to the truths of the historically marginalized, including women, minorities, the voiceless and dispossessed. They focus on texts in terms of the cultural practices, structures of thought and the historical and material context in which they occurred rather than on methodology. R. G. Collingwood, Jacques Derrida, Michel Foucault, Julia Kristeva, Jacques Lacan. See J. A. Cuddon and Michael Bentley in Selected References.

6. LITERARY CONCEPTS

CONCEPTS AND PHRASES:

Aesthetic distance: the reader or viewer's simultaneous involvement with, and critical detachment from, a work, so that it can be appreciated aesthetically but not conflated with reality. J. A. Cuddon.

Affective fallacy: judging a work by its emotional effect on the reader or viewer. See Catharsis and Pathos in Concepts.

Afflatus ("to blow upon"): the divine breath of poetic inspiration.

Alienation effect: a technique in which the author or a character interrupts the work, steps outside the narrative and directly addresses the reader to remind it that the work is an illusion and to preserve a sense of detachment. The technique was used in Miguel de Cervantes' *Don Quixote*, Henry Fielding's *Tom Jones*, Lord Byron's *Don Juan*, Luigi Pirandello' s *Six Characters* and works by Jorge Luis Borges, Bertolt Brecht, Vladimir Nabokov and others. See Metafiction and Self-referentiality/reflexivity in Concepts.

Allegory: a story that uses character-types and projects at least two levels of meaning: a primary, or surface, meaning and a secondary, or below-the-surface, meaning, which are usually linked on a one-to-one basis. See *Pilgrim's Progress* in Concepts for an example.

Anagnorisis: the hero's tragic revelation or realization of the true nature of things. See 1. Aristotle in Details.

Anticlimax: the deliberate or unintended deflation of the rising dramatic tension by an abrupt, unexpected or trivial declension.

Anti-hero: a protagonist who does not project the traditional heroic qualities of bravery, good looks, charm, moral rectitude, etc. Antiheros range from the ordinary to the comic to the villainous; examples include Falstaff, Don Quixote, Leopold Bloom, Sam Spade, Holden Caulfield, Columbo and Shrek.

Apocrypha ("hidden away"): works whose authenticity has been questioned or ruled to be outside the officially recognized canon, such as the *Gospel of Thomas*.

Apologia: a formal defense of a belief or doctrine.

Aporia ("impassable path"): an impasse, puzzle or point of self-contradiction. For deconstructionists, it is the point at which the text undermines, dismantles and deconstructs itself. Jacques Derrida; J. A. Cuddon, William Harmon, Christopher Norris. See 3. Deconstructionism in Details.

Archetypes: in Jungian psychology, the innate, unconscious, universal symbols or pre-existent mental forms that are shared in the collective unconscious by all humans and are represented in myths, rituals and folklore; for example, the Hero, the Great Mother, the Warrior, the Mentor, the Martyr, the Trickster. Carl Jung; Joseph Campbell. See 7. Carl Jung in Psychology Details.

Aristotle's *Poetics*: see 1. Aristotle in Details.

Ars est celare artem ("it is true art to conceal art)": a phrase attributed to the Roman poet Ovid.

Art for art's sake (Aestheticism): the doctrine that every work of art provides its own unique, autonomous and intrinsic truth and aesthetic pleasure without reference to any didactic, moral or functional purpose. Edgar Allan Poe, James McNeill Whistler, Oscar Wilde; Harold Bloom, Walter Pater, Edmund Wilson. See Autotelic, Formalism, New Criticism and Symbolism in Concepts and Edgar Allan Poe in Quotations.

Autotelic: the proposition that each work of art tells its own truth in its own terms without reference to the biographical details of its creator or its cultural and historical context; a tenet of New Criticism and Formalism. It is presented in opposition to utilitarian, ideological and didactic art. See Art for art's sake, Formalism and New Criticism in Concepts and Edgar Allan Poe in Quotations

Bathos: overreaching sublimity or pathos, the effect of which is unintentionally humorous or absurd.

Belles-lettres ("beautiful letters"): fiction, poetry, drama, essays and letters that are light and entertaining, and are valued as much for their aesthetic qualities as for their informative or didactic value.

Biographical fallacy: that the character and biographical details of a writer's life can be read or inferred from the fictional works of the writer. See New Criticism in Concepts.

Black comedy/black humor (*humour noir*): a form of comedy in which horrific events, such as murder, suicide, cannibalism, nuclear war, etc. are portrayed in a comic or satirical manner. Examples are provided by Jonathan Swift's *Modest Proposal*, Stanley Kubrick's *Dr. Strangelove* and *Monty Python's The Meaning of Life*.

Catharsis: the purging, purifying or cleansing of the emotions, which is one of the purposes of art, according to Aristotle. See 1. Aristotle in Details.

Cautionary tale: a story in which the main character disregards a warning or social prohibition, performs a forbidden act and meets an unpleasant end. The genre was used in folklore to foster conformity to social norms.

Cento: a patchwork poem; a poem that contains passages drawn from other authors and works.

Character development: the process by which the central character changes and evolves during the course of the narrative and reaches a point of insight or understanding.

Chorus: in ancient Greek drama, a group of 12 to 24 performers who sang and danced as they provided commentary on the narrative as it unfolded and guided the audience in its emotional reaction to the action. The music track in a modern film is somewhat analogous.

Closet drama: a work that is intended to be read privately rather than performed on stage.

Codex: a book; a manuscript with flat sheets of paper or parchment that are folded, stacked and bound in a book format. The codex developed from the Roman wooden writing tablet and superseded the continuous scroll, which had been the preferred format of the ancient world until 300 to 500 CE. The book (German for "beech") format is associated with early Christians who preferred it for their Bible (Greek for "books") rather than the scroll, because it could be accessed randomly rather than sequentially and because both sides of the paper could be written on.

Comedy of manners: a form of comedy that satirizes the manners and affectations of a social class.

Comic relief: the insertion of a comic character or a humorous scene into a serious work in order to relieve the dramatic tension.

Commedia erudita: learned comedy, which was usually written by academics and performed by amateurs; versus *commedia dell'arte all'improvviso*: comedy of craft, which was improvised and performed by professional actors.

Content analysis: see Textual analysis in Concepts.

Content providers: writers and artists who provide artistic and creative content for the cultural production process. See Commodification in Art Concepts.

Critical theory: a term that refers to two different, but overlapping, schools of thought: (1) Neo-Marxist sociological criticism, which is a synthesis of Kant, Hegel, Marx, Weber and Freud and which is concerned with forms of social dominance and transformation (see 9. Cultural Materialism in Sociology Details); and (2) critical literary criticism, which is concerned with textual analysis, explanations and meanings; it uses hermeneutics to analyze and interpret texts and symbolic expressions and incorporates insights from Neo-Marxism, psychoanalysis, feminism, semiotics, structuralism, post-structuralism and deconstructionism. Jurgen Habermas.

Cultural hegemony: the dominant class's ideology, world view and construction of reality, which governs the text and validates and re-enforces cultural practices, according the tenets of cultural materialism. Antonio Gramsci, Raymond Williams. See 9. Cultural Materialism in Sociology Details.

Cultural literacy: the knowledge of, and familiarity with, a common body of cultural knowledge. The concept is usually identified with the Western cultural tradition and canon and has been criticized as being too Euro- and male-centric and for ignoring multiculturalism and the contributions of women and other historically marginalized groups. Mortimer Adler, Allan Bloom, E. D. Hirsch, and others. See Feminist criticism and Western canon/great books curricula in Concepts and 4. Post-structuralism in Details.

Death of the author/birth of the reader: a major tenet of deconstructionism and post-structuralism that the author is not the primary source of meaning for a text because individual readers bring their own cultural biases and assumptions to it, which creates multiple, fluid meanings; that the text is appropriated for meanings beyond the author's intention. Roland Barthes. See Reader-response theory in Concepts and 3. Deconstructionism and 4. Post-structuralism in Details.

Decode: to interpret the meaning of culturally encoded signs, symbols, texts and structures; a central feature of deconstructionism. See Deconstructionism in Concepts and 3. in Details.

Deconstructionism: a school of literary theory that focuses on the text ("there is nothing outside the text"). To deconstruct a text is to "undo" or dismantle it in order to identify and analyze the contradictions behind the text and to demonstrate the fundamental ambiguity, instability and indeterminacy of language. It asserts that every text has multiple, elusive, unstable and contradictory meanings that diverge from the author's intended meanings. Roland Barthes, Jacques Derrida. See Death of the author/birth of the reader in Concepts and 3. Deconstructionism in Details.

Denouement ("to untie"): the final unraveling, resolution or revelation of the plot, in which the mystery is solved, the villains are apprehended, peace is restored and the man and the woman live happily ever after.

Deus ex machina ("god from the machine"): a plot device in which an unsolvable problem in the drama is unexpectedly resolved in a contrived and improbable manner.

Didactic: a work whose purpose is to provide moral or educational instruction, as well as to entertain, which is a heresy, according to the tenets of New Criticism and the proponents of art-for-art's-sake.

Digital revolution/information technology: a technological and social revolution in which small lap-top boxes and hand-held mobile devices enable and empower social networks and virtual communities, as well as provide instantaneous access to global databases containing the sub-total of virtually all recorded human experience (down to the genetic level) via search engines, online digital libraries, electronic books, "aggregated" news, real-time video, peer networking and social media. The revolution has led to the decline of printed media, including books, magazines and newspapers, and has

fostered the breakdown of social and political hierarchies.
Marshall McLuhan, John Naisbitt. For the ways in which
technology has altered human cognition and social structures,
see Printing press in Concepts, Marshall McLuhan in
Quotations, 10. Economic/Technological Determinism in
Economics Details and 23. Marshall McLuhan and 24.
Information Technology/Metaphor of the Machine in
Sociology Details.

Dramatic irony: a literary device in which the audience is aware
of a critical dramatic point but the protagonist is not. See
Irony in Concepts.

Dramatis personae: the characters in a drama.

Emendations: corrections and/or improvements to a text.

Épistème (Greek for "knowledge"): the underlying, often
unconscious, knowledge structure, or set of beliefs and
assumptions, that govern social behavior, such as *a priori* rules
of grammar. This underlying structure, which consists of
binary oppositions (e.g., male/female, rational/emotional,
signifier/signified), shapes and makes experience meaningful
through the use of concepts, language and signs. Jacques
Foucault. See New Historicism in Concepts and 2.
Structuralism in Details.

Errata: errors in the text that are identified by the author,
publisher or others.

Exegesis: a critical analysis, explanation or interpretation of a text.

Exegete: an official interpreter of dreams, omens and sacred texts;
a cultural critic.

Faust: a fictional scholar who sold his soul to the devil for 24
years in return for unlimited knowledge and worldly pleasures.
Christopher Marlowe, Johann Wolfgang von Goethe.

Feminist criticism: a school of literary criticism that raises "new
questions of old texts" from a feminist perspective. It focuses
on power relationships, the rediscovery of women writers and
how women have been represented in literature. It discusses
the notion of an *écriture feminine* and whether there is a
characteristic feminine imagination, language and style.
Simone de Beauvoir, Mary Ellman, Margaret Fuller, Sandra
Gilbert, Susan Gubar, Julia Kristeva, Kate Millett, Toril Moi,

Judith Newton, Elaine Showalter, Lisa Tuttle, Virginia Woolf. See 4. Post-structuralism in Details.

Figures of speech: words or phrases that transcend their literal meaning. Generally, figures of speech are classified as (1) **metaphors** (in which something is described in terms of something else, such as "all the world is a stage"); (2) **similes** (in which two objects are compared, using like or as, such as "she sings like an angel"); (3) **hyperbole** (exaggeration and overstatement, such as "he eats like a horse"); (4) **irony** (in which the intended meaning is the opposite of the literal meaning, such as "he looks malnourished"); (5) **meiosis/litotes** (understatement, such as "she eats like a bird"); (6) **metonymy** (in which an attribute or something closely associated with it is substituted for the thing itself, such as "the stage," "the press," "the throne," "the bench"); (7) **personification** (in which an abstract concept or an inanimate object is endowed with human qualities, such as "beauty's ignorant ear") and (8) **synecdoche** (a form of metonymy in which the part stands for the whole; e.g., "hired hand" for employee). See Trope in Concepts and J. A. Cuddon in Selected References.

Folio: a book or pamphlet that consists of full sheets of paper on each of which is printed four pages of text, two on each side. Folding the folio once, produces two leaves and four pages. *Recto* is the page on the right and *verso* is the page on the left.

Formalism: a school of criticism in which the value of a work is determined by its form, structure and essence rather than by its content or context. See Autotelic and New Criticism in Concepts.

Genetic fallacy: that the explanation of an subject can be found it its origins or essence; versus existentialism, in which its meaning is found in its immediate existence, action and effect. See 37. Existentialism in Philosophy/Religion Details.

Gothic novel: a genre that was popular in the late 18th and early 19th Centuries. It featured supernatural tales of mystery and horror; was often set in the Middle Ages and was populated with dark forests, castles and dungeons, hidden passageways, ghosts, witches, villains, torture, bloodshed, etc. Charles Brockden Brown, Edgar Allen Poe, Ann Radcliffe, Mary Shelley, Horace Walpole.

Heresy of paraphrase: a tenet of New Criticism, which is that, since a poem is autonomous, autotelic and indivisible and provides a statement of experience rather than a statement about experience ("a poem should not mean but be"), it cannot be reduced or paraphrased. Cleanth Brooks, Archibald MacLeish. See New Criticism and Ontology in Concepts and Aura in Art Concepts.

Hermeneutics/hermeneutic circle: the analysis, interpretation and explanation of written texts (originally, religious texts) in order to understand their symbolic and, often, hidden or secret meaning. The circle refers to the fact that, often, the whole text can only be understood in reference to its parts, and its parts can only be understood in reference to the whole. Wilhelm Dilthey, Jürgen Habermas, Martin Heidegger, Paul Ricœur, Max Weber. See Semiotics and Deconstructionism in Concepts.

Higher criticism: the study of the authorship and meaning of Biblical texts by using historical evidence, scientific techniques, literary criticism, comparative analysis, etc.; versus **lower criticism**: the study of the textual accuracy of Biblical texts, including the identification and elimination of transcription errors.

Homily: a sermon; the commentary following the reading of scripture.

Horizon of expectations: a shared set of assumptions that, at a given point in time, is used in judging a work. Hans Jauss. See Reader-response theory in Concepts.

Hypertexts/hypermedia: electronic texts that are dynamically linked to other texts, images, maps and sounds and can be instantly cross-referenced. Hyperlinks replace "*q.v.*" (an abbreviation of *quod vide*, for "which see"), which, in printed texts, reference related terms found elsewhere in the same work. George Landow. See Intertextuality in Concepts and 24. Information Technology/Metaphor of the Machine in Sociology Details.

Illuminated manuscripts: handwritten manuscripts decorated with elaborate and colorful rubrics, illustrations, marginalia and lettering, often in gold leaf. They were produced primarily in monasteries but also, later, in commercial scriptoria during the 1200s through the 1400s. It is thought that medieval scribes copied or reproduced as few as two manuscripts a year. See Codex, Printing press and Scriptorium in Concepts.

Implied reader: in reader-response theory, the hypothesized ideal reader who is necessary for the text to achieve its full effect; versus the actual reader who may be unwilling or unable to accept the assumptions of the text. See Reader-response theory in Concepts.

Incunabula: books and pamphlets that were printed before 1501.

Indeterminacy: the concept that texts have no fixed meaning and can be interpreted in multiple ways; a tenet of post-structuralism. See 4. Post-structuralism in Details.

In medias res ("into the middle of things"): a narrative that begins in the middle of the action, as occurred in Homer's *Iliad*, which started during the middle of the Trojan war; as opposed to **ab ovo**, a narrative that begins at the beginning or origin (or "egg") of the action.

Intentional fallacy: that a work reflects its creator's intentions. See Death of the author and *Lacuna* in Concepts and 3. Deconstructionism in Details.

Interior monologue: the expression of a character's thoughts as they occur, which may be in the form of stream of consciousness, in which half-thoughts, impressions and perceptions, often ungrammatical and illogical, are expressed. The technique was used by T. S. Eliot, James Joyce, Marcel Proust and Virginia Woolf.

Intertextuality: the post-structural concept that every text is an interdependent mosaic of fragments and quotations that represents the absorption and transformation of other texts; or, to paraphrase Jacque Derrida, the endless chain of signifiers leading to other signifiers. Jacques Derrida, Julia Kristeva. See Hypertexts/hypermedia and Trace in Concepts.

Irony ("dissimulation" or "feigned ignorance"): a literary device in which the literal meaning is the opposite of the intended meaning; in which what is said is the opposite of what is meant. In classical Greek theater, the *eirôn* was a self-deprecating character who would defeat his boastful adversary by pretending to be more ignorant and naive than he was, thereby inducing his opponent to reveal his contradictions and absurdities. See Dramatic irony in Concepts and Socratic irony in 11. Philosophy/Religion Details.

Lacuna: a gap or missing portion in the text; in deconstructionism, the gap between what the text "means to say and what it is . . . constrained to mean." Jacques Derrida. See 3. Deconstructionism in Details.

Legenda: a group or list of "things to be read." It is usually constrained by a lower asymptotic limit that approaches but never reaches zero.

Library: traditionally, a collection of books, manuscripts, printed and visual materials, records and documents. The ancient library of Alexandria may have contained 200,000 or more papyrus scrolls. It was destroyed in 391 CE, perhaps, by order of Theophilus, Christian Bishop of Alexandria. The United States Library of Congress contains approximately 30 million books. Online universal digital libraries, such as that maintained by Google, contain approximately 30 million scanned books. See Digital revolution/information technology in Concepts.

Ligne donnée: an inspirational "line given" to a poet by God or a muse. Paul Valéry. See Afflatus in Concepts.

Linguistics: the study of language, which includes (1) **grammar** (the rules governing the use of words, clauses and sentences), (2) **syntax** (the construction of sentences), (3) **phonetics** (speech sounds), (4) **semantics** (the study of meanings), (5) **etymology** (the origin and evolution of words and their meanings) and (6) **pragmatics** (how meaning is inferred from context and intention).

Literary immortality: a concept that is associated with the 18th Century Enlightenment's belief in posterity as a substitute for the loss of faith in God and an afterlife. The historian Will Durant reminds us that literary immortality represents a couple of seconds in geological time. Carl Becker. See Posterity as a substitute for God and immortality in Historiography Concepts.

Literati: men and women of letters; intellectuals who read, write and comment on literature and the public issues of the day. See Public intellectual and Republic of letters in Concepts and Intelligentsia in Sociology Concepts.

Literature of silence: Ihab Hassan's meditation on Samuel Beckett, the art of nothingness and the roots of postmodernism. See Cage's *4'33"* in Art Concepts, Federico Fellini in Art Quotations and 25. Postmodernism in Art Details.

Magical realism: a type of fiction that mixes realism and surrealism by introducing imaginary, fantastic, dream-like characters, images and sequences into the natural world of the narrative and treating them as real. Jorge Luis Borges, Gabriel Garcia Marquez.

Magnum opus: an artist's "great work." See Masterpiece in Concepts.

Marginalia: comments or annotations that are made in the margins of a book.

Masterpiece: originally, a work produced by a journeyman to qualify for advancement to a master craftsman in his guild, such as a gold cup or salt cellar for a goldsmith's guild; now, an outstanding work of an artist or writer. See Guild system in Economics.

Mentalités: the term used by the *Annalistes* to describe the attitudes, collective psychology, world view and mindset of a particular culture at a particular time See 6. Annales School in Historiography Details.

Metafiction: fiction that reflexively refers to itself as a work of fiction by having, for example, the story or the characters within the story comment on the story itself. Examples are provided in the works of John Barth, Jorges Luis Borges, Lord Byron, Miguel de Cervantes, Geoffrey Chaucer, Henry Fielding, Vladimir Nabokov, Luigi Pirandello and Kurt Vonnegut. See Alienation effect and Romantic irony in Concepts.

Meta-language: language about language. Roland Barthes. See 2. Structuralism, 3. Deconstructionism and 4. Post-structuralism in Details.

Metaphor ("carrying from one place to another"): a thing that is described in terms of something else, e.g., "all the world is a stage." See Figures of speech in Concepts.

Mock epic: a form of satire in which a trivial subject, such as a lock of hair or a common bodily function, is treated in a grand, inflated, satirical manner. Alexander Pope, Mark Twain.

Morality play: one that portrays the struggle between good and evil; **miracle play**: one that depicts the lives of Christian saints and divine miracles and **mystery play**: one that represents the Crucifixion and the Last Judgment.

Narratee: the reader or audience to whom the narration is addressed.

Narrative: the plot or storyline; the sequence of events in a story, with a beginning, middle and end; the exposition, development, climax and conclusion. See Plot in Concepts.

Narrative point of view: the perspective from which the story is told. The narration may be in (1) the **first-person** ("I"/"we"), in which the narrator is a character in the story, or (2) the **third-person** ("he"/"she"/"they"), in which the narrator may be (a) **omniscient** (i. e, as one who knows the thoughts and feelings of all the characters); (b) **limited** (who knows what's going on in the mind of one character) or (c) **objective** (who describes only the external events, behaviors, dialogue and actions of the characters, but not their thoughts and feelings).

New Criticism: a school of literary criticism that emphasizes the autonomy of the work itself, independent of its creator's biographical details or its historical context, and focuses on a close reading of the text; versus New Historicism. See Autotelic, Biographical fallacy, Formalism, Heresy of paraphrase and New Historicism in Concepts.

New Historicism: a school of literary criticism that was influenced by the Annales School, in which texts are understood in terms of the cultural practices, structures of thought (*épistèmes*) and historical and material contexts in which they occur and views literature as inseparable from its cultural and historical context; versus the tenets of New Criticism. Louis Althusser, Clifford Geertz, Stephen Greenblatt, Raymond Williams. See New Criticism in Concepts, 4. Post-structuralism in Details and 6. Annales School in Historiography Details.

Objective correlatives: the means by which a particular emotion is evoked in the reader, according to T. S. Eliot; the external factors which elicit an emotion; that is, "a set of objects, a situation, a chain of events, which shall be the formula of that particular emotion."

Ontology: the texture and structure of a poem that give it "being." John Crowe Ransom. See Heresy of paraphrase and New Criticism in Concepts and Aura in Art Concepts.

Oral tradition: in non-literate societies (i.e., those without a written language), the primary method for transmitting cultural traditions and history from one generation to the next, using speeches, songs, poems and folktales. The *Iliad*, for example, was recited from memory and not written down until the 8th Century BCE, approximately 400 years after the events it celebrates.

Oxymoron: a rhetorical paradox; a figures of speech in which two contradictory concepts are combined; for example, Oscar Wilde's "life is too important to be taken seriously," or "it is only the superficial qualities that last."

Palimpsest: a piece of paper or parchment whose original text has been scrapped away so that it can be used again. In some cases, the original underwriting, or *scriptio inferior*, can be deciphered under the subsequent texts.

Paperback revolution: a landmark in the democratization of knowledge, since it made both popular works and literary classics affordable to mass audiences. It began with *The American Library of Vital Knowledge* in the early 19th Century, continued with the pamphlets, railroad yellow-backs and dime novels of the late 19th Century, and culminated in the inexpensive paperbacks of Penguin and Pocket Books in the 1930s and the Modern Library in the 1950s. See Digital revolution/information technology in Concepts.

Parent-poems: those that represent the poet's influence by, and attempt to achieve independence from, precursor or father/mother-poems. Harold Bloom.

Parody: an exaggerated or satirical imitation of another work.

Pathetic fallacy: ascribing human qualities and emotions to nature.

Pathos ("suffering"): appealing to an audience's emotions; evoking pity, sympathy or sorrow. See Affective fallacy and Catharsis in Concepts.

Peripeteia: the turning point or reversal of circumstances; the hero's tragic reversal of fortune. Aristotle.

Persona ("mask"): an individual's public character, social role or identity. See Persona in Psychology Concepts and 7. Carl Jung in Psychology Details.

Picaresque novel: a genre that portrays the adventures of a carefree rogue or rascal who lives by his wits on the lower margins of society.

Pilgrim's Progress (1678): John Bunyan's allegory of "Christian," the protagonist, and his pilgrimage from the City of Destruction through the Slough of Despond to Vanity Fair and the Celestial City, and the characters he meets along the way, including Mr. Worldly Wiseman, Prudence, Faithful, Lord Hate-Good, Mrs. Timorous, Mrs. Light-Mind and Mr. Stand-Fast. See Allegory in Concepts.

Pirandello's *Six Characters in Search of an Author*: a 1921 play by Luigi Pirandello in which six unfinished characters unexpectedly show up at the rehearsal for another play in search of an author to finish their own play, forming a play within a play and representing an early example of the theater of the absurd. See Alienation effect and Metafiction in Concepts.

Plot: the pattern or sequence of events in the movement of a story; the narrative structure, which consists of the exposition (in which background information and the premise of the story are presented), development, rising action, conflict, climax and turning point, falling action and resolution. See Narrative in Concepts.

Poetic justice: a condition in which virtue is rewarded and vice is punished, often by the vice itself, as when, for example, in *Hamlet*, the villains are hoisted by their own petard (an explosive device), or, alternately, by their own flatulence ("petar").

Post ironic: a term derived from postmodernism in which, since everything is presumed to be ironic, any overt expression of irony is thought to be redundant.

Postmodernism: a vernacular style and a cultural philosophy. See 25. Postmodernism in Art Details.

Post-structuralism: a critical literary theory that is often, but incorrectly, identified with and subsumed under postmodernism. See 4. Post-structuralism in Details.

Presence: see Ontology and Trace in Concepts and Aura in Art Concepts.

Printing press: a machine that uses moveable metal type which was invented by Johannes Gutenberg in the 1440s and is used in the mass production of books, pamphlets, newspapers and tracts. The invention created a social revolution by: (1) popularizing books and other forms of printed materials by making them less expensive than hand-written versions; (2) democratizing learning by encouraging literacy and facilitating the study of vernacular (i.e., non-Latin) languages; (3) enabling the printing of vernacular Bibles and religious and secular literature and (4) accelerating the spread of the Protestant "heresy" in the 16th and 17th Centuries. Today approximately 300,000 new books titles are printed in the United States each year. See Digital revolution and Scriptorium in Concepts, Ecclesiastes in Quotations and 10. Economic/Technological Determinism in Economics Details and 18. Protestant Reformation in Philosophy/Religion Details.

Readerly versus **writerly texts**: the former contain recognizable characters and events which the reader accepts passively without having to make much effort to understand as the work is "consumed"; the latter focuses the reader's attention on the text itself and how it is written and requires the reader to make an effort to find meaning and "produce" the text. Roland Barthes; J.A. Cuddon.

Reader-response theory: that the reader is an active agent who brings his or her own cultural biases and assumptions to the text, which creates multiple, fluid meanings and, thus, insures that the text is appropriated for meanings beyond the author's intention. It is a major tenet of deconstructionism and post-structuralism. Roland Barthes, Hans-Robert Jauss. See Death of the author/birth of the reader in Concepts and 3. Deconstructionism and 4. Post-Structuralism in Details.

Reading revolution: the shift in practice, beginning in the mid-18th Century, from reading a small number of books repeatedly and, often, aloud to a small audience to reading many books extensively and alone. The term also refers to the Protestant Reformation's emphasis on the scriptures as a means of individual salvation, which led to vernacular translations of the Bible from Latin, an increase in popular literacy and the ideal of a learned clergy. Rolf Engelsing.

Read-write asymmetry: the relative ease in reading, appreciating or criticizing a work of literature compared to the difficulty in writing one.

The Real Thing: the title of a short story by Henry James, Jr. in which the author suggests that the artistic illusion is often more authentic than the reality itself. In the story, an artist's professional models portray an older patrician couple in genteel poverty with much more verisimilitude than the actual patrician couple themselves, who are self-conscious about being painted.

Republic of letters: a virtual community of men and women of letters in the 18th Century Enlightenment who exchanged ideas and engaged in the "free examination of questions" across international and social boundaries. See 27. 18th Century Enlightenment in Philosophy/Religion Details.

Roman à clef ("novel with a key"): a novel or film that portrays real people and actual events but with fictitious names; Orson Welles' *Citizen Kane* is an example.

Romantic irony: the critical awareness by the author that his or her work is not to be taken literally or seriously, and invites the reader to share this ironic and, even, comic point of view. Examples include works by Jorges Luis Borges, Miguel de Cervantes, Geoffrey Chaucer, Henry Fielding, Vladimir Nabokov, Luigi Pirandello, Johnathan Swift and Mark Twain.

Scriptorium: a room in medieval monasteries in which scribes copied manuscripts by hand, perhaps as few as two a year. Today, approximately 300,000 new book titles are published each year. See Printing press in Concepts and Ecclesiastes in Quotations.

Self-referentiality/reflexivity: self-awareness; works that reference themselves and their creators; for example, those by Jorge Luis Borges, Miguel de Cervantes, Vladimir Nabokov, Luigi Pirandello and Kurt Vonnegut. See Alienation effect, Metafiction and Romantic irony in Concepts.

Semiotics: the study of systems of communication and modes of signification (meaning); the study of signs as a method of conveying information and their relationship to meaning. In semiotics, signs (signifiers) are ascribed meaning (signification) through structures, codes and systems, which serve to convey information through media as varied as spoken and written language, pheromones, body language, hand gestures, food, clothing, traffic signs, etc. For example, a bottle of wine or a picture of a bottle of wine (the signifier) may evoke a mental image of a quiet, relaxing drinking experience or an image of an elitist snob snacking on hors d'oeuvres or an image of a French chateau and vineyard (the signified). Roland Barthes, James Gleick, Charles Peirce, Ferdinand de Saussure. See 2. Structuralism in Details and Sexual/courtship displays and rituals in Anthropology Concepts.

Source analysis: tracing the influences of other artists on a particular work; also, analyzing and interpreting the content, context and significance of a work's sources.

Stream of consciousness: see Interior monologue in Concepts. William James, James Joyce.

Subtext: that which is implied or suggested but not explicitly stated in the text itself. See 3. Deconstructionism in Details.

Symbol: something that stands for something more than its literal self; a concrete object or image which is used to represent or convey multiple meanings. Examples include Miguel de Cervantes's windmills, Herman Melville's great white whale, Nathaniel Hawthorne's scarlet letter and Marcel Proust's madeleine.

Symbolic consciousness: the ability to symbolize, to see one thing in terms of another, to invest meaning in the world, which represents "the most characteristic mental trait of mankind," according to Susanne Langer (*q.v.* in Quotations).

Symbolism/Imagism: a school of literature represented by the works of Charles Baudelaire, T. S. Eliot, James Joyce, Edgar Allan Poe, Marcel Proust, Arthur Rimbaud, Gertrude Stein, Paul Valery, W. B. Yeats and Auguste Villiers, whose images and symbols have been described by Edmund Wilson (in *Axel's Castle*) as evocative, dreamlike, fantastical, symphonic, opaque and ineffable. In the case of Villiers, Baudelaire and Rimbaud, the artists renounced the external world and lived in interior exile, since "reality never equals the dream." See Edmund Wilson in Selected References.

Text (Latin for "fabric" or "to weave"): written information that is conveyed through various media such as letters, pamphlets, books, traffic signs, e-mails or tweets. "After you have chosen your words, they must be weaved together into a fine and delicate fabric [*textum*]" -- Quintilian. See 2. Structuralism in Details.

Textual analysis/criticism: (1) New Criticism's close reading of the text, with minimal references to the author or the cultural context; or (2) Neo-Marxism's critical theory and post-structuralism's use of hermeneutics to analyze and interpret the social or hidden meaning of texts and symbolic expressions, their relationships to power structures and their fluid and indeterminate nature. Jurgen Habermas. See New Criticism in Concepts and 4. Post-structuralism in Details.

Theater of the absurd: a school of drama that offers a tragicomic view of the seemingly meaninglessness and absurdity of human existence. The school is represented in the works of Edward Albee, Samuel Beckett, Jean Genet, Eugene Ionesco and Luigi Pirandello. See Tragic fallacy in Concepts and 37. Existentialism in Philosophy/Religion Details.

Trace: Jacques Derrida's concept that every sign contains traces (or connotations) of other signs. Since speech and writing lack "pure presence," the trace echoes this absence of presence and exposes the "*differance*," or contradiction, between the sign and its binary opposite, leading to an endless chain of signifiers leading to other signifiers. See Intertextuality and Semiotics in Concepts and 3. Deconstructionism in Details.

Tragedy (Greek for "goat song," which may have referred to the prize awarded to the winning entry in a drama contest): see 1. Aristotle in Details.

Tragic fallacy: that, to the modern temper, the concept of man's nobility is absurd. Joseph Wood Krutch. See 37. Existentialism in Philosophy/Religion and 4. Sigmund Freud in Psychology Details.

Tragic flaw: see 1. Aristotle in Details.

Trans-historical: the timelessness of a work of art; a pejorative term when used by postmodernists. Mieke Bal, Hans-Georg Gadamer. See Ontology in Concepts.

Trope: a figure of speech; also, a commonly used theme, motif, literary device or cliché. See Figures of speech in Concepts.

Understatement: that which deliberately and ironically minimizes the significance of something, thereby exaggerating its rhetorical effect. See Figures of speech in Concepts.

Universal in the particular: one of the effects of a work of art, which is to reveal a universal truth or an insight through the particularities of the work itself. See Aristotle and Pablo Picasso in Art Quotations.

Variorum: a compilation of various editions of a literary work, which compares textual variants and emendations and provides critical notes and commentary.

Vernacular: originally, a form of Latin that was spoken by native-born slaves; now, generally, a native language or dialect that is spoken or written in an informal, conversational style. The term also applies to the functional, utilitarian art and culture of everyday life. See Vernacular tradition in Art Concepts.

Western canon/great books curricula: a set of "classic" literary and scientific works that represents the orthodox canon or cultural tradition of Western civilization. The concept has been criticized as being too Euro- and male-centric and for ignoring multiculturalism and the contributions of women and other historically marginalized groups. Mortimer Adler, Allan Bloom, E. D. Hirsch. See Cultural literacy and Feminist criticism in Concepts and 4. Post-structuralism in Details.

Willing suspension of disbelief: the willingness of the reader or the audience to accept the implausibility or unreality of the narrative; the *sine qua non* of storytelling. Samuel Coleridge.

QUOTATIONS:

- *Of the making of many books there is no end. .--* Ecclesiastes.

- *Therefore, Simplicio, come either with arguments and demonstrations and bring us no more texts and authorities, for our disputes are about the sensible world, and not one of paper.* -- Galileo.

- *The greatest possible merit of style is, of course, to make the words absolutely disappear into the thought.* -- Nathaniel Hawthorne.

- *We have taken it into our heads . . . to write a poem simply for the poem's sake. . . . Would we but permit ourselves to look into our own souls we should immediately there discover that under the sun there neither exists nor can exist any work more thoroughly dignified, more supremely noble, than this very poem, this poem per se, this poem which is a poem and nothing more, this poem written solely for the poem's sake.* -- Edgar Allan Poe.

- *When I use a word . . .* it means just what I choose it to mean. – Humpty Dumpty in Lewis Carroll' s *Through the Looking Glass.*

- *Everything in the world exists to end up in a book.* -- Stéphane Mallarmé.

- *A complete poem is one where an emotion has found its thought and the thought has found its words.* -- Robert Frost.

- *The power of understanding symbols, i.e. of regarding everything about a sense-datum as irrelevant except a certain form that it embodies, is the most characteristic mental trait of mankind. It issues in an unconscious, spontaneous process of abstraction, which goes on all the time in the human mind: a process of recognizing the concept in any configuration given to experience, and forming a conception accordingly.* -- Susanne Langer.

- *The real is what resists symbolization absolutely.* -- Jacques Lacan.

- *Schizophrenia may be a necessary consequence of literacy.* -- Marshall McLuhan.

- *The printing press, the computer, and television are not therefore simply machines which convey information. They are metaphors through which we conceptualize reality. . . . We do not see the world as it is. We see it as our coding systems are.* -- McLuhan.

- *There is nothing outside the text.* -- Jacques Derrida.

- *Interpretation is the revenge of the intellect upon art.* -- Susan Sontag.

- *Deconstruction is an attempt to go through the looking glass, to get beyond or behind language. . . . We bring to a text mental habits that fix the meaning of the words, and then we attribute that meaning to the words.* -- Louis Menand.

LITERARY CONCEPTS DETAILS: (1) Aristotle, (2) Structuralism, (3) Deconstructionism and (4) Post-structuralism.

1. **Aristotle** defined art as the imitation (*mimesis*) and perfection of nature. In *Poetics*, he proposed that the purpose of drama is to purge, purify and cleanse the emotions (*catharsis*). He identified the essential elements of the drama as (1) character (*ethos*), (2) plot (*mythos*), (3) dialogue or speech (*lexis*), (4) spectacle (*opsis*), (5) the hero's miscalculation or tragic flaw (*hamartia*), (6) the reversal of fortune (*peripeteia*) and (7) the hero's tragic revelation or realization (*anagnorisis*) of the true nature of things.

2. **Structuralism** is a school of thought that studies the underlying, often unconscious, structures, or sets of beliefs and assumptions that govern social behavior, such as kinship patterns, rituals, myths

and *a priori* rules of grammar. These underlying structures (or *épistèmes*), which consist of binary oppositions (e.g., male/female, rational/emotional, speech/writing, signifier/signified), shape and make experience meaningful through the use of concepts, language and signs.

In semiotics, signs (signifiers) are ascribed meaning (signification) through these structures, codes and systems, which serve to convey information through means as diverse as spoken and written language, pheromones, body language, hand gestures, food, clothing, traffic signs, etc. For example, a bottle of wine or a picture of a bottle of wine (the signifier) may evoke a mental image of a quiet, relaxing drinking experience or an image of an elitist snob snacking on hors d'oeuvres or an image of a French chateau and vineyard (the signified).

Structuralism has been criticized for being (1) two-dimensional (with a one-to-one relationship between the signifier and the signified) and (2) deterministic (with the meaning fixed as constant and universal) and for failing to recognize (3) the hegemonic/power relationships from which those structures are derived. Roland Barthes, Noam Chomsky, Michel Foucault, Immanuel Kant, Julia Kristiva, Thomas Kuhn, Claude Lévi-Strauss, Charles Peirce, Ferdinand de Saussure. See Cultural hegemony and Semiotics in Concepts, 4. Post-structuralism in Details and J. A. Cuddon in Selected References.

3. **Deconstructionism** is a school of post-structural critical thought that focuses on the text ("there is nothing outside the text"). To deconstruct a text is to "undo" or dismantle it by identifying and analyzing the contradictions behind it and the *"différances"* (or variances) in its elements, thereby demonstrating the fundamental ambiguity, instability and indeterminacy of language and the deferral of meaning. Deconstructionism asserts that every text has multiple, elusive and contradictory meanings that diverge from the author's intended meanings through the decentering, displacement and "death of the author" and the "birth of the reader." According to Louis Menand, "deconstruction is an attempt to go through the looking glass, to get beyond or behind language. . . . We bring to a text mental habits that fix the meaning of the words, and then we attribute that meaning to the words." Roland Barthes, Paul de

Man, Jacques Derrida; Jacques Lacan. See Death of the author/birth of the reader and Reader-response theory in Concepts.

4. **Post-structuralism** is a school of critical thought that encompasses and extends deconstructionism by focusing on the context as well as on the text; that is, it studies both the object (the text) and the systems of knowledge that produced the object. It explores the ways in which history, cultural assumptions and norms and social hierarchies and hegemonic relationships serve to condition underlying structures and conceptual relationships. It contends that language and meaning are fluid and unstable; that texts are social constructs that reflect power relationships and point to other texts, not to an external, objective reality, and defends the validity of multiple truths and alternative interpretations.

    Post-structuralists focus on the ways in which "language is oppression" and attempt to undermine the hierarchical nature of structuralism's binary opposites of dominate and subservient elements. They celebrate "the insurrection of subjugated knowledges" (Michel Foucault) by showing, for example, that gender identity and gender differences are socially coerced constructions that enforce cultural hegemony (Judith Butler). Roland Barthes, Judith Butler, Jacques Derrida, Michel Foucault, Julia Kristeva, Jacque Lacan. See Critical theory, Feminist criticism, New Historicism, Indeterminacy and Intertextuality in Concepts, Decentered self in Psychology Concepts and J. A. Cuddon in Selected References. Post-structuralism has been criticized for being relativistic and nihilistic (see, for example, Alan Sokal in Sociology Quotations).

    Post-structuralism should not to be confused with **postmodernism**, although both share a common conceptual framework of indeterminacy and the belief that there is no objective truth; that reality is socially constructed and that social dynamics and power hierarchies play a critical role in conceptual relationships. Post-structuralism is a literary theory and school of critical thought, while postmodernism is a broader, more inclusive cultural term and, more specifically, a cultural philosophy and a vernacular style. See 25. Postmodernism in Art Details.

7. PHILOSOPHY/RELIGION

CONCEPTS AND PHRASES:

Agape: divine or altruistic love; God's love for humans and humans love for God and for one another; "God is love" (John 4). See Situational ethics in Concepts.

Agency: the capacity to make free, independent decisions and choices. See Autonomy, Cultural hegemony and Reflexivity in Concepts.

Age of Reason/18th-Century Enlightenment: an intellectual movement, philosophy and world view that celebrated human reason, science and progress; it was optimistic, secular and humanistic and opposed religious dogma, ignorance and superstition. See 28. 18th-Century Enlightenment in Details.

Agnosticism: the doctrine that the existence of God cannot be proven or disproven.

Anima: Latin for breath, soul, life or spirit.

Animism: the belief that all entities and objects in nature have a soul or spiritual essence.

Anthropomorphic god: see Greek cosmology in Concepts.

Anticlerical: a term that originated in the 18th Century and was applied to those who opposed the Roman Catholic Church for its political power, secrecy, censorship and patriarchy, as well as its sanction of reactionary governments and its opposition to the separation of church and state. More recently, the term has been applied to those who oppose Islamic clerics and theocrats.

Antinomianism: the belief that those who are "chosen" or "elected" by God are above traditional social constraints; a form of spiritual anarchism. The abolitionist William Lloyd Garrison, for example, described himself as "a minority of one with God"; to Paul Tillich, "love is the ultimate law." Anne Hutchinson, Henry David Thoreau, Bob Dylan. See Autonomy, Civil disobedience, Higher

law and Situational ethics in Concepts and Perry Miller and Stow
Persons in Selected References.

Apocalypse (Greek for "uncovering" or revelation): popularly, the
"end time" or the end of the world, in which, in various Abrahamic
traditions, after a period of tribulations, the Messiah will return and
the righteous will receive everlasting life. See Armageddon,
Eschatology and Millennialism in Concepts.

Apostate: one who renounces or abandons one's faith.

Arete: to the ancient Greeks, excellence, valor, virtue, knowledge;
fulfilling one's potential. See Eudemonia in Concepts and 13.
Aristotle in Details.

Argument from design: the doctrine that the existence of God can be
deduced from the intelligent design of the universe; that a watch
implies a watchmaker. See Deism in Concepts and 27. 18th
Century Enlightenment/Age of Reason in Details.

Arianism: the belief that Christ is the son of God but not God himself;
that God the Father is separate from, and greater than, Christ the
Son. Arianism was declared to be a heresy by the Council of
Nicaea in 325 CE; versus **Athanasianism/Trinitarianism**: the
belief that God, Christ and the Holy Spirit are equal aspects of the
same substance, or "one God in three persons," which is the
official doctrine of the Roman Catholic Church as promulgated in
the Nicene Creeds of 325 and 381. See Trinitarianism versus non-
Trinitarianism in Concepts.

Armageddon: the final, decisive battle between the forces of good and
the forces of evil, as prophesized in the Book of Revelation. See
Apocalypse and Millennialism in Concepts.

Asceticism (Greek for "exercise" or "training"): the practice of
abstaining from worldly pleasures in order to achieve a higher
level of spirituality.

Ataraxia (Greek for "tranquility"): the Epicurean concept of
tranquility, peace of mind, freedom from anxiety and emotional
conflict. See Epicureanism in Concepts.

Atonement: to provide reparation for an offense, injury or
transgression; the pardoning or forgiving of sins and
transgressions. For Christians, it is achieved through the
crucifixion and resurrection of Jesus Christ and his teachings and
moral example ("and forgive us our debts, as we forgive our
debtors"), but also through prayer, confession, repentance, fasting
and leading a virtuous life. For Jews, it is achieved through
repentance, service, sacrifice, confession, restitution, fasting and

prayer, tribulations and punishment or death. For Moslems, it is achieved through prayer, alms-giving, fasting and pilgrimage. See Confession, Penance and Repentance in Concepts.

Autonomy (Greek for "self" and "law"): moral self-determination; "the ability to impose objective moral law on oneself" -- Immanuel Kant. See Agency, Antinomianism, Higher law and Situational ethics in Concepts.

Banality of evil: Hannah Arendt's thesis that horrific acts of evil can be carried out by ordinary people who identify with an evil leader or an evil ideology; "the normalizing of the unthinkable." According to Arendt, the horrors of the Holocaust were committed by amoral, if dedicated, knowledgeable and zealous bureaucrats in the mundane manner of an impersonal, factory assembly line. Arendt's thesis has been challenged on the grounds that the subject of her inquiry, Adolf Eichmann, although not a psychopath, was a zealous anti-Semite who believed in Nazi ideology and the Final Solution. Hannah Arendt, Edward Herman.

Bhagavad Gita: the Hindu epic poem, scripture and devotional text, which was composed in the 5th or 4th Century BCE. See *Bhagavad Gita* in Quotations.

Bodhisattva: in Buddhism, an enlightened being; one who is on the path to enlightenment, or one who delays enlightenment in order to help others achieve enlightenment.

Bodhi tree: the fig tree under which Siddhartha Gautama (563-483 BCE), the founder of Buddhism, attained enlightenment.

Brahma: in Hinduism, the creator of the world.

Calvinism/Reformed tradition: a major branch of Protestantism, which originated in Switzerland in the early 16th Century and whose followers believe in original sin (i.e., innate human depravity), predestination and salvation through God's grace (i.e., justification by faith), rather than through good works. Puritanism (Congregationalism and Presbyterianism) is the Anglo-Scottish-American version of Calvinism. See 18. Protestant Reformation in Details and 10. Puritanism in American History Details.

Cartesian method: the starting point of modern philosophy, which is to doubt everything except the proposition that "I think, therefore I am" (*cogito ergo sum*). See 19. René Descartes in Details.

Categorical imperative: the proposition that one should act as though one's action would become a universal law. See 26. Immanuel Kant in Quotations.

Christ: see Historical Jesus and Messiah in Concepts.

Civil disobedience: acting in an illegal but non-violent manner to achieve social change; a method of asserting a higher moral law by submitting to the civil consequences (including arrests, fines and jail) for violating, in a nonviolent manner, what is perceived to be an unjust or immoral human law or a pervasive public practice, such as a fugitive slave law or a poll tax or a racially segregated public transportation system. Henry David Thoreau, Mahatma Gandhi, Martin Luther King, Jr. See Higher law and Situational ethics in Concepts and 32. Civil Rights/Black Freedom Movement in American History Details.

Civil religion: a mixture of nationalistic and Judeo-Christian symbols, rituals, traditions and practices that are used in secular celebrations; e.g. religious invocations at Presidential inaugurations and state funerals; the national anthem at sporting events; pledges of allegiance to the flag, and the veneration of the Founding Fathers, military veterans and past wars. According to Jean-Jacques Rousseau, ritualistic expressions of nationalism and patriotism serve as a form of social cement. Robert Bellah.

Climate of opinion: the *zeitgeist* or world view of a particular culture at a particular time and place. Immanuel Kant, G. W. F. Hegel; Carl Becker, Arthur Lovejoy, Alfred North Whitehead.

Collective immortality: the belief, suggested by Walt Whitman in *Leaves of Grass* and other poets and philosophers, that, although the individual leaf may die, the collective organism lives on. It is predicated on the belief in the immanence of the divinity in all life and that in every individual "is the soul of the whole [or, Over-Soul] . . . to which every part and particle is equally related, the eternal One" (Ralph Waldo Emerson). See Over-Soul, Pantheism, Reincarnation and Universalism in Concepts, Baruch Spinoza and Emerson in Quotations and 20. Baruch Spinoza and 29. New England Transcendentalism in Details.

Confession: acknowledging one's transgressions in order to atone for them; to assuage guilt and anxiety and resolve internal conflict by confessing one's shortcomings. There are Roman Catholic, psychoanalytic, autobiographical, twelve-step and pop-cultural versions of "the talking cure." See Atonement, Penance and

Repentance in Concepts and Cathartic method in Psychology Concepts.

Cosmologies: myths, theories, stories and beliefs that explain the origin and nature of the universe.

Covenant theology: a series of contracts between God and individuals and religious communities who considered themselves to be his "chosen people," specifically, the Israelites and, later, the Puritans and other Protestant denominations. See 10. Puritanism in American History Details and Stow Persons in Selected References.

Creationism: generally, the belief in the literal truth of the Biblical account of the creation of the universe in six days. See Karen Armstrong in Selected References.

Creative life force: *anima mundi, vis vitae, élan vital.* See Vitalism in Concepts and 3. Pantheism in Details.

Crimes against humanity: the systematic and widespread use of murder, extermination, enslavement, deportation, imprisonment, torture, rape, persecution and other acts of inhumanity committed or condoned by a government or a de facto authority against a civilian population. See Genocide and Holocaust in Concepts.

Cultural hegemony: the doctrine that cultural norms and values are social constructs that are imposed by the dominant class, but are perceived to be universally true by the general population; that the ideology at any given time of the ruling class (e.g., patriarchy, emperor worship, slavery, feudalism, the divine right of kings, laissez-faire capitalism, Social Darwinism, dialectical materialism, the cult of personality) causes the general population to falsely believe in the universality and immutability of that world view, to accept their subordinate status and to act in ways which are antithetical to their own self-interest; Antonio Gramsci; versus **post-hegemonic synthesis**, which ascribes free will, agency, autonomy and reflexivity, or self-awareness, to individuals as they make their political and cultural choices, and sees cultural hegemony in layered social structures rather than as a monolithic value system; Peter Berger and Thomas Luckmann, Anthony Giddens, Raymond Williams. See Agency, Autonomy, Determinism versus Free will, and Reflexivity in Concepts.

Death of God: see Slave morality and Transvaluation of values in Concepts and 33. Friedrich Nietzsche in Details.

Decalogue (Greek for "ten words"): the Ten Commandments of the Judeo-Christian Bible.

Deductive reasoning: a form of "top down" logic that starts with one or more general statements, or premises, which are presumed to be self-evident, to reach a conclusion. For example, (1) all men are mortal; (2) Socrates is a man; (3) therefore, Socrates is mortal; a form of *a priori* reasoning; versus **inductive reasoning**: a form of "bottom up" logic in which observed particular facts are used to reach a general conclusion; it is the basis of *a posteriori* reasoning and the scientific method. See Empiricism and Syllogism in Concepts, 17. Scholasticism in Details and 1. Scientific Method in Science Details.

Deism: an 18ᵗʰ Century religion and philosophy that viewed God as the First Cause, as the rational, benevolent creator of the universe, who conforms to the laws of nature, does not intervene in human affairs and can be known through science and reason rather than through revelation, dogma or scripture. Benjamin Franklin is said to have converted to Deism by reading arguments against it. See Theism in Concepts and 27. 18ᵗʰ Century Enlightenment in Details.

Determinism: the doctrine that all events are controlled by an immutable chain of cause and effect, with little human free will or choice and no random variation or chance; see Predestination in Concepts, 16. Augustine and 18. Protestant Reformation in Details; versus **fatalism**: the doctrine that events are governed by fate, destiny, an unseen power and/or random chance; see Fortuitism, Radical contingency and Tychism in Concepts; Population Bottleneck in Anthropology Concepts; Alternative histories in Historiography Concepts; and Broken symmetry, Chaos theory, Multiverse, Schrodinger's cat, Stochastic, Uniformitarianism versus catastrophism/neo-catastrophism and Vacuum genesis in Science Concepts; versus **free will**: the doctrine that individuals have the capability to make free, independent choices and moral judgments; see Agency, Autonomy, Cultural hegemony versus post-hegemonic synthesis, Pelagian heresy and Reflexivity in Concepts.

Dharma: in Buddhism, the cosmic moral order; the right way of living; the path to enlightenment.

Dialectical method: a method of formal reasoning in which a proposition is examined and shown to be true, partially true, inconsistent, contradictory or false, or its antithesis is shown to be true or false. Also a logical model of thesis, antithesis and synthesis that was developed by Johann Fichte and G. W. F. Hegel and adopted by Karl Marx. See Unity of opposites in Concepts and 11. Socrates, 30. Hegel and 32. Marx in Details.

Diaspora: the historical migration, movement or dispersion of an ethnic population from its ancestral homeland. Traditionally, it refers to the exile and dispersion of the Jews by the Babylonians in 587 BCE and by the Romans in the 1st and 2nd Centuries CE following the First and Second Revolts against Roman rule. The term also applies to other groups, including the African Diaspora of West Africans who were enslaved and shipped to the Americas in the Atlantic slave trade from the 1500s to the 1800s.

Distributed guilt: the doctrine that every harmful or evil act is associated with a web of causes and responsibilities, including apathy and indifference. Thus, for example, responsibility for a fatal, catastrophic fire in a Third World sweatshop cannot be disassociated from the purchase of its products by individual consumers in the developed world. Or, the catastrophic effects of climate change cannot be disassociated from the individual choices and actions of governments, producers and consumers. See Categorical imperative in Concepts and Infinite regression in Historiography Concepts.

Divine grace: for Christians, God's gift of love, forgiveness, mercy and salvation to an innately sinful humanity, which is provided through the example and sacrifice of Jesus Christ, as well as through church sacraments, faith, good works and/or a personal religious conversion experience.

Dualism: in a religious context, the division of the world into good and evil; in philosophy, the classification of things into binary opposites, such as self and non-self, male and female, life and death, good and evil, yin and yang, reason and emotion, ideal and material, universal and particular, objective and subjective, determinism and free will, nature and nurture, etc. See Manichean dualism and Unity of opposites in Concepts, Ralph Waldo Emerson in Quotations, 19. Descartes and 22. Leibniz in Details and 4. Post-Structuralism in Literary Concepts Details.

Elect: those who are chosen or "elected" by God; in Judaism, the children of Israel; among Protestant Christians, those individuals and groups who identify themselves as having been chosen and saved by God from innate sin and eternal damnation, usually through a personal conversion experience. William James, Stow Persons. See Religious conversion experience in Concepts.

Elysian Fields: in Greek mythology, the final, eternal resting place of the virtuous.

Emergent divinity: a concept in humanistic thought that views humans as evolving toward a higher state of consciousness. Also, the view that the creative life spirit or force that created the universe is in the process of becoming, or evolving toward a state of self-realization; "the creator is his own creation" (LeRoi Jones). See *In statu viae*, Pantheism and Theomorphism in Concepts.

Empiricism: the doctrine that all knowledge is derived through the senses from the "irreducible brute facts" of experience, i.e., from observation, experimentation, inductive reasoning and the application of scientific methods, rather than from *a priori* theories or pre-established principles; Williams James, John Locke; see 21. John Locke and 35. Pragmatism in Details; versus **rationalism**: the doctrine that reason is superior to experience as a source of knowledge and that the exterior world can only be known through the mind, not the senses; see Rationalism and Rational empiricism in Concepts.

End justifies the means: the doctrine that evil or harmful acts are justified if they advance a higher ideal or goal; see Paradox of evil in Concepts; versus **means justify the end**: that violence leads to violence, and nonviolence leads to peace; "hatred is increased by being reciprocated, and can on the other hand be destroyed by love" -- Baruch Spinoza. Martin Luther King, Jr.

Epicureanism: a Hellenistic school of philosophy that held that pleasure, based on moderation and self-control, should be the goal of human life.

Epiphenomenon: an event that accompanies another event that may or may not have caused it; also, a secondary mental phenomenon that accompanies and is presumed to have been caused by a primary physical or mental phenomenon.

Eschatology: the study of "last things," the end of time; for Christians, the Second Coming of Christ and the Last Judgment; for Muslims, the last judgment and the end of time; for other religions, the end of one cycle and the beginning of another. See Apocalypse and Millennialism in Concepts.

Essentialism: the doctrine that there are unchanging essences, attributes or properties that are inherent in any class of entities. Essentialist philosophies have been used to characterize and justify national, racial, class and gender differences; see 12. Plato and 13. Aristotle in Details; versus **existentialism** and **post-essentialism**, in which identities and roles are, respectively, defined by individual choice and action or are socially constructed; see Post-essentialism in Concepts, 37. Existentialism in Details and 4. Post-structuralism in Literary Concepts.

Ethicalism: the belief that moral principles have an inherently sacred quality; that it is not necessary to rely on a transcendent deity or the promise or threat of supernatural rewards or punishments to uphold human moral behavior. Buddhism, Confucianism, Unitarianism, Universalism and humanism are forms of ethicalism. See Autonomy and Moralizing gods hypothesis in Concepts; 5. Humanism in Details; Anterior insula and Prosocial behavior in Anthropology Concepts and 12. Violence and Human Nature in Anthropology Details.

Ethics: a set of moral principles; the precepts for ethical conduct. See Normative ethics versus meta-ethics in Concepts.

Eudemonia: to ancient Greeks, the sense of excellence, happiness and well-being that is derived from living a life of reason, knowledge and virtue. See *Arete* and Pythagorean ideal in Concepts and 13. Aristotle in Details.

Evangelicalism: a form of Protestant Christianity that stresses the centrality of the "born again" religious conversion experience. It celebrates the death and resurrection of Jesus Christ as the basis for personal salvation and the remission of sins, and proselytizes its beliefs to others as "the good news." Karen Armstrong, Kevin Phillips. See Great Awakening cycle/revivalism and Religious conversion experience in Concepts.

Faith: the trust or belief in a religious power, person, doctrine or teaching, which may be beyond reason, experience, physical evidence or proof. See 2. Religion in Details.

Fertility cults: religious sects whose beliefs, rituals and practices involved physical and symbolical re-enactments of sexual and reproductive behaviors, which were used to maintain and celebrate fertility.

Fifth Bardo: in Tibetan tradition, the transitional state between an individual's last breath and its rebirth into its next life, during which the mindstream, or consciousness, becomes dissociated from the physical body, which allows a spiritual period of luminosity, transcendence, peace, insight and awareness. *The Tibetan Book of the Dead.*

Five Pillars of Islam: the five obligations of the faithful, as defined in the Quran, which are (1) acknowledging one God and Muhammad as his messenger, (2) praying five times daily, (3) giving alms, (4) fasting on Ramadan and (5) making a pilgrimage to Mecca.

Fortuitism: the doctrine that the universe, evolution and human history are driven by random chance rather than by design. See Determinism versus fatalism, Radical Contingency and Tychism in Concepts; Population Bottleneck in Anthropology Concepts; Alternative histories and Radical contingency in Historiography Concepts; Richard White in Historiography Quotations and Broken symmetry, Chaos theory, Multiverse, Schrödinger's cat, Stochastic, Tychism, Uniformitarianism versus catastrophism/neo-catastrophism and Vacuum genesis in Science Concepts.

Four Noble Truths of Buddha: see 6. Buddhism in Details.

Free thinker: generally, one who believes that truth is derived from science, experience and human reason rather than from church dogma or religious orthodoxy, and who is skeptical of supernatural explanations.

Free will: see Agency, Cultural hegemony, Determinism and Pelagian heresy in Concepts.

Fundamentalism: in Christianity, the belief in the literal and infallible truth of the Bible, including the creation of the universe in six days, the virgin birth of Jesus, the miracles performed by Jesus, the resurrection and the Second Coming. Karen Armstrong.

Gaia: in Greek mythology, the primal Earth-Mother; the goddess who gave birth to the earth and whose marriage to her son Uranus, god of the sky, created the race of Titans, and whose grandson was Zeus.

Garden of Eden: in the Judeo-Christian tradition, the divine garden where the first man and first woman ate the forbidden fruit from the tree of knowledge, for which they were expelled. See Knowing versus being and Paradise in Concepts.

Genetic fallacy: that the explanation of a subject can be found it origin or essence, in contrast to **existentialism**, in which meaning is found in its immediate existence, action and effect. See Essentialism in Concepts and 37. Existentialism in Details.

Genocide: the deliberate and systematic destruction, usually through mass murder, of a political, racial, religious, national or ethnic group. The 20th Century witnessed the genocide of Armenians and Greeks by Ottoman Turks during the First World War; Jews and others in the Holocaust by Nazi Germans and their allies during the Second World War; Cambodians by the Khmer Rouge in 1975-79; Tutsi Rwandans by Hutu Rwandans in 1994 and Moslem Bosnians by Serbs in 1995. See Crimes against humanity and Holocaust in Concepts.

Gnosticism (Greek for "knowledge"): a syncretic blend of religious beliefs and practices that, possibly, originated in the 2nd Century of the Common Era as a branch of early Christianity. It was influenced by Platonism, Judaism and, later, Persian Zoroastrianism. Gnosticism posited a dualistic universe of upper and lower worlds, good and evil, the spiritual and the material, the eternal and the ephemeral. Its adherents practiced philanthropy, poverty and sexual abstinence in their search for knowledge and enlightenment.

God above God: Paul Tillich's proposition that God is not the highest existing Being, since he would then be a creature and not the source of all being. Rather, he is the ground of Being-itself, and beyond the distinction between eternal essence and existing being. See Panendeism in Concepts.

Goddess worship: the worship, throughout history and pre-history, of female deities, as represented by earth and mother goddesses, fertility cults, Venus figures and goddesses from different traditions, such as Ceres, Freyja, Gaia, Ishtar, Neith and the Virgin Mary. Joseph Campbell. See Venus/goddess figurines in Anthropology Concepts.

God's chosen people: originally, the "children of Israel"; the concept was later appropriated by the Puritans and other religious and secular groups. See 6. American Exceptionalism in American History Details.

Golden mean: the middle way between two extremes; the ethical injunction to be moderate and avoid extremes. Pythagoras, Confucius, Socrates, Plato, Aristotle, Maimonides.

Golden rule: that one should do not do to others what ones does do not want done to oneself; an ethic that is honored in nearly all religious and ethical traditions. See Anterior insula in Anthropology Concepts; 5. Social Intelligence in Anthropology Details and Theory of Mind, Reflexivity and Mirror neurons in Psychology concepts.

Great Awakening cycle/revivalism: periodic movements of religious renewal, which reflect the waxing and waning of religious enthusiasm in the United States. The core of the revival is the immediate, personal and intensely emotional religious experience that participants undergo as they are possessed by the "holy spirit," accept Jesus as their personal savior and are freed from sin and the threat of eternal damnation. Sidney Ahlstrom, Thomas Kidd, William McLoughlin. See Religious conversion experience in Concepts and 17. Great Awakening Cycle in America History Details.

Great chain of being: the medieval concept of the cosmos as a fixed hierarchy, with God at the top and, in descending order, angels, stars, the moon, kings, princes, nobles, men, wild animals, domesticated animals, trees, plants, precious stones and other minerals.

Great heresy: the Copernican hypothesis (1543) that the earth revolves around the sun, which, in the 16th Century Christian world, was punishable by excommunication, torture and death. See *Index Librorum Prohibitorum* and Inquisition in Concepts.

Greek cosmology: a system of legends and myths that involved divine intervention into human affairs by a pantheon of serio-comic, anthropomorphic gods, who competed with one another to assist their favorite mortals and thwart their worldly and other-worldly opponents. These gods used various methods that were often channeled through natural phenomena, including the human *psyche* (self, soul, spirit, personality) and the human *soma* (body). The *Iliad* and *Odyssey* portray these melodramatic conflicts between humans and humans, gods and humans and gods and gods. E. R. Dodds. See 2. Ancient Greeks and the Irrational in Psychology Details.

Hades: to the ancient Greeks and Romans, the underworld and the god who ruled it; the home of the dead.

Hajj: the annual Muslim pilgrimage to Mecca.

Hegira: the flight of Mohammed from Mecca to Medina in 622 CE, which marks the beginning of the Islamic calendar.

Hell: a place of eternal woe, anguish and damnation.

Heresy: a belief or doctrine that is not in accordance with official religious doctrine and is punishable by penance, excommunication, and, in some cases, torture and death. Heresies are denounced and punished in nearly all religious faiths, including Judaism,

Christianity, Islam and Buddhism. See Arianism, Great heresy, *Index Librorum Prohibitorum* and Inquisition in Concepts.

Hermeneutics/hermeneutic circle: the analysis, interpretation and explanation, or exegesis, of written texts (originally, religious texts) in order to understand their symbolic and, often, hidden or secret meaning. The circle refers to the fact that, often, the whole text can only be understood in reference to its parts, and its parts can only be understood in reference to the whole. Wilhelm Dilthey, Jürgen Habermas, Martin Heidegger, Paul Ricœur, Max Weber. See Deconstructionism in Literary Concepts.

Higher law: a universal, divine, moral or natural law or principle that is above man-made laws. The concept was invoked by American abolitionists to protect runaway slaves from the Fugitive Slave Act in the antebellum period, and, in the 20th Century, was legally applied against those who were complicit in crimes against humanity during World War II. See Civil disobedience and Situational ethics in Concepts.

Historical Jesus: the biographical Jesus of Nazareth, a Galilean Jew who lived from approximately 4 BCE to approximately 30 CE and preached in the Roman province of Judea. His life and death is the basis of the Christian religion, as well as the subject of a school of research that focuses on his humanity and ethical teachings in their historical and cultural context. John Dominic Crossan.

Holism: the sense of spiritual connectedness, wholeness and oneness; the integration of the individual into the larger whole. Also, the view that natural and social systems function as integrated wholes and should be viewed as such rather than as a collection of individual parts. Jan Smuts. See Dualism, Ying and yang and Unity of opposites in Concepts and Ralph Waldo Emerson in Quotations.

Holocaust (also known as the Shoah, the Hebrew word for "catastrophe"): the historical event from 1939 to 1945 that involved the systematic, state-sponsored murder by Nazi Germans and their allies of six million European Jews (including one million children) and five million Polish and Soviet citizens and prisoners-of-war, political opponents, gypsies, homosexuals, Jehovah's Witnesses, and the physically and mentally disabled. See Crimes against humanity, Genocide and Neo-Orthodoxy in Concepts; Winston Churchill and T. S. Eliot in Quotations and Infinite Regression in Historiography.

Holy wars: religious and territorial wars, including (1) the Muslim conquest of the Arabian Peninsula, Central Asia, the Middle East, North Africa and the Iberian Peninsula in the 7th through 15th Centuries; (2) the Christian Crusades in the 12th and 13th Centuries; (3) the Christian *Reconquesta* of Moorish Spain from the 9th through the 15th Centuries; (4) the French Wars of Religion between Catholics and Protestants in the 16th Century; (5) the Thirty Years War of the 17th Century and (6) the Muslim *jihads* in the 20th and 21th Centuries.

Humanism: see 5. Humanism in Details.

I Ching: the Book of Changes; a Chinese book of divination and prophesy, which dates from 1000 BCE or earlier. It is based on 64 sets of hexagrams of 6 lines each, the subject of which are concepts such as Creating, Leading, Humbling, Persevering, Retiring, Ascending, Infiltrating, Converting.

Iconoclast: initially, in 8th Century Byzantium, one who destroyed religious icons and sacred images in order to prevent their veneration, based on the Biblical injunction against worshiping "graven images"; the term now refers to one who attacks conventional beliefs and institutions. Those who venerate such religious images are called **iconophiles**.

Ideology: a conceptual framework; a pattern of thought; a world view; a system of ideas, attitudes, values, assumptions and beliefs that serves to justify, explain and provide coherence to experience and, in many cases, to furnish the inspiration and motivation for action. According to cultural materialists, ideology reflects the economic self-interests of the dominant class and is falsely endowed with universality and immutability, which allows that class's construction of reality to be generalized and infused throughout society. See Cultural hegemony versus post-hegemonic synthesis in Concepts and 11. Counterarguments to Economic/Technological Determinism in Economics Details.

Index Librorum Prohibitorum: a list of publications that were prohibited by the Roman Catholic Church from 1559 to 1966 in order to protect the faithful from theological error and immoral thoughts. It included works by writers such as Dante, Bruno (who was burned alive at the stake for professing Copernicus' theory that the earth revolved around the sun), Galileo, Kepler, Milton, Pascal, Locke, Voltaire, Rousseau, Kant, Gibbon, Stendhal, Victor Hugo, Flaubert and Sartre.

Infidel (from Latin for "one without faith"): a disbeliever; for Christians and Muslims, one who is not a member of their respective religions.

Inner light the divine spirit, or Holy Spirit, that shines on and dwells in all humans, according to the Religious Society of Friends, or Quakers; "that of God in everyone," according to George Fox. See Over-Soul, Quakers, Unitarianism, Universalism and Vitalism in Concepts and 29. New England Transcendentalism in Details.

Inquisition: a system of tribunals administered by the Roman Catholic Church to root out heresy, identify crypto-Jews and Muslims and enforce religious purity and orthodoxy. At one time, it tortured and burned people alive at the stake. It is estimated that 150,000 were investigated and 5,000 were executed, primarily during the 15th to the 17th Centuries. The tribunal is now called the Congregation for the Doctrine of the Faith.

In statu viae: a tenet of Roman Catholic theology that the world is a work-in-progress, that "the universe was created 'in a state of journeying' . . . toward an ultimate perfection yet to be attained, to which God has destined it."

Inverse law of moral significance: that the relatively blameless are often burdened with guilt, while evil-doers operate with a clear conscience. See Ends justify the means and Paradox of evil in Concepts and Pol Pot in Quotations.

Islam: an Abrahamic religion in which the main tenet is submission to God's will, as defined in the Quran and the teachings of Muhammad (570-632 CE). In Islam, Muhammad is considered to be a prophet, a messenger of God, not God himself, in contrast to some versions of Christianity, in which Jesus is believed to be a triadic form of God incarnate. See Five Pillars of Islam, People of the Book and Quran in Concepts.

Jehovah/Yahweh (Hebrew for "he who causes to be"): the God of Israel.

Jen/Ren: Confucius's first principle of goodness, kind-heartedness and benevolence.

Jihad (Arabic for "striving," "struggling" or "persevering" in the service of God): a Muslim holy war. See Holy wars.

Justification by faith: the belief that faith is the precondition, but not the cause, of salvation, which is predestined by God and awarded through divine grace alone, not through good works or free will; a major tenet of St. Augustine, Calvinism, Puritanism and many

Protestant denominations; versus **sanctification/justification by good works**: the belief that humans can earn salvation by leading a sanctified (that is, virtuous) life and performing good deeds.

Kabbalah: a set of mystical, esoteric Jewish teachings and beliefs.

Karma: the Buddhist moral law of cause and effect. Good deeds create good karma, which leads to happiness; bad deeds create bad karma, which leads to suffering. See 6. Buddhism in Details.

Kenosis*:* Jesus's humbling and emptying himself of his own will in order to receive the will of God; analogous to the Buddhist concept of *sunyata* (*q.v.* in Concepts).

Knowing versus **being**: two mutually exclusive mental states and a paradigm of the human condition, according to D. H. Lawrence. Since the "blood-knowledge" of pure being (i.e., animal instinct) was corrupted by the "mind-knowledge" of knowing when Adam and Eve ate from the tree of knowledge and transformed a natural act into a self-conscious, sinful act, humans are inevitably divided within themselves, which is symbolized by the Christian cross.

Krishna (Sanskrit for "dark" or "black"): one of the most popular Hindu deities, an incarnation of Vishnu, who is represented variously as a child-god, the prankster, the herdsman, the divine lover with a flute, the Supreme Being.

Law **of compensation**: a tenet of Ralph Waldo Emerson and New England Transcendentalism that "for everything you have missed, you have gained something else; and for everything you gain, you lose something." See 29. New England Transcendentalism in Details.

Lethe: the River of Forgetfulness in Hades, from which, according to Greek mythology, travelers drank in order to erase the memory of their former lives.

Liberation theology: a movement within the Roman Catholic Church that developed in Latin American in the 1950s and 1960s and seeks to apply the teachings and mission of Jesus to help the poor and marginalized and to work for social justice; it has been criticized by some as a form of Christian Marxism. See Social Gospel in American History Concepts and Social justice in Sociology Concepts.

Lisbon earthquake (1755): an event in which from 10,000 to 100,000 people died as result of the temblor and the subsequent fire and tsunami. It had a profound impact on Enlightenment thinkers, comparable to that of the Holocaust in the 20th Century, since it challenged the idea of a benevolent deity and the belief that this is "the best of all possible worlds." It led to a shift in focus from divine intervention in human affairs and natural events to the scientific inquiry into the causes of natural and social phenomena.

Liturgy: prescribed forms of church ritual; the practices and forms of worship of various religions.

Liturgy of silence: the practice of some religious groups, including Buddhists and Quakers, of not speaking in certain religious settings in order to open the mind to spiritual insight.

Logos: word, speech, narrative, rational discourse; according to Karen Armstrong, a mode of thought that is represented by scientific rationalism, secular humanism, Enlightenment values and the belief in social progress and universal human rights; versus *mythos*: a sacred story; a mode of thought that is expressed in myth, spirituality, ritual, transcendental truth, ecstasy and the sense of the sacred. Armstrong's dichotomy parallels the Apollonian-Dionysian cultural dichotomy of Nietzsche (*q.v.* in Art Concepts). Karen Armstrong.

Manichean dualism: a cosmology that views the world as a struggle between absolute good and absolute evil, the kingdom of light versus the kingdom of darkness. Manichaeism was a syncretistic religion that originated in Persia in the 3rd Century CE and borrowed many of its tenets from Hinduism, Judaism, Buddhism, Christianity and Zoroastrianism.

Marianism: the veneration of Mary, the mother of Jesus. In Roman Catholic theology, the Blessed Virgin Mary is worshiped as the Mother of God. See Goddess worship in Concepts.

Materialism: the philosophical doctrine that nothing exists except physical matter; that mental phenomena are the products of physical processes; versus **idealism**: two schools of philosophy that posit that reality consists of either (1) ideas in the mind or (2) ideals or forms beyond the world of the senses; that is, that material objects have no independent existence except as projections of the subjective, internal mental world or reflections of the objective, external ideal world. See Realism in Concepts and 4. Philosophical Idealism in Details.

Mechanomorphism: the belief that the universe is governed by the physical laws of nature; also, the belief that god, or the devil, takes the form of a machine (*deus in machina* or *diabolis in machina*).

Messiah (the "anointed one" in Hebrew, which was translated as *Christos* in Greek): in Judaism, the king, the savior, the liberator, the promised prophet; in Christianity, Jesus of Nazareth, the savior and redeemer of mankind.

Metta: the Buddhist concept of loving kindness, compassion and good will.

Millennialism: the Christian eschatological belief, as described in the Book of Revelation, that the tribulations, the Second Coming of Christ and the Battle of Armageddon will occur before the thousand-year reign of Christ on earth, which will then be followed by the Last Judgment, the end of the world and the eternal New Jerusalem.

Moral philosophy: ethics; the study of right and wrong conduct and the ways in which to live a virtuous life.

Moralizing gods hypothesis: that the development of powerful, all-seeing, punitive, moralizing deities who (1) could see inside a person's mind, (2) encouraged prosocial behavior, (3) punished selfishness and cruelty and (4) demanded rituals and costly displays of devotion was the result of a shift from nomadic, hunter-gathering societies to large-scale, agricultural settlements, which needed such supernatural agents to enforce social cooperation and a sense of solidarity among large groups of people. Although religious beliefs and sacred rituals reinforced in-group trust and solidarity, they also promoted mistrust and conflict with outgroups and provided the moral imperatives to kill and die for a cause. Scott Atran, Jeremy Ginges, Ara Norenzayan.

Muslim: a practitioner of Islam; one who resigns oneself to God's will. Muslims are "people of the book" (i.e., the Bible, along with Jews and Christians), who worship the God of Abraham as the one and only God; refer to the Torah and the Gospels as sources of divine revelation; recognize Abraham, Moses, John the Baptist and Jesus as prophets, or messengers of God, and view the Quran as the final synthesis of the Scriptures. See Islam and Five Pillars of Islam in Concepts.

Mysticism: a belief in direct, personal communion with the spiritual world; the belief that religious truths can be known through insight, revelation and intuition, rather than through reason and sacred texts.

Mythology: a collection of sacred stories that serve to define a world view, explain natural phenomena, such as the origin of the universe, and establish models of social behavior. Also, a system of beliefs that represents the psycho-poetic expression of human consciousness in response to the mysteries of life. According to Carl Jung, myths are a set of archetypal themes and structures that are embedded in the collective unconscious and are common across all cultures. Carl Jung, Joseph Campbell. See 7. Carl Jung in Psychology Details.

Naturalistic fallacy: that that which is found in nature is inherently right and good. See 28. Romanticism and 29. New England Transcendentalism in Details, 12. Violence and Human Nature (the Hobbes-Rousseau Dichotomy) in Anthropology Details and 25. Social Darwinism in American History Details.

Neo-Orthodoxy: the post-World War I/post-Holocaust/post-Hiroshima climate of opinion, temper of thought and school of religious philosophy that embraces St. Augustine's doctrine of original sin and rejects Thomas Aquinas' reconciliation of faith and reason. Neo-Orthodoxy is characterized by irony, ambiguity, tragedy and paradox. Karl Barth, Reinhold Niebuhr, Lionel Trilling. See Post-Enlightenment in Concepts, Death instinct in Psychology Concepts and 12. Violence and Human Nature in Anthropology Details.

New England Transcendentalism: an early 19th Century American philosophical movement that believed in the immanence, or presence, of the divinity in all life, the infinitude of the private man and the law of moral compensation. See Pantheism and Universalism in Concepts and 29. New England Transcendentalism in Details.

Nihilism: a belief in "nothing," or *nada*; that existence is without meaning or purpose. See 37. Existentialism in Details.

Nirvana: a mystical state of oceanic being, of transcendental peace; the feeling of being at one with the universe. In Buddhism and Hinduism, it is the profound peace of mind that comes from extinguishing the fires of desire, ignorance and attachment; the liberation from the cycle of birth and death. In psychoanalytic theory, it is associated with the unconscious, thalassal-regressive wish to return to the blissful nirvana of the prenatal, oceanic womb. Norman O. Brown, Jonathan Edwards, Sándor Ferenczi, Sigmund Freud, Romain Rolland.

Nominalism: the doctrine that reality consists entirely of concrete particulars; that universals and abstract objects do not exist; that universals are only words imposed on groups of particulars. The concept is personified by the Jorge Luis Borges' character, Funes the Memorious, who could remember every detail in his life, including every leaf on every tree that he passed, and, therefore, could never generalize about anything because that would require the forgetting of differences. It is also represented in British Prime Minister Margaret Thatcher's assertion that "there is no such thing as society: there are individual men and women, and there are families." See Suzanne Langer and Jacques Lacan in Art Quotations and Historical nominalism in Historiography Concepts.

Nonconformists/dissenters: Puritans (Congregationalists and Presbyterians), Separatists, Baptists, Quakers and Methodists, who, beginning in the 16th Century, refused to follow the practices of the established Church of England. After Congregationalism became the established state religion in the Massachusetts Bay Colony, it persecuted other dissenting religionists, particularly Quakers. See Antinomianism and Soul libertie in Concepts and 10. Puritanism in American History Details.

Normative ethics: first-order knowledge of what is right and wrong, which based on values that could be conflated with emotions and prejudices; versus **meta-ethics**, second-order knowledge that examines the nature and meaning of moral terms, systems and judgments.

Noumena versus *phenomena*: Kant's distinction between things as they are in themselves versus things as they appear through the senses. See 26. Kant in Details.

Objectivism: a philosophy of rational, amoral egoism that was developed by Ayn Rand and influenced by Friedrich Nietzsche. It (1) celebrates the heroic virtues of individualism and the ruthless selfishness of the *Ubermensch*; (2) disdains the idea of moral obligation and public good; (3) demonizes the welfare state and (4) provides the philosophical justification for secular, laissez-faire capitalism and libertarianism. Jennifer Burns.

Ontology: a branch of philosophy that studies the nature of existence and being. It is concerned with questions of universals and particulars, the objective and the subjective, eternality and flux, determinism and non-determinism, idealism and materialism.

Original sin/innate human depravity: the theological doctrine that humans are inherently sinful. It is the starting point of Roman Catholicism (through St. Augustine) and many forms of Protestantism. According to Catholic theology, individual redemption from sin is provided by the death and resurrection of

Jesus Christ, baptism and other church sacraments and an individual's efforts to lead a virtuous life. According to Calvinism and other forms of Reformed Protestantism, an individual's salvation from innate depravity and eternal damnation is predetermined and only occurs through God's grace, and not through good works. See Justification by faith and Pelagian heresy in Concepts and 12. Violence and Human Nature in Anthropology Details.

Overdetermination: the proposition that an action or event is often determined by multiple causes, any one of which, by itself, could have caused the event. Sigmund Freud; Louis Althusser.

Over-Soul: the divine spirit, universal soul or Holy Spirit that is shared by, and dwells in, all human beings, according to the precepts of New England Transcendentalism. It is similar to the inner light of the Quakers (*q.v.* in Concepts). See Pantheism, Universalism and Vitalism in Concepts, Ralph Waldo Emerson in Quotations and 29. New England Transcendentalism in Details.

Pagan: one who is not a Jew, Christian or Muslim; that is, one who is not a member of the "people of the Book"(i.e., those who recognize the prophets of the Bible); a pejorative term that was applied by Christians to Greco-Roman polytheists and indigenous and non-Abrahamic religionists. See Infidel and People of the Book in Concepts.

Panendeism: the belief that the universe is part, but not the whole, of God. See God above God in Concepts.

Pantheism: the belief in the immanence, or presence, of the divinity in all life; that God, the universe and nature are one; versus a theistic or anthropomorphic god. See Theism and Vitalism in Concepts, Baruch Spinoza and LeRoi Jones in Quotations and 3. Pantheism and 29. New England Transcendentalism in Details.

Paradise (Persian for "walled enclosure" or "royal park"): the restored Garden of Eden; heaven; the blissful afterlife; the kingdom of God, where the righteous will live forever.

Paradox of evil: that horrific acts of evil are often rationalized by their agents as motivated by idealism, moralism or the belief that the ends justify the means. Adolph Eichmann, the zealous Nazi bureaucrat who helped to organize the mass murder of six million Jews during the Holocaust, claimed that "I was an idealist" before he was executed for his crimes against humanity. Pol Pot asserted that "my conscience is clear" twenty years after he and the Khmer

Rouge presided over the execution and starvation of two million fellow Cambodians. See Ends justify the means, the Inverse law of moral significance, Moralizing gods hypothesis and the Problem of evil in Concepts; 12. Violence and Human Nature in Anthropology Details and 5. Freud's Defense Mechanisms in Psychology Details.

Paradox of humanism: Joseph Wood Krutch's term for the modern human condition in which humans have consciousness over so much but control over so little; that humanism and nature are fundamentally antithetical. In *Civilization and Its Discontents* (1930), Sigmund Freud portrayed the irreconcilable contradiction between human nature (with its innate sexual and aggressive impulses) and human culture (with its demands for conformity, repression and sublimation).

Passover: the Jewish religious observance that honors their deliverance from slavery in Egypt.

Pelagian heresy: the theological doctrine that humans have the free will to choose right or wrong; that salvation can be achieved through good works and that the atonement of Jesus absolves mankind of original sin. It contradicts St. Augustine's doctrine of innate human depravity and was declared a heresy by the Roman Catholic Church at the Council of Ephesus in 431 CE. See Justification by faith versus sanctification by good works in Concepts.

Penance: confession, acts of contrition, prayer and/or punishment for acts of wrongdoing. See Atonement and Confession in Concepts.

Pentecostalism: a charismatic movement within Protestant Christianity in which believers are possessed by the Holy Spirit, experience God or Jesus directly, are filled with religious enthusiasm and ecstasy and, in some cases, are able to speak in tongues, faith-heal and prophesize. See Religious conversion experience, Evangelicalism and Great Awakening cycle in Concepts and Karen Armstrong in Selected References.

People of the Book (that is, the Bible): Jews, Christians and Muslims, who worship the God of Abraham as the one and only God and view the Bible as a source of divine revelation. Muslims recognize Abraham, Moses and Jesus as prophets, and view the Quran as the final synthesis of the Scriptures.

Les philosophes: 18th-Century Enlightenment philosophers, scientists, *encyclopédistes*, scholars, historians, economists, public intellectuals, reformers and men and women of letters who celebrated human reason, science, progress, social improvement, representative government and secular liberalism, and opposed religious dogma and political absolutism. See Republic of letters in Literary Concepts and 27. 18th Century Enlightenment in Details.

Polytheism: the belief in more than one god. Polytheism was common among pastoral and nomadic hunter-gatherer societies and was characteristic of Greek, Roman and Indian cosmologies; versus the monotheism of Judaism, Christianity and Islam. See Greek cosmology in Concepts.

Positivism: a school of philosophy that views science as the definitive source of knowledge and celebrates human reason and the scientific method as the highest form of social evolution. See 31. Auguste Comte in Details and 4. Positivism in Sociology Details.

Post-Enlightenment: a term applied to the 20th and 21th Centuries, a period that is said to be characterized by the erosion of the Enlightenment values of reason, order, optimism, secularism and faith in science, human progress and social improvement. The Post-Enlightenment *zeitgeist* is thought to be the result of world wars, mass movements, totalitarianism, genocide, the threat of nuclear annihilation and the rise of religious fundamentalism. See Neo-Orthodoxy in Concepts, 4. Sigmund Freud in Psychology Details and 16. Mass Society and 17. Erich Fromm in Sociology Details.

Post-essentialism: the doctrine that identities and roles are socially constructed. See Essentialism in Concepts, 37. Existentialism in Details and 4. Post-structuralism in Literary Concepts Details.

Post-hegemonic synthesis: see Cultural Hegemony in Concepts.

Practical philosophy: an ethical or moral philosophy that provides the precepts for leading a life of reason, knowledge and virtue. See Ethicalism, *Eudemonia*, Moral philosophy and Scottish Common Sense Realism in Concepts.

Predestination: the doctrine that every event is foreordained by God, including an individual's personal salvation. It was a basic tenet of St. Augustine, Calvinism, Puritanism and other forms of Protestantism. See Determinism, Original sin and Pelagian heresy in Concepts.

Pre-established harmony: see 22. Gottfried Leibniz in Details.

Priesthood of all believers: a concept derived from Martin Luther's belief that personal salvation is the responsibility of the individual and is not mediated by priests, saints nor the authority of the church. Protestantism's emphasis on the scriptures as a means of individual salvation led to vernacular translations of the Bible from Latin, an increase in popular literacy and the ideal of a learned clergy. See 18. Protestant Reformation in Details.

Problem of evil: the contradiction between the reality of evil in the world and the belief in God's omnipotence and/or benevolence. The contradiction can be resolved by accepting the benevolence but not the omnipotence of God, or by viewing the ultimate goodness of the universe as reflected in the evolution of life toward a higher state of being. See Emergent divinity, *In statu vitae*, Theodicy and Vitalism in Concepts, Epicurus/David Hume in Quotations and 20. Baruch Spinoza in Details.

Promised Land: the land promised by God to Abraham and his descendants, which is described in Exodus as the land between the Nile and the Euphrates rivers. See God's chosen people in Concepts.

Proselytize: to share the gospel or "good news" with others; to attempt to persuade, "save" or convert others to one's own religion. It is one of the central features of Protestant evangelicalism.

Protestant ethic: a complex of values and personality traits that is associated with religious and economic individualism, the work ethic, self-reliance, temperance, and thrift. According to Max Weber, it laid the foundation for the rise of capitalism. Max Weber, William Tilden. See Protestant ethic and the rise of capitalism in Economics Concepts, 6. Freud's Anal Personality Traits in Psychology Details and Benjamin Franklin's Table of virtues in American History Concepts.

Protestant Reformation: see 18. Protestant Reformation in Details.

Purgatory: according to Catholic doctrine, a temporary or transitional place between death and the final judgment; a place of remorse, suffering, purification and atonement.

Puritanism: the Anglo-Scottish-American form of Calvinism. "Precisionists," as the Puritans were called, were 17th and 18th Century Nonseparating Congregationalists, who sought to purify and reform the Church of England of it "papist" practices from within; versus Separatists/ Brownists (including Pilgrims) who formally separated from the Church of England. Congregationalism and Presbyterianism are the spiritual and institutional descendants of Puritanism. See 10. Puritanism in American History Details.

Pythagorean ideal: that one should lead a life of passionate, sympathetic contemplation (as paraphrased by Bertrand Russell).

See 8. Pythagoras in Details and Bertrand Russell in Selected References.

Q source: the hypothesized collection of Jesus's sayings written in 40 or 50 CE that may have served as the original textual source for the Gospels of Matthew and Luke.

Quakers: members of the Religious Society of Friends, which originated in England in the mid-17th Century. Quakers are egalitarian, pacifistic, quietist and universalist and believe that the divine spirit, or inner light, shines on and dwells within all humans ("that of God in everyone," according to George Fox). Quakers have no clergy or church hierarchy and their meetings often consist of silent, "unprogrammed" worship. See Liturgy of silence and Universalism in Concepts.

Quetzalcoatl: Plumed Serpent; the paramount god of Native Mesoamericans, including the Aztecs.

Quietism: the belief that spiritual peace is attained through the quieting or diminution of the emotions and the human will; the peaceful withdrawal from the conflicts of the world in order to contemplate the divine and the eternal.

Quran (Arabic for "the recitation"): Islam's holy book, as revealed by God to Muhammad from 609 CE to 632 CE. It focuses on a living, monotheistic God; the rules for leading a virtuous life; the afterlife and the day of judgment. It refers to the Torah and the Gospels as sources of divine revelation and recognizes Abraham, Moses, John the Baptist and Jesus as prophets, or messengers of God. See Islam and the Five Pillars of Islam in Concepts.

Radical contingency: the doctrine that small, initial, random differences and dependencies can have enormous consequences. For example, had the asteroid that struck the earth and killed the dinosaurs 66 million years ago arrived a few months earlier or a few months later, it may have missed the earth, and the world would still be ruled by dinosaurs. According to Richard White, "the inevitability of the present violates the contingency of the past, which involves alternative choices and outcomes that would have produced alterative presents." Jorge Luis Borges, Blaise Pascal, Richard White, Thornton Wilder and others. See Fortuitism and Tychism in Concepts; Population Bottleneck in Anthropology Concepts; Alternative histories in Historiography Concepts and Broken symmetry, Chaos theory, Multiverse,

Uniformitarianism versus catastrophism/neo-catastrophism and Vacuum genesis in Science Concepts.

Ramadan: the Muslim holy month of fasting, purification and reflection.

Rapture: in Christian eschatology, the belief that, with the Second Coming, the righteous will be "caught up" and "meet the Lord in the clouds." 1 Thessalonians.

Rational empiricism: the doctrine that knowledge is derived from the application of human reason, including the scientific method, to sensory experience. It represents the reconciliation of rationalism and empiricism (*qq.v.* in Concepts).

Rationalism: the doctrine that reason is superior to experience as a source of knowledge, and that the exterior world can only be known through the mind, not the senses. It often employs deductive and *a priori* reasoning; versus empiricism. See Empiricism and Rational empiricism in Concepts.

Realism: the doctrine that things exist independently of the mind and its perception of them; versus idealism.

Reductionism: the doctrine that complex systems can be explained by reducing them to their smallest, most fundamental components or essences. See Essentialism and Holism in Concepts.

Reflexivity: self-awareness; an individual's recognition of the personal, social and environmental influences that shaped it, as well as the individual's autonomous ability to change and re-shape its own views and norms; the circular relationship between cause and effect. "Man is both knowing subject and the object of his own study" -- Michel Foucault. See Agency and Cultural hegemony in Concepts.

Reification: the fallacy of treating an abstraction or an object as if it had a real, concrete, material existence. See Reification in Economics Concepts.

Reincarnation: a tenet of many Eastern religions that, after the death of the body, the spirit takes up a new life in a new body, thus, perpetuating the cycle of life, death and rebirth.

Religion: see 2. Religion in Details.

Religion as universal obsessional neurosis: Sigmund Freud's definition of religion, which he described as irrational, ritualistic, obsessive and compulsive and represents the regressive, infantile wish for a powerful, protective, idealized parental authority figure. See Nirvana in Concepts.

Religion of humanity: a secular religion founded by Auguste Comte in the mid-19th Century, which celebrated altruism, order and scientific progress. It was described by Thomas Huxley as "Catholicism minus Christianity." See Positivism in Concepts, Edmund Burke in Quotations, 5. Humanism in Details and 4. Auguste Comte/Positivism and 6. John Stuart Mill/Utilitarianism in Sociology Details.

Religious conversion experience: the personal experience of religious salvation, spiritual regeneration and/or psychic rebirth. For many "born again" Christian evangelicals and other members of Protestant denominations, the experience is intensely emotional and the central event of their spiritual lives, during which they are visited by God or Jesus, forgiven for their sins, infused with the Holy Spirit, spiritually "re-born" and promised eternal life. For first-generation Puritans, the individual conversion experience, after it was publically examined and confirmed, conferred membership into the community of the "elect," with the right of male members to vote and hold public office. Karen Armstrong, William James, Stow Persons, Kevin Phillips, Herbert Schneider. See Evangelicalism, Great Awakening cycle and Twice-born in Concepts.

Religious enthusiasm: the emotional fervor derived from being possessed or inspired by the divine spirit, which is often associated with Protestant evangelicalism. See Religious conversion experience and Great Awakening cycle/revivalism in Concepts.

Religious relics: in Roman Catholicism, venerated objects or body parts of saints, martyrs and other revered persons, which are usually stored or displayed in reliquaries in cathedrals.

Religious truth: a spiritual truth, belief or insight that, according to differing traditions, may be derived from (1) scripture or sacred texts; (2) the authority of the church; (3) faith; (4) reason; (5) personal revelation; (6) intuition; (7) meditation and contemplation; (8) ritualistic practices; (9) hallucinogenic drugs and trances; (10) science or (11) nature. See 2. Religion in Details.

Repentance: in Christian theology, "to turn away from sin"; to feel regret or contrition for wrongdoing. See Atonement, Confession and Penance in Concepts.

Revelation: the revealing of a divine truth.

Rites of spring: rituals that celebrate the miraculous return of life after death, of the verdure and abundance of spring after the death and dormancy of winter; the regeneration and transcendence of freedom over slavery, of life over death and suffering. For Jews, it is Passover and the escape from slavery in Egypt; for Christians, it is Easter and the Resurrection; for African-Americans, it is Juneteenth and Emancipation Day when they were freed from slavery.

Rosh Hashanah: the Jewish New Year.

Sacrifice: a ritual offering of food, objects, animals and/or humans to thank, please or appease a deity. It may be (1) an expression of worship, (2) a statement of gratitude, (3) a request for divine assistance, (4) a declaration of contrition, (5) an act of appeasement to avoid divine retribution or (6) an expression of social dominance and control by the ruling elite to impress or intimidate its subjects.

Samadhi: in Hinduism and Buddhism, single-minded concentration, meditation or absorption, in which the subject merges with the object of attention, the individual with the eternal or divine.

Satan: the personification of evil; the devil; Lucifer; a fallen angel; the serpent; the tempter; the great deceiver; the obstructer; the adversary; Beelzebub.

Satori: in Buddhism, spiritual awakening or enlightenment; seeing and understanding the true nature of things.

Scottish Common Sense Realism: a school of philosophy that rose during the 18th Century Enlightenment. It enshrines the principles of common sense and assumes that ordinary people know intuitively the existence of the self, the existence of real objects and the basic principles of morality and religion. Today, it serves as the de facto, vernacular philosophy of Anglo-American culture. See 35. Pragmatism/Instrumentalism in Details.

Sectarianism: the conflicts and schisms that arise within a religion. In Protestantism, (1) the Protestant Reformation's emphasis on the individual's responsibility for his or her personal salvation (the "priesthood of all believers"), (2) the primacy of scripture and (3) the loss of the absolute doctrinal authority of the Roman Catholic Church led to an unending series of schisms and fissions, which, in turn, led to the creation of a multiplicity of denominations, sects and factions, often based on minor and narrow, but very strongly held, differences in scriptural interpretation, doctrine or practice (which Sigmund Freud called the "narcissism of small differences"). Other major religions have also been subjected to such centrifugal forces (Islam's Sunni and Shia, for example), but not to the same extent as Protestant Christianity. See Sunni-Shia schism in Concepts, 18. Protestant Reformation in Details and Narcissism of small differences in Psychology Concepts.

Secularism: a socio-political order in which there is a formal separation between church and state; in which individuals have freedom of thought and conscience and in which governmental and other public institutions are not controlled by religious leaders or institutions. "The wall of Separation between the Garden of the Church and the Wilderness of the world" should be absolute so that the profanity of the state would not contaminate the purity of the church, according to Roger Williams. The separation is based on the principles that (1) "religion is a matter which lies solely between Man and his God" (Thomas Jefferson), and (2) a government should not establish, endorse, support or interfere with religion and, conversely, that "no religious body [should] seek to impose its will directly or indirectly upon the general populace or the public acts of its officials" (John F. Kennedy). In the United States, religious toleration and secularism were derived from (1) the multiplicity of religious denominations (see Voltaire in Quotations); (2) a belief in "soul libertie" (Roger Williams), that is, freedom of thought and conscience; (3) cultural pluralism and (4) the reaction against the tyranny, persecution and orthodoxy that, historically, was associated with single, state-supported religions. Roger Williams, Thomas Jefferson; John Barry. See Soul libertie in Concepts and 27. 18th Century Enlightenment in Details.

Seekers: members of a 17th Century religious sect who considered all organized religions to be spiritually corrupt. The term was also informally applied to individuals such as Roger Williams who were outside an established, state-supported church but who sought religious truth and revelation. John Barry.

Septuagint: the Greek version of the Hebrew Bible, which was translated in approximately 250 BCE.

Shaman: a spiritual or holy person, who may possess a gift for healing.

Shantih: in Buddhism, calmness, tranquilly, bliss; the peace that passes all understanding.

Shiva: the Hindu god of destruction and reproduction, who is usually portrayed with four arms and surrounded by fire.

Sin: a perceived offense or transgression against God. In Roman Catholic theology, a mortal sin is a rupture of the bond with God, which kills the soul and leads to eternal damnation unless it is repented; a venial sin, on the other hand, is a forgivable transgression that injures, but does not break, the bond with God.

Situational ethics: an ethical system based on the altruistic love of humans for other humans, which may transcend traditional moral codes and human laws in certain situations. It is illustrated, for example, by Mark Twain's Huckleberry Finn, who decides not turn in his friend Jim, a runaway slave, to the authorities; or by those in German-occupied countries during World War II who, at great risk to themselves, flouted Nazi laws in order to protect Jews and others fleeing from the Nazis. "Love is the ultimate law" (Paul Tillich). Joseph Fletcher. See Agape, Antinomianism, Autonomy, Civil disobedience, Ethicalism and Higher law in Concepts.

Skepticism: the doctrine that reality and truth are unknowable. See Solipsism in Concepts and 24. David Hume in Details.

Slave morality: Nietzsche's description of Christianity, which, in his view, elevated the weak over the strong and repressed natural, life-affirming human instincts. See Objectivism and Transvaluation of values in Concepts and 33. Nietzsche in Details.

Solipsism: the doctrine that the individual mind knows nothing outside itself; that nothing is true; that if it were true it would be unknowable, and that if it were knowable it would be incommunicable -- Gorgias (c. 483–375 BC), as paraphrased by Sextus Empiricus and Bertrand Russell.

Soul libertie: liberty of conscience; freedom of religion and thought; the doctrine that the government should have no role in regulating religious thought or practice, which was a radical and heretical idea when it was advanced in the 17th Century. Roger Williams; John Barry. See Secularism in Concepts.

Special providences: special events, incidences or signs that are perceived to be evidence of God's intervention into human affairs and natural events.

Sunni-Shia schism: the division between the two major denominations of Islam, which originated in a dispute over the successor to the Prophet Mohammed, who died in 632 CE. Sunni Muslims recognize Mohammed's father-in-law as the first caliphate, while Shia Muslims recognize Mohammed's first cousin and son-in-law as the legitimate caliphate and imam. Sunni Islam, which constitutes the largest denomination in Islam, tends to be theologically orthodox, traditional and conservative and views its religious leaders as temporal and under the control of state authority. Shia Islam, which constitutes 10-15% of the world's

Islamic population (concentrating in Iran, Pakistan, India and Iraq), views its religious leaders as divinely appointed; it is associated with a messianic spirit and, historically, has suffered persecution and martyrdom.

Sunyata (from Sanskrit for "emptiness"): in Buddhism, a state in which the mind is empty, without boundaries, free of worldly concerns and open to the infinite; the emancipation that is achieved from emptying the self and the mind. See *Kenosis* in Concepts.

Syllogism: a type of deductive reasoning in which a conclusion is deduced from a major and minor premise. For example: (1) all men are mortal; (2) Greeks are men; therefore, (3) all Greeks are mortal. See Deductive reasoning in Concepts and 17. Scholasticism in Details.

Syncretism: the blending of two or more religious traditions and sets of beliefs.

Tao: in Confucianism and Buddhism, the path or the way; the fundamental nature or essence of the universe, the objective of which, in spiritual practice, is to harmonize and become one with.

Teleology (from Greek *telos*, for "purpose" or "goal"): the purpose or final cause of things.

Theism: commonly, the monotheistic belief in a personal God who actively governs the universe.

Theocracy: a government that is directed and controlled by the leaders of the official, established, state-sponsored religion; versus secularism (*q.v.* in Concepts).

Theodicy (Greek for "god trial"): schools of thought that attempt to reconcile the existence of a just, omnipotent and/or benevolent God with the reality of evil in the world. Justifications include: (1) God is morally perfect, but the disobedience of Adam and Eve and their descendants is the source of all evil; that human suffering is punishment for original sin and the evil inherent in human nature (Augustine of Hippo); (2) justice will be served at the end of the world with the Second Coming, the resurrection of the dead and the Last Judgment (Gospel of Matthew, Book of Revelation); (3) suffering is necessary for human development (Irenaeus), (4) humans have an inherent need to believe that the universe has meaning and order, despite the evidence to the contrary (Peter Berger, Max Weber), and (5) a benevolent, although not omnipotent, God and the goodness of the universe is reflected in the evolution of life toward a higher state of being and consciousness (emergent deity); versus **anti-theodicy**: the view that, in light of the Holocaust and other horrific crimes against humanity, as well as natural disasters, the relationship between God and evil is irrelevant; that the role of humans is to live a godly life and to build a world where goodness will prevail (Emmanuel Levinas). See Emergent divinity, Ethicalism, *In statu viae*, Problem of evil, and Vitalism in Concepts and Epicurus Winston Churchill and T. S. Eliot in Quotations.

Theomorphism: the belief that humans are made in God's image; to love God and other human beings is to love oneself. See Emergent Divinity in Concepts and Baruch Spinoza and LeRoi Jones in Quotations.

Theosophy (Greek for "divine wisdom"): an eclectic and esoteric school of thought that emphasizes individual enlightenment, illumination and awareness in order to discover the deeper meaning and connections between nature, humanity and the divine world. Jakob Boehme.

Torah: the authoritative collection of Jewish religious teachings, including the Pentateuch, the first five books of the Hebrew Bible.

Totemism: among hunter-gathering groups, the veneration of an animal or plant as the symbolic or spiritual ancestor or emblem of a group, clan or tribe. The modern use of an animal or plant (e.g., an eagle, bear, lion, dove, lily, rose or maple leaf) as an emblem to represent a kingdom, dynasty, nation-state, corporation, school or sports team is a vestige of this tribal expression.

Transubstantiation: the doctrine that the bread and wine of the Eucharist are physically transformed into the actual flesh and blood of Christ, which is the official doctrine of the Roman Catholic Church; versus **consubstantiation**: the belief that the body and blood of Christ are present along with the bread and wine in the Eucharist.

Transvaluation of values: Nietzsche's call to replace Christianity's system of moral values (which, in his view, are hostile to life, elevate the weak over the strong, are revengeful, and focus on the struggle against sin and the repression of natural instincts) with a more life-affirming set of values that honor the natural instincts. The term has also been applied more generally to the re-evaluation and transformation of one set of values with another.

Trinitarianism: the belief that God, Jesus ("very God of very God") and the Holy Spirit are equal aspects of the same substance, or "one God in three persons," which is the official doctrine of the

Roman Catholic Church as promulgated by the Councils of Nicaea in 325 and 381; versus **non-Trinitarianism**: the belief that to worship Jesus as God is idolatrous and blasphemous and a form of polytheism; it emphasizes, instead, the humanity and ethical teachings of Jesus. See Arianism and Unitarianism in Concepts.

Twice-born: the term used by William James to describe those who have suffered a mental breakdown or a "crisis of meaning" and, afterward, experience a profound sense of renewal and a deeper appreciation for life; analogous to the "born again" religious experience of Christians.

Tychism: the doctrine that the universe is ruled by random chance. Since Darwin's variations and Mendel's genetic mutations are random and accidental, evolution is seen as driven "by chance and the destruction of bad results." Charles Peirce. See Determinism versus fatalism, Fortuitism and Radical contingency in Concepts; Population Bottleneck in Anthropology Concepts; Alternative histories and Radical contingency in Historiography Concepts and Broken symmetry, Chaos theory, Multiverse, Stochastic, Uniformitarianism versus catastrophism/neo-catastrophism and Vacuum genesis in Science Concepts.

Typology: the doctrine that New Testament events were prefigured in Old Testament events; also, the study of cultural types, including human personality types (*q.v.* in Psychology Details).

Unitarianism: a religion that rejects Trinitarianism (i.e., that God, Jesus and the Holy Ghost are "one God in three persons"), original sin and predestination, and, instead, celebrates God's love and man's potential excellence. It emphasizes the humanity and ethical teachings of Jesus rather than his divinity, his miracles or the resurrection. Unitarianism developed in the late 18th Century and early 19th Century in England and New England partially in reaction to the pessimism and determinism of Calvinism/ Puritanism, but also as a re-affirmation of the rational, benevolent deity of the 18th Century Enlightenment. Unitarianism is a version of universalism and served as the starting point for New England Transcendentalism. William Ellery Channing, Ralph Waldo Emerson. See Inner light, Over-Soul, Trinitarianism versus non-Trinitarianism and Universalism in Concepts, Ralph Waldo Emerson in Quotations, and 3. Pantheism and 29. New England Transcendentalism in Details.

Unity of opposites: the doctrine that every element is united with its opposite in a larger monism. See Dialectical method, Dualism and Ying and yang in Concepts, Emerson in Quotations and 9. Heraclitus, 20. Baruch Spinoza and 30. G. W. F. Hegel in Details.

Universalism: an inclusive, humanistic, syncretic set of beliefs that focuses on the universality and commonality of all religions and, in some forms, proposes that the divine spirit resides in all humans. See Ethicalism, Inner light, New England Transcendentalism, Quakers and Unitarianism in Concepts.

Utilitarianism: the doctrine that (1) every action should be judged by its utility, that is, whether it increases happiness, satisfaction and usefulness, and (2) social policies should seek to achieve the greatest happiness, or the least harm, for the greatest number of people. Jeremy Bentham, John Stuart Mill. See 35. Pragmatism/Instrumentalism in Details and 6. John Stuart Mill/Utilitarianism in Sociology Details.

*V***edas**: Hindu religious texts or scriptures.

Vishnu (Sanskrit for "the All Pervading One"): one of the central gods of Hinduism, who was reincarnated as Krishna and Rama, and is portrayed as having four arms.

Vitalism: *élan vital* (vital force); *anima mundi* (the world soul or creative spirit of the universe); the belief that the universe and all living organisms are united and guided by a creative life-force. Plato, Baruch Spinoza, G. W. F. Hegel, Ralph Waldo Emerson, Henri Bergson. See Inner light, Over-Soul and Universalism in Concepts and 3. Pantheism and 29. New England Transcendentalism in Details.

*W***eltanschauung**: world view. See Ideology in Concepts.

Will to meaning: the belief that humans are driven to find meaning in life. Viktor Frankl.

*Y***ing and yang** (Chinese for "shady side" and "sunny side"): the Chinese concept of polar opposites, which are complementary and interdependent and, together, form an indivisible whole that is greater than the sum of its parts. See Dualism, Holism and Unity of opposites in Concepts.

Yoga (Sanskrit for join, unite, attach or yoke): a system of exercises and breathing and meditation practices by which the practitioner seeks to liberate and unite the self with the divine spirit.

Yom Kippur: the Jewish day of atonement.

Zen Buddhism: the way of enlightenment; a religious philosophy that focuses on the struggle to transcend suffering through meditation, detachment and simple living. See 6. Buddhism and 40. Ram Dass in Details.

Zeus: in Greek cosmology, the "father of gods and men" and the ruler of heaven and earth. Zeus was the son of the Cronus and Rhea and the grandson of the sky god Uranus and the earth goddess Gaia.

QUOTATIONS:

- *I know one thing, that I know nothing.* -- Socrates.

- *Whirl is king, having deposed Zeus.* -- Aristophanes.

- *Men create gods after their own image, not only with regard to their form but with regard to their mode of life.* -- Aristotle.

- *When a sensible man ceases to see different identities due to different material bodies and he sees how beings are expanded everywhere, he attains to the Brahman conception.* -- *Bhagavad Gita.*

- *Is* [God] *willing to prevent evil, but not able? Then he is impotent. Is he able, but not willing? Then he is malevolent.* -- Epicurus as paraphrased by David Hume.

- *Credo quia absurdum* [I believe because it is absurd]. -- Tertullian.

- *Our life is what our thoughts make it.* -- Marcus Aurelius.

- *Here I stand. I cannot do otherwise.* -- Martin Luther.

- *Cogito, ergo sum* [I think, therefore I am]. -- René Descartes.

- *The intellectual love of the mind towards God is part of the infinite love wherewith God loves himself.* – Baruch Spinoza.

- *If there were only one religion in England there would be danger of despotism, if there were two, they would cut each other's throats, but there are thirty, and they live in peace and happiness.* -- Voltaire.

- *Act only according to that maxim whereby you can, at the same time, will that it should become a universal law.* -- Immanuel Kant.

- *The only religion I profess is that of universal humanity and benevolence.* -- Edmund Burke.

- *Within man is the soul of the whole; the wise silence; the universal beauty, to which every part and particle is equally related, the eternal ONE. And [in] this deep power in which we exist and whose beatitude is accessible to all . . . the act of seeing and the thing seen, the seer and the spectacle, the subject and the object are one. We see the world piece by piece, as the sun, the moon, the animal, the tree; but the whole, of which these are shining parts, is the soul.* -- Ralph Waldo Emerson.

- *It is not the consciousness of men that determines their existence, but on the contrary, their social existence determines their consciousness.* -- Karl Marx.

- *The philosophers have only interpreted the world, the point is to change it.* – Marx.

- *Religion is the love of life in the consciousness of its impotence.* -- George Santayana.

- *The crime that has no name.* -- Winston Churchill.

- *After such knowledge, what forgiveness?* -- T. S. Eliot.

- *There is but one truly serious philosophical problem and that is suicide. Judging whether life is or is not worth living amounts to answering the fundamental question of philosophy.* -- Albert Camus.

- *God loves the world through us.* -- Mother Teresa.

- *My conscience is clear.* -- Pol Pot.

- *The universe . . . bends toward justice.* -- Martin Luther King, Jr. and Theodore Parker.

- *The creator is his own creation.* -- LeRoi Jones.

- *I am so past enlightenment.* -- one Buddhist monk strolling with another monk (*New Yorker* cartoon).

PHILOSOPHY/RELIGION DETAILS: (1) Philosophy, (2) Religion, (3) Pantheism, (4) Philosophical Idealism, (5) Humanism, (6) Buddhism, (7) Confucianism, (8) Pythagoras, (9) Heraclitus, (10) Parmenides, (11) Socrates, (12) Plato, (13) Aristotle, (14) Stoicism, (15) Marcus Aurelius, (16) Augustine of Hippo, (17) Scholasticism, (18) Protestant Reformation, (19) René Descartes, (20) Baruch Spinoza, (21) John Locke, (22) Gottfried Leibniz, (23) George Berkeley, (24) David Hume, (25) Jean-Jacques Rousseau, (26) Immanuel Kant, (27) 18th Century Enlightenment/Age of Reason, (28) Romanticism, (29) New England Transcendentalism, (30) G. W. F. Hegel, (31) Auguste Comte, (32) Karl Marx, (33) Friedrich Nietzsche, (34) Max Weber, (35) Pragmatism/Instrumentalism, (36) Phenomenology, (37) Existentialism, (38) Logical Positivism, (39) Analytic Philosophy, (40) Ram Dass and (41) Four World-View Typologies.

1. **Philosophy** (Greek for "love of wisdom") is the rational and systematic study of a set of foundational concepts, including those concerned with (1) aesthetics (the nature of art and beauty); (2) cosmology (the origin and nature of the universe); (3) epistemology (the nature of knowledge and perception; how we know what we know); (4) ethics (the nature of good and evil, right and wrong, and the precepts for ethical conduct); (5) logic (the principles of rational argument and formal reasoning); (6) metaphysics (the nature of reality); (7) ontology (the nature of existence and being) and (8) teleology (the purpose and final cause of things).

2. **Religion** is a faith or belief system, which is often expressed through narratives, symbols, traditions and sacred stories. Religion (1) serves as a means of expressing spirituality and reverence for the divine; (2) provides a method for explaining the origin, nature and purpose of the universe, the mysteries of life and death and the relationship between humans and the supernatural and the divine; (3) sanctions systems of ethics and moral values that are intended to give meaning, direction and purpose to life and to reinforce ethical behavior, altruism, social justice and self-sacrifice; (4)

offers the hope and compensation of an afterlife, and (5) provides aid and comfort to the suffering, the poor, the marginalized and the dispossessed.

Critics of religion have described it as (1) a socially constructed cultural system (Clifford Geertz); (2) the opium of the people (Karl Marx); (3) a manifestation of universal obsessional neurosis and wishful thinking (Sigmund Freud) and (4) a means of reinforcing the dominant ideology of the ruling class. At various times in history, religion has been associated with superstition and magical thinking, blood sacrifice, patriarchy, dogma, schism, intolerance, censorship, anti-intellectualism, antipathy to rational empiricism and secular pluralism, religious wars, torture and terrorism.

3. **Pantheism** is the belief in the immanence, or presence, of the divinity in all life; that God, the universe and nature are one (Baruch Spinoza). It is reflected in such concepts as animism (the belief that all entities and objects in nature have a soul or spiritual essence); *vis vitae* (vital force -- Posidonius); *anima mundi* (the world soul or creative spirit of the universe -- Plato); the-will-to-live (Arthur Schopenhauer); *élan vital* (the creative life force -- Henri Bergson) and the divine Over-Soul (Ralph Waldo Emerson). See Baruch Spinoza, Ralph Waldo Emerson and LeRoi Jones in Quotations

4. **Philosophical Idealism** is a school of philosophy that has two fundamental divisions: (1) the external, or objective, idealism of Pythagoras, Plato, G. W. F. Hegel and others, in which reality consists of absolute Ideas or Forms beyond the world of the senses, and (2) the internal, or subjective, idealism of George Berkeley, Jonathan Edwards and others, in which reality consists of ideas in the mind. In each case, material objects have no independent existence except as reflections of the external ideal world or projections of the internal mental world.

5. **Humanism** is an ethical philosophy that exalts the dignity of men and women and celebrates human reason, ethics, social justice, scientific progress and social improvement. It rejects divine intervention, institutional religion, supernatural explanations and religious dogma as the basis of morality. Historically, it was represented in classical and Renaissance humanism ("man is the

measure of all things" -- Protagoras), the 18th Century
Enlightenment (see 27. in Details), positivism, utilitarianism, social
Marxism, representative democracy and cultural pluralism. See
Religion of humanity in Concepts.

6. **Buddhism** is a non-theistic religion of enlightened consciousness
that was founded in India by Siddhartha Gautama (563-483 BCE),
who was known as the Buddha ("the awakened one"). Buddhism's
Four Noble Truths assert that life is suffering (*dukkha*), which is
caused by cravings, ignorance and attachment. Suffering ceases
when nirvana, the profound peace of mind, is achieved through the
spiritual practices of the Noble Eightfold Path (of right
understanding, right thought, right speech, right action, right
livelihood, right effort, right mindfulness and right concentration).

On the path to enlightenment and liberation from suffering,
students of Buddhism focus on developing a sense of mindfulness;
that is, on the direct involvement of consciousness in the present
moment, without attachments or distractions and beyond words or
logic. Buddhists practice *samatha* (calmness and concentration)
and *vipassana* (insight and mindfulness) meditation. They are
advised to cease being spectators of their own actions, to remember
to forget, that the arrow releases itself and that one should not cross
the river before one gets to the river. Karen Armstrong, Ram Dass,
Rupert Gethin, Peter Harvey, Damien Keown, D. T. Suzuki. See
40. Ram Dass in Details.

7. **Confucianism** is a humanistic, non-theistic system of ethics that
was founded in China by Confucius (551-478 BCE). It (1)
provides the precepts for living a virtuous life; (2) promotes social
harmony and the cultivation of virtue and knowledge and (3)
celebrates altruism, propriety, honesty, loyalty, kindness and filial
piety. Historically, it was associated with the ideal of a
meritocracy (which included a system of written civil service
examinations) and served as the official state ideology of pre-
Communist China.

8. **Pythagoras** (c. 570-495 BCE) advocated a life of passionate,
sympathetic contemplation (as paraphrased by Bertrand Russell).
His philosophy represented a combination of rationalism and
mysticism (including the transmigration of immortal souls) and

celebrated an objective world of ideals revealed to the intellect but not to the senses; that numbers ("all things are numbers") and geometric forms are exact and eternal truths beyond the world of the senses, which anticipated Plato's ideal Forms.

9. **Heraclitus** (c. 535-475 BCE) proposed that all is flux; that everything is perpetually changing (for example, you cannot step twice in the same river); that fire is the primordial element and that harmony is achieved through the unity of opposites (good and evil are one; to God, all things are fair and good and right; but men hold some things wrong and some right).

10. **Parmenides** (born c. 515 BCE) proposed that all things are fixed and nothing changes; that all sensible things are illusions; that the only true being is the One, which is infinite and indivisible, and that cold means not hot.

11. **Socrates** (c. 469-399 BCE) was the father of Western philosophy. He proposed that the starting point of wisdom and philosophical inquiry is the awareness of one's own ignorance ("I know one thing, that I know nothing"). He associated virtue with the search for knowledge and truth and believed that the unexamined life is not worth living. Socrates employed what came to be known as the Socratic method, which is a dialectical process of critical thinking that involves asking a series of questions, pointing out contradictions, eliminating some hypotheses and arriving at the truth. "Socratic irony" is a method in which the questioner professes to be ignorant of the issues involved in order to invite further discussion and critical thinking. See Irony in Literary Concepts.

12. **Plato** (c. 424-348 BCE) was a student of Socrates who developed a philosophy of idealism in which reality consists of eternal, unchanging Ideas, Forms or Essences behind the veil of worldly appearances. His philosophy is illustrated by the allegory of the cave in which prisoners chained in a cave with their backs to the entrance perceive the flickering shadows on the back of cave wall to be reality, not the true objects outside in the sunlight, from which the shadows are projected. Plato is also known for his concept of philosopher-kings, the intellectual ruler-guardians

whose love of wisdom and knowledge would guide them as they governed the ship of state.

13. **Aristotle** (384-322 BCE) was a student of Plato who (1) proposed that the essential nature of things is determined by their purpose; (2) delineated four types of causes (in building a ship, for example, [a] the formal cause is the design of the ship, [b] the material cause is the material used to build the ship, [c] the efficient cause is the tools and workmen who actually build it and [d] the final cause is the intended purpose of the ship); (3) developed the concepts of *arete* (excellence, valor; virtue; living up to one's potential) and *eudemonia* (the sense of happiness and well-being derived from living a life of reason, knowledge and virtue) and (4) described art as the imitation and perfection of nature whose purpose is to purify and cleanse the emotions (*catharsis*). See 4. Aristotle in Art Details.

14. **Stoicism** was a school of moral philosophy that was popular in the Greek and Roman world from the 3rd Century BCE to the 6th Century CE. It was derived from the teachings and writings of Zeno, Seneca, Epictetus and Marcus Aurelius. Stoics taught that one should accept the world as it is, cultivate indifference to pleasure and pain and live a life of reason, virtue and harmony with nature and the divine will. See 15. Marcus Aurelius in Details.

15. **Marcus Aurelius** (121-180 CE) was a Stoic philosopher and Roman emperor who, in his *Meditations*, counseled to "hold fast to the divine spirit within you"; live "simply and spontaneously"; "accept all things with a kindly smile"; "adapt yourself to the environment in which your lot has been cast, and show true love to the fellow-mortals with whom destiny has surrounded you," and, finally, "forget your thirst for books, so that when your end comes you may . . . meet it with good grace and unfeigned gratitude in your heart to the gods."

16. **Augustine of Hippo** (354-430) was a philosopher-theologian who provided the intellectual foundations for Roman Catholic theology, as well as the Protestant Reformation, by developing the doctrines of original sin, predestination and salvation through faith and divine grace. He contrasted the eternal City of God (which he identified with the spiritual Christian church) with the temporal

City of Man (which he identified with the earthly city of Rome, which had been sacked and pillaged in 410 by the Visigoths).

17. **Scholasticism** (1100s to 1300s) was a school of critical thought that employed deductive and syllogistic reasoning to teach and defend Roman Catholic doctrine. It was used by academic "schoolmen," or "scholastics," of the medieval universities, such as Thomas Aquinas (1225-1274), one of the Church's greatest theologians and philosophers, who used deductive logic to reconcile reason with faith, and Aristotelian thought with Christian orthodoxy. Thomas demonstrated the rational basis of Catholic doctrine and showed that God could be known through "natural reason," as well as through faith and revelation. The scholastic method has been criticized for using an *a priori*, dialectical approach to justify pre-established principles and dogma, for ignoring inductive methods and empirical data and for over-relying on disputations and subtle verbal distinctions.

18. **Protestant Reformation** (1500s and 1600s) was a religious reform movement that broke away from the Roman Catholic Church, which led to the formation of a series of Protestant denominations. It began in 1517 with the posting of the *Ninety-Five Theses* by Martin Luther (1483-1546) on the church door at Wittenberg ("Here I stand"). Protestant reforms focused on issues such as the sale of indulgences (which offered to reduce the time spent in purgatory), simony (the selling of church offices), corruption, transubstantiation, papal supremacy, priestly celibacy, the veneration of saints, confessions, liturgy and rituals. Protestants believed in original sin, predestination, personal salvation by faith through the grace of God and the priesthood of all believers (that is, that each person was their own priest and was responsible for their own salvation). They focused on inward devotion and the believer's direct, personal relationship with God rather than the authority of the church, outward ceremony or a relationship with God that was mediated through the church, priests, saints or others.

Historically, the Protestant Reformation was associated with (1) the rise of an urban middle class and (2) proto-nationalist (largely Anglo-German-Dutch) resentment against the power and authority of Rome, and resulted in (3) the confiscation of Catholic church properties by Protestant secular authorities. The Reformation precipitated the Roman Catholic Counter-Reformation and led to a series of religious wars, which lasted for over one hundred years. The spread of Protestant "heresies" (including vernacular [i.e., on-Latin] versions of the Bible) was facilitated by the invention of the printing press in Europe in the 1440s. The Protestant Reformation laid the foundation for scientific empiricism, republicanism and the rise of capitalism. See Protestant ethic and the rise of capitalism in Economics Concepts.

The Protestant emphasis on the individual's direct, personal relationship with God, written scripture and the vernacular Bible, led to (1) an increase in popular literacy, (2) the rise of an educated middle class and (3) the ideal of a learned clergy. However, the emphasis on written scripture as a means to personal salvation and the absence of the absolute doctrinal authority of the Roman Catholic Church led to an endless series of Protestant fissions and schisms, many over minor doctrinal issues, and the proliferation of Protestant denominations and sects, including Lutherans, Calvinists, Anabaptists, Anglicans, Puritans (Congregationalists and Presbyterians), Separatists/Brownists, Baptists, Quakers, Methodists, Unitarians, Mormons, Adventists, Jehovah's Witnesses and Pentecostals.

19. **René Descartes** (1596-1650) was the father of modern philosophy, who was associated with (1) Cartesian doubt (doubt everything, except "I think, therefore I am"), which is the starting point and first principle of modern philosophy; (2) mind-matter dualism (the mental and the material/physical worlds are separate, parallel, independent and predetermined, and only appear to interact by coincidence); (3) rationalism (reason is superior to experience as a source of knowledge; the exterior world can only be known through the mind, not the senses) and (4) the invention of coordinate geometry.

20. **Baruch Spinoza** (1632-1677) was "the noblest and most lovable of the great philosophers," according to Bertrand Russell. Spinoza (1) was a proponent of rationalism, determinism and pantheism (God and the material universe are the same substance); (2) believed that "love towards God must hold the chief place in the mind"; (3) suggested that "hatred is increased by being reciprocated, and can on the other hand be destroyed by love" and

(4) proposed that things cannot be other than what they are since negation (evil, sin, suffering) exists only from the point of view of finite creatures, and everything is part of the whole and is necessary for the goodness of the whole.

21. **John Locke** (1632-1704) was the father of British empiricism, in which knowledge of the external world is derived through the senses from experience and scientific observation. From his theory of the mind at birth as a *tabula rasa*, or blank tablet, it followed that there are no innate ideas, no innate depravity and no original sin, and, thus, all men are created equal. This provided the justification for the 18th Century Enlightenment's concepts of science, natural rights and the social compact (in which government is based on the consent of the governed), which, in turn, provided the philosophical basis for the American and French Revolutions, the Declaration of Independence, the United States Constitution and the French Declaration of the Rights of Man. See 27. 18th Century Enlightenment/Age of Reason in Details.

22. **Gottfried Leibniz** (1646-1716) was a proponent of rationalism. He (1) proposed that matter consists of an infinite number of atom-sized, "windowless" monads, which are discrete mortal souls that do not interact with each other and only appear to do so coincidentally; (2) developed the concept of pre-established harmony (that is, that mind and matter, the mental and physical worlds, are parallel and absolutely independent of each other; for example, that I will my finger to move and it then moves represent two separate, predetermined events that are coincidentally, but not causally, connected); (3) invented differential and integral calculus independently of Newton and (4) believed that this is the best of all possible worlds (for which he was caricatured as Dr. Pangloss in Voltaire's *Candide*).

23. **George Berkeley** (1685-1753) developed the philosophy of subjective idealism, that is, that reality consists of ideas in the mind and has no existence independent of the mind; that material objects are reflections of internal mental states, and that nothing exists unless it is perceived ("to be is to be perceived"). His "westward the course of empire makes its way" led to the naming of the city and campus at the University of California after him.

24. **David Hume** (1711-1776) was an 18th Century empiricist and radical skeptic who believed that (1) knowledge is acquired through experience and the senses rather than through reason or innate ideas; (2) reality is unknowable since there is no inherent connection between cause and effect other than that ascribed by mental habit and (3) human behavior is governed by passions rather than by reason.

25. **Jean-Jacques Rousseau** (1712-1 778) developed a version of the **social contract** in which the state reflects the "general will" of the people. He believed that people in a state of nature are essentially good and possess a natural, innate moral sense that has been repressed and corrupted by the decadence of civilization and the inequity of private property. Rousseau has been described as the father of the Romantic movement. See 28. Romanticism in Details and 12. Violence and Human Nature (the Hobbes-Rousseau Dichotomy) in Anthropology Details.

26. **Immanuel Kant** (1724-1804) sought to reconcile empiricism (that is, that knowledge of external reality is derived through the senses from experience and scientific observation) with rationalism (that is, that innate, human reason is the source of all knowledge). He proposed that *noumena* (the objective things-in-themselves) can only be known through *phenomena* (things as they appear through the senses) as they are filtered through the innate, *a priori* categories of the mind and through transcendental intuition. In contrast to Locke's theory of the mind at birth as a *tabula rasa*, or blank tablet, which passively receives sense impressions, Kant believed that the mind actively filters, interprets and judges experience through pre-established concepts and mental categories, such as cause and effect, space and time. He distinguished between reason and understanding and developed the precept of the categorical moral imperative, which is that one must act as though that action would become a universal law.

27. **18th Century Enlightenment/Age of Reason** was an intellectual movement, climate of opinion and world view of the late 17th and 18th Centuries. It consisted of scientists, *philosophes, encyclopédists,* men and women of letters and the reading public who celebrated the power of human reason, science and progress to

triumph over religious dogma, the authority of the church, divine-right monarchy, ignorance, superstition and intolerance.

The Enlightenment was associated with (1) humanism and the perfectibility of man; (2) faith in human reason and rational empiricism to discover the laws of nature and nature's God; (3) a belief in the inevitability of human progress and social improvement; (4) the doctrine of natural rights; (5) the social compact (in which government is based on the consent of the governed) and representative government; (6) religious toleration; (7) a rational, benevolent, orderly God who obeys the laws of nature and does not intervene in human affairs (Deism); (8) merchant capitalism and free trade (see 3. Adam Smith/Classical/Free Market Economics in Economics Details); (9) music, art and architecture that was characterized by its order, form, harmony and restraint (see 12. 18th Century Neoclassicism in Art Details); (10) the view of history as philosophy teaching by example, of universal man stripped of the particulars and accidents of time and place (David Hume) and (11) a belief in posterity as a substitute for God and immortality.

Enlightenment ideas were spread through the "public sphere" (*q.v.* in Political Science Concepts) by the "republic of letters," a virtual, international community of readers, writers and intellectuals, and were discussed and exchanged in universities, scientific societies and academies, the *Encyclopédia*, newspapers and journals, such as *The Tatler* and *The Spectator*, the salons of Paris, coffeehouses ("penny universities"), bookshops, athenaeums, debating societies and Free Mason lodges. The Enlightenment's humanistic, anticlerical and egalitarian ideals of liberty, fraternity and equality were adopted by educated elites (*les grands* and *gens de letters*) who, however, also distrusted "mob rule" and the multitudes as much they did censorship, absolute monarchy and church dogma (Robert Darnton; Daniel Roche). Enlightenment ideals are reflected in the Declaration of Independence, the United States Constitution and the Bill of Rights, the French Declaration of the Rights of Man, the French Revolutions of 1789, 1830 and 1848, the Latin American wars for independence in the 19th Century and the wars for national liberation and independence in the 20th Century. The Enlightenment laid the intellectual foundation for the modern, democratic, secular, progressive social state. The ideas and values of the Enlightenment are represented in the works of George Berkeley, Denis Diderot, Benjamin Franklin, Edward Gibbon, David Hume, Thomas Jefferson, Immanuel Kant, Wilhelm Leibniz, John Locke, James Madison, Montesquieu, Isaac Newton, Thomas Paine, Jean-Jacques Rousseau, Adam Smith and Voltaire. See Post-Enlightenment in Concepts, 12. 18th Century Neoclassicism in Art Details and Carl Becker, Peter Gay and Jonathan Israel in Selected References.

28. **Romanticism** was an intellectual, literary and artistic movement in the first half of the 19th Century that has been viewed as a reaction against the scientific rationalism and orderliness of the 18th Century Enlightenment. It celebrated the primacy of feelings, the extremes of emotion, the value of intuition, originality and the imagination, and the unique, subjective experience of the individual. Romanticism (1) stressed the heroic nature of the individual genius; (2) revered the beauty, sublimity and spirituality of nature; (3) abhorred the evils of industrialism and urbanization and their incursion into nature; (4) exalted the mystical, supernatural and irrational; (5) honored the Dionysian spirit with its imperatives of the heart (emotion) over those of the head (reason); (6) re-discovered Gothic medievalism and indigenous folk cultures and (7) inspired and sanctified romantic nationalism. Representative figures include Jane Austen, William Blake, the Brontes, Lord Byron, Thomas Cole, Samuel Taylor Coleridge, James Fenimore Cooper, Emily Dickinson, Ralph Waldo Emerson, Johann Fichte, Margaret Fuller, Johann Wolfgang von Goethe, Francisco Goya, Nathaniel Hawthorne, G. W. F. Hegel, Johann Herder, Victor Hugo, Washington Irving, Immanuel Kant, John Keats, Herman Melville, Edgar Allan Poe, Jean-Jacques Rousseau, George Sand, Friedrich Schiller, Walter Scott, Mary and Percy Shelley, Henry David Thoreau, J. M. W. Turner, Walt Whitman and William Wordsworth. See 13. Romanticism in Art Details.

29. **New England Transcendentalism** was a literary and philosophical movement of the second quarter of 19th Century that served as the quintessential expression of American Romanticism. It has been viewed as a reaction against both the original sin and religious orthodoxy of Puritanism/Calvinism, on the one hand, as well as the scientific rationalism of the 18th Century Enlightenment, on the other. It celebrated (1) individualism

("enjoy an original relation with the universe"; "the infinitude of the private man"); (2) self-reliance ("trust thyself"); (3) the immanence of the divinity (or Over-Soul) in all life; (4) the beauty and sublimity of nature ("nature is the symbol of the spirit"); (5) the moral law of compensation; (6) "double consciousness," i.e., the reflective self (in the world of ideas) over the actual self (in the here and now) and understanding over reason; (7) antinomianism, civil disobedience and the imperatives of a higher law and (8) a life of spiritual simplicity and integrity ("simplify, simplify"; "live deliberately"; "the mass of men lead lives of quiet desperation" and "desperate haste"; "to be awake is to be alive"; "I was determined to know beans"). New England Transcendentalism is represented in the works of Bronson Alcott, Emily Dickinson, Ralph Waldo Emerson, Margaret Fuller, Herman Melville, Henry David Thoreau, Jones Very and Walt Whitman.

30. **G. W. F. Hegel** (1770-1831) developed these concepts: (1) dialectical idealism, in which the conflict between a thesis and its antithesis leads to a new synthesis; (2) the unity of opposites, in which every notion includes its own negation and (3) the idea of the material world as a manifestation of the Absolute Mind or Spirit.

31. **Auguste Comte** (1798-1857) was the founder of positivism, a school of thought that views science as the definitive source of knowledge and in which truth is derived from the application of scientific methods and empirical techniques to all phenomena, including human social behavior, which laid the foundation for modern sociology. See Religion of humanity in Concepts and 4. Positivism in Sociology Details.

32. **Karl Marx** (1818-1883) inverted Hegel's dialectical idealism and incorporated it into his socio-economic philosophy of dialectical materialism. The latter is driven by class dynamics and changes in the material/economic substructure, which drive changes in the superstructure (art, religion and ideology; social, cultural, political and legal institutions). See 9. Karl Marx/Dialectical Materialism and 10. Economic/Technological Determinism in Economics Details.

33. **Friedrich Nietzsche** (1844-1900) developed these concepts: (1) the will to power; (2) *Übermensch* (Superman); (3) beyond good and evil; (4) the death of God; (5) Christianity as a slave morality; (6) the transvaluation of values (*q.v.* in Concepts); (7) the herd instinct and (8) the Apollonian-Dionysian cultural dichotomy of reason and harmony versus instinct and passion (*q.v.* in Art Concepts).

34. **Max Weber** (1864-1920) stressed (1) the importance of religion and ideas, rather than economic and material conditions, as factors in historical causation and (2) the primacy of subjective meanings that individuals attach to their actions. Weber proposed that a socio-religious system of values (the Protestant ethic of industry, frugality and capital accumulation) laid the foundation for an economic system (capitalism). He also developed the concepts of *charisma* (the "gift of grace") and *verstehen* ("insight), and borrowed Friedrich Schiller's term "disenchantment" to describe the loss of magic, mystery, spirituality and "sublime values" in modern, rational, secular, bureaucratic society. See 14. Max Weber/Protestant Ethic in Economics Details and 14. Max Weber in Sociology Details.

35. **Pragmatism/Instrumentalism** is a school of radical empiricism that was developed in the United States in the late 19th and early 20th Centuries. It proposed that (1) knowledge is derived from the "irreducible brute facts" of experience; (2) truth is a process, not an essence; (3) truth is determined by its usefulness and its practical outcomes, that is, its "cash value" and (4) effective learning is derived, not from a "spectator theory of knowledge," in which the student plays a passive role, but from active experimentation, problem-solving, the practical application of knowledge ("learning by doing") and the usefulness of the results. Instrumentalism is the doctrine that scientific theories should be evaluated by how effectively they explain and predict phenomena, not whether or not they accurately describe objective reality.

The discovery of radioactivity and Einstein's theories of relativity in the early 20th Century destroyed the Newtonian "block universe" of an enclosed, monistic, cosmic machine. Philosophical pragmatism offered, instead, an open-ended universe of individual freedom and choice, novelty, variety, spontaneity, flux, indeterminacy and chance. It (1) stressed the creative role and boundless potentiality of the individual; (2) contradicted the determinism and moral absolutism of Calvinism and the Social Darwinism of the late 19th Century and (3) laid the philosophical foundation for 20th Century progressive reform movements. John Dewey, William James and Charles Peirce are the founders of philosophical pragmatism and instrumentalism. See Richard Hofstadter and Stow Persons in Selected References. For the informal identification of pragmatism with practicality and expediency, see Scottish Common Sense Realism and Utilitarianism in Concepts and Frederick Jackson Turner in American History Quotations.

36. **Phenomenology** is a school of thought that focuses on the structures of consciousness and subjective experience, including perceptions, judgments and emotions. It is derived from Kant's distinction between *noumena* (objects as things-in-themselves which cannot be experienced directly) and *phenomena* (objects as interpreted by human understanding or consciousness). It views man not an isolated object, but as a continuum or field of being, and proposes that the mind interacts with the "lived experience" of everyday life "just as it appears" and is presented to consciousness ("being-in-the world"). Phenomenology is associated with Martin Heidegger and Edmund Husserl.

37. **Existentialism** is an "anti-philosophy" philosophy of the 20th Century. It proposes that (1) existence precedes essence (Jean-Paul Sartre), that is, that individuals define themselves in the moment by their choices (versus the genetic proposition that explanations are found in origins or pre-defined essences) and (2) the individual is free and responsible for giving meaning to his or her life in the face of an absurd and seemingly meaningless universe and for living that life passionately and sincerely.

Existentialism is identified with the following concepts: (1) the individual's quest to achieve self-hood in the face of anxiety, dread, despair, alienation, boredom, nausea and nothingness (Sartre); (2) authenticity (Søren Kierkegaard); (3) the leap of faith (Kierkegaard); (4) the limit-situation (that is, the extreme, intense experience on the edge of despair, madness, danger or death in which the self is exposed to the limits of conventional constraints and allows itself to abandon those limits and expose itself to new forms of consciousness; Karl Jaspers); (5) the repetition-compulsion (that is, the urge to repeat, re-enact or re-live an original trauma; Sigmund Freud), (6) grace under pressure and the moment of truth (Ernest Hemingway); (7) the myth of Sisyphus (who finds meaning and purpose in a pointless, unending task; Albert Camus) (8) the question of suicide ("there is only one truly serious philosophical problem, and that is suicide," according to Camus) and (9) the obsession with death ("death forces us to forego the demand for an explanation of everything and to concentrate on giving meaning to life through action," according to Jaspers as paraphrased in John Killinger).

Existentialism can be viewed as a response to the 20th Century horrors of world wars, totalitarianism, genocide, the rise of religious fundamentalism, the threat of nuclear annihilation and the erosion of the Enlightenment values of reason, optimism, secularism and faith in science and human progress.
Existentialism is represented in the works of Albert Camus, Martin Heidegger, Ernest Hemingway, Karl Jaspers, Søren Kierkegaard, Jean-Paul Sartre and others.

38. **Logical Positivism** is a school of thought that (1) proposes that the objective of philosophy is the logical clarification of thought and (2) rejects metaphysical speculations and (3) insists that all propositions be logically consistent and empirically verifiable. Logical positivism is considered to be an antecedent to, and subset of, Analytic philosophy. Bertrand Russell.

39. **Analytic Philosophy** is a school of philosophy that proposes that knowledge must be based on logical inferences from observable facts. It uses the formal language of mathematical symbols and rules to solve problems in logic and to achieve clarity and precision in philosophical discourse.

40. **Ram Dass** (b. 1931) is a spiritual teacher who counsels his followers to project love; to live in harmony with the present; to let the mind sit quietly and do its thing; to float down the stream of life in a state of higher consciousness and unity, with no overlay of self-consciousness; to recognize that "your enemies wake you up

to a place you are not," and to "clear your mind, center your body, open your heart and ask god." See 6. Buddhism in Details.

41. **Four World Views** is a method of classifying the paradigms, or basic conceptual frameworks, that seek to justify, explain and provide meaning and coherence to what Max Weber called the "world process." These four world views are: (1) scientific-rationalism (that truth is found through methodical, scientific inquiry), (2) neo-romanticism (that truth is found through harmony with nature and spiritual exploration of the self), (3) social-traditionalism (that truth is found through religious and secular institutions and traditions), and (4) postmodernism (that truth is a social construct). Walter Truett Anderson.

8. POLITICAL SCIENCE

CONCEPTS AND PHRASES:

Absolute monarchy: a form of government in which all power
resides in a single, usually, hereditary sovereign, who derives all
his or her authority from God and has few legal constraints; "the
monarch is the law"; versus limited or constitutional monarchy.
Edward Coke, Robert Filmer, Thomas Hobbes. See Divine right of
kings in Concepts.

Acquisitive mentality versus **civic responsibility**: the conflict in
political and cultural values between private gain and public good,
between economic individualism and social responsibility; a
fundamental conundrum of American democracy. John Kenneth
Galbraith. See Individualism in Concepts.

Anarchism: the term applied to a range of political philosophies whose
common goal is to abolish the state.

Anticlerical: a term that originated in the 18th Century and was applied
to those who opposed the Roman Catholic Church for its political
power, secrecy, censorship and patriarchy, as well as its sanction of
reactionary governments and its opposition to the separation of
church and state. More recently, the term has been applied to those
who oppose Islamic clerics and theocrats.

Arab Spring: a series of spontaneous, grass-roots movements in North
Africa and the Middle East, beginning in 2011, for democracy and
social change and the overthrow of authoritarian governments.
The uprisings were facilitated by the use of Internet technology
and electronic social media. See 2. Patterns of Political-Social
Revolutions in Details.

Aristocracy: a social system and form of government which is
controlled by a small, privileged class, whose power is usually
hereditary and based on landed wealth; versus a plutocracy, in
which the wealth may or may not have been inherited. See

Oligarchy and Plutocracy in Concepts and 15. Elites/Oligarchies in Sociology Details.

Authoritarian personality: see 16. Authoritarian personality in Psychology Details. Theodor Adorno, Richard Hofstadter.

Authoritarian state: a government in which political power is concentrated in a single individual, a cabal of individuals or a single party, and which uses military power, political repression, patronage and corruption to perpetuate itself in power. Generally, it differs from totalitarianism in that it is usually less intrusive and ideological and allows a limited number of social and economic institutions that are not under its direct control. See Totalitarianism in Concepts.

Autocracy: a government in which absolute power resides in one person.

Balance of power: (1) the leverage exerted by a smaller third group over two larger opposing groups, which compete for its support; (2) an alliance among smaller groups or individuals against a larger group; (3) a situation in which no one group is strong enough to dominate other groups. See 5. Social Intelligence/Social Brain Hypothesis in Anthropology Details.

Balance of terror: the stasis between two or more thermonuclear powers, whose ability to annihilate each other and the rest of civilization is balanced by the certainty of their mutual destruction. See 31. Cold War in American History Details.

Balanced government: a government of checks and balances that is based on (1) the **separation of powers** between the three branches of government (the legislative, executive and judicial) and (2) the **division of powers** between the national government and the states or provincial governments. In the United States, the concept of a balanced government was derived from the skeptical view of human nature held by the framers of the Constitution, who distrusted both tyranny and mob rule (or, the "perpetual vibration between the extremes of tyranny and anarchy," according to Alexander Hamilton). Thus, a major disadvantage of a balanced government is that, not infrequently, legislation which would benefit the common good is paralyzed by political wrangling, inertia, inefficiency, obstructionism, gridlock and the disproportionate power wielded by small, powerful economic interest groups (the tyranny of the minority). Aristotle, John Locke, Montesquieu, John Adams, James Madison, Alexander

Hamilton. See Dual/shared sovereignty and Federalism in Concepts.

Benevolent dictatorship: a term of self-justification applied by or to an authoritarian leader who is portrayed as acting for the benefit of the nation and the "general will" of the people rather than for himself, his family or a small coterie.

Big Brother: the fictional dictator of a nightmarish totalitarian state in which each citizen is under constant "telescreen" surveillance. It is based on George Orwell's dystopian novel *1984*, which was published in 1949.

Bill of Rights: the first Ten Amendments to the Constitution of the United States, which guarantee freedom of religion, speech and press; the right to assembly peacefully and to bear arms; protection from unreasonable searches and seizures, double jeopardy and self-incrimination and the right to due process and a speedy and public trial by an impartial jury.

Blood and iron: the term used by Otto von Bismarck in 1862 to describe the use of Prussian military power, rather than "speeches and majority decisions," to achieve German national unification.

Brave New World: Aldous Huxley's 1932 satirical novel of a futuristic "World State" that is built on the technocratic principles of Henry Ford and whose citizens are characterized by their passive, blissed-out hedonism, apathy and nihilism. The title is taken from Shakespeare's *The Tempest*.

Bread and circuses (*panem et circenses*): the use of cheap food and lavish entertainment to keep a populace passive and supportive of the ruling social order. Juvenal; Suzanne Collins.

British political model: a political system that is characterized by parliamentary democracy, compromise, toleration of dissent, loyal opposition and public spiritedness, but also, at one time, by imperialism, bigotry, provincialism and class privilege.

Broker state: a political system in which the national government serves as a mediator or power broker between competing special interest groups, such as organized labor and big business. The interests of the public at large, consumers, the marginalized and the un-enfranchised are, generally, not addressed in this model. John Chamberlain. See Countervailing powers in Economics Concepts for examples of competing interest groups.

Campaign finance reform: legislative proposals, including campaign spending limits, public financing of candidates, full disclosure and the requirement that public media allocate air time to candidates (which is the largest source of campaign expenditures). The reforms are intended to democratize the political process and limit the influence of corporations, unions and the wealthy donor class. Campaign finance reform was upended by the Supreme Court decision *Citizens United* in 2010, which held that money donated to political candidates and issues is free speech and, thus, is protected by the First Amendment to the Constitution and cannot be limited by legislative action. See Donor class, Lobbyists, Machine politics, Patronage system, Plutocracy, Political campaign contributions and Super PACs in Concepts.

Caudillo/**man on horseback**: the archetypal, charismatic, authoritarian leader who saves his country from political divisions and turmoil and unilaterally rules in the national interest. The term was commonly applied to Latin American dictators.

Charismatic leader: a leader who possesses what Max Weber called *charisma*, the "gift of grace," whose authority and power is derived from his exceptional personal qualities, "by virtue of which he is set apart from ordinary men and treated as endowed with supernatural, superhuman, or at least specifically exceptional powers." See Cult of personality in Concepts and 14. Max Weber in Sociology Details.

City-states: early, independent cities, their citizens and their regional network of villages and dependent territories, such as those in Mesopotamia, Egypt, Phoenicia, Greece, Rome, Carthage and Mesoamerica and, later, the Italian Renaissance city-states of Venice, Milan and Florence. Not infrequently, city-states sought to extend their sphere of influence through alliances, conquest and annexation, which led, in some cases, to the rise of empires. City-states were enabled and constrained by the unique circumstances of their natural geography (rivers, harbors, deserts, mountains, sea, etc.). In ancient Greece, for example, independent city-states developed because they were initially shielded from invasion by mountains and the sea. See *Civitas*, Greek democracy and *Polis* in Concepts and 10. Rise of Urban Civilizations in Anthropology Details and 4. Geographical Determinism in Historiography Details.

Civil discourse: public dialogue among members of a political entity regarding public policy and the common issues of the day. It also refers to the courteous and respectful nature of the dialogue, in contrast to the bombastic and polarizing rhetoric of the culture wars of the day. Edward Shils. See Culture wars and Public sphere in Concepts.

Civil disobedience: acting in an illegal but non-violent manner to achieve social change; a method of asserting a higher moral law by submitting to the civil consequences (including arrests, fines and jail) for violating, in a nonviolent manner, what is perceived to be an unjust or immoral human law or a pervasive public practice, such as a fugitive slave law or a poll tax or a racially segregated public transportation system. Non-violent forms of direct action include demonstrations, marches, strikes, blockades, sit-ins, boycotts and tax resistance. Henry David Thoreau, Mohandas Gandhi, and Martin Luther King, Jr. See Higher law and Natural rights in Concepts and 32. Civil Rights/Black Freedom Movement in American History Details.

Civitas: the Roman concept of a social body of citizens with rights and responsibilities who are united by a common set of laws and customs.

Class politics versus **status politics**: the Richard Hofstadter-Seymour Lipset thesis that economic and class issues are paramount during periods of depression, whereas status anxieties (including the fear of declining social status by displaced social groups) prevail during times of prosperity. See Status anxieties/displaced social groups in Concepts.

Class warfare: see James Harrington, Benjamin Franklin, Thomas Jefferson and James Madison in Quotations and 4. Karl Marx/Dialectical Materialism in Details.

Client state: a satellite or puppet state; a country that is under the political and economic influence of another country and serves as its proxy in the region.

Coalitional politics: fluid, informal arrangements between two or more political groups to work together for their mutual benefit. In parliamentary forms of government and in multi-party systems, the arrangements are more formalized than those in two-party systems, and parties may join to form a coalition government. Coalitional arrangements are deeply rooted in human social behavior, dating back to hunter-gatherer bands, and may have played a critical role in the evolution of human social intelligence as a result of the complexities and challenges of living in groups, which involved cooperative hunting, food sharing, mutual grooming, reciprocal altruism, personal alliances, balances of power, etc. See Balance

of power and Log-rolling in Concepts and 5. Social
Intelligence/Social Brain Hypothesis in Anthropology Details.

Colonialism: the colonization and political and economic rule of one
country or territory by another, often from a distant metropolis, in
which the mother country and its ruling minority in the colony
presumes its own cultural superiority and inherent right to rule.
Historically, indigenous populations in the colonized countries
were exposed to diseases and death from the exogenous minority
and were subjected to unequal social relationships of dependency,
oppression, exploitation and servitude. Colonialism is associated
with imperialism, mercantilism and global capitalism. See
Imperialism and Neo-Colonialism in Concepts.

Common law: a system of laws that is guided by custom, tradition,
precedents and previous court decisions (*stare decisis*), which is
based on the assumption that similar cases should be decided by
similar principles. These laws "arise gradually, in the emergence
of a consensus from a multitude of particularized prior decisions"
(Oliver Wendell Holmes, Jr.), and are derived inductively from
particular facts rather than from "pre-established truths of universal
and inflexible validity" (Benjamin Cardozo). "The life of the law
has not been logic; it has been experience" (Holmes). Benjamin
Cardozo, Edward Coke, Oliver Wendell Holmes, Jr.

Commonwealth (derived from "common well-being"): a political
community formed for the common good; also, an association of
nations.

Communism: an economic-political system in which the means of
production are held in common. See 4. Karl Marx/Dialectical
Materialism in Details.

Conflict of interest: a situation in which a public official uses the
power of his or her office for personal benefit or gain. See
Political campaign contributions in Concepts, 6. Public Regulation
Quandary in Details and Crony Capitalism in Economics Concepts.

Conservatism: see 3. Conservatism in Details.

Convergence theory: that, because of technological developments,
capitalism and socialism have merged and been superseded by the
new technocratic, bureaucratic state. See End of ideology in
Concepts. Daniel Bell, John Kenneth Galbraith, Clark Kerr, Max
Weber.

Cooperative commonwealth: an envisioned, morally just and gender-
and racially-inclusive society based on cooperative labor which
would replace the wage system. The concept was taken from the

title of an influential book on American socialism written in 1884 by Laurence Gronlund and promoted by the Knights of Labor (*q.v.* in American History Concepts) in the late 19th Century. See Utopian socialists in Concepts and Freedom's ferment, Oneida community and Utopian communities in American History Concepts).

Corporate state: a government dominated by big business interests and a wealthy, corporate elite. See Managerial revolution, Military-industrial-university-media complex and State monopoly capitalism in Concepts.

Corporate welfare: governmental subsidies, price supports, loan guarantees, tax breaks, contracts and preferential treatment given to large businesses.

Counterrevolution: a conservative or reactionary revolution that attempts to reverse an earlier series of reforms or revolution and to restore the *status quo ante*. See 2. Patterns of Political-Social Revolutions in Details.

Coup d' état/golpe de estado: a strike or blow against the state; the sudden and often violent overthrow of a legitimate, elected government, usually by a military leader or a small group, or *junta*, of military officers, and the imposition of military control over the country.

Cult of personality: the hero-worship of a political leader; the use of mass media and other opinion-making institutions to project a heroic or god-like image of a political leader or dictator. See Charismatic leader and Totalitarianism in Concepts.

Cultural hegemony: the doctrine that cultural norms and values are socially constructed and imposed by the dominant class, but are perceived to be universally true by the general population; that the prevailing ideology at any given time of the ruling elite (e.g., patriarchy, emperor worship, slavery, feudalism, the divine right of kings, laissez-faire capitalism, Social Darwinism, dialectical materialism, the cult of personality) causes the general population to falsely believe in the universality and immutability of that world view, to accept their subordinate status and to act in ways which are antithetical to their own self-interest; Antonio Gramsci; versus **post-hegemonic synthesis**, which ascribes agency, free will, autonomy and reflexivity, or self-awareness, to individuals as they make their political and cultural choices, and sees cultural hegemony in layered social structures rather than as a monolithic value system; Peter Berger and Thomas Luckmann, Anthony Giddens, Raymond Williams.

Culture wars: the "culture struggle" (*kulturkampfe*) between those who hold opposing sets of values, assumptions, ideals and world views. Currently, in the United States, culture wars are being waged over such polarizing social issues as women's rights, abortion, homosexuality, immigration, gun control, global warming, the separation of church and state, etc. Patrick Buchanan, James Hunter.

Cycles of corruption and purification, materialism and idealism, private self-interest and public good: the cyclical nature of American political and social history. Lincoln Steffens, Arthur M. Schlesinger, Jr. See 36. American Generational Cycles in American History Details.

Demagogue: a political leader who uses personal charisma, impassioned rhetoric and half-truths and falsehoods to appeal to the fears, emotions and prejudices of the people. The angry rhetoric is often directed at alleged conspiracies by perceived enemies and scapegoated out-groups.

Democratic socialism: a system of government that combines political democracy with centralized economic planning by the state and the national ownership of the means of production.

Détente: the relaxation of tensions between two hostile nations.

Dialectical materialism: see 4. Karl Marx/Dialectical Materialism in Details.

Dictatorship of the bourgeoisie: see 4. Karl Marx in Details.

Dictatorship of the bureaucracy: see 14. Max Weber in Sociology Details.

Dictatorship of the proletariat: the precursor to the classless, stateless society of pure communism, according to Karl Marx. See 4. Karl Marx in Details.

Disenfranchised: those who are without political or social power. See Franchise in Concepts.

Divine right of kings: the doctrine that the monarch derives his or her power directly from God and is not subject to the will of the people, the nobility nor the church; thus, opposition to the monarch is an act of religious heresy as well as an act of political treason. Robert Filmer. See Absolute monarchy in Concepts.

Dollar Diplomacy: the term coined by Theodore Roosevelt to describe the United States' economic, diplomatic, and, not infrequently, military intervention to protect American business interests abroad; a foreign policy dominated by the protection of overseas markets and sources of raw materials, including oil, for American corporate interests. Charles Beard, Joyce and Gabriel Kolko, Walter La Feber, William Appleman Williams. See Gunboat/Big Stick diplomacy, Imperialism, Neo-Colonialism and Neo-Conservatism in Concepts.

Donor class: wealthy individuals and families who give massive amounts of money to political parties, candidates, issues and causes. With the Supreme Court decision in *Citizens United* in 2010 and the advent of super PACs (political action committees), the top 100 individual super PAC donors accounted for more than 60% of the $349 million raised in the 2012 election. The infusion of massive sums of money by the donor class into the political process has (1) displaced the traditional role of political parties; (2) allowed a few individuals to exert enormous influence over political candidates and public policy and (3) subverted the democratic principle of equal representation for all. David Brock, Jane Mayer, Kevin Phillips. See Campaign finance reform, Lobbyists, Machine politics, Patronage system, Plutocracy, Political campaign contributions and Super PACs in Concepts.

Dual/shared sovereignty: a political system in which sovereignty is shared, to varying degrees, by a central or national authority, on one hand, and regional, provincial or state authorities, on the other, as is the case in the "federal" division of powers in the United States. It reflects the tension between centralization and decentralization and the balance of power between the center and the periphery. In the 18th Century, for example, British North American colonial legislatures considered themselves to be coordinate and coequal with Parliament, united by a common sovereign, with the exclusive right to levy taxes. In the first half of the 19th Century, Southern states considered themselves to be sovereign entities within a federated system with the right to withdraw or secede from the United States. In both cases, the issue of shared sovereignty was resolved only by war, specifically, the American War of Independence (1775-1783) and the American Civil War (1860-1865). See Balanced government in Concepts.

Economic trade leads to political liberalization: Bernard Bailyn's thesis that the breakdown of Puritan orthodoxy and political hegemony in New England in the 17th and 18th Centuries was the result of commercial contact and trade with other cultures; an argument that was used in later historical contexts, including foreign policies which encouraged trade and détente with hostile, authoritarian and fundamentalist nations. Bailyn's thesis is built on the classical free market premise that economic interests generally transcend ideology and religious orthodoxy.

Elites/oligarchies: social and political systems that are controlled by elites, who maintain their power through force, manipulation, ideology, the need for united action against a perceived enemy and the apathy and indifference of the general population. Vilfredo Pareto, Jane Mayer, Robert Michels, C. Wright Mills. See Cultural hegemony in Concepts and 15. Elites/oligarchies in Sociology Details.

End of ideology: the thesis by some historians and social scientists that political ideologies in the United States are irrelevant and exhausted, and that public policy will be driven, instead, by technocratic issues. The thesis was echoed in Francis Fukuyama's 1989 essay, "The End of History," in which he argued that, with the end of the Cold War and the triumph of capitalism, history had reached "the end point of mankind's ideological evolution and the universalization of Western liberal democracy [which is] the final form of human government." Daniel Bell, Francis Fukuyama, Max Weber. See Convergence theory in Concepts and 4. Consensus Schools in American History Details.

Entitlements: social programs that provide for basic human needs, such as food, health care, public education, unemployment insurance and pensions.

Escape from freedom: Erich Fromm's thesis that the freedom of modern men and women from the web of medieval restrictions and the customs and traditions of pre-industrial societies has created a sense of alienation, isolation, *anomie* and anxiety, which has caused some to escape or abandon their freedom by seeking the purposefulness, emotional certainty and security provided by totalitarian groups and religious movements. See Totalitarianism and True believers in Concepts and 16. Mass Society and 17. Erich Fromm in Sociology Details.

Ethics of responsibility versus **ethics of ultimate ends**: see Pragmatic versus utopian liberalism in Concepts. Daniel Aaron, Theodore Roszak, Arthur Schlesinger, Max Weber.

Fabian socialism: a political movement that seeks to achieve democratic socialism gradually through incremental reforms rather than through class conflict or violent revolution. The Fabian Society, which was founded in England in the late 19th Century, took its name from the Roman general, Favius Maximus, who successfully fought Hannibal in a war of attrition by a series of delaying tactics and avoiding direct frontal assaults and pitched battles.

Fascism: see Totalitarianism in Concepts.

Federalism: a political system in which sovereignty is shared between the "federal" (i.e., the national or central) government and the state or provincial governments through the division of powers. See Balanced Government and Dual/shared sovereignty in Concepts.

Franchise: the right to vote. In the British North American colonies in the 17th and 18th Centuries, the franchise was extended only to white males who owned property and met specific religious criteria. In the United States, (1) universal white male suffrage was not achieved until the abolition of property qualification in the early 19th Century during the era of Jacksonian democracy; (2) *de jure* (i.e., according to the law) but not *de facto* (i.e., according to actual practice) universal male suffrage was achieved after the Civil War by the 15th Amendment in 1870, but was nullified for most African-Americans in many states by poll taxes, intimidation, terrorism and other extra-legal means; (3) white female suffrage was achieved nationally during the Progressive Era with the adoption of the 19th Amendment in 1920; (4) the *de facto* right to vote was not achieved for all African-Americans until the passage of the Voting Rights Act of 1965, and, (5) because they were subject to the military draft at the time, the right to vote was granted to those who were 18 years of age and older by the 26th Amendment in 1971. See Stake-in-society in Concepts.

Geographical determinism: a school of thought that proposes that climate, natural resources and geography are the foundations of a natural economy, which, in turn, shapes and determines a culture. See Geographical Determinism in 8. American History Details and 4. Historiography Details.

Geopolitics: the relationship between a nation's geography (including its location, size, topography, demography and natural resources) and its power (particularly its military and naval power) and position in world politics. Also, the use of demographic, economic, diplomatic, military and naval power to achieve territorial hegemony and nationalistic ends. Alfred Thayer Mahan. See Dollar Diplomacy, Gunboat/Big Stick diplomacy, *Lebensraum*, Neo-Conservatism, *Realpolitik* and Sphere of Influence in Concepts and Geographical Determinism in 8. American History Details and 4. Historiography Details.

Germ theory of liberty: that the Anglo-Saxon traditions of liberty and self-government were born in the Teutonic forests of pre-history. Tacitus, Herbert Baxter Adams, Francis Parkman, Theodore Roosevelt.

Gerontocracy: a form of government in which political power is held by the oldest members of society.

Glasnost and ***perestroika*** (Russian for "openness" and "restructuring"): a series of reforms instituted by Mikhail Gorbachev in the 1980s to relax Soviet censorship and repression, to make the one-party government more transparent and to institute limited market reforms, which led, eventually, to the dissolution of the Soviet Union in 1991 and the end of the Cold War.

Grassroots movements: political and social movements that begin, usually, at the local level. They represent expressions of public spiritedness and participatory democracy and are usually associated with single, ad hoc issues, such as Mothers Against Drunk Driving, the Tea Party, Occupy Wall Street and Black Lives Matter. The scope and scale of their influence has been magnified exponentially by the use of Internet technology and social media, which has partially offset the enormous financial resources injected into the public sphere by powerful economic interest groups (which, in some cases, have co-opted and funded some of the grass-roots organizations in a process known as astroturfing). See Arab Spring and Participatory democracy in Concepts and 3. Alexis de Tocqueville in American History Details.

Greek democracy: a form of direct democracy in which all adult males in the city-state (*polis*), except resident foreigners (*metics*) and slaves, gathered in popular assemblies and voted on the affairs of state, including legislation, executive appointments, treaties and declarations of war. In 5th Century BCE Athens, for example, approximately 10% to 20% of the total population of 300,000 (which included, perhaps, 150,00 slaves) were eligible to vote and participate directly in the governance of the state. See City-states and *Polis*.

Gunboat/Big Stick diplomacy: the conspicuous display of military and naval power ("showing the flag") in order to demonstrate a nation's military and/or economic dominance in a region. The term is derived from Theodore Roosevelt's "speak softly, and carry a big stick." Theodore Roosevelt and Alfred Mahon. See Dollar Diplomacy, Geopolitics, Imperialism, Neo-Conservativism, *Realpolitik* and Sphere of Influence in Concepts.

Hegemony: the economic, political, military and cultural dominance of one nation over others. See Sphere of influence in Concepts.

Higher law: a universal, divine, moral or natural law or principle that is above man-made laws. The concept was invoked by American abolitionists to protect runaway slaves from the Fugitive Slave Act in the antebellum period, and, in the 20th Century, was legally applied against those who were complicit in crimes against humanity during World War II. See Civil disobedience in Concepts.

Ideal types: Max Weber's classification of political authority and leadership into the following categories: (1) charismatic, (2) traditional (e.g., a monarchy), and (3) rational-legal (the modern bureaucratic state). See Charismatic leader in Concepts and 14. Max Weber in Sociology Details.

Identity politics: the politics of self-identified, often marginalized, social groups who seek to empower and articulate their interests and identities in the face of the indifference or oppression by the mainstream culture. It includes those of women, African-Americans, Latinos, seniors and LGBTs.

Ideology: a conceptual framework; a world view; a system of ideas, attitudes, values, assumptions and beliefs that serves to justify, explain and provide coherence to experience and, in many cases, to furnish the inspiration and motivation for action. See Cultural hegemony in Concepts, 11. Counterarguments to Economic/ Technological Determinism in Economics Details and 14. Max Weber in Sociology Details.

Imperialism: the military, economic, political and cultural domination and control of one or more countries or territories by another. See Colonialism, Dollar Diplomacy, Gunboat Diplomacy, Neo-Colonialism and Neo-Conservatism in Concepts.

Individualism: an American cultural value and trait. It is associated with self-reliance, social and geographical mobility, the ideal of

the self-made man and the distrust of collective action. The term
was coined by Alexis de Tocqueville in his *Democracy in America*
(1835-40), which he defined as the "feeling which deposes each
citizen to isolate himself from the mass of his fellows and
withdraw. . . . . He gladly leaves the greater society to look for
itself." See Antinomian personality in American History
Concepts; 3. Alexis de Tocqueville, 11. Frederick Jackson
Turner/Frontier Thesis, 21. New England Transcendentalism in
American History Details and Narcissism of small differences in
Psychology Concepts. For economic individualism, see
Objectivism, Positive central state versus laissez-faire
individualism and Rugged individualism in Concepts and 4.
Conservatism: Laissez-faire/Economic Individualism in Details.

Industrial democracy: an umbrella term for socio-economic systems
in which workers participate in their company's decision-making
processes to various degrees, ranging from team-building, quality
circles, consultation and collective bargaining to profit-sharing and
representation on the board of directors to partial or full ownership
and control of the company. On a macro-level, the term also refers
to a political economy in which all members have equal economic
and political power to influence how their society, including the
workplace, is governed.

Jingoism: chauvinism; bellicose patriotism; aggressive nationalism.
In the United States, the term originated with the emotional fervor
that led to the war with Spain in 1898, which was precipitated by
what later proved to be an accidental internal explosion on the *USS
Maine*, which caused it to sink in the harbor of Havana, Cuba. The
resulting war fever was fed by the sensationalist "yellow
journalism" of the Hearst and Pulitzer newspapers ("Remember the
Maine!") and by the "Big Stick" rhetoric of Theodore Roosevelt.
The use of warmongering to sell newspapers was also employed
successfully in the Mexican-American War of 1846 and the First
World War in 1917 and, later, to raise television and cable news
ratings in the invasion of Iraq in 2003.

Just and equal laws: see Mayflower Compact in Concepts.

Kleptocracy (Greek for "rule by thieves"): a form of government in
which patronage, nepotism and corruption is systemic and whose
purpose is to increase the personal wealth of the ruling class and

government officials at the expense of the general population. See Crony capitalism in Economics Concepts.

Laissez-faire ideology: the doctrine that the government should not regulate businesses nor interfere in the operations of the marketplace. See 3. Conservatism in Details and 3. Adam Smith/Classical/Free Market Economics in Economics Details.

LDCs: less developed countries, many of which are characterized by extreme poverty, authoritarian governments, cronyism, corruption and ethnic strife.

Lebensraum (German for "living space"): an argument that was used by Nazi Germany to justify its occupation and colonization of Eastern Europe. The concept was foreshadowed in the doctrine of Manifest Destiny in the United States and has since been implicitly employed by other expansionist ideologies in other countries. See Manifest Destiny in American History Concepts and Territoriality in Anthropology Concepts.

Legislation cannot change mores/folkways: an argument that has been used by Social Darwinists, states' rights advocates, libertarians and social conservatives to defend the status quo and to counter the efforts of reformers seeking to end racism, sexism, homophobia and xenophobia. William Graham Sumner. See 25. Social Darwinism and 26. Reform Darwinism in American History Details.

Levellers and Diggers: 17th-Century Protestant nonconformists and dissenters who advocated social democracy, universal male suffrage and agrarian communism.

Leviathan state: the central feature of Thomas Hobbes's 17th Century political philosophy, according to which people in a state of nature live in a state of perpetual "war of all against all," and, therefore, voluntarily give up their natural rights and enter into a social contract to establish a civil society, thereby ceding their liberty to the Leviathan state under an absolute monarchy in order to prevent violence and anarchy and protect themselves from their own natural depravity. Hobbes' theory stands in opposition to Jean-Jacques Rousseau's 18th Century's counter-theory that people in a state of nature are essentially good and have an innate moral sense. An alternative to both theories was provided by the framers of the Constitution of the United States, who were skeptical of both human nature and absolute political power, and, therefore, designed a form of representative self-government with an elaborate system of checks and balances. See Balanced government in Concepts, Thomas Hobbes in Quotations and 12. Violence and Human Nature (the Hobbes-Rousseau Dichotomy) in Anthropology Details.

Libertarianism: a political philosophy that is now identified with individual freedom, minimal governmental regulation and taxation, private property rights and laissez-faire capitalism. In the 19th Century, it was associated with religious antinomianism (*q.v.* in Philosophy/Religion Concepts), abolitionism, women's rights, free thought and free love. See Objectivism and *The Road to Serfdom* in Concepts, and 3. Adam Smith/Classical/Free Market Economics in Economics Details.

Lobbyists: "the Third House of Congress"; paid professionals who represent powerful economic and social interest groups. Lobbyists raise and make political campaign contributions to favored candidates, sponsor events, draft policy statements and gain access for their clients and advocate on their behalf to elected officials and policy makers. In the United States, political campaign contributions are not considered to be bribes if there is no direct quid pro quo exchange. See Campaign finance reform, Donor class, Machine politics, Patronage system, Plutocracy, Political campaign contributions and Super PACs in Concepts.

Local/regional oligarchies: local and regional elites, usually in semi-rural areas or in countries with weak or distant central governments. They are often supported by private, armed militias and use extralegal means to enforce social codes, monopolize trade, adjudicate disputes, tax commerce, wage war and summarily punish their opponents. See 15. Elites/Oligarchies in Sociology Details.

Log-rolling: trading favors, votes and mutual aid among politicians to promote each other's pet projects. See Coalitional politics in Concepts.

Machiavellian: using cynical, unscrupulous, amoral means and techniques, including deception and manipulation, to obtain and retain political power. See Demagogue in Concepts and Machiavelli in Quotations.

Machine politics: the use of private, tightly controlled political organizations, or "machines," run by bosses and their subordinates to influence local and state politics by selecting candidates, raising money, getting out and directing the vote, monitoring the election polls and, in some cases, manipulating the results, in return for bribes, patronage, government jobs, favorable legislation and government contracts. Since the 2010 Supreme Court decision in *Citizens United*, many of these functions have been taken over on the state and national level by super PACs and their networks of super rich donors. See Campaign finance reform, Donor class, Lobbying, Patronage system, Plutocracy, Political contributions and Super PACs in Concepts.

Madisonian pluralism: the coexistence of diverse and competing political, economic, cultural, and religious groups in society, each with the freedom to contribute to the marketplace of ideas, which prevents the monopoly of any one point of view. The concept is derived from *The Federalist No. 10*, in which James Madison proposed that it is better to have many competing factions in order to prevent any one faction from dominating the political system. When the influence is wielded asymmetrically by a few powerful groups, the system is described as **elite pluralism**. According to some cultural materialists, the ideology of democratic pluralism, of society being held together by common norms and the promise of equal opportunity, is a myth, a pretense, an "illusion of control," a social construct of the ruling class. Stuart Hall, Joseph Stiglitz. See Cultural hegemony and Separation of church and state in Concepts.

Managerial revolution: a society in which the ruling elite of corporate executives and managers achieves social dominance, political power and privilege by controlling the means of production. James Burnham.

Mass society: the subject of a school of thought that is critical of modern society for its weak communal ties, *anomie*, alienation, ignorance, passivity, mindless conformity, cultural mediocrity, materialism and "crowd psychology," and its manipulation by, and receptivity to, demagogues and mass movements. See Escape from Freedom in Concepts and 16. Mass Society in Sociology Details.

Mayflower Compact: the governing document and social compact of the Plymouth Colony, in what is now Massachusetts, which was signed in 1620 by the adult men onboard the *Mayflower* to "covenant and combine ourselves together into a civil body politic . . . to enact, constitute, and frame such just and equal laws . . . for the general good of the colony." It established the principles of self-government, the right to choose one's leaders and majority rule in the British North American colonies.

Military-industrial-university-media complex: the central thesis of a school of thought that political and economic power in the United States is exercised in concert by an interlocking power elite of political, corporate, military, academic and media leaders, who share a common world view and move easily between institutions. The complex originated in the massive public military expenditures and research and development projects during World War II and the Cold War of the 1950s and the 1960s. President Dwight Eisenhower first identified the complex and named its first two components. Jane Mayer, C. Wright Mills. See Permanent warfare economy in Economics Concepts and 15. Elites/Oligarchies in Sociology Details.

Military junta: a group or committee of military officers who rules a country, usually through martial law. See *Coup d'état* in Concepts.

Nationalism: the identification with, and sense of belonging to, a particular nation or group; a shared sense of national identity; also, the aggressive promotion of the interests of one nation at the expense of others. See 19. Origins of American Nationalism in American History Details.

Nation-state: primarily, a 19th and 20th Century historical development and construct in which cultural and ethnic groups with fluid identities and boundaries coalesced into modern states with relatively fixed boundaries, a centralized government and common cultural identities. See 19. Origins of American Nationalism in American History Details.

Natural aristocracy of talent: Thomas Jefferson's ideal form of representative government, which would be ruled by a meritocracy based on education, training and talent rather than by an **"artificial aristocracy" of birth and wealth** or an **"aristocracy of our moneyed corporations."** See Philosopher-kings and Technocracy in Concepts.

Natural rights: universal human rights, which are based on natural laws that exist anterior to, and independent of, a state's authority to grant them. Thomas Jefferson, John Locke, Jean Jacques Rousseau. See Higher law in Concepts and 27. 18th Century Enlightenment in Philosophy/Religion Details.

Negative versus **positive liberty**: freedom from external restraints ("I am slave to no one") versus the freedom to act with agency and free will ("I am my own master"); the right to be left alone versus the right of self-realization (for example, the right to vote or freedom from discrimination). Isaiah Berlin, Erich Fromm, Robert Self.

Neo-Colonialism: a system of economic and political domination by multinational corporations over underdeveloped nations, which are exploited as sources of cheap labor and raw materials and as markets for surplus goods.

Neo-Conservatism: a political movement and school of thought that began in the last quarter of the 20th Century. It was composed of "defense intellectuals," or "war hawks," who opposed détente with the Soviet Union, supported the Vietnam War and endorsed the preemptive invasion of Iraq in 2003. Its organization, the Project for the New American Century, advocated American military intervention to "challenge regimes hostile to our interests" and to promote "political and economic freedom abroad." It represented a combination of preemptive militarism and Wilsonian idealism and has been described as seeking to "spread democracy by the sword," as well as to obtain oil and extend American influence in the Middle East. See Dollar Diplomacy, Geopolitics, Gunboat Diplomacy and *Realpolitik* in Concepts and 6. American Exceptionalism in American History Details.

New England town meeting: an early and enduring form of direct democracy in the United States in which town members meet periodically to express their opinions on local issues with government officials. Frank Bryan. See Grassroots movements, Greek democracy and Participatory democracy in Concepts.

Objectivism: a philosophy of rational, amoral egoism that was developed by Ayn Rand and influenced by Friedrich Nietzsche. It (1) celebrates the heroic virtues of individualism and the ruthless selfishness of the *Ubermensch*; (2) disdains the idea of moral obligation and public good; (3) demonizes the welfare state and (4) provides the philosophical justification for secular, laissez-faire capitalism and libertarianism. Jennifer Burns.

Old Guard: those in the political establishment who oppose changes to the status quo; versus **Young Turks**: those who are impatient to change the established political order. The term originally applied to Turkish nationalist reformers who wanted to abolish the absolute monarchy of the Ottoman empire. It now applies to insurgents in a political party who are eager to take control of it.

Oligarchy: a form of government in which power is held by a small group of people, often based on their wealth, birth, family ties or military or corporate connections. See Aristocracy, Elites and Kleptocracy in Concepts and 15. Elites/Oligarchies in Sociology Details.

Paranoid style in American politics: a common theme, a style of thought and a major psychological undercurrent in the American political tradition. Historically, it was expressed in (1) colonial resistance to Parliamentary taxation after the French and Indian War (1754-1763) to pay off the enormous British war debt, which led to the American Revolution; (2) the antebellum South's fear of a "Black Republican" party plot to incite slave rebellions and abolish slavery; (3) the post-Civil War South's fear of African-Americans' social and political power; (4) the Populist's belief that economic depressions were caused by an international conspiracy of bankers and Jews; (5) the popular belief that munitions-makers started the First World War; (6) the fear and paranoia of an internal Communist conspiracy and domestic subversion during the McCarthy era and the Cold War of the 1950s and 1960s and (7) the Islamophobia that followed the September 11, 2001 attacks on the World Trade Center and the Pentagon. Daniel Bell, Richard Hofstadter, Kathryn Olmstead, William Tilden. See McCarthyism, Red Scare and Salem Witch Trials in American History Concepts and Litigious paranoia in Psychology Concepts

Participatory democracy: a social-political system in which all members of society are equally and effectively empowered to participate in the political process and influence public policy; grassroots democracy at the local, regional and national level. Internet technology and social media have increased the scope, scale and effect of popular participation (recent examples include the Tea Party, Occupy Wall Street and Black Lives Matter movements), which partially offsets the enormous financial resources injected into the public sphere by powerful economic interest groups to elect candidates and influence legislation and public policy. See Grassroots movements, Greek democracy, Mayflower Compact, New England town meeting, Plutocracy and Super PACs in Concepts.

Patronage system: originally, a system in which kings, churchmen and the nobility provided direct financial support to musicians, painters, sculptors and other artists. In a later political context in the United States, it referred to the spoils system ("to the victor belong the spoils"), in which the victorious political party dismissed incumbent public officeholders of the opposing party and rewarded its supporters with government jobs and contracts. With the advent of super PACs, the term has reverted to its original meaning in which a wealthy "patron" or donor serves as a "financial angel" and personally subsidizes individual political candidates, issues and causes. David Brock, Jane Mayer, Kevin Phillips. See Campaign finance reform, Donor class, Lobbyists, Machine politics, Plutocracy, Political campaign contributions and Super PACs in Concepts.

Permanent warfare economy/military Keynesianism: the theory that (1) the economic recovery from the Great Depression in the United States was caused by the massive military expenditures of World War II, beginning with the Lend Lease program in 1941, and (2) the economic prosperity and technological innovations in the decades following World War II, including the Cold War *mentalité* supporting foreign military interventions, were driven by massive public expenditures on defense industries, the space race, regional wars and the military-industrial-university-media complex. Norman Chomsky, Michael Kidron, C. Wright Mills, Rebecca Thorpe. See Military-industrial-university-media complex in Concepts and Rise and fall of great powers: the 16th Century Spanish paradigm in Historiography Concepts.

Philosopher-kings: Plato's intellectual ruler-guardians, whose love of wisdom and knowledge would guide them as they governed the ship of state. See Thomas Jefferson's Natural aristocracy of talent in Concepts.

Plutocracy: a form of government in which power is held by the wealthy, both (1) directly through their influence in the government (by campaign contributions to candidates and causes [primarily through super PACs], lobbying, providing jobs to former government officials, and serving as members of Congress, ambassadors and other government officials) and (2) indirectly through their influence in the media and opinion-, policy- and decision-making institutions, such as think tanks, journals, academic programs, fellowships and advocacy and "grass-roots" organizations, the funding for which is channeled through private, tax-exempt political foundations. According to John Jay, the first Chief Justice of the Supreme Court, "the people who own the country ought to govern it." Currently, nearly half the members of congress are millionaires. With the Supreme Court decision in *Citizens United* in 2010 and the advent of super PACs (political action committees), the top 100 super PAC donors accounted for more than 60% of the $349 million raised in the 2012 election. The condition reflects the contradiction in American values between the ideal of social and political equality and the reality of economic and political inequality. David Brock, Jane Mayer, Kevin Phillips. See Economic inequality/concentration of wealth in Concepts and Donor class, Patronage system and Super PACs in Political Science Concepts and Louis Brandeis in Political Science Quotations.

Police state: see Totalitarianism in Concepts.

Polis: the ancient Greek city-state, including the citizens who composed it. See City-states and Greek democracy in Concepts.

Political campaign contributions: money given to political candidates and the organizations that support them. In the United States, political campaign contributions to candidates are not considered bribes as long as they adhere to the election laws and there is no explicit quid pro quo exchange of a contribution for a favor. Political campaigns are very expensive: the average Senatorial candidate in the United States spends over $10 million on an election, which is approximately 60 times the annual salary of the office he or she is seeking. The total expenditures for the 2012 election was $6 billion, according to the Center for Responsive Policies. See Campaign finance reform, Donor class, Lobbying, Machine politics, Patronage system, Plutocracy and Super PACs in Concepts.

Political conservatism: see 3. Conservativism in Details.

Political correctness (or "PC"): a pejorative term directed against those who oppose racism, sexism, homophobia, global warming, etc.

Political economy: the original term for the study of economics, which acknowledges the intimate, reciprocal relationship between economic and political power. James Harrington, Adam Smith, Benjamin Franklin, Thomas Jefferson, James Madison, John Stuart Mill, Karl Marx; Kevin Phillips. See Harrington, Franklin, Jefferson and Madison in Quotations.

Political parties: political organizations with a common set of principles or interests which seek to influence public policy by having their candidates elected to run the government and set public policy. In the United States, political parties are based on

(1) differing economic and class interests, according to James Madison, Charles Beard, Vernon Louis Parrington and Arthur M. Schlesinger, Jr.; (2) patronage and personalities as much as on principles and ideology, according to Richard Hofstadter or (3) cultural, ideological, religious and ethnic differences, according to Lee Benson, Lisa McGirr and others. The power of traditional political parties and their candidates has been superseded by the ascendency of super PACs (political action committees) and the infusion of massive amounts of private money into the political process by wealthy, largely anonymous patrons. See Donor class, Lobbyists, Patronage, Plutocracy, Political contributions and Super PACs in Concepts and James Madison and John Jay in Quotations.

Politics as /entertainment: Richard Hofstadter's thesis that the real economic and social issues in political elections are often hidden and offstage and are intentionally overshadowed by the personalities and the political dramas of the day. See 4. Consensus Schools of American Historiography in American History Details.

Politics of civility: see Civil discourse in Concepts. Edward Shils.

Populist: originally, a member of the People's Party, which was formed by Midwestern wheat and Southern cotton farmers in response to the economic depression of the 1890s. It advocated a wide range of political and social reforms (e.g., a graduated income tax, an eight-hour day, the direct election of U. S. senators) that were later adopted by the Progressive movement, but were dismissed at the time as agrarian radicalism and "hayseed socialism." Now, it is a generic term used to describe a popular or radical leader of the political left or right who speaks, in some contexts demagogically, on behalf of ordinary people against elites and the establishment. See 28. Populism and 29. Progressivism in American History Details.

Positive central state: the central feature of political philosophies that support a strong, national government to promote social and economic progress, provide for the national defense, insure the common welfare and redress social injustice. It was a central component of Progressivism (1890-1920) and New Deal and post-New Deal liberalism (1933-1968). Alexander Hamilton, Herbert Croly, Lester Ward; Theodore Roosevelt, Woodrow Wilson, Franklin D. Roosevelt, Harry Truman, John F. Kennedy, Lyndon B. Johnson. See Progressivism and Reform Darwinism in Concepts, 5. Progressive/Liberalism in Details and 26. Reform Darwinism, 28. Populism, 29. Progressivism and 30. New Deal in

American History Details; versus **laissez-faire individualism**: an economic and political philosophy that advocates minimumal governmental regulation and taxation and enshrines political liberty and economic individualism as the fountainheads of social progress. William Graham Sumner, Herbert Hoover, Ayn Rand, Barry Goldwater, Ronald Reagan. See Objectivism and Social Darwinism in Concepts, 3. Conservatism in Details, 25. Social Darwinism in American History Details and 3. Adam Smith/Classical/Free Market Economics in Economics Details.

Power elite: an interlocking political, corporate, military, academic and media elite who share a common world view and move easily between institutions. Jane Mayer, C. Wright Mills. See Military-industrial-university-media complex and Permanent warfare economy in Concepts and 15. Elites/Oligarchies in Sociology Details.

Power of the periphery: the theory that revolutionary change originates on the margins, not at the core, of dominant civilizations. Alexander Motyl.

Pragmatic versus **utopian liberalism**: two separate strands of American progressivism: (1) **pragmatic reformers** are described as practical, realistic and, if necessary, willing to compromise and accept limited, incremental reforms, while (2) **utopian reformers** are characterized as idealistic and uncompromising and seek to achieve broader, more inclusive social reforms; one accepts a half-loaf of reform, while the other demands the whole loaf. The two traditions are analogous to Weber's **ethics of responsibility** versus the **ethics of ultimate ends**. The categories are relative and time-bound since reforms that are termed "utopian" in one generation (e.g., the abolition of slavery, the 8-hour day, child labor laws, the right of women to vote, social security, medical insurance) are often taken for granted in the next. The division between pragmatic realists and ideological purists is also found among political conservatives. Daniel Aaron, Michael Kazin, Christopher Lasch, Vernon Louis Parrington, Arthur Schlesinger, Max Weber. See 5. Progressivism/Liberalism in Details.

Privatism and the fall of the public man: the withdrawal of citizens from public involvement. Richard Sennett, Philip Slater. See Culture of contradictions and Pursuit of loneliness in American History Concepts and 3. Tocqueville in American History Details.

Progressivism: an early 20th Century middle-class reform movement that implemented a series of reforms, including child labor laws;

women's suffrage; trust-busting; the initiative, referendum, recall; the direct election of U. S. senators; pure food and drug laws; workplace safety regulations; federal regulation of interstate commerce and the conservation and preservation of natural resources. John Morton Blum, Eric Goldman, Alonzo Hamby, Samuel Hays, Richard Hofstadter, William Leuchtenburg, Arthur Link, George Mowry, Robert Wiebe. See 29. Progressivism in American History Details.

Public opinion: the aggregate attitudes of the public concerning various political and social issues of the day. It wasn't until the rise of the public sphere in the 18th Century that what average people thought about public issues became important to those who governed. It's influence on public policy and its vulnerability to manipulation by the media and various interest groups is the subject of many studies. James Bryce, Benjamin Ginsberg, Jill Lepore, Walter Lippmann, Alexis de Tocqueville. See Public sphere.

Public regulation quandary: the question of who, in a regulated economy, effectively controls the regulatory machinery governing large-scale economic organizations (including trusts, monopolies, oligopolies and large corporations) to maintain competition and protect the public interest. See 6. Public Regulation Quandary in Details.

Public rights: those that are asserted in opposition to private property rights, as when, for example, in 1739, Ben Franklin and his neighbors petitioned the Pennsylvania Assembly to prohibit a Philadelphia tannery from dumping its wastes in public spaces.

Public sphere: the arena of public discourse. Beginning in the 18th Century Enlightenment, the "realm of communication was marked by new arenas of debate, more open and accessible forms of urban public space and sociability, and an explosion of print culture" (Jürgen Habermas). The public sphere was characterized by "rational, critical and genuinely open discussion of public issues" in coffeehouses, book stores, libraries, athenaeums, and Free Mason lodges. The media in the public sphere were associated with the rise of popular literacy, a free press, the democratic diffusion of knowledge, political debate and cultural pluralism. Jurgen Habermas, James Melton, Paul Starr. For the impact of Internet technology and electronic social media on the public sphere, see 24. Information Technology/Metaphor of the Machine in Sociology Details.

Quantitative versus **qualitative liberalism**: the distinction made by Arthur Schlesinger, Jr. between "bread and butter" reforms that improve economic well-being, such as the minimum wage and unemployment insurance, and those that improve the quality of life, such as education, civil rights and environmental protections.

Reactionary: one who opposes or seeks to reverse political, economic and social reforms and restore the *status quo ante*. See Counterrevolution in Concepts and 2. Patterns of Political-Social Revolutions in Details.

Realpolitik: international power politics; a nation's expedient and often cynical use of diplomatic alliances, economic power and military coercion to achieve its national interests, often at the expense of democratic ideals, common humanitarian values, the rule of law and the principle of self-determination. Otto von Bismarck, George Kennan, Henry Kissinger, Klemens von Metternich. See Blood and iron, Geopolitics, Gunboat/Big-Stick diplomacy, Neo-Conservativism and Sphere of Influence in Concepts.

Red versus **blue states**: those states in which the majority of voters vote for, respectively, Republican or Democratic candidates and issues. The designations are derived from the colored maps used by the television news media to depict the election returns from each state. The terms are also used to describe the differences in cultural values between those two groups. Ironically, throughout most of modern history, the association was reversed, and red denoted revolution and blue denoted conservatism. See Culture wars in Concepts.

Reform Darwinism: a counter-movement to Social Darwinism, which laid the intellectual foundations for the Populist and Progressive reform movements of the late 19th and early 20th Centuries. It asserted that group-level selection, social cooperation and altruism are as important in human evolution as competition, and that biological ('genetic") evolution has been replaced by purposeful, social ("telic") evolution, in which humans can collectively plan and control their own destinies, reform society and end social injustice through collective action and the positive liberal state. Edward Bellamy, Herbert Croly, Henry George, Walter Rauschenbusch, Theodore Roosevelt, Lester Ward; Eric Goldman, ˙Richard Hofstadter. See Social Darwinism in Concepts and 26. Reform Darwinism in American History Details.

Revanchism: the desire of a defeated nation for revenge and the restoration of its lost territories through force. The rise of Nazism in Germany, for example, has been linked to its humiliation from the events that followed its defeat in the First World War. Norbert Elias.

Revolution of rising expectations: the theory that revolutions occur, not at the depths of oppression, but when society starts to improve as a result of economic gains, social mobility, rising literacy rates, improved communications, education, etc. Crane Brinton. See 2. Patterns of Political-Social Revolutions in Details.

Right of self-determination: the right of individuals and countries to determine their own destiny without outside interference; a principle enshrined in the Declaration of Independence, the Monroe Doctrine, the Open Door Notes, Wilson's Fourteen Points and the Truman and Nixon Doctrines. Ironically, the principle has often been used by the United States to justify its military intervention and covert action in other countries. George Kennan. See Sphere of influence in Concepts.

Rites of legitimization: the ceremonies and rituals that validate the ruler's right to rule.

The Road to Serfdom: Friedrich von Hayek's influential book, published in 1944, which warned that central economic planning inevitably leads to totalitarianism and servitude. It serves as one of the pillars of libertarianism, but has been challenged by empirical studies that show that Western social-welfare states provide high levels of political freedom, social equality and quality-of-life services.

Rugged individualism: the term coined by Herbert Hoover to contrast the American tradition of self-reliance with the "European philosophy" of paternalism and state socialism. Hoover used the concept to justify his laissez-faire economic policies and to deny direct federal assistance to those who were devastated by the Great Depression.

Ruling class/ruling elites: see Cultural hegemony, Elites and Plutocracy in Concepts and 15. Elites/oligarchies and 20. Class Structure in Sociology Details. Fred Block, William Domhoff, James Madison, Karl Marx, Jane Mayer, C. Wright Mills, Vilfredo Pareto, Kevin Phillips.

Separation of church and state: "the wall of Separation between the Garden of the Church and the Wilderness of the world," so that the profanity of the state would not contaminate the purity of the church (Roger Williams); the principle that a government should not establish, endorse, support or interfere with religion and, conversely, that "no religious body [should] seek to impose its will directly or indirectly upon the general populace or the public acts of its officials" (John F. Kennedy). It is based on the premise that "religion is a matter which lies solely between Man and his God" (Thomas Jefferson). John Barry. See Madisonian pluralism and Soul libertie in Concepts and Secularism in Philosophy/Religion Concepts.

Separation of powers: the checks and balances between the three branches of government, the executive, judiciary and legislature, which is derived from Montesquieu's *trias politica* that incorporates elements of monarchy, aristocracy and democracy. See Balanced government in Concepts.

Social contract: the doctrine that society is a contractual relationship between its members based on their free will and mutual consent. Also, the expectations by members of a society that, under the terms of the social contract, they have the responsibility to be good, lawful, productive citizens and it, society, in turn, has a reciprocal responsibility to protect its members' natural rights and insure that their basic human needs are met, such as an education, a decent living and health care. Thomas Hobbes, Thomas Jefferson, John Locke, Jean-Jacques Rousseau. See Mayflower Compact and Social justice in Concepts.

Social Darwinism: a social-economic theory and world view popular in the late 19th and early 20th Centuries that was loosely based on Charles Darwin's theory of evolution, the struggle for existence (Robert Malthus), natural selection (Darwin and Alfred Russel Wallace) and the survival of the fittest (Herbert Spencer). According to the tenets of Social Darwinism, humanitarianism, social justice and, even, philanthropy were futile since they interfered with natural laws and would permit the poor and "unfit" to reproduce, thus, impeding human progress (William Sumner). The theory represented a synthesis of Calvinism (predestination, the inevitability of suffering, the fit are the elect) and classical laissez-faire capitalism (economic scarcity, the struggle for existence, self-seeking individualism, competition and "antagonistic cooperation"). Social Darwinism was, and is, used to justify political and economic domination by the wealthy (the richest are the fittest), the sanctity of private property, anti-labor legislation, resistance to social reforms and support for militarism and imperialism (might makes right). Eric Goldman, Richard Hofstadter. See Reform Darwinism in Concepts and 25. Social Darwinism and 26. Reform Darwinism in American History Details.

Social justice: a movement that seeks to insure the rights, dignity and equality of all humans. It is grounded in religious and humanitarian traditions, including those of St. Thomas Aquinas, John Locke, Thomas Jefferson, the Social Gospel and liberation theology. It seeks the "equitable distribution of resources to ensure that all have full opportunities for personal and social development" (Green Party). Its objectives are to end poverty and extreme inequality, to insure human rights and equal opportunity for all and to provide public education, health care, a living wage, unemployment insurance, pensions and child-care assistance. John Rawls.

Soul libertie: liberty of conscience; freedom of religion and thought; the doctrine that the government should have no role in regulating religious thought or practice, which was a radical and heretical idea when it was proposed in the 17th Century. Roger Williams; John Barry.

Special interests: economic, political and social groups that lobby government officials to adopt policies that favor their interests and objectives, such as industries, corporations, financial institutions, small businesses, unions, etc. See Lobbyists, Political campaign contributions and Super PACs in Concepts.

Sphere of influence: the political, economic and military domination of one nation over others in a region; an expression of geopolitics and *realpolitik*. Examples include the regional hegemony of the United States over all other countries in the Western Hemisphere in the 19th and 20th Centuries as a result of the Monroe Doctrine, and the Soviet Union's domination of Central and Eastern European countries after World War II; versus the right of self-determination. See Geopolitics and *Realpolitik* in Concepts.

Stake-in-society: the 17th and 18th Century doctrine that only those who have a financial investment in the community should be allowed to govern it; that ownership of real property (commonly a forty shilling freehold in England and colonial America) provided "sufficient evidence of permanent common interest with and attachment to the community"(John Locke) that established a white man's right to vote and hold public office. Property qualifications provided the basis for the republican form of government, as well as the means for protecting the **"better and wiser sort"** from majority rule and government by the **"meaner sort."** Many property-less white males were excluded from voting or holding public office until the 1820s and the 1830s and the rise of Jacksonian democracy; women were denied the vote on the national level until 1920 and African-Americans in many states were effectively disenfranchised until the Voting Rights Act of 1965. See Franchise in Concepts.

State: generally, a sovereign nation. In the United States, the term refers to a political subdivision of the nation, specifically one of 50 political entities, such as Alabama, California, Idaho, Illinois, Massachusetts, New Hampshire, New York, Texas and West Virginia, which, under a federal system, share sovereignty with the national (or "federal") government. See Dual/shared sovereignty in Concepts.

State monopoly capitalism: "state socialism turned on its head"; a partnership between the national government and large corporations in which the government intervenes to protect the interests of big businesses, sometimes against those of workers, consumers and environmentalists. Although it violates the tenets of classical, laissez-faire, free market capitalism, it is defended for creating jobs, investments and "trickle down" prosperity. Murray Rothbard. See Corporate state, Managerial revolution, Military-industrial-university-media complex and Power elite in Concepts.

States as laboratories for social experimentation: a principle established during the Progressive Era of the early 20th Century in which many states adopted reforms, such as women's suffrage, child labor laws, health and safety regulations and the income tax, before the national government.

Status anxieties/displaced social groups: the anxieties associated with the decline in social status of one group (say, lower middle-class white males without a college education) relative to other groups (for example, immigrants, women, minorities, white collar workers, public employees and the college educated). Status anxieties have been identified as a causal factor in, and the dynamic basis of, both reform and reactionary movements. Daniel Bell, David Donald, Richard Hofstadter and George Mowry. See 29. Progressivism in American History Details.

Stern/authoritarian parent versus **nurturing/permissive parent**: the prototype, mechanism and First Cause by which, respectively, a child's conservative or liberal temperament and world view is modeled and developed, according to several theories. John Gillis, George Lakoff, William Tilden. See 16. Authoritarian Personality in Psychology Details.

Super PACs: political action committees, which, since the Supreme Court decision in *Citizens United* in 2010, can raise unlimited funds from individuals, corporations and unions, but are not allowed to coordinate their activities with, or make direct contributions to, individual candidates or political parties (since doing so could be considered a quid pro quo exchange). With the advent of super PACs, networks of private, anonymous superrich donors are now larger and more powerful than the traditional two political parties that they have displaced and provide many of the same services, such as selecting and tutoring candidates, developing strategies and policy statements, raising money, funding media campaigns (including "attack ads") and getting out the vote. David Brock, Jane Mayer, Kevin Philipps. See Campaign finance reform, Donor class, Lobbyists, Machine politics, Patronage system, Plutocracy and Political contributions in Concepts.

Superpower: a nation-state that is able to project its influence and power on a global scale.

Symbolic groups: those that are identified by their social and ideological significance as much as by their economic and class interests, although some control the opinion- and decision-making institutions of society. Examples include antebellum Southern plantation owners, post-Civil War captains of industry, Wall Street financiers, Main Street businessmen, family farmers, blue-collar workers, urban professionals, college students, retired persons, military veterans, religious groups, sports celebrities, NRA members, soccer moms, GLBTs, etc. Daniel Bell.

Technocracy: (1) a government in which public policy and decision-making is guided by professional experts, governmental administrators, scientists, engineers and specialists and by the application of scientific methods to social issues; (2) a meritocracy which is based on education, training and talent (see Jefferson's Natural aristocracy of talent in Concepts) and/or (3) an economy which is driven by technological innovations. Jacques Ellul, Walter Lippmann, Lester Ward, Max Weber.

Theocracy: a government that is directed and controlled by the leaders of the official, established, state-sponsored religion. See Separation of church and state and Soul liberties in Concepts.

Third World: undeveloped and developing, or emerging, countries. Originally, the term was applied to those countries that were not aligned with either the Western bloc or the Sino-Soviet bloc during the Cold War.

Totalitarianism: a government that is characterized by (1) a single, monolithic party; (2) a charismatic leader and the cult of personality; (3) an emotional and all-encompassing ideology; (4) coercive, police-state methods; (5) pervasive social control, including absolute control of the media and surveillance over every aspect of the public and private lives of its citizens; (6) a privileged in-group and a hated, scapegoated, dehumanized out-group. Hannah Arendt. See Big Brother, *Brave New World* and Escape from freedom in Concepts and 16. Mass Society and 17. Erich Fromm in Sociology Details.

True believers: those who, according to Eric Hoffer, are in flight from the "blemished self" and, thus, seek meaning and purpose in their lives by joining totalitarian groups and religious movements. See Escape from freedom and Mass society in Concepts and 16. Mass Society and 17. Erich Fromm in Sociology Details.

Tyranny of the minority: the fact that, in a balanced government of checks and balances, with its separation and division of powers and its bicameral legislatures, not infrequently, proposed legislation that would benefit the common good is paralyzed by political wrangling, obstructionism, gridlock and the disproportionate influence wielded by powerful economic interest groups. See Balanced government and Lobbyists in Concepts.

Tyranny of opinion/tyranny of the majority: see 3. Tocqueville in American History Details.

United Nations: an international organization of 193 member nations whose goal is to promote international cooperation, world peace, human rights and social and economic development.

Utopia: an ideal community or society. It includes those envisioned by Plato, Thomas More, Edward Bellamy and B. F. Skinner; versus the **dystopias** portrayed in George Orwell's *1984* and Aldous Huxley's *Brave New World*.

Utopian socialists: the term applied to those who, in the 19th Century, lived in small, socialist communities, held property in common and produced collectively on a small scale. The term was used pejoratively by Marx and Engels against those who believed that socialism could be achieved without class struggle or revolution. Edward Bellamy, Charles Fourier, Thomas More, John Humphrey Noyes, Robert Owens, Saint-Simon; Alice Felt Tyler. See Cooperative commonwealth in Concepts and Freedom's ferment, Oneida community and Utopian communities in American History Concepts.

Vox populi, vox dei ("the voice of the people [is] the voice of god"): an aphorism attributed to Alcuin, an 8th Century English abbot, the full quotation of which was: "And do not listen to those who keep saying, 'the voice of the people is the voice of God,' because the tumult of the crowd is always close to madness."

War as an antidote to materialism: Theodore Roosevelt's rationale for supporting the United States' entry into the First World War.

War as endemic: see Thomas Hobbes in Quotations and 12. Violence and Human Nature (the Hobbes-Rousseau Dichotomy) in Anthropology Details.

War as the nemesis of reform: Richard Hofstadter's thesis that the United States' participation in the First World War led to the death of Progressivism and a reaction against the moral idealism that had been used to justify it. The thesis was applied to the Vietnam War of the 1960s and 1970s and its effects on Lyndon Johnson's War on Poverty and post-World War II liberalism. William Jennings Bryan, Richard Hofstadter.

Warlords: leaders of local and regional militias, who often operate independently of the national government. See Local/regional oligarchies in Concepts.

Welfare state: a government that insures the economic and social well-being of its citizens by providing public education, health care, full employment at a living wage, and pensions; the "middle way" between capitalism and communism. Lester Ward. See Positive central state and Social justice in Concepts and 28. Populism, 29. Progressivism and 30. the New Deal in American History Details.

World-systems theory: a school of thought that focuses on the study of, and posits the locus of social change in, global systems, not nation states. Immanuel Wallerstein.

QUOTATIONS:

- *Man is by nature a political animal.* -- Aristotle.

- *The most perfect political community is one in which the middle class is in control, and outnumbers both the other classes.* -- Aristotle.

- *A prince should . . . appear to be pious, faithful, humane, honest and religious . . . as long as one keeps in mind that when the need arises you can and will change into the opposite.* -- Niccolò Machiavelli.

- *During the time men live without a common power to keep them all in awe, they are in that condition which is called war; and such a war as is of every man against every man. . . . The life of man* [in a state of nature is] *solitary, poor, nasty, brutish, and short.* -- Thomas Hobbes.

- *Power always follows property.* -- James Harrington.

- *Superfluous property is the creature of society. . . . By virtue of the first laws part of the society accumulated wealth and grew powerful, they enacted others more severe, and would protect their property at the expense of humanity. This was abusing their powers, and commencing a tyranny.* – Benjamin Franklin.

- *The opinions of men are almost as various as their faces . . .* [but] *when men differ in opinion both sides ought equally to have the advantage of being heard by the public and . . . when truth and error have fair play, the former is always an overmatch for the latter.* -- Franklin.

- *The establishment of our new government seemed to be the last great experiment for promoting human happiness by reasonable compact in civil society. It was to be, in the first instance, in a considerable degree a government of accommodation as well as a government of laws. Much was to be done by prudence, much by conciliation, much by firmness.* -- George Washington.

- *The happiness of society is the end of government.* -- John Adams.

- *All men are created equal.* -- Thomas Jefferson.

- *I hope we shall crush . . . in its birth the aristocracy of our moneyed corporations, which dare already to challenge our government to a trial of strength and bid defiance to the laws of our country.* – Jefferson.

- *The most common and durable source of factions has been the various and unequal distribution of property. Those who hold and those who are without property have ever formed distinct interests in society.* -- James Madison, *Federalist No. 10.*

- *Ambition must be made to counteract ambition. . . . If men were angels, no government would be necessary.* -- Madison, *Federalist No. 51.*

- *Give all power to the many, they will oppress the few. Give all power to the few, they will oppress the many.* -- Alexander Hamilton.

- *The people who own the country ought to govern it.* -- John Jay.

- [In the United States,] *I am not sure that the people would choose men of superior abilities even if they wished to be elected, but it is certain that candidates of this description do not come forward.* -- Alexis de Tocqueville.

- *A party of order or stability, and a party of progress or reform, are both necessary elements of a healthy state of political life.* – John Stuart Mill.

- *All political movements are slaves to symbols of the past.* – Karl Marx.

- *Power tends to corrupt, and absolute power corrupts absolutely. Great men are almost always bad men.* -- Lord Acton.

- *The ultimate good desired is reached by the free trade in ideas -- that the best test of truth is the power of the thought to get itself accepted in the competition of the market.* -- Oliver Wendell Holmes, Jr.

- *Democracy substitutes election by the incompetent many for appointment by the corrupt few.* -- George Bernard Shaw.

- *We can have democracy in this country, or we can have great wealth concentrated in the hands of a few, but we can't have both.* - Louis Brandeis.

- *Do political institutions flourish only where the family is weak, or is it the other way around?* -- Luigi Barzini.

- *From out there on the moon, international politics look so petty.* -- Edgar Mitchell.

- *We're an empire now, and when we act, we create our own reality. And while you're studying that reality, . . . we'll act again, creating other new realities, which you can study too, and that's how things will sort out. We're history's actors . . . and you, all of you, will be left to just study what we do.* – an official in the George W. Bush administration.

- *Every election is a morality play.* -- Jill Lepore.

POLITICAL SCIENCE DETAILS: (1) Political Science, (2) Patterns of Political-Social Revolutions, (3) Conservatism, (4) Karl Marx/Dialectical Materialism, (5) Progressivism/Liberalism and (6) Public Regulation Quandary.

1. **Political Science** is the study of governments and political systems, processes, leaders and behaviors.

2. **Patterns of Political-Social Revolutions** is Crane Brinton's thesis that revolutions often adhere to the following paradigm: the historical stage is set with (1) the moral and financial bankruptcy of the old regime, which is accompanied by (2) the alienation of the intellectuals and (3) the loss of nerve by the ruling class, which,

with (4) the rising expectations of the lower and marginalized classes, leads to (5) a political revolution. After (6) a brief honeymoon and rule by the moderates, this is followed by (7) a *coup d' état* by radicals and extremists (i.e., the revolution overflowing its banks), (8) a reign of terror and virtue, then (9) a conservative, Thermidorean counterrevolution and the rule by a tyrant and, finally, (10) a period of repression, restoration (of the old regime) and reaction.

3. **Conservatism** in the United States has been represented by at least four major, overlapping and, sometimes, conflicting traditions:
    1) **Traditional/Social Conservatism** is identified with traditional values, the preservation of social hierarchy and order (of the "rich and well-born"), the distrust of majority rule, incremental change, historical continuity and social conservatism. It initially developed as a reaction against the excesses of the French Revolution of the late 18th Century and, later, as a response to Progressive and New Deal critiques of wealth and plutocracy (as embodied in the 16th Amendment's graduated income tax). Edmund Burke, Alexander Hamilton, Peter Viereck. See Kevin Phillips in Selected References.
    2) **Religious/Moral Conservatism** is associated with Protestant fundamentalism and evangelicalism and Roman Catholicism, which developed in response to evolutionism and, later, the moral relativism manifested in the social, racial, gender and sexual revolutions of the 20th and 21th Centuries It is grounded in a Biblical world view, distrusts scientific theories such as evolution and global warming, and opposes the strict separation of church and state and the technocratic rule by professionals and experts. It is identified with strict moral codes (including opposition to pre-marital sex, abortion [and, in the case of Roman Catholicism, artificial contraception], homosexuality and transgender identifications), the preservation of traditional, heterosexual family values and roles and the return to the *status quo ante* the 1960s. It maintains a skeptical view of human nature, but is not necessarily hostile to social justice, incremental reforms and social improvement. See Evangelicalism, Great Awakening cycle/revivalism and the Religious conversion experience in Philosophy/Religion Concepts and Karen Armstrong and Kevin Philips in Selected References.

3) **Corporate State Conservatism** seeks to maintain an alliance between big business and the national government for favorable tax treatment, subsidies, opposition to organized labor and the avoidance of governmental oversight, taxation and regulation, particularly environmental, financial and labor regulations. It is modeled after the American System developed by Tench Coxe and Alexander Hamilton in the early 19th Century, although its economic self-interests have shifted from protectionism to free trade. Since the Great Depression, it has lobbied for large public investments in the military-industrial complex and the permanent warfare economy (military Keynesianism). See Corporate welfare, Managerial revolution, Military-industrial-university-media complex, Permanent warfare economy/military Keynesianism, Power elite and State monopoly capitalism in Concepts and 20. American System in American History Details.

4) **Laissez-faire/Economic Individualism** celebrates dynamic, competitive, laissez-faire economic individualism and political libertarianism. It advocates the primacy of private economic self-interest and opposes governmental taxation and regulation. It embraces free market economics and accepts the reality of business cycles (Schumpeter's "creative destruction"), economic inequality, social hierarchies and political elites. Paradoxically, it also often supports pro-business governmental programs and massive public expenditures for a strong, national defense. Adam Smith, William Graham Sumner, Joseph Schumpeter, Ayn Rand, Ronald Reagan. See Individualism, Libertarianism and Objectivism in Concepts; 25. Social Darwinism in American History Details and 3. Adam Smith/Classical/Free Market Economics in Economics Details.

Throughout American history, some strands of conservatism have supported a strong, national government to conduct an aggressive military and foreign policy (see Neo-Conservatism in Concepts), while others have advocated protectionism, isolationism and the avoidance of foreign entanglements and wars. Additionally, the division between ideological purists and pragmatic realists that is often found among political progressives is also found among political conservatives.

4. **Karl Marx/Dialectical Materialism** is an economic, social and political philosophy that proposes that:
   1) Societies change in dialectical stages because of the struggle, between socio-economic classes (for example, between the landed aristocracy and the urban bourgeoisie, and between the bourgeoisie and the industrial proletariat).
   2) The mode of production consists of (a) the factors of production (land and other natural resources, labor, capital and technology) and (b) the (social) relations of production.
   3) Changes in the economic/technological base or substructure drive changes in the superstructure (that is, art, ideology and religion, and social, cultural, political and legal institutions).
   4) The dictatorship of the bourgeoisie (the capitalist class) will inevitably be destroyed by its internal contractions and ever greater financial crises, and will be replaced by the dictatorship of the proletariat (the working classes), which will lead, eventually, to a classless, stateless society of pure communism.

   Karl Marx, Friedrich Engels; Antonio Gramsci Louis Althusser. See 10. Economic/Technological Determinism in Economics Details.

5. **Progressivism/Liberalism** is a political philosophy of reform and social improvement that is derived from the 18th-Century Enlightenment's faith in human reason, science, progress, natural rights and social amelioration. It is characterized by optimism, humanism, secularism and faith in the power of collective action to achieve social justice.

   Historically, liberalism was associated with the urban bourgeoisie's opposition to the landed, feudal aristocracy, hereditary privileges and religious orthodoxy and, initially, supported laissez-faire capitalism and entrepreneurial opportunity. Later, in response to the excesses of industrial capitalism in the 19th and 20th Centuries, it advocated middle-class social reforms and a strong, positive central government to regulate capitalism, insure equal opportunity, correct social injustices, soften the business cycle and provide a safety net for children, seniors, the disabled and the unemployed. Progressives have worked for social inclusiveness (of immigrants, the poor, women, racial minorities, the marginalized) and against economic inequality and social prejudice. Jane Addams, Jeremy Bentham, John Dewey, Benjamin

Franklin, J. S. Mill; Thomas Jefferson, Andrew Jackson, Theodore Roosevelt, Woodrow Wilson, Franklin Roosevelt, John F. Kennedy, Lyndon Baines Johnson, Bill Clinton, Barack Obama. See 26. Reform Darwinism, 28. Populism, 29. Progressivism and 30. New Deal in American History Details and 16. Keynesian Economics in Economics Details.

6. **Public Regulation Quandary** arises from the question of who, in a regulated economy, effectively controls the regulatory machinery governing large-scale economic organizations (including trusts, monopolies, oligopolies and large corporations) to maintain competition and protect the public interest: (1) the elected executive, (2) the legislative body, (3) the regulatory agencies, (4) disinterested experts and public servants, (5) special interest groups, (6) the regulated industries themselves, or (7) no one? For example, after the Interstate Commerce Commission was established in 1887 to regulate railroad rates, it came under the control of the very industry it was enjoined to regulate. Today, the Securities and Exchange Commission, state public utilities commissions and many other state and federal regulatory agencies are often influenced, dominated and, even, controlled by the industries that they are charged with regulating in the public interest. Walter Lippmann and others.

9. PSYCHOGLOGY

CONCEPTS AND PHRASES:

Affective: involving feelings and emotions; versus **cognitive**: involving perceiving, learning, thinking, reasoning, judging and remembering.

Agency: the capacity to make free, independent decisions and choices. See Autonomy, Ego Psychology, Reflexivity, Post-hegemonic synthesis and Self-actualization in Concepts.

Agoraphobia (Greek for "fear of the marketplace"): the fear of crowds and public places.

Amotivational syndrome: a condition that is characterized by apathy, the lack of motivation and the absence of goal-oriented behavior.

Anal phase of childhood development: in Sigmund Freud's paradigm, the second phase in the child's psycho-sexual development (after the oral and before the phallic and genital phases, *qq.v.*), which usually occurs between the ages of one and three years, the age of toilet training. During this training process, conflicts often arise over issues involving parental authority, rebellion, conformity, independence, power and control. Fixation at this stage of development is thought to be the result of harsh, rigid or premature toilet training, in which the child is forced, at times, against its will, to regulate the time and place of defecation. Character traits derived from this fixation include obstinacy/rebelliousness, frugality/retentiveness and orderliness/cleanliness and their corresponding reaction-formations of opposite traits. Freud; Karl Abraham, Ernest Jones, William Tilden. See Retentiveness/hoarding in Concepts and 6. Freud's Anal Personality Traits in Details.

Analytical versus **existential schools of psychology**: very broadly, a method for categorizing depth and behavioral schools of psychology. The former uses analytical and introspective methods to reveal and resolve repressed feelings in the unconscious and buried memories from the past. The latter focuses on the outwardly observable behavior in the here and now and attempts to modify those behaviors. More narrowly, "analytical" refers to a school of psychology founded by Carl Jung, and "existential" refers to a school of psychology that is derived from existential philosophy, which seeks to make sense of the world in the face of the meaninglessness of life and the inevitability of death. See Depth psychology versus Behavioral/cognitive psychology in Concepts, 7. Carl Jung In Details and 37. Existentialism in Philosophy/Religion Details.

Anti-social personality disorder: a disorder that is characterized by a lack of concern for the rights and feelings of others, as well as by deceit, manipulation, aggression, impulsive behavior, failure to accept responsibility, lack of remorse, a low threshold for frustration and the inability to maintain enduring relationships. See Sociopathy in Concepts.

Aphasia (Greek for "speechlessness"): a language disorder that involves an impaired ability to read, write, speak and/or comprehend language.

Apperception: the process by which new experience is perceived and absorbed into the mind through the framework of past experience; also, the mind as conscious of its own consciousness.

A priori **mental categories**: innate, pre-established structures and mental categories through which the mind actively filters, interprets and judges experience, such as cause and effect, space and time, the rules of grammar, cultural archetypes, etc.; see Structuralism in Concepts, 7. Carl Jung and 14. Constructivism in Details and 26. Immanuel Kant in Philosophy/Religion Details; versus the mind as a *tabula rasa*: John Locke's theory of the mind at birth as a blank tablet, which passively receives sense impressions from which it builds simple and complex ideas. See Sensational psychology versus *a priori* structuralism in Concepts.

Archetypes: according to Carl Jung, the innate, unconscious, universal symbols, or pre-existent mental forms, that are shared in the collective unconscious by all humans and are represented in myths, rituals and folklore; e.g., the Great Mother, the Hero, the Mentor, the Martyr, the Trickster. See Collective unconscious in Concepts and 7. Carl Jung in Details.

Attachment theory: that mental disorders in adulthood, including depression, are derived from difficulties in bonding with a parent or caregiver in early childhood; that the early loss, separation or perceived rejection by a parent conveys to the child that it is unlovable and attachment figures are untrustworthy. Albert Bandura, Aaron Beck, John Bowlby, Albert Ellis, Anna Freud. See Object relations theory in Concepts and 12. Cognitive Models of Depression in Details.

Authoritarian personality: see 16. Authoritarian personality in Details.

Autonomy (Greek for "self" and "law"): moral self-determination; "the ability to impose objective moral law on oneself" -- Immanuel Kant. See Agency and Self-actualization in Concepts.

Behavioral/population sink: the thesis that increased population densities lead to increased social pathologies, aggression and personality disorders. (Paradoxically, in the laboratory experiments from which these conclusions were drawn, there was plenty of food and water available to the laboratory animals in the less populated parts of the experimental area, but most of them chose to congregate in the more densely populated areas.) John B. Calhoun. See 15. Urbanization and 16. Anti-Urban Cultural Tradition in American History Details.

Behaviorism: see 9. Behaviorism in Details.

Behavior modification: changing or unlearning harmful or dysfunctional behavior patterns (such as fears or phobias or substance abuse) by modifying the immediate social environment and employing techniques that are goal-oriented and focus on the here and now, such as using daily journals, rehearsed responses to problematic situations and meditation techniques. See 11. Cognitive Behavioral Therapy in Details and Benjamin Franklin's Table of Virtues in American History Concepts.

Bipolar disorder: a mental illness that was formerly known as manic-depression. It is characterized by alternating moods of depression and elevated energy levels, euphoria, pressured speech, racing thoughts, grandiosity and insomnia. Hypomania is a milder form of the mania phase.

Birth trauma: the prototype for all subsequent trauma and anxiety, according to Otto Rank. See Nirvana principle and Repetition-compulsion in Concepts.

Borderline personality disorder: a term applied to those who are emotionally volatile, easily bored and harbor feelings of emptiness and thoughts of suicide. The disorder may be linked to substance abuse, dysfunctional relationships or, possibly, hormonal fluctuations.

Castration anxiety: according to Sigmund Freud, the feelings that arise in the phallic stage of a child's psycho-sexual development, usually between the ages of three and six, when it discovers its genitalia. The discovery by the male child that females have no penises leads him to fear castration by the powerful father because of his attraction to his mother (the Oedipal complex) and, therefore, to shift his attraction to other females. The realization by the female child of her lack of external genitalia leads her to blame the lack on the mother as punishment for her attraction to her father (the Electra complex). According to Freud, the fear of such punishment is one of the main sources of repression and the origin of the conscience, or superego. Freud, Carl Jung; Norman O. Brown. See Phallic stage in Concepts.

Cathartic method: psychoanalysis's use of free association, dream analysis and psychotherapy, or the "talking cure," to reveal repressed feelings and conflicts, which can then be analyzed and resolved. See 4. Sigmund Freud in Details.

Character/personality traits: the traits, attributes and patterns of behavior that identify and characterize an individual. The degree to which personality traits are genetically inherited and/or environmentally conditioned is the subject of many studies, including cross-cultural studies on child-rearing practices and comparative studies of twins reared apart. Various models of personality types are discussed in Psychology Details.

Co-dependency: a relationship in which an individual's own needs are subordinated to the excessive needs, care and attention of another person, often to support or enable the second person's addiction, irresponsible behavior or narcissism; narcissists are said to be natural magnets for co-dependents. Co-dependency is a type of dependent personality disorder (*q.v.* in Concepts).

Cognition: the mental processes involved in perceiving, learning, thinking, knowing, reasoning, judging and remembering.

Cognitive behavioral therapy: see 11. Cognitive Behavioral Therapy in Details.

Cognitive dissonance: the mental conflict that arises when an individual holds two or more incompatible values or beliefs simultaneously; or when new information is presented that contradicts or is inconsistent with existing information or beliefs.

Dissonance occurs, for example, when a member of a sports team is expected to be both competitive and cooperative, or when an honors student receives an average grade, or when a trusted authority figure is discovered to have committed a disgraceful act. Leon Festinger. See Role conflict in Concepts.

Cognitive models of depression: see 12. Cognitive Models of Depression in Details.

Cognitive negative bias: a self-reinforced mental schema in which individuals are predisposed to view themselves and the world in negative terms and to blame themselves for negative results. See Self-fulfilling prophesy in Concepts and 11. in Cognitive Models of Depression in Details.

Collective unconscious: according to Carl Jung, in addition to the individual unconscious, "there exists a second psychic system of a collective, universal, and impersonal nature which is identical in all individuals" and contains the innate, unconscious, pre-existent mental forms, or archetypes that are shared by all humans. See 7. Carl Jung in Details.

Compulsive urge to disparage: one of the attributes of the neurotic personality, according to Karen Horney.

Conditioned response: one in which a response is conditioned by rewards for a desired behavior and punishment for an undesired behavior. See 9. Behaviorism in Details.

Constructivism: see 14. Constructivism in Details.

Counterintuitive: something that initially appears to be untrue but which, in fact, may be true, as, for example, the fact that the earth revolves around the sun, or that humans can influence global climate.

Countertransference: the therapist's unresolved feelings that are directed at the client. See 5. Freud's Defense Mechanisms in Details.

Critical thinking/self-awareness: thinking about thinking; the process of examining one's own assumptions and methods; seeking an objective understanding of oneself. See Apperception, Reflexivity and Theory of Mind in Concepts and Robert Burns in Quotations.

Cultural hegemony: the doctrine that ideas are class-based; that cultural norms and values are social constructs that are imposed by the dominant class, but are perceived as universally true by the general population; that the ideology at any given time of the ruling elite causes the general public to falsely believe in the universality and immutability of that world view, to accept their subordinate status and to act in ways which are antithetical to their own self-interest; versus Agency and Post-hegemonic synthesis (*qq.v.* in Concepts). Antonio Gramsci.

Cultural stereotype: an oversimplified perception, expectation, generalization or belief, usually negative and prejudicial, about another social group.

Death instinct: Sigmund Freud's thesis that human aggression is innate -- the original sin, as it were -- and the aim of all life is death. In this view, aggression is the death instinct turned outward, while depression is the death instinct turned inward. To Sandor Ferenczi, the death instinct is identified with the unconscious, thalassal-regressive wish to return to the blissful nirvana of the prenatal, oceanic womb. Norman O. Brown, Sandor Ferenczi, Sigmund Freud, Karl Jaspers, Ernest Hemingway. See Repetition-compulsion and Nirvana principle in Concepts; 12. Violence and Human Nature in Anthropology Details and 37. Existentialism in Philosophy/Religion Details.

Decentered self: the theory that knowledge is derived from one's relationships with others and from one's social systems, and not from the individual mind acting as an autonomous knower. In meta-cognitive mindfulness therapy, it refers to the non-judgmental, decentered self who practices mindfulness by focusing on the present moment and observing, experiencing and releasing thoughts as they occur. Jacques Lacan. See Social psychology in Concepts and 13. Mindfulness-based Cognitive Therapy in Details, 4. Post-structuralism in Literary Concepts Details and Sociological assumption in Sociology Concepts.

Defense mechanisms: see 5. Freud's Defense Mechanisms in Details.

Dementia praecox (Latin for "premature madness"): the original term for schizophrenia. See Schizophrenia in Concepts.

Dependent personality disorder: one in which an individual relies excessively on another person for acceptance and approval. Because of low self-esteem and the fear of separation, such people often attach themselves to a stronger person and assume the role of the passive, submissive, self-sacrificing caregiver who is excessively devoted to their partner's needs. Co-dependency (*q.v.* in Concepts) is a type of dependent personality disorder. Karen Horney.

Depression: melancholia; a mood disorder that is characterized by a chronic sense of sadness, hopelessness and depression. Symptoms include lethargy, insomnia, despair, lack of enthusiasm and motivation, the inability to experience pleasure, feelings of emptiness and worthlessness and thoughts of suicide. The condition may have a physiological basis. See 11. in Cognitive Models of Depression in Details.

Depth psychology: schools of psychology, such as psychoanalysis and analytical psychology, that focus on the psychodynamics of internal mental states, including the unconscious and buried memories of the past, and use various analytical and introspective methods to reveal, analyze and resolve repressed feelings and conflicts; Sigmund Freud, Carl Jung, Melanie Klein; versus **behavioral/cognitive therapy**: schools that focus on outwardly observable behavior and attempt to change the dysfunctional aspects of that behavior by employing techniques that are goal-oriented and focus on the here and now; see 9. Behaviorism, 10. Cognitive Psychology, 11. Cognitive Behavioral Psychology, 12. Cognitive Models of Depression and 13. Mindfulness-based Cognitive Therapy in Details.

Dissociation: a mental state in which the mind appears to be detached from the body and the emotions. "I stand outside myself, watching myself watching myself" (Jack Gurney in *The Ruling Class*).

Double-bind: a situation in which the overt verbal message is contradicted by the nonverbal, subtextual message, or in which two mutually contradictory messages are presented simultaneously; for example, a solicitous expression of sympathy that is delivered with an underlying tone or body language that suggests sarcasm, insincerity or indifference; or a hurtful remark that is presented in a humorous manner. Gregory Bateson.

Double consciousness: the"sense of always looking at one's self through the eyes of others" (E. B. Du Bois); for example, a woman watching herself being watched, or a black man as he imagines himself being watched by a white person. John Berger, E. B. Du Bois, Ralph Waldo Emerson. See Looking-glass effect and Reflexivity in Concepts and Du Bois' full quotation in American History Quotations.

Dreams: in psychoanalytic theory, the manifestations of unconscious fears, desires and repressed memories, as well as a means of wish fulfillment. To Sigmund Freud, dreams represent "the royal road to the unconscious," and dream analysis is used to elicit and analyze repressed feelings and conflicts in the unconscious. See 4. Sigmund Freud in Details.

DSM: *Diagnosis and Statistical Manual of Mental Disorders*; the
   official canon of the American Psychiatric Association, which
   provides standardized criteria for classifying mental disorders.
Dysfunctional families: those that exhibit a range of negative
   attributes, including chronic conflict, abuse, misbehavior,
   delinquency, disrespect, co-dependency, abandonment, etc. Leo
   Tolstoy observed that "happy families are all alike, [but] every
   unhappy family is unhappy in its own way." Such families are
   associated with a range of parenting styles, including abusive,
   withholding, neglectful, disciplinarian, perfectionist, overly
   egalitarian, cheerleading, appeasing, parent-child role reversal, etc.
   In such situations, the child may assume a reactive role in order to
   cope with the dysfunctional parenting style. These roles include
   the Good Child, the Problem Child, the Rebel, the Caretaker, the
   Friend, the Jokester, the Manipulator, the Mascot, the Lost One.
   Gregory Bateson, Murray Bowen, Lynn Hoffman, Salvator
   Minuchin, Peggy Papp, Virginia, Satir. See Family romance in
   Concepts.

Ego (Latin for "I"): in Sigmund Freud's structural model, that part of
   the mind that represents reason, forethought and the cognitive and
   executive functions. It is partially conscious and partially
   unconscious, and corresponds, roughly, to the functions performed
   by the prefrontal cortex. See Id, ego and superego and Triune
   brain in Concepts and 4. Sigmund Freud in Details.
Ego psychology: a Neo-Freudian school of psychology that is based on
   the premise that the individual is endowed with a measure of free
   will and possesses a number of autonomous ego functions
   (including reality testing, impulse control and object relationships)
   that are not dependent on unconscious mental processes. Gordon
   Allport, Erik Erikson, Anna Freud, Karen Horney. See Id, ego and
   superego and Neo-Freudianism in Concepts.
Electra complex: the daughter's attraction for her father, often in
   competition with her mother; analogous to the son's attraction for
   his mother. Carl Jung.
Epistemology: a branch of philosophy that examines the nature of
   knowledge and perception; that is, how we know what we know.

Family romance: Freud's theory that, in the process of freeing itself
   from the authority of its family, the pre-adolescent child becomes

estranged and critical of its parents and imagines that he or she is the offspring of a superior, noble or aristocratic family.

Father/mother figure: a substitute parental figure; a person of authority with whom a person identifies and views as a source of protection and/or emulation. See Identification and Transference in 5. Freud's Defense Mechanisms in Details.

Free association: a therapeutic method used in psychoanalysis that encourages the patient to relate everything that comes to mind without censorship or judgment, which allows repressed feelings and conflicts to emerge and become available for analysis and resolution. Josef Breuer, Sigmund Freud, William James, James Joyce, Virginia Woolf. See Stream of consciousness in Concepts.

Generalized other: the imagined spectator, who represents the social conventions and common expectations that others have of the individual; an individual's imagined understanding of the roles and expectations of it and its interactions with other actors in a shared social system; analogous to Freud's superego. George Herbert Mead. See Theory of mind in Concepts.

Genital phase of childhood development: in Sigmund Freud's paradigm, the fourth stage of an individual's psycho-sexual development, which begins at puberty, in which sexual thoughts and urges are re-awakened after a period of latency, and the individual directs its sexual energies toward its peers. Healthy sexual relationships develop if the individual has not been fixated at an earlier stage of development and has not had to struggle excessively with repression and other forms of parental and cultural restrictions and taboos.

Gestalt: holism; the complete form; the totality of perception; the belief that the whole is greater than the sum of its parts.

Holistic psychology: a school of psychology that focuses on the spiritual sense of connectedness and oneness; the integration of the individual into the larger whole; Alfred Adler, Carl Jung, Jan Smuts; versus **reductive psychology**: schools that focus on the psychodynamics of the individual and its internal mental states; see Depth psychology in Details.

Id, ego and superego: the three major components of Sigmund Freud's structural model of the mind: (1) the **id** represents the unconscious instinctual drives and passions; (2) the **ego** represents reason, forethought and the cognitive and executive functions; it is mostly conscious (like the tip of an iceberg), but also, partially, unconscious and preconscious; it attempts to mediate the demands of the id and the superego and navigate through the realities of the external world and (3) the **superego** represents the conscience, the ego-ideal, the inner critic, the moralizing self, the internalized societal and parental standards of right and wrong. See Prefrontal cortex and Triune brain in Concepts and 4. Sigmund Freud in Details.

Identification: see 5. Freud's Defense Mechanisms in Details.

Identity: the defining features of an individual's character and personality, both as the individual perceives itself and as others perceive it; also, the sense of selfhood as a distinct personality, with a sense of uniqueness as well as a sense of affiliation within a larger, concentric superset of social groups, from which are derived one's family, gender, cohort, ethnic, class, cultural, national, human and spiritual identities. See Looking-glass effect, Persona, Reflexivity and Social psychology in Concepts and Robert Burns in Quotations.

Identity crisis: the challenges and conflicts that occur, usually during adolescence but also in midlife, in developing and maintaining a strong, cohesive sense of identity. Erik Erikson.

Identity diffusion: the lack of a clearly defined self-image; versus **identity foreclosure**, in which the ego identity is defined and fixed prematurely. James Marcia.

Individual psychology: schools of psychology that focus on the mind, emotions and behavior of the individual; versus **social psychology**: those that focus on the ways in which human behavior is shaped and conditioned by social groups and institutions ("the individual mind can exist only in relation to other minds with shared meanings" -- George Herbert Mead). See Social psychology in Concepts.

Inferiority complex: see 8. Alfred Adler in Details.

Innate versus **learned behavior**: see Nature-nurture continuum in Concepts.

Interpersonal skills: social and behavioral skills that involve verbal and nonverbal communication and interaction with others. See Social cognition/social intelligence in Concepts.

Introjected parent of the opposite sex: see 5. Freud's Defense Mechanisms in Details.

Introspection looking inward; examining one's own thoughts and feelings. Carl Jung. See Critical thinking and Reflexivity in Concepts.

Irrational: non-rational; not in accordance with reason; outside rational consciousness, self-awareness or self-control; also, behavior that is illogical, inflexible, unrealistic and self-defeating.

Knowing versus **being**: two mutually exclusive mental states and a paradigm of the human condition, according to D. H. Lawrence. Since the "blood-knowledge" of pure being (i.e., animal instinct) was corrupted by the "mind-knowledge" of knowing (symbolized by Adam and Eve's eating from the tree of knowledge, which transformed a natural act into a self-conscious, sinful act), humans are inevitably divided within themselves.

Libido: the instinctual, psycho-sexual energy or force that drives mental activity and behavior, according to psychoanalytic theory. More commonly, it is used as a synonym for the sex drive. Sigmund Freud, Carl Jung.

Litigious paranoia: displaying an obsessive concern for minor, perceived injustices, as well as an inordinate, inappropriate and extreme disputatiousness, often defined in monetary terms and manifested in extensive litigation and accompanied by fears of conspiracy and persecution. Litigious paranoia has been described as an expression of quid pro quo "sphincter morality," which is common among anal personality types. Daniel Bell, James Bryce, Sigmund Freud, Charles Grant, Richard Hofstadter, William Tilden. See Paranoia in Concepts, 6. Freud's Anal Personality Traits in Psychology Details and Paranoid style in American politics in American History Concepts.

Looking-glass effect: a habit of mind in which an individual perceives itself as it imagines others perceive it. Also, the reverse, in which an individual is perceived by others as that individual perceives itself. Charles H. Cooley. See Double consciousness and Theory of mind in Concepts and Robert Burns in Quotations.

Manifest versus **latent dream content**: the text and subtext of dreams, which are decoded through dream analysis and psychoanalysis. Sigmund Freud. See Dreams and Cathartic method in Concepts.

Megalomania: a personality disorder that is characterized by fantasies and delusions of power, omnipotence and domination. See Narcissistic personality disorder in Concepts.

Mindfulness-based cognitive therapy: see 13. Mindfulness-based Cognitive Therapy in Details.

Mirror neurons: those brains cells that are activated when an individual performs a specific action or, more importantly, when it observes another individual performing the same action. The mirroring in the mind (by firing the same neurons) of the individual observing the action is thought to be the psychological mechanism underlying such behaviors as intention decoding, imitation and empathy and the basis for theory of mind (*q.v.* in Concepts).

Moral indignation: an expression of repressed envy, according to Svend Ranulf. See Reaction-formation in Concepts.

Narcissism of small differences: the urge to exaggerate the minor differences between similar individuals or groups in order to preserve a sense of uniqueness, separation and otherness. Freud used the term to suggest that human aggression is innate. The concept is often applied to groups with adjoining territories who are constantly at war with each other, such as the Protestants and Catholics in Northern Ireland, the Palestinians and Israelis in the West Bank, and the Crips and the Bloods in East Los Angeles. The sense of uniqueness and superiority, and the feelings of antipathy directed at those who are virtually similar, may be derived from the fact that the "other" is unconsciously perceived as a sexual or resource competitor. Sigmund Freud; Ernest Crawley, Glen Gabbard. See Individualism in American History Concepts and Male coalition violence, Territoriality and Tribalism in Anthropology Concepts.

Narcissistic personality disorder: a personality disorder that is characterized by an inflated sense of self-worth, self-love and, not infrequently, self-doubt, as well as by arrogance, grandiosity, charm, deceit, manipulation and a strong sense of entitlement. Narcissism originates in childhood and may be derived from a parent's lack of empathy ("I am grandiose because I feel unlovable . . . I fear I cannot be loved unless I am perfect and omnipotent"). There are overt and covert forms of narcissism. Sigmund Freud, Karen Horney, Melanie Klein.

Nature-nurture continuum: the spectrum, or range, of complex interactions between (1) nature (i.e., hereditary, biological and genetic factors) and (2) nurture (i.e., environmental, relational and social factors) and the extent to which each determines, conditions or influences human behavior. The continuum is influenced by the degree of agency, autonomy and free choice exercised by the individual between those two poles. See Agency, Autonomy, Ego Psychology, Neo-Freudianism, Post-essentialism, Post-hegemonic synthesis, Reflexivity, Self-actualization, Sensational psychology, Social psychology and Sociobiology in Concepts.

Negative identification: the identification with (i.e., the emulation of) a non-ideal other, or the dislike of an ideal other. Those with negative identities often engage in anti-social behavior.

Neo-Freudianism: a school of psychoanalytic thought that accepts the basic tenets of Sigmund Freud but also emphasizes the social and cultural influences on individual personality development as much as instinctual drives. To paraphrase Erich Fromm, it attempts to explain the psychic structure as it is defined by the social structure. Neo-Freudians tend to be more optimistic and less fatalistic about human nature than orthodox Freudians and grant the ego a measure of autonomy and free will. Erik Erickson, Erich Fromm, Karen Horney, Henry Stack Sullivan. See Ego psychology in Concepts.

Neurosis: a personality disorder that is not accompanied by delusions or hallucinations and whose symptoms are usually expressed within the boundaries of acceptable behavior. The disorder may be accompanied by anxiety, depression, low self-esteem and/or mental confusion. The term "neurosis" has been replaced by "personality disorder" or "anxiety disorder" in the *DSM*. Personality disorders include obsessive-compulsiveness, narcissism, hysteria, phobias, avoidance and schizoid isolation.

Nirvana principle: in religion, a mystical state of oceanic being; the feeling of being at one with the universe. In Freudian psychology, it is identified with the unconscious, thalassal-regressive wish to return to the blissful nirvana of the prenatal, oceanic womb. Norman O. Brown, Jonathan Edwards, Sándor Ferenczi, Romain Rolland.

Nomothetic: studies that focus on broad social patterns and trends, use empirical methods and quantitative data to demonstrate causal relationships, and draw generalizations and conclusions about social groups and personality typologies, such as Max Weber's ideal types or Carl Jung's introversion-extroversion dichotomies or

Sigmund Freud's oral, anal and phallic personality types; Gordon Allport, Allan Johnson; various personality typologies are listed in Details; versus **idiographic**: studies that focus on individual case studies.

Nomothetic fallacy: that by identifying and naming a problem or personality disorder it can be recognized and resolved, if only because an individual becomes aware of and identifies with it.

Object relations theory: a school of psychoanalysis that focuses on the internal, mental representations of the self and others. It proposes that the way we relate to people as adults is derived from our earliest experiences and interactions with "objects" such as our parents or caregivers, who are embedded in our unconscious as internalized images and who may or may not be accurate representations of the actual others. Melanie Klein, Otto Rank; Ronald Fairbairn.

Obsessional neurosis: the preoccupation with unpleasant, repetitive or intrusive thoughts, such as those associated with death, punishment, violence or sex. Compulsive behavior is often used to relieve the anxiety associated with the obsessive thought. Freud characterized religion as a form of universal obsessional neurosis.

Obsessive-compulsive disorders ("OCDs"): anxiety disorders that are associated with intrusive thoughts and ritualistic, repetitive or compulsive behaviors. OCD symptoms may include hoarding; obsessive religious, sexual or violent thoughts; excessive hand-washing or nail-biting, compulsive counting, etc. See Retentiveness/hoarding in Concepts.

Oedipal complex: the attraction of the son for the mother, which may or may not be accompanied by competitive and, even, murderous thoughts toward the father. Sophocles, Sigmund Freud. See Castration anxiety in Concepts.

Oral phase of childhood development: in Sigmund Freud's paradigm, the first phase of the infant's psycho-sexual development, from birth to age two, in which nursing, weaning and teething occur and in which the mouth is the first erogenous zone. Fixation at this stage of development is manifested later in such behavioral patterns as dependency, talkativeness, food obsessiveness, overeating, dieting, smoking, drinking, nail-biting, breast fixations and oral forms of sadism ("biting" remarks, verbal cruelty, sarcasm, manipulation, glibness, etc.).

Overcompensation: attaining a sense of superiority or excellence in one area in order to compensate for feelings of inferiority, inadequacy or incompetence in another. Alfred Adler, Melanie Klein.

Paranoia: a severe mental disorder that is characterized by delusions and irrational fears of persecution and conspiracy and the belief that others are intent on harming one. According to Freudian psychology, paranoia is associated with the unconscious fear that the "other" (i.e., the love-hate object) will be incorporated into the body and, not infrequently, the unconscious fear of passive submission to that other. Sigmund Freud, Karl Abraham, Sandor Ferenczi. See Litigious paranoia in Concepts and 6. Freud's Anal Personality Traits in Details.

Parapsychology: the study of paranormal and psychic phenomena, including telepathy, clairvoyance, extra-sensory perception, precognition, near-death experiences, communication with the dead, reincarnation, psycho-kinesis, etc.

Passages: a personality development model that describes the changes and challenges encountered in successive phases of adulthood, including (1) pulling up roots; (2) seeking a world view; (3) the urge to merge; (4) rooting and extending; (5) the mid-life crossroads and (6) generativity, renewal and approval. Roger Gould, Gail Sheehy.

Passive-aggressive: expressing anger or resentment in a passive, indirect way, including avoidance, procrastination, inefficiency, obstructionism, helplessness, victimization, negativity, sulking and surliness. The behavior is usually manifested in environments in which it is unsafe for the individual to assert itself directly or to openly express anger or frustration.

Peer group/nurture assumption: Judith Rich Harris' thesis that the critical, formative determinates of a child's personality, in addition to genetic factors, are the child's peer groups, rather than its home environment, parents, teachers, other adults or society at large.

Persona (Latin for "mask"): an individual's social role or identity. According to Carl Jung, identification with the persona inhibits personal development, and its disintegration and reconstruction into a more flexible and realistic persona is necessary for individualization and personal growth. See Identity in Concepts and 7. Carl Jung in Details.

Personality disorders: functional mental disorders whose symptoms are usually expressed within the boundaries of acceptable behavior. These include antisocial, borderline, narcissistic, obsessive-compulsive and schizotypal disorders. "Personality disorder" has replaced the term "neurosis" (*q.v.* in Concepts) in the *DSM.*

Phallic phase of childhood development: in Sigmund Freud's paradigm, the third stage of the child's psycho-sexual development (after the oral and anal phases and before the genital phase), from the age three to six years, in which the child's libido focuses on the genitalia as the primary erogenous zone. The male child's discovery that females have no penises leads him to fear castration by the powerful father because of his attraction to the mother (the Oedipal complex) and, therefore, to shift his attraction to other females. The realization by the female child of her lack of external genitalia leads her to blame the lack on the mother as punishment for her attraction to the father (the Electra complex). Males fixated at the phallic stage of development tend to be vain, assertive and ambitious, while females fixated at this stage tend to be seductive and either domineering or unusually submissive, with low self-esteem. The phallic stage is followed by a period of latency, after which the genital stage emerges during puberty with re-awakened sexual feelings.

Pleasure principle: Sigmund Freud's thesis that the id seeks to attain immediate pleasure and avoid pain; versus the **reality principle**, in which the ego seeks to mediate the conflicting demands of the id and the superego and to navigate the realities of the external world. Sigmund Freud. See Id, ego and superego in Concepts.

Polymorphously perverse: Sigmund Freud's thesis that infants and young children derive uninhibited, undifferentiated sexual pleasure from various parts of their bodies as they pass through the oral, anal and phallic erogenous phases of development, and from bisexual and incestuous feelings, until they are constrained, shamed and repressed by social conventions, norms and taboos. Norman O. Brown, Sigmund Freud, Herbert Marcuse.

Post-essentialism: the theory that personalities, identities and roles are socially constructed rather than biologically determined. See Nature-nurture continuum in Concepts and 4. Post-structuralism in Literary Concepts.

Post-hegemonic synthesis: a school of thought that ascribes free will, agency, autonomy and reflexivity, or self-awareness, to individuals as they make choices within given cultural and social structures and biological constraints. Peter Berger and Thomas Luckmann, Anthony Giddens, Raymond Williams. See Agency, Autonomy, Cultural hegemony, Ego psychology, Nature-nurture continuum and Reflexivity in Concepts.

Post-hoc perceptual bias: the thesis that people often cannot imagine the probability or consequences of a harmful action until after it has occurred. It is reflected in the disparity between the enormous personal and economic losses incurred by society from dysfunctional, anti-social and criminal behavior, and the small investment made by society in identifying and preventing the causes. Prevention and proactive intervention are hindered by social inertia, indifference, denial and fatalism, as well as by post-hoc perceptual biases.

Prefrontal cortex: that part of the human brain that performs executive functions, such as planning, decision-making, orchestrating complex actions, inhibiting impulsive and socially unacceptable behavior and deferring gratification. It corresponds roughly to the ego in Freud's structural model. See Id, ego and superego and Triune Brain in Concepts.

Prosocial behavior: behavior that is intended to benefit others. It may be motivated by empathy, altruism or anticipated reciprocity and may be associated with parental nurturing, trust, social cooperation and the maternal hormone oxytocin. Patricia Churchland, Philip Kitsch, Donald Pfaff, Frans de Waal. See Mirror neurons, Social psychology and Theory of mind in Concepts and 5. Social Intelligence/Social Brain Hypothesis in Anthropology Details.

Psyche (Greek for "soul," "breath," or "spirit"): the conscious and unconscious mind. See Unconscious in Concepts and 2. Ancient Greeks and the Irrational and 4. Sigmund Freud in Details.

Psychosis: any severe form of mental disorder that involves the loss of contact with reality and which may be accompanied by delusions, hallucinations, disorganized thoughts and speech and, in some cases, catatonia. The term is applied to severe forms of schizophrenia, paranoia, bipolar disorders and the effects of substance abuse.

Reaction-formation: a defense mechanism in which an unpleasant, anxiety-inducing unconscious impulse or thought is mastered by outwardly expressing its exact opposite in an exaggerated fashion. For example: (1) over-solicitousness may be a reaction-formation against unconscious anger and hostility; (2) cheerfulness, humor and wittiness may disguise inner feelings of despair and depression; (3) excessive cleanliness or orderliness may be a reaction-formation against unconscious feelings of uncleanliness and impurity or disorder and chaos; (4) homophobia may be a reaction-formation against unconscious feelings of attraction for members of the same sex. Calvin Hall. See 5. Freud's Defense Mechanisms in Details.

Reflexivity: self-awareness; an individual's recognition of the personal, social and environmental influences that shaped it, as well as the individual's autonomous ability to change and re-shape its own views and norms. Thus, culture shapes character, and character shapes culture. "Man is both knowing subject and the object of his own study" -- Michel Foucault. See Agency, Autonomy, Post-hegemonic synthesis and Theory of mind in Concepts.

Repetition-compulsion: the urge to repeat or re-live a traumatic experience. According to Freud, the repetition of a harmful event or a dangerous pattern of behavior does not change until the underlying internal conflicts associated with that trauma are resolved. See 37. Existentialism in Philosophy/Religion Details.

Residues: inner and, often, illogical and irrational psychological sentiments, motivations and instincts; versus **derivatives**: the outward manifestations, logical explanations and rationalizations of those residues. Vilfredo Pareto.

Retentiveness/hoarding: a manifestation of parsimony, one of Freud's three fundamental character traits of the anal-retentive personality (the others are obstinacy/rebelliousness and orderliness/cleanliness). Retentiveness is thought to originate in a child's fixation at the anal stage of development as a result of harsh, rigid or premature toilet training and the dispossession of the products of the child's labor by an authority figure. The anally-fixated personality compensates for the original loss of his or her possessions by collecting, retaining or hoarding their unconscious analogues (or "copro-symbols"), such as money, stamps, shells, coins, jewelry, books, words, time, facts and statistics. "All collectors are anal-erotics, and the objects collected are nearly always typical copro-symbols," according to Ernest Jones. Hoarding is an obsessive-compulsive disorder and an extreme form of retentiveness. See Anal phase of childhood development and Obsessive-compulsive disorders in Concepts, 6. Freud's Anal

Personality Traits in Details and William Tilden in Selected References.

Role conflict: the conflict that is experienced by an individual who holds two or more contradictory social roles or sets of expectations, such as those of being a good mother, a successful career woman and a sexually attractive wife. Also, a single role with multiple, conflicting expectations, such as being a good boss. See Cognitive dissonance in Concepts.

Sadomasochism: the pleasure derived from, respectively, inflicting or receiving pain; aggression turned outward versus aggression turned inward. Havelock Ellis, Sigmund Freud, Richard von Krafft-Ebing.

Schizoid personality disorder: a term used to describe those who are excessively reserved, aloof, withdrawn, indifferent, avoidant or passive, and who have difficulty in expressing feelings and establishing relationships. Eugen Bleuler, Karen Horney. See Secret/covert schizoid in Concepts.

Schizophrenia (Greek for "split mind"): a severe mental disorder that was once known as *dementia praecox*. It is characterized by paranoid delusions, auditory hallucinations, disorganized thoughts and speech ("word salad"), dysphoria, social withdrawal, deficits in emotional response (the "blunted effect"), a lack of motivation and displays of "safety behaviors" to avoid perceived threats. It has been linked to a physiological process in the development of the adolescent brain in which weak or redundant connections between the neurons are excessively pruned or eliminated.

Secret/covert schizoid: a term applied to those who are outwardly engaging, sociable, available and interactive but who are inwardly detached, emotionally cold, passive and withdrawn, and require other people for a sense of security and stability and prefer partners who make few emotional or intimate demands. Ralph Klein.

Self-actualization: the process of realizing one's full potential; "to express and activate all [one's] capacities," including the ability to act independently, autonomously, spontaneously and stoically; to embrace a sense of wonder and a sense of fellowship with others, a sense of comfort in solitude and a sense of humor; and to accept the shortcomings of oneself and the world, "thereby transcending rather than just coping with them" -- Abraham Maslow. Maslow, Carl Rogers.

Self-fulfilling prophecy: "a false definition of the situation evoking a new behavior which makes the original false conception come true" (Robert Merton); the circular relationship between an expectation and a self-validating behavior; for example, the belief among some depressives that the self is worthless, the world is unfair and the future is hopeless (Aaron Beck). Robert Merton. See 12. Cognitive Models of Depression in Details.

Sensational psychology: John Locke's theory of human knowledge and understanding, which is based on the premise that the mind at birth is a *tabula rasa*, or blank tablet, and that there are no innate ideas, and, thus, that the individual personality is entirely shaped by experience, sensory impressions and environmental influences; versus the *a priori* **structuralism** of Immanuel Kant, Claude Levi-Strauss and Norm Chomsky, who propose that the mind actively filters, interprets and judges experience through innate, pre-established concepts and mental categories (such as cause and effect, the rules of grammar, etc.). See *A priori* mental categories, Nature-nurture continuum, Sociobiology and Structuralism in Concepts and 14. Constructivism in Details.

Separation anxiety: the anxiety generated by the child's early, primal, traumatic separation from its mother or "significant other," with whom it had formed an emotional attachment. It serves as the prototype for all subsequent anxiety and neuroses, according to Karen Horney. See Attachment theory and Object relations theory in Concepts.

Sexual etiology of neuroses: Freud's theory that the blocked discharge of libidinous desire leads to frustration, repression, anxiety, regression, fixation, etc. Jean Martin Charcot, Sigmund Freud. See 4. Sigmund Freud in Details.

Significant other: the primary caregiver, usually the mother, with whom the child has formed a strong emotional attachment. Harry Stack Sullivan.

Social cognition/social intelligence: the knowledge, skills and proficiency with which an individual understands, empathizes with and interacts with other humans. Social intelligence is thought to be the driving force in human evolution, and is derived from the challenges and complexities of living in groups. Among hunter-gatherers, these challenges involved cooperative hunting, food sharing, mutual grooming, reciprocal altruism, coalitional politics, alliances, balance of power, etc. Robin Dunbar, Nicholas Humphrey, Richard Leakey. See Interpersonal skills, Mirror neurons, Prosocial behavior, Reflexivity, Social psychology and Theory of mind in Concepts and 5. Social Intelligence/Social Brain Hypothesis in Anthropology Details.

Social psychology: the study of human behavior in its social context. It is based on the assumption that human behavior is inherently relational, that is, that it is shaped and/or determined by its social environment, or, to paraphrase Eric Fromm, the psychic structure as it is defined by the social structure. Since society is "an intricate web of multiple relations between individuals" (George Simmel), and, since all individuals belong to groups (family, friends, neighbors, school-mates, church-members, business associates, community members, political affiliates, citizens, etc.), their behavior is shaped and conditioned by those groups. "The individual mind can exist only in relation to other minds with shared meanings" (George Herbert Mead). Social psychology focuses on the dynamics and behavior patterns of individuals in relation to those groups and institutions and the ways in which individuals are embedded in and conditioned by social systems; versus **individual and depth psychology**, which focuses on the behavior, feelings and internal mental states of the individual *per se*. George Herbert Mead. See Social cognition/social intelligence in Concepts, 5. Social Intelligence/Social Brain Hypothesis in Anthropology Details and 18. Structural Functionalism in Sociology Details.

Sociobiology: a school of scientific thought that maintains that individual and social behavior is largely inherited, that is, that it is the product of genes and natural selection. Inherited behaviors include those associated with gender, aggression, territoriality, mating, reciprocal altruism, social cooperation, intelligence, anxiety/stress-response and introversion. Sociobiology has been criticized as a form of biological determinism, and has been challenged by studies that demonstrate a reciprocal relationship between nature and nurture, biology and the environment. Steven Pinker, Edward O. Wilson. See Nature-nurture continuum in Concepts and 10. Epigenetics/Gene Expression and 11. Adaptive/Developmental Plasticity in Science Details.

Sociopathy: a personality disorder that is characterized by anti-social behavior. Sociopaths can be charming, manipulative, deceitful, grandiose, narcissistic, impulsive, callous and tyrannical. They are contemptuous of social norms, lack empathy, a sense of remorse or the capacity to love and are driven by the need for constant stimulation. See Anti-social personality disorder in Concepts.

Stream of consciousness: the mindstream or mindflow; the uninterrupted flow of thoughts, half-thoughts, feelings, impressions and perceptions, many of which are illogical, inconsistent and contradictory. Psychoanalysis uses free association and the "talking cure" to allow the patient's repressed feelings and conflicts to emerge from the stream of thought and become available for analysis and resolution. Sigmund Freud, William James. See Free association in Concepts and Interior monologue in Literary Concepts.

Structuralism: a school of thought that maintains that societies are governed by underlying, often unconscious, structures that guide social behavior, such as kinship patterns, rituals, myths and *a priori* rules of grammar. Noam Chomsky, Jonathan Culler, Claude Lévi-Strauss, Ferdinand de Saussure. See 2. Structuralism in Literary Concepts Details.

Substitute gratification: the substitution of an acceptable pleasure for an unacceptable or unattainable one; for example, ice cream for sex, money for love, flowers for babies, art for immortality.

Suicide: see Albert Camus in Philosophy/Religion Quotations and 13. Emile Durkheim in Sociology Details.

Symbolic consciousness: the ability to symbolize, to see one thing in terms of another and to invest meaning in the world, which represents "the most characteristic mental trait of mankind," according to Susanne Langer (*q.v.* in Art Quotations).

Theory of mind: an individual's ability to apprehend the mental states of others; the ability to put oneself in another's place. Social cognition is one of the driving forces in human evolution. See Mirror neurons, Prosocial behavior, Reflexivity and Social cognition in Concepts and 5. Social Intelligence/Social Brain Hypothesis in Anthropology Details.

Triune brain: a neuro-anatomical model of the brain, which consists of three parts: (1) the **R-complex**, that is, the primitive, reptilian brain, which is the source of aggression, dominance, territoriality, rigid and stereotyped behaviors, and courtship and mating displays and rituals; (2) the **limbic system**, or mammalian brain, which is the source of the emotions, memory and parental behavior, including maternal bonding and nurturing, attachments, affiliation and mutuality and (3) the **prefrontal cortex**, which governs reasoning, planning, decision-making and impulse control. Fan Amini and Richard Lannon, Thomas Lewis, Paul D. MacLain, Steven Pinker.

Twice-born: the term used by William James to describe those who have suffered a mental breakdown or a "crisis of meaning" and, afterward, experience a profound sense of renewal and a deeper appreciation for life; analogous to the "born again" religious experience.

Unconscious: that part of the mind that is outside human awareness and is, largely, "the province of the id," with its instinctual drives and passions. See Id, ego and superego in Concepts, Sigmund Freud in Quotations and 4. Sigmund Freud in Details.

Will to meaning: the belief that humans are driven to find meaning in life. Viktor Frankl.

Wishful thinking/magical thinking: the implicit belief in a causal relationship between a thought or ritual and a subsequent effect.

QUOTATIONS:

- *Know thyself.* -- inscription on the Temple of Apollo at Delphi.

- *All human actions have one or more of these seven causes: chance, nature, compulsions, habit, reason, passion, desire.* -- Aristotle.

- *Our life is what our thoughts make it.* -- Marcus Aurelius.

- *We are such stuff*
  As dreams are made on, and our little life
  Is rounded with a sleep. -- Shakespeare, *Tempest.*

- *O would some power the gift to give us to see ourselves as others see us.* – Robert Burns.

- *It is not the consciousness of men that determines their existence, but on the contrary, their social existence determines their consciousness.* -- Karl Marx.

- *When we remember that we are all mad, the mysteries disappear and life stands explained.* -- Mark Twain.

- *In the end, one experiences only oneself.* -- Friedrich Nietzsche.

- *It seems to be my fate to discover only the obvious.* -- Sigmund Freud.

- *The poets and philosophers before me discovered the unconscious; what I discovered was the scientific method by which the unconscious can be studied.* -- Freud.

- [Psychoanalysis] *is in essence a cure based* [on] *love.* -- Freud (in a letter to Carl Jung, 1906).

- *I am myself and my circumstances.* -- José Ortega y Gasset.

- [With] *a little madness* [you can] *cut the rope and be free.* -- Nikos Kazantzakis.

- *You're born, you deconstruct your childhood, then you die.* -- a patient on a couch to her therapist (*New Yorker* cartoon).

PSYCHOLOGY DETAILS: (1) Psychology, (2) Ancient Greeks and the Irrational, (3) Hippocrates' Four Temperaments, (4) Sigmund Freud, (5) Freud's Defense Mechanisms, (6) Freud's Anal Personality Traits, (7) Carl Jung, (8) Alfred Adler, (9) Behaviorism, (10) Cognitive Psychology, (11) Cognitive Behavioral Therapy, (12) Cognitive Models of Depression, (13) Mindfulness-based Cognitive Therapy, (14) Constructivism, (15) Herbert Marcuse and Cultural Materialism, (16) Authoritarian Personality, (17) Max Weber's Ideal/Personality Types, (18) William Sheldon's Somatotypes, (19) Erich Fromm's Five Personality Orientations, (20) Abraham Maslow's Hierarchy of Needs, (21) David Riesman's Three Personality Types, (22) Five Factor Model of Personality Traits, (23) Merrill-Reid's Five Personality Types, (24) Myers-Briggs Type Indicator and (25) Keirsey Temperament Sorter.

1. **Psychology** is the study of the human mind.

2. **Ancient Greeks and the Irrational** refers to E. R. Dodds's study of the ways in which the ancient Greeks explained mental phenomena. The Greek cosmology consisted of a system of legends and myths that involved divine intervention into human affairs by a pantheon of serio-comic, anthropomorphic gods who competed with one another to assist their favorite mortals and thwart their worldly and other-worldly opponents. These gods used various methods to influence human behavior that were channeled through natural phenomena, including the human *psyche* (the spirit or soul) and the human *soma* (body). These methods included *âte* (in which the mind was temporally blinded or clouded by an irrational impulse), *hubris* (pride/arrogance), *katharsis* (purification), *koros* (complacency), *menos* (mysterious energy), *moira* (lot, fate, destiny), *nemesis* (an avenging agent), *phthonos* (jealousy) and *thumos* (the inner voice or conscience).

3. **Hippocrates'** (460-370 BCE) **Four Temperaments** posits four basic personality types, which are based on the four "humors," or bodily fluids, and the four elementary substances, which are: (1)

sanguine (blood/air), (2) choleric (yellow bile/fire), (3) melancholic (black bile/earth) and (4) phlegmatic (phlegm/water).

4. **Sigmund Freud** (1856-1939) was the founder of psychoanalysis, who developed a theory of the mind based on the following concepts:

1) The id (Latin for "it"), which represents the unconscious instinctual drives and passions. It is the reservoir of unconscious, irrational, repressed, sexual and aggressive thoughts, feelings, memories and impulses, and acts in accordance with the pleasure principle of seeking immediate gratification.

2) The ego (Latin for "I"), which represents reason, forethought and the cognitive and executive functions. It is mostly conscious, but is also partially unconscious and preconscious, and acts in accordance with the reality principle, which seeks to mediate the conflicting demands of the id and the superego and navigate the realities of the external world.

3) The superego, which represents the conscience, that is, the ego-ideal, the inner critic, the moralizing self, the internalized societal and parental standards of right and wrong.

4) The libido, which is the instinctual, psycho-sexual (mental and emotional) energy that drives mental activity and behavior.

5) The pleasure principle, whose objective is to attain pleasure and avoid pain; it is the driving force of the id.

6) The reality principle, which governs the ego and seeks to mediate the conflicting demands of the id and the superego and the realities of the external world.

7) The death instinct, which is based on the premise that human aggression is innate (*q.v.* in Concepts).

8) The importance of early childhood: that the personality is formed by events in early childhood as well as by "dispositional" forces.

9) Infantile sexuality: that infants and young children derive undifferentiated sexual pleasure from all parts of their bodies as they pass through the oral, anal and phallic erogenous phases of development.

10) Infantile narcissism, which is derived from childhood feelings of omnipotence. See Narcissistic personality disorder in Concepts and 8. Alfred Adler in Details.

11) Separation anxiety: see Separation anxiety in Concepts.

12) The Oedipal complex: see Oedipal complex in Concepts.

13) The significance of dreams: that dreams are "the royal road to the unconscious," which represent manifestations of unconscious desires, fears and repressed memories, as well as a means of wish fulfillment.

14) The sexual etiology of neuroses: that the blocked discharge of a libidinous desire leads to frustration, repression, anxiety, regression, fixation, etc.

15) Defense mechanisms: see 5. in Details.

16) The nirvana principle and the thalassal regressive trend: see Nirvana principle in Concepts.

17) The castration complex: see in Concepts.

18) Religion is a form of universal obsessional neurosis, which represents wishful or magical thinking, is irrational, ritualistic and compulsive, and reflects the regressive, infantile wish for a powerful, protective, idealized parental/authority figure. See Nirvana principle in Concepts.

Based on his theory of the mind, Freud developed a therapeutic method of psychoanalytic treatment that consisted of the "talking cure," free association, introspection and dream analysis to reveal and bring into consciousness repressed feelings and conflicts in order that they could be analyzed and resolved.

In his *Civilization and Its Discontents* (1930), Freud portrayed the irreconcilable contradiction between human nature (with its innate sexual and aggressive impulses) and human culture (with its demands for civility, conformity, repression and sublimation). Recent studies in neuroscience have confirmed that anger and violence originate in the ancient circuitry of the subcortical brain (particularly, the amygdala and the hypothalamus; or, in Freudian terms, the id), which is triggered by perceived threats to the self, family, tribe, status, territory, etc., which the pre-frontal cortex (in Freudian terms, the ego) struggles to control. R. Douglas Fields. Sigmund Freud; Karl Abraham, Norman O. Brown, Anna Freud, Calvin Hall, Ernest Jones, Melanie Klein. See Paradox of humanism in Philosophy/Religion Concepts and 12. Violence and Human Nature in Anthropology Details.

5. **Freud's Defense Mechanisms** are the means that the ego unconsciously employs to deal with anxieties arising from the

conflicting demands of the id, the superego and the realities of the external world. These include:

1) **Displacement**: re-directing feelings of anger and frustration to a less threatening object.

2) **Fixation**: the obsessive attachment to a person, idea or object.

3) **Identification**: to like, or to wish to become like, an ideal other; the emotional attachment to, and the emulation of, an ideal other.

4) **Introjection**: incorporating another (often, a parent, teacher, coach or therapist) into one's own identity.

5) **Projection**: ascribing one's own negative or uncomfortable thoughts and feelings to others. For example: "I would like to have an extramarital affair" becomes "my spouse is cheating on me"; "I am selfish and greedy" becomes "those people are selfish and greedy."

6) **Rationalization**: self-justification.

7) **Reaction-formation**: the exaggerated, outward expression of the exact opposite repressed, unconscious feeling. For example: homophobia for homosexual attraction; solicitude for anger; cheerfulness for depression; indignation for envy; obsessive cleanliness and orderliness for feelings of uncleanliness and impurity or chaos and disorder.

8) **Regression**: mentally retreating or withdrawing to an earlier stage of personal development; behaving in an infantile or childish manner.

9) **Repression**: denial; keeping or forcing negative or uncomfortable ideas or images into the unconscious and preventing them from reaching conscious awareness.

10) **Sublimation**: re-directing unconscious impulses and sexual energy into socially acceptable channels; for example, aggression into sports; eroticism into art or cooking, fear of death or punishment into religion.

11) **Transference**: the redirection of one's feelings for a person (usually, a parent) to another person (for example, a teacher, coach or therapist).

6. **Freud's Anal Personality Traits** are a complex of related, but often contradictory, personality traits that are summarized in Freud's fundamental triad of *orderliness, parsimony* and *obstinacy*, which are thought to be derived from harsh, rigid or premature toilet training that causes the child to be fixated at this stage in its

psycho-sexual development. These traits include obstinacy, rebelliousness, retentiveness, frugality, hoarding, orderliness, cleanliness, neatness and punctuality (and their corresponding reaction-formations of conformity, slovenliness and procrastination), as well as, paradoxically, but not infrequently, prodigality and wastefulness, and generosity and philanthropy (in which the eliminative mode prevails over the retentive one). Retentiveness and obstinacy are frequently manifested later as anger and resistance to parental/authority figures and constraints as represented by governmental regulations and taxation, which represent a threat to the individual's autonomy and the unfair dispossession of the products of its labor.

The anally-fixated personality compensates for the original loss of the products of his or her labor by collecting, retaining or hoarding their unconscious analogues (or "copro-symbols"), such as money, stamps, shells, coins, jewelry, books, words, time, facts and statistics. "All collectors are anal-erotics, and the objects collected are nearly always typical copro-symbols" (Ernest Jones). Hoarding is an obsessive-compulsive disorder and an extreme form of retentiveness.

The cultural imperative to regulate the time and place of defecation is a universal, if unspoken, precondition of all sedentary cultures and may have emerged when humans gave up a nomadic life style and settled down in permanent agricultural villages and urban centers. One anthropologist, Geza Roheim, has stated that all urban cultures are "based on sublimations or reaction-formations of anal trends." Character traits described by Freud and his colleagues are expressed in various cultural forms according to the unique historical and cultural contexts in which they are transmitted. For example, in cultures in which material scarcity and the memory of scarcity are present, the traits of frugality and orderliness are predominate; in cultures with relative abundance and social mobility, the traits of obstinacy, rebelliousness and prodigality and wastefulness are manifested. Sigmund Freud; Karl Abraham, John Bourke, Norman O. Brown, Erik Erikson, Otto Fenichel, Sandor Ferenczi, Ernest Jones, Lou Andreas-Salomé, William Tilden. See Anal phase of childhood development, Litigious paranoia, Retentiveness/hoarding, and Obsessive-compulsive disorders in Concepts and Scarcity Psychology in Economics Concepts.

7. **Carl Jung** (1875-1961) was the founder of the analytical school of psychology, who developed the following concepts:
   1) The collective unconscious: in addition to the individual unconscious, "there exists a second psychic system of a collective, universal, and impersonal nature which is identical in all individuals. This collective unconscious does not develop individually but is inherited, and consists of pre-existent forms, the archetypes."
   2) Archetypes: the innate, unconscious, universal symbols, or pre-existent mental forms or patterns, which are shared in the collective unconscious by all humans and are represented in myths, rituals and folklore; e.g., the Great Mother, the Hero, the Mentor, the Martyr, the Trickster.
   3) Complex: a group or constellation of unconscious feelings and beliefs, which have " a powerful inner coherence" and influence an individual's attitudes and behavioral patterns.
   4) Electra complex: the daughter's attraction for the father, often in competition with the mother.
   5) Persona: an individual's social "mask," role or identity. See Identity and Persona in Concepts.
   6) Shadow: the repressed or disowned qualities of the conscious self, which lead to denial, projection, integration or transmutation.
   7) Intuition: the apprehension of something in an unconscious way that is independent of reason.
   8) *Anima*: the unconscious female component in the male, and *animus*: the unconscious male component in female.
   9) Extroversion-introversion, sensation-intuition, and thinking-feeling dichotomies. See 24. Myers-Briggs Type Indicator in Details.
   10) Self-realization: awakening to elements in the unconscious psyche and achieving wholeness through the integration of the conscious and unconscious self.
   11) *Scotomata*: perceptual blind spots about oneself and others.
   12) Synchronicity: meaningful coincidences.
   13) Second puberty: a period that occurs in late adulthood when concerns about the self are shifted to those about the community, spirituality and humanity.

8. Alfred Adler (1870-1937) developed the following concepts:
    1) The inferiority complex, which originates in the child's
        feelings of helplessness and dependency and which the
        unconscious self strives to convert into feelings of superiority
        or completeness, but which may lead to overcompensation and
        narcissism.
    2) Teleological psychodynamics: that the human personality is
        creatively guided by goals; if you explain the goal, you explain
        the behavior.
    3) Holistic psychology: the spiritual sense of oneness; the
        integration into the whole.
    4) The importance of birth order in personality development: the
        oldest child is dethroned, the middle is neglected and the
        youngest is overindulged.

9. **Behaviorism** rejects the introspective methods of depth
    psychology (which explores feelings, internal mental states and the
    unconscious) and focuses, instead, on outwardly observable human
    behavior, which, it posits, is driven by stimulus and response and
    consists of a set of habits that are learned through conditioning and
    can be modified through conditioning; that is, by using rewards for
    desired behavior and punishments for undesired behavior. Ivan
    Pavlov, B. F. Skinner, John Watson.

10. **Cognitive Psychology** is related to behaviorism in that it rejects
    the use of introspective methods (such as those used by
    psychoanalysis) but accepts the existence and influence of internal
    mental states (desires, beliefs, etc.) and views the mind in
    computational terms as an information processing machine.

11. **Cognitive Behavioral Therapy** is a "rational therapy" that
    incorporates behavioral and cognitive psychology and focuses on
    behavior modification, that is, on changing or unlearning harmful
    or dysfunctional mental and behavior patterns (such as fears or
    phobias or substance abuse) and modifying the immediate social
    environment. It employs techniques that are goal-oriented and
    focus on the here and now, and stresses the alleviation or
    elimination of symptoms through the use of daily journals,
    exposure to the feared stimuli, medication, relaxation, meditation

and other techniques. See Benjamin Franklin's Table of Virtues in American History Concepts.

12. **Cognitive Models of Depression** are based on a range of views, theories and assessments, including the following:

1) Recurrent patterns of depressive thinking or schemas are derived from a triad of negative thoughts: (a) the self is worthless, (b) the world is unfair and (c) the future is hopeless. Aaron Beck.

2) Depression is a form of learned helplessness from which the individual cannot escape because of the initial, learned lack of control. Martin Seligman.

3) Depression is derived from deficits in bonding with the parent/caregiver in early childhood (attachment theory). "Experiences of early loss, separation and rejection by the parent or caregiver (conveying the message that the child is unlovable) may all lead to. . . . internal cognitive representations of the self as unlovable and of attachment figures as unloving, untrustworthy" -- John Bowlby.

4) Depressed individuals often blame themselves for negative outcomes and do not take credit for positive ones, based on negative beliefs about themselves and their experiences of failure. Albert Bandura.

5) Depressive patterns are characterized by cognitive distortions and negative thoughts, including all-or-nothing thinking (false dichotomies), over-generalizations, discounting or filtering out positive experiences, jumping to conclusions, magnifying others' positive attributes and minimizing their negative ones, personalizing responsibility for events over which they have no control. David Burns. See Cognitive negative bias in Concepts.

13. **Mindfulness-based Cognitive Therapy** uses meta-cognitive awareness and meditation, in addition to traditional methods of cognitive behavior therapy, to address issues of depression by teaching patients to develop the ability to observe and accept all thoughts and feelings as they pass through the mind without becoming attached to or reactive against them; to become disengaged and nonjudgmental, and to focus on the present; that is, to observe, experience and release the thoughts and feelings as they occur. Meta-cognitive awareness is informed by the tenets and

practices of Buddhism. Zindel Segal, John Teasdale, C. Mark
Williams.

14. **Constructivism** is an epistemological theory, cognitive model and
learning method that is based on the principle that the human mind
is not a passive receptacle that receives information from the
environment, but, in learning and the act of knowing, actively
creates meaning and gives order to reality through a series of
individual constructs, or filters, which impose order on the chaos
of experience. In personal-construct psychology, "individuals
encounter problems not because life is inherently problematic but
because of the way they frame their problems, or the way people
make sense of events that occur in their life; the way we expect to
experience the world alters how we feel about it and act. . . . In
other words, we order ourselves by ordering our thoughts. The
goal of this therapeutic approach, therefore, is to allow the clients
to explore their own minds, acting as a facilitator but not
intervening" (George Kelly). Immanuel Kant; John Dewey, Ernest
von Glasersfeld, George Kelly.

15. **Herbert Marcuse and Cultural Materialism** is a synthesis of
Neo-Marxism and Neo-Freudianism, in which the material culture
(the economic/productive and sexual/reproductive relationships in
the substructure) determines the superstructure (art, ideology and
religion; social, cultural, political and legal institutions). Marcuse
asserted that (1) irrationality is inherent in technology and (2) the
hyper-rationalized industrial process is characterized by production
for waste and destruction (war) and the exploitation of regimented,
repressive, stupefying labor. He proposed, instead, that the
productive process should be based on nonrepressive sublimation,
that is, sublimation without desexualization and work as play. See
9. Cultural Materialism in Sociology Details.

16. **Authoritarian Personality** is a complex of personality traits and is
characterized by rigidity of thought, stereotyped thinking,
intolerance of ambiguity, the need to conform and appear
respectable, unquestioned obedience to authority and prejudice and
paranoia. Authoritarianism and excessive conformity is thought to
be the outward manifestation of a reaction-formation that
originates in childhood, during which the child outwardly
assimilates strict and rigid parental controls, but inwardly and

unconsciously hates both the controls and those who fail to conform to them. Theodor Adorno, Gordon Allport, Daniel Bell, Erich Fromm, Richard Hofstadter, Daniel Riesman. See Paranoia and Reaction-formation in Concepts, 6. Freud's Anal Personality Traits in Details and Stern/authoritarian parent in Political Science Details.

17. **Max Weber's Ideal/Personality Types**: (1) goal-rational, (2) value-rational, (3) emotion-rational and (4) traditional (custom/habit-driven). See 14. Max Weber in Sociology Details.

18. **William Sheldon's Somatotypes**: (1) ectomorphs (thin and nervous; a high ratio of skin/surface area to body mass), (2) endomorphs (fat and phlegmatic; a low ratio of skin/surface area to body mass) and (3) mesomorphs (muscular and athletic; a balanced ratio of skin/surface area to body mass).

19. **Erich Fromm's Five Personality Orientations**: (1) hoarding, (2) exploitative, (3) receptive, (4) marketing and (5) productive.

20. **Abraham Maslow's Hierarchy of Needs** (in which the lower level of need must be satisfied before the next higher level can be achieved): (1) physiological (food, water and shelter), (2) safety and a sense of security, (3) love and a sense of belonging, (4) recognition and a sense of self- esteem and (5) self-actualization (the process of realizing one's full potential). See Self-actualization in Concepts.

21. **David Riesman's Three Personality Types**: (1) tradition-directed, (2) inner-directed and (3) outer-directed.

22. **Five Factor Model of Personality Traits**: (1) curious/open to experience versus cautious/consistent; (2) conscientious/self-disciplined/organized versus spontaneous/careless; (3) extroverted versus solitary/reserved; (4) agreeable/friendly/cooperative/compassionate versus suspicious/cold/antagonistic and (5) nervous/anxious/depressed/vulnerable versus secure/self-confident. Gordon Allport, Raymond Cattell, Ernest Tupes and Raymond Christal.

23. **Merrill-Reid's Five Personality Types**: (1) analytical, (2) competitive/ambitious, (3) sociable/gregarious, (4) artistic/expressive and (5) socially conscious.

24. **Myers-Briggs Type Indicator** (based on Jung's four principal psychological functions of sensation, intuition, feeling and thinking):
    1) Extroversion (outward-turning, action-oriented) versus introversion (inward-turning, reflective and thoughtful).
    2) Sensation (perception or judging through the sense organs) versus intuition (perception or judging in an unconscious way).
    3) Thinking (rational perception or judging using logical cognition) versus feeling (perception or judging through subjective estimation).
    4) Perception (information gathering) versus judgment (decision-making).
    See 25. Keirsey Temperament Sorter in Details.

25. **Keirsey Temperament Sorter** of 16 basic temperaments based on the Jung/Myer-Briggs typology of Extroversion-Introversion, Sensation-iNtuition, Thinking-Feeling, Perception-Judgment: (1) Inspector (ISTJ), (2) Protector (ISFJ), (3) Counselor (INFJ), (4) Mastermind(INTJ), (5) Crafter (ISTP), (6) Composer (ISFP), (7) Healer (INFP), (8) Architect (INTP), (9) Promoter (ESTP), (10) Performer (ESFP), (11) Champion (ENFP), (12) Inventor (ENTP), (13) Supervisor (ESTJ), (14) Provider (ESFJ), (15) Teacher (ENFJ), (16) Field Marshal (ENTJ).

10. SCIENCE

CONCEPTS AND PHRASES:

Absolute zero: the temperature at which kinetic energy nearly reaches zero, which is -459 degrees Fahrenheit, -273 degrees Celsius and 0 degrees Kelvin. The average temperature of the universe is 2.73 degrees Kelvin above absolute zero. See Entropy in Concepts.

Accelerating universe: the validated theory that the universe is expanding at an accelerating rate, which may be driven by an anti-gravity force called "dark energy." See Cosmological constant and Dark energy in Concepts.

Adaptation: the evolutionary process by which an organism adjusts to the imperatives and constraints of its environment, or a trait that enhances that adjustment, the success of which is measured by its "fitness," that is, its enhanced ability to survive and pass along its genes. For example, humans who migrated to the northern latitudes developed paler skin, which allowed them to synthesize vitamin D from less sunlight, which is needed for the absorption of calcium. See Natural selection and Sexual selection in Concepts.

Aether: the heavenly fifth element, or quintessence (earth, air, fire and water are the other four), which was once thought to be the medium through which light traveled.

Allele: one member of a pair of genes that reside at the same corresponding location, or locus, on a pair of chromosomes, one inherited from the mother and one inherited from the father. If the two genes are identical, they are termed homozygous and, if not, heterozygous; the gene may be dominant, co-dominant, or recessive.

Anthropocene epoch: the informal name given to the era in which we are now living, which is characterized by extensive human modifications to the natural environment. The epoch is associated with mass extinctions, pollution, deforestation, overfishing, ozone depletion, global warming and climate change. Although the impact of humans on the environment can be traced back to (1) the migration of anatomically modern humans around the globe, which began approximately 60,000 years ago, and the subsequent extinction of mega-fauna, and (2) the Neolithic/Agricultural Revolution, which began approximately 11,000 years ago, the impact of humans on the environment increased exponentially during (3) the Industrial Revolution, which began in approximately 1750 CE and has accelerated rapidly since with the introduction of anthropogenic greenhouse gases, primarily from the burning of fossil fuels to generate steam and electricity and to power internal combustion engines. The Anthropocene era overlaps the more formally named Holocene interglacial period. Paul Cruzen.

Anthropogenic/greenhouse gases: those that trap solar radiation and heat in the atmosphere and are the driving force of global warming and climate change. They include carbon dioxide, which is produced by burning fossil fuels, as well as water vapor, methane and nitrous oxide.

Anti-matter: particles with identical masses but opposite charges of their counterparts. For example, a positron is an electron with a positive charge. The relative absence of anti-matter in the universe is a mystery. See 7. Standard Model in Details.

Astronomical unit: the average distance between the earth and the sun, which is approximately 93 million miles.

Asymptotic freedom: the freedom of movement of certain subatomic particles in relation to each other, which varies inversely with their distance, much like that of a stretched rubber band. See Entanglement in Concepts.

Atomic number: the number of positively charged protons in an atom's nucleus, which equals the number of negatively charged electrons in its orbit; **atomic mass**: the total mass of protons, neutrons and electrons in an atom; **isotopes**: atoms of the same chemical element which have the same number of protons but a varying number of neutrally charged neutrons in the nucleus; for example, carbon-12 has 6 protons and 6 neutrons in its nucleus, while carbon-14 has 6 protons and 8 neutrons.

Baryonic matter: ordinary matter, mostly protons and neutrons, which constitutes approximately 5% of the mass-energy of the universe (dark matter constitutes 27%, and dark energy 68%). Recent studies suggest that only 10% of baryonic matter resides in the galaxies, with the remainder residing in diffuse, intergalactic gas.

Base pairs: the chemical compounds adenine and thymine (A-T) and cytosine and guanine (C-G), which are strung together like beads on a string to form the double-stranded DNA molecules, which, in humans, comprise the 46 chromosomes that reside in the nucleus of every cell in the body. Human DNA consists of 3 billion base pairs, of which approximately 20,000 are protein-encoding genes. Thus, genes are those segments on the DNA molecules/chromosomes that provide instructions for making the thousands of proteins (from twenty or so amino acids) that are responsible for building and maintaining the body's structures and functions. The non-coding segments of the DNA molecules were once thought to be "junk DNA," but it is now known that they play a critical role in regulating gene expression (that is, if, when and for how long a gene is turned on or off). See Epigenetics and Nucleotides in Concepts and 8. Human Genes/DNA in Details.

Big Bang theory: one that describes the birth of the universe approximately 13.8 billion years ago from a hot, dense singularity; also, a television comedy series. See Inflation theory and Vacuum genesis in Concepts.

Biomass: the combined weight of all living things in a given geographical area.

Black hole: a gravitational singularity; a very dense mass, usually from a collapsing star, with a gravitational field so strong that no light or matter can escape from it. A supermassive black hole known as Sagittarius A* with a mass of four million suns occupies the center of our Milky Way galaxy.

Boyle's law: that, in a closed system, at a given temperature, the volume and pressure of a gas vary inversely.

Broken symmetry: a condition in which small fluctuations (or "noise") in a disordered system pass a critical threshold, or bifurcation or tipping point, and force the system to assume one of two mutually-exclusive states. See Schrödinger's cat, Superposition and Vacuum genesis in Concepts.

Chaos theory: a methodology used to describe underlying structures and patterns in seemingly random, unpredictable, nonlinear systems. The initial conditions dependency, or butterfly effect, is a central tenet of chaos theory, in which infinitesimal differences in initial conditions (say, a butterfly flapping its wings in Brazil) can have a large, cumulative, nonlinear effect on subsequent outcomes (say, a hurricane in Florida). Fractals (*q.v.* in Concepts) are also an inherent part of chaos theory.

Chirality: left or right handedness. In physics, it denotes the direction of spin: a right-handed particle spins in the same direction as its motion; a left-handed particle spins in the direction opposite to its motion.

Clade: a biologically related group consisting of an ancestor and all its descendants.

Continental drift: see 6. Plate Tectonics/Continental Drift in Details.

Convergent evolution: the independent development of a physical trait that is found in two or more unrelated species; for example, the independent evolution and adaptation of wings by insects, birds and bats.

Cosmological constant: the expansionary, anti-gravity force, or "dark energy"; a factor that Einstein plugged into his equations to account for the fact that the universe does not collapse on itself. See Accelerating universe and Dark energy in Concepts.

Cosmology: the study of the origin and nature of the universe.

Dark energy: the anti-gravity force that is thought to be the reason that the universe is expanding at an accelerating rate. Dark energy may be (1) an inherent property of a vacuum, that is, the negative pressure of empty space itself, which stretches space; (2) a force field of vibrating electromagnetic energy that radiates through empty space; (3) an as yet undetected, extremely lightweight "quintessence" particle or (4) a modified form of gravity which, on extremely large scales, becomes a repulsive force. Dark energy is thought to constitute 68% of the mass-energy of the universe. See Accelerating universe and Cosmological constant in Concepts.

Dark matter: heavy, slow-moving and, as yet, undiscovered, subatomic particles that do not absorb or emit light and are thought to be much heavier than protons. They provide the extra gravity needed to keep the galaxies from flying apart and are thought to constitute 27% of the mass-energy of the universe.

Doomsday asteroids: those that have the potential for destroying or significantly modifying the earth's biosphere. The asteroid that struck the Yucatan Peninsula 66 million years ago measured approximately 10 kilometers (6 miles) in diameter and is thought to have caused the extinction of the non-avian dinosaurs. Near-earth objects (NEOs), which include asteroids, meteoroids and

comets, are identified and tracked by an international consortium
of scientists. See Uniformitarianism versus Catastrophism/Neo-
Catastrophism in Concepts.

Doppler effect: the increase in frequency or pitch of a light or sound
wave as it approaches an observer and the decrease as it recedes.

Drake equation: a formula that attempts to estimate the number of
extraterrestrial civilizations in our galaxy that have the capability
of communicating with us. See Earth-like planets in Concepts.

Earth-like planets: planets outside our solar system ("exoplanets")
which may support life. Statistical extrapolations from the Kepler
mission suggest that there may be 10 billion Earth-size planets
within their stars' habitable zones (i.e., those which could support
liquid water and life) in our Milky Way galaxy. The search for
Earth-like planets within these habitable, or "Goldilocks," zones is
motivated by the search for extraterrestrial life. See Drake
equation in Concepts.

Ecology/bionomics: the study of the relationships, interactions,
reciprocal dependencies and long-term sustainability of organisms
and their environment. Se Anthropocene epoch in Concepts.

Entanglement/nonlocality: in quantum physics, the relationship
between two subatomic particles over long distances in which a
change in the state of one particle is accompanied simultaneously
by a corresponding change in state of the other.

Entropy: the process by which energy dissipates and disorder
increases in a closed system until a thermodynamic equilibrium is
reached, much like that of an ice cube melting in a warm room.

Epigenetics/gene expression: the processes that regulate if, when and
for how long a gene is turned on or off. Since genes provide the
instructions for the production of proteins, which, in turn, regulate
morphology, growth and other biological functions, regulating
gene expression allows the developing organism to respond
relatively rapidly and dynamically to changes in the environment
without altering the underlying gene structure. See 10.
Epigenetics/Gene Expression and 11. Adaptive/Developmental
Plasticity in Details.

Exaptation: a trait serving a function other than the one for which it
was originally selected. For example, feathers evolved for
insulation and were later adapted for flight.

Extremophiles/lithophiles: life forms that survive in extreme
environments, such as those that live deep within granite

batholiths, under ice sheets, or near hydrothermal vents on ocean floors. They serve as exemplars of the tenacity of the life force.

Force field: the area or extension of space-time through which a force acts. The force, or interaction, between subatomic particles is mediated by wave-like, or "virtual" particles, which convey discrete quanta, or bundles, of energy (represented by "excitations" or ripples in the force field) and mediate the interaction by exchanging (emitting and absorbing) these quanta. Photons are quantum excitations of electromagnetic fields; gluons are excitations of strong nuclear fields; and W and Z bosons are excitations of weak nuclear fields. See 7. Standard Model in Details.

Forces: (1) the **electromagnetic force** (which includes gamma rays, X-rays, ultraviolent radiation, visible light, infrared radiation, microwaves and radio waves), (2) the **strong nuclear force** (which binds protons and neutrons in the nucleus), (3) the **weak nuclear force** (which is responsible for a form of radioactive decay) and (4) **gravitation**. The interactions of the first three forces are described by the Standard Model and the fourth by Einstein's general theory of relativity. The theory of everything (*q.v.* in Concepts) would unify the Standard Model's three forces with Einstein's theory of gravity. See 7. Standard Model in Details.

Fractals: forms with self-similar patterns that repeat themselves over different scales, such as those in leaves, trees, rivers, blood vessels, broccoli, clouds and snowflakes. See Chaos theory in Concepts.

Gaia hypothesis: that the earth is a living, self-regulating super-organism. John Lovelace.

General theory of relativity: Einstein's theory that gravity is curved space-time.

Genes: the basic units of inheritance, which are discrete segments of base pairs (adenine-thymine and cytosine-guanine) on the DNA molecules that make up chromosomes. They provide the instructions for making the thousands of proteins (from twenty or so amino acids) that are responsible for building and maintaining the body's structures and functions. See Base pairs and Nucleotide in Concepts and 8. Human Genes in Details.

Genetic drift: random genetic changes or mutations in a population. In a small, isolated, "founder" population, genetic variants can more easily increase in statistical frequency until they become "fixed" in that population. Thus, it is postulated that small, isolated populations serve as laboratories for evolutionary change, especially if adaptive traits established in them are later transferred through migration to larger populations. See 8. Human Genes in Details and Founder's effect in Anthropology Concepts.

Genetic markers: unique variants or mutations in the DNA that are associated with certain physical characteristics (including risk factors for certain medical conditions) or are used to identify and trace specific haplogroups (i.e., population groups who are descended from a common ancestor and share a unique pattern of genetic variants). Genetic markers, or signatures, allow geneticists and historians to trace the origins, history, movement and relationships among various population groups. See 12. Genetic Markers and Human Migrations in Details.

Genome editing: using an RNA guide to target a specific DNA sequence and an enzyme to remove and/or replace a defective gene. If the editing is done to the sperm, egg or stem cells of the embryo, the changes are heritable and passed down to the descendants of that organism.

Genomic imprinting: an organism's ability to tag and switch a gene on or off depending on whether it was inherited from the mother or the father.

Genotype: the inherited, genetic constitution of an organism. The term generally refers to the organism's entire sequence of DNA, including the protein coding and non-coding sections; versus **phenotype**: the observable characteristics or traits of an organism; the physical manifestation of the genotype.

Global climate change: the unprecedented rise in global temperatures and increasingly extreme weather patterns, which is outside the normal range of climate variability. It is associated with the introduction of anthropogenic greenhouse gases, beginning with the Industrial Revolution around 1750 CE, from burning coal and oil to generate steam and electricity and to power internal combustion engines. The overwhelming consensus of the scientific community is that this climate change has been driven by human activity. See Anthropocene epoch and Anthropogenic/ greenhouse gases in Concepts.

Gravitational lensing: the bending or warping of an image from a distant object by an intervening object, which provides a means of triangulating its distance.

Gravitational waves: ripples in the fabric of spacetime, which was predicted by Albert Einstein's theory of general relativity.

Group-level selection: a form of social evolution in which the advantage of natural selection is conferred on the group rather than the individual. Altruism, cooperation and self-sacrifice among individuals within a group reinforce that group's cohesion and solidarity, provide an advantage to the group in trade and war with other groups and increase the chances that the genes of at least some its members will be successfully transmitted to future generations; versus **individual selection**, in which selfishness, competition and egoism confers an evolutionary advantage to an individual by enhancing its chances of surviving, reproducing and passing along its genes within the group but, perhaps, at the expense of the group's chances of survival and, thus, the individual's. See Kinship selection in Concepts and 5. The Darwinian-Mendelian Evolutionary Paradigm in Details and 25. Social Darwinism in American History Details.

Half-life: the time it takes for one-half of a given quantity of a radioactive material to decay into an isotope or another element. For example, carbon-14 (which is absorbed from the carbon dioxide in the atmosphere by plants and the animals that eat those plants) decays into to carbon-12 at a steady rate and has a half-life of 5,730 years. Since the ratio of carbon-14 to carbon-12 in living plants and animals is known, and since an organism stops absorbing carbon-14 from the atmosphere when it dies, the ratio can be used to calculate (or radiocarbon date) the year the plant or animal died, since 1/2 of the original carbon-14 in the sample will remain after 5,730 years, 1/4 after 11,460 years, 1/8 after 17,190 years, 1/16 after 22,920 years, and so on. See Photosynthesis in Concepts.

Haplogroup: a population group that is descended from a common ancestor and is identified by its unique genetic pattern of mutations or variants on given segments of DNA. See 12. Genetic Markers/Human Migration in Details.

Heisenberg's principle of uncertainty/indeterminacy: that both the position and momentum of a subatomic particle cannot be known simultaneously. More popularly, it is used as a metaphor to suggest the reciprocal, interactive relationship between the observer and the observed; that the very act of observing affects the object that is being observed. See William Butler Yeats in Quotations.

Heliotropism/hydrotropism: the tendency of a plant to bend or grow toward, respectively, the sun or a water source; the movement is guided by plant hormones called auxins.

Holocene interglacial period: the geological epoch in which we are now living, which began at the end of the last ice age, approximately 12,000 years ago. The term Anthropocene (*q.v.* in Concepts) is informally applied to part of the Holocene in recognition of the significant impact of human activity on the natural environment, especially climate change.

Inertia: Isaac Newton's first law of motion, which states that an object at rest or in a uniform state of motion will remain in that state unless acted on by an outside force. See 4. Isaac Newton in Details.

Inflation theory: that the universe began as an infinitely dense singularity, smaller than an atom (the "primeval atom"), perhaps arising from a quantum energy fluctuation in empty space, and, after a fraction of a second, expanded faster than the speed of light, after which it cooled and continued to expand, but at a slower rate. See Big Bang theory, Broken symmetry and Vacuum theory in Concepts.

Isotropic: a system that is uniform in all directions, as, for example, a volume of water; versus **anisotropic**: a system that varies according to the direction from which it is measured, as, for example, the grain of wood or the layers of a sedimentary rock.

Kinship selection: a form of group-level selection applied at the extended family level. Strategies that enhance the survival and reproductive success of the extended family, even at the expense of individual members, by facilitating altruism, cooperation and self-sacrificing behavior among close relatives, increase the likelihood of an individual's passing along, through its surviving kin, at least some of his or her genes. See Group-level selection in Concepts and 5. The Darwinian-Mendelian Evolutionary Paradigm in Details.

Lamarckianism: the discredited theory that directly acquired traits are inheritable; for example, that a mother giraffe who continually stretches her neck to reach for fruit high in the trees can pass along the acquired trait of a longer neck to her offspring, or that a man or woman who work out daily in the gym will produce trim, muscular children. See 11. Adaptive/Developmental Plasticity in Details.

Light year: the distance light travels in one year at a rate of 186,000 miles per second (or 670,000,000 miles per hour), which is approximately 6 trillion miles. The distance from the sun to the earth is approximately 8 light minutes and from the nearest star is approximately 4 light years.

Mass-energy equivalence: that energy equals mass times the speed of light squared, according to Einstein's special theory of relativity.

Mechanics: the study of forces and motions. See 4. Isaac Newton in Details.

Momentum: the mass of an object multiplied by its velocity. See 4. Newton's laws of motion in Details.

Morphology: the form and structure of an organism.

M-theory: a proposed synthesis of string theories using higher dimensional surfaces called membranes or banes. See Superstring theory in Concepts.

Multiverse/meta-universe: a hypothesized set of multiple universes, or parallel or alternative universes. The fact that at least six critical variables are necessary for our own universe, the stars and life to exist suggests the existence of other, perhaps aborted, universes that fall outside those parameters. Martin Rees.

Mutations/genetic variants: random, permanent changes or variants to one or more base pairs that make up the DNA strand on each chromosome. They may occur spontaneously or through environmental damage or transcription or copying errors, such as duplications, insertions, deletions, inversions and translocations. See 9. Mutations/Genetic Variants in Details.

Natural history: until the 19th Century, the term applied to the study of botany, zoology, geology, paleontology and meteorology; and **natural philosophy**: the term applied to the study of physics, chemistry and astronomy. "Scientist" was not coined until 1833.

Natural selection: the mechanism by which evolution occurs, according to Charles Darwin's theory of evolution. Because organisms struggle for existence and compete for limited natural resources, those traits or adaptations that arise from random genetic mutations and confer positive competitive advantages to their hosts are more likely to be passed along through their genes to their offspring and, thus, increase in frequency throughout the population. See 5. The Darwinian-Mendelian Evolutionary Paradigm in Details.

Nature-nurture continuum: among humans, the spectrum, or range, of complex interactions between (1) nature (that is, hereditary; biological and genetic factors) and (2) nurture (that is, environmental, relational and social systems) and the extent to which each determines, conditions or influences human behavior. The continuum is influenced by the degree of agency, autonomy and free choice exercised by the individual between those two poles. See Sociobiology in Concepts and Agency, Reflexivity and Sociological assumption in Sociology Concepts.

Nebular hypothesis: that stars and their planetary systems were formed by the contraction of giant molecular clouds into flattened, rotating disks which accreted into stars at their cores and into planets along their rings. See Stellar/supernova nucleosynthesis in Concepts.

Newton's celestial mechanics: a paradigm, or conceptual system, that describes the motions of planets in their orbits around the sun, which are governed by the laws of gravity and motion. The Newtonian "block universe" of the 18th Century Enlightenment has been compared to that of an orderly, symmetrical, perfectly reciprocating machine, such as a watch or an orrery. Carl Becker, William James. See 27. 18th Century Enlightenment in Philosophy/Religion Details.

Non-Euclidian space: curved, four-dimensional space-time, such as that described by Albert Einstein in his general theory of relativity.

Occam's razor: the principle of parsimony applied to scientific hypotheses, according to which the simplest, adequate explanation or hypothesis is usually the best; the "razor" refers to the process of shaving away unnecessary assumptions.

Ontogeny recapitulates phylogeny: the theory that the development of an individual organism recapitulates the development of its species; that, in developing from an embryo to an adult, an organism goes through successive stages resembling the evolution of its ancestors.

Pangea: the primal super-continent that existed from approximately 300 million to 175 million years ago. It split apart and evolved into the seven continents of today through a process of rifting (spreading) of the continental and oceanic plates. See 6. Plate Tectonics/Continental Drift in Details.

Paradigm shift: the observation that scientific revolutions occur when inconsistencies and anomalies in the old paradigm and accumulated new observations reach a critical tipping point and the old model is supplanted by a new one. Examples include the transition from a Ptolemaic cosmology to a Copernican one in the 16th and 17th Centuries, or from Newtonian mechanics to Einstein's theories of relativity in the 20th Century. Immanuel Kant, Thomas Kuhn, Malcolm Gladwell. See John Maynard Keynes in Quotations.

Parallax: the difference in apparent position of an object when viewed from two different positions or angles, which permits, by triangulation, the calculation of its distance.

Periodic table: a chart or matrix in which the 118 known chemical elements are systematically arranged in horizontal rows by ascending atomic numbers and in which the resulting groupings of vertical columns denote similar classes of elements with similar chemical properties, such as copper, silver and gold or helium, neon and argon.

Phase transition: the discontinuous, quantitative or qualitative change in the equilibrium of a system, such as that which occurs in the transition between a liquid and a gas. In quantum physics, it is represented by the quantum "leap" that occurs when an electron "jumps" from one orbit or energy level to another, during which discrete packets, or "quanta," of photons are emitted or absorbed.

Phenotype: the observable characteristics or traits of an organism; the physical manifestation of the genotype. See Genotype in Concepts.

Photons: quanta, or force-carriers, of electromagnetic energy, including light. Photons (1) have no mass, (2) exhibit properties of both waves and particles and (3) convey the electromagnetic force by exchanging (emitting and absorbing) discrete quanta, or bundles, of energy. See 7. Standard Model in Details.

Photosynthesis: the process by which sunlight, water and carbon dioxide in the atmosphere are converted by plants into organic compounds and oxygen; the master motor of life on earth.

Plate tectonics/continental drift: see 6. Plate Tectonics/Continental Drift in Details.

Ptolemaic cosmology: the geocentric model advanced by the Greco-Egyptian Ptolemy in the 2nd Century, in which the sun, planets and stars revolve around the earth; versus the **Copernican cosmology**, in which the earth and the planets revolve around the sun in elliptical orbits. Nicolaus Copernicus's heliocentric model, which was proposed in 1543, was declared to be a heresy by the Catholic Church because it contradicted Church doctrine, and those whose who subscribed to it could, and were, be burned alive at the stake, including the astronomer Giordano Bruno in 1600. See Galileo in Quotations and Great Heresy and Inquisition in Philosophy/Religion Concepts.

Punctuated equilibria: the theory that evolution proceeds slowly through long periods of stasis that are infrequently punctuated by rapid bursts of change and episodic speciation. Niles Eldredge and Stephen Jay Gould. See Uniformitarianism versus Catastrophism/Neo-Catastrophism in Concepts.

Quantum leap: the phase transition that occurs, for example, when an electron "jumps" from one orbit, or energy level, to another, during which discrete packets, or "quanta," of photons are emitted or absorbed. See Phase transition in Concepts.

Quantum loop gravity: a theory that attempts to reconcile the Standard Model of particle physics with Einstein's theory of general relativity, which describes gravity as the curvature of spacetime . The theory of quantum loop gravity views space as a thin network of woven, quantized loops of gravitational fields called spin networks, or spin foam.

Quarks (pronounced "kworks"): a class of subatomic particles in six flavors (up, down, strange, charm, bottom and top). A proton, for example, is composed of two up quarks and one down quark. The term is derived from James Joyce's "three quarks for Mister Mark!" in *Finnegan's Wake*, which refers to a bar call for three quarts of beer. See 7. Standard Model in Details.

Reproductive strategies: those that are employed by various species to maximize their reproductive success, which, in the evolutionary calculus of sociobiology, is defined as successfully passing along one's genes: **r-selected species** are those with high reproductive rates, high predation rates and short life spans, such as insects and rodents; versus **K-selected species**, which are those with few offspring, high parental investment, low predation rates and long life spans, such as large mammals. Robert MacArthur, Edward O. Wilson.

Schrödinger's cat: an iconic thought experiment of quantum physics in which a cat, in a sealed box with a vial of poison gas that can be activated by a random event such as the decay of a subatomic particle, exists in a superposed state of dead-and-alive until the box is opened and the cat is observed, at which time the cat collapses into an either-or state of dead or alive. See Stochastic and Superposition in Concepts.

Science schmaltz: Steven Pinker's term for scientific studies that eulogize and overstate the importance of peaceful tribes, altruistic apes, neuroplasticity, epigenetics, group-level selection, mirror neurons "and other distortions of science for dubious moral uplift."

Scientific method: see 1. Scientific Method in Details.

Sexual selection: the process by which males compete with other males of the same species for access to, and selection by, sexually-receptive females. Reproductive success allows those traits of the selected male and female to be passed along through their genes to their offspring, which, thus, increases their frequency throughout the population. See Sexual/courtship displays in Anthropology Concepts.

Singularity: a gravitational black hole; an infinite curvature of space-time, with zero volume and infinite mass.

Snowball earth: a condition in which, for four extended periods, more than 600 million years ago, the surface of the earth, including, possibly, the tropical oceans, was covered in ice to a depth of a kilometer or more.

SNPs: single nucleotide polymorphisms; genetic variants or mutations in the DNA sequence involving single nucleotides. See Base pairs in Concepts and 9. Mutations/Genetic Variants in Details.

Sociobiology: a school of scientific thought that maintains that individual and social behavior is largely inherited, i.e., that it is the product of genes and natural selection. Inherited behaviors include those associated with gender, aggression, territoriality, mating, reciprocal altruism, social cooperation, intelligence, anxiety/stress-response, introversion, etc. Sociobiology has been criticized as a form of biological determinism and has been challenged by studies that demonstrate a reciprocal relationship between nature and nurture, biology and the environment. Steven Pinker, Edward O. Wilson. See Nature-nurture continuum in Concepts and 10.

Epigenetics/Gene Expression and 11. Adaptive/Developmental Plasticity in Details.

Special theory of relativity: Einstein's theory that the speed of light remains uniform for all observers (although length may contract and time may dilate) and the equivalency of mass and energy. See Mass-energy equivalence in Concepts.

Standard Model: the paradigmatic model of particle physics, which describes the three fundamental forces (the electromagnetic force, the strong nuclear force and the weak nuclear force), but not gravitation, dark energy nor dark matter. It is populated by a virtual zoo of subatomic particles, including quarks, leptons, gluons, photons, etc. See 7. Standard Model in Details.

Stellar/supernova nucleosynthesis: the process by which the heavier chemical elements in the universe are created in the cores of stars and from stellar explosions. The matter ejected into interstellar space provides the heavier materials for future stars and planetary systems such as ours. Thus, we and everything on our planet and our solar system consist of recycled stardust.

Stochastic: behaviors or processes that are random, uncertain, variable and probabilistic, rather than absolute, fixed and determined; for example, the roll of the dice on the craps table or the arrival rate of customers at the post office.

Stratigraphy: in geology, the study of the layers of rock, which is based on the law of superimposition, in which upper strata are presumed to be younger and lie above the lower and, thus, older strata.

Subduction/obduction: respectively, the under-thrusting and over-thrusting of converging and colliding tectonic plates, usually with the oceanic crust (which is denser) subducting under the continental crust (which is lighter). See 6. Plate Tectonics in Details.

Superconductivity: the lack of electrical resistance in certain materials that have been cooled below a critical threshold.

Superposition: a condition in quantum physics in which a system exists in all possible states simultaneously until it is measured or observed, whereupon it "collapses" into a single state. See Schrödinger's cat in Concepts.

Superstring/M-theory: a theory that attempts to reconcile the Standard Model (which describes the electromagnetic, strong nuclear and weak nuclear forces) with the general theory of relativity (which describes gravitation), according to which, in addition to four-dimensional space-time, the universe consists of condensed, tightly curled, vibrating strings in six or more dimensions. M refers to higher dimensional surfaces called membranes or banes. Brian Greene, Timothy Ferris.

Symbiosis: the mutually beneficial relationship between organisms of two different species.

Taxonomy: the hierarchical classification of organisms into (1) domains (e.g. Eukarya), (2) kingdoms (e.g., Animals), (3) phyla (e.g., Vertebrates), (4) classes (e.g., Mammals), (5) orders (e.g., Primates), (6) families (e.g., Hominids), (7) genera (e.g., Homo) and (8) species (e.g., Sapiens).

Telomeres: the bead-like ends of chromosomes, which protect the genes and shorten over time as the cells divide, much like the worry-beads of time.

Theory of everything: one which would unify the standard model of particle physics, which describes the three fundamental forces (the electromagnetic, strong and weak nuclear forces) with Einstein's general theory of relativity, which describes gravity. Dark energy is not addressed in either theory. See Superstring/M-theory in Concepts.

Thermohaline circulation: the conveyor belt of ocean currents, in which colder temperatures and higher salinity increase the density and drive the circulation of deep-water currents around the globe. In global warming, additional fresh water from melting glaciers is thought to dilute ocean salt water to the degree that it could upset the conveyor mechanism and flip the planet into an ice age.

Thought experiments: "theoretical experiments-in-the-imagination" that are used to explore, in the mind, the consequences of imagined scenarios or hypotheses without having to conduct actual physical experiments. Albert Einstein, Carl Hempel.

Tychism: the doctrine that the universe is ruled by random chance. Since Darwin's variations and Mendel's genetic mutations are random and accidental, evolution has been viewed as driven "by chance and the destruction of bad results" (Charles Peirce). See Broken symmetry, Chaos theory, Multiverse/meta-universe, Stochastic, Uniformitarianism versus catastrophism/neo-catastrophism and Vacuum genesis in Concepts; Alternative histories and Radical contingency in Historiography Concepts and Determinism versus fatalism and Fortuitism in Philosophy/ Religion Concepts.

Uniformitarianism: gradualism; the widely accepted paradigm in geology that natural laws operate in the same manner throughout time, although not necessarily at uniform rates, and that geological processes such as volcanism, earthquakes, glaciation, erosion and sedimentation occur over very long time-frames; Charles Lyell; versus **catastrophism/neo-catastrophism**: that the earth's natural history is driven by sudden, violent catastrophic events such as asteroid impacts, mass extinctions, earthquakes, volcanic eruptions, glacial flooding, human induced climate change, etc. Although catastrophism was initially discredited because it was associated with the belief in divine intervention, such as the Biblical account of the Flood, catastrophic events have been recognized and incorporated into the paradigm of uniformitarianism, which allows that gradual, natural processes are punctuated by occasional, natural, catastrophic events. These include, for example, (1) the volcanic eruptions from the Siberian Traps, which are linked to the Permian–Triassic boundary extinctions 250 million years ago and (2) the Chicxulub asteroid impact event, which may have triggered the volcanic eruptions from the Deccan Traps in the Indian subcontinent and is associated with the Cretaceous-Paleogene boundary extinctions of non-avian dinosaurs 66 million years ago. See Doomsday asteroids and Punctuated equilibria in Concepts.

Vacuum genesis: the theory that the universe began as a quantum energy fluctuation in the vacuum of empty space. See Big Bang theory, Broken symmetry and Inflation theory in Concepts.

Valence: the number of unoccupied electron "slots" in the outer shell of an atom, which allows it to share electrons and bond with other atoms.

Vector (Latin for "to carry" or "convey"): a quantity that represents both magnitude and direction, such as velocity; versus **scalar**: a quantity that represents magnitude but not direction, such as the lines on a topographical map.

Velocity: a physical quantity that indicates both magnitude (speed) and direction.

Wallace, Alfred Russel: the co-discoverer of evolution through natural selection concurrently with, but independently of, Charles

Darwin. He was an "unselfish man in the shadow of Darwin." E. B. Poulton, U. Kutschera. See 5. The Darwinian-Mendelian Evolutionary Paradigm in Details.

Wave-particle duality: the observation that subatomic particles, such as photons, exhibit properties of both waves and particles.

Waves: carriers of energy; periodic oscillations or vibrations that transmit energy from one point to another. Waves are measured by their length, amplitude and frequency. Common types of wave motion include reflection (which involves a wave's change in direction), refraction (which involves a change in speed and direction as the wave passes through another medium), diffraction (in which the wave spreads out after passing through a gap), and interference (in which waves overlap one another). Electromagnetic waves consist of gamma rays, x-rays, ultraviolet light, visible light, infra-red light, microwaves and radio waves. See 7. Standard Model in Details.

QUOTATIONS:

- *The half of knowledge consists of being able to put the right question.* -- Roger Bacon.

- *But still, it moves.* – attributed to Galileo after he was forced to recant Copernicus' hypothesis that the earth revolves around the sun.

- *Why should that apple always descend perpendicularly to the ground? Why should it not go sideways, or upwards but constantly to the earth's centre? Assuredly, the reason is, that the earth draws it. There must be a drawing power in matter. . . . If matter thus draws matter, it must be in proportion of its quantity, therefore the apple draws the earth, as well as the earth draws the apple.* – Isaac Newton.

- *I seem to have been only like a boy playing on the sea-shore, and diverting myself in now and then finding a smoother pebble or a prettier shell than ordinary, whilst the great ocean of truth lay all undiscovered before me.* -- Newton.

- *If I have seen further . . . it is by standing upon the shoulders of Giants.* -- Newton.

- *The small part of ignorance that we arrange and classify we give the name of knowledge.* -- Ambrose Bierce.

- *How can we know the dancers from the dance?* -- William Butler Yeats.

- *The most beautiful thing we can experience is the mysterious. It is the source of all true art and science.* -- Albert Einstein.

- *The difficulty lies not so much in developing new ideas as in escaping old ones.* -- John Maynard Keynes.

- *It requires a very unusual mind to make an analysis of the obvious.* -- Alfred North Whitehead.

- *The universe is expanding and expanding. . . . (It makes you feel sort of <u>insignificant</u>, doesn't?) -- Monty Python's The Meaning of Life.*

SCIENCE DETAILS: (1) Scientific Method, (2) Two Cultures, (3) the Universe, (4) Isaac Newton, (5) the Darwinian-Mendelian Evolutionary Paradigm, (6) Plate Tectonics/Continental Drift, (7) the Standard Model, (8) Human Genes, (9) Mutations/Genetic Variants, (10) Epigenetics/Gene Expression, (11) Adaptive/Developmental Plasticity, (12) Genetic Markers, Paleo-/Archaeogenetics and Human Migration Patterns.

1. **Scientific Method** is the structured process by which a problem or question is identified and defined, a hypothesis is formulated, a research plan is developed, observations and other empirical data are collected and analyzed, conclusions are drawn, results are independently replicated and predictions are tested and confirmed.

2. **Two Cultures** is C. P. Snow's term for the "gulf of mutual incomprehension" that exists between the sciences and the humanities.

3. **The Universe** is 13.8 billion years old. It consists of approximately 5% baryonic, or ordinary, matter (mostly protons and neutrons), 27% dark matter and 68% dark energy. The universe may contain 1 billion trillion stars (assuming that there are 100 billion stars in each galaxy and 10 billion galaxies in the observable universe) and is expanding at an accelerating rate. Our Milky Way galaxy contains approximately 100 billion stars, of which 1 to 10 billion stars may contain Earth-size planets that may support liquid water and life. See Earth-like planets in Concepts.

4. **Isaac Newton** (1642-1726) discovered universal gravitation (from Latin *gravitas*, for weight or heaviness), an invisible force that acts over vast distances, and the laws of motion, which explain the elliptical orbits of planetary objects around the sun. He demonstrated the power of human reason and empirical methods to discover the laws governing the natural world and laid the

foundation for the Enlightenment's view of the universe as an efficient, harmonious machine, rationally designed by a benevolent, supreme being. Newton developed the three laws of motion (see below); studied optics and the refraction of light and invented calculus.

Newton's father was an illiterate farmer who died before his son was born, and, as a young child, Newton was virtually abandoned by his mother and step-father. Newton was reclusive, celibate, may have suffered from Asperger syndrome and had a nervous breakdown later in life. He was a member of the Royal Society, Master of the Mint (who vigorously prosecuted counterfeiters) and a secret Non-Trinitarian (which was a heresy at the time, since it denied that Jesus was God). He experimented with alchemy and studied Biblical prophecy, eschatology and the occult. See James Gleick in Selected References.

Newton's three laws of motion are: (1) an object at rest or in a uniform state of motion remains in that state unless acted on by an outside force (the law of inertia); (2) the acceleration (change in velocity of an object) is directly proportional to the magnitude of the force applied to it and inversely proportional to its mass, and (3) for every action there is an equal and opposite reaction.

5. **The Darwinian-Mendelian Evolutionary Paradigm** is based on the following principles: because organisms compete for limited resources, a "struggle for existence" occurs (Thomas Malthus), which results in the natural selection (Charles Darwin, Alfred Wallace) of those traits that arise from random genetic variants or mutations (Gregor Mendel) that confer a competitive advantage to their hosts and, thus, are more likely to be passed along through their genes to their offspring, which results in the "survival of the fittest" (Herbert Spencer). For example, a slight genetic modification to a bird's beak that allows it to capture and eat insects as well as seeds and nuts confers an advantage to that bird and its offspring compared to its conspecifics in an environment with two such food sources. Evolution through natural selection is a pillar of modern science. Thomas Malthus (1766-1834), Charles Darwin (1809-1882), Gregor Mendel (1822-1884), Alfred Russel Wallace (1823-1913). See 9. Mutations/Genetic Variants in Details.

6. **Plate Tectonics/Continental Drift** is the theory, which has been validated by empirical studies, that the surface of the earth consists of two types of vast, moving, colliding plates:

    1) Thin, dense **oceanic plates** that make up the ocean floor and are up to 7-10 km (4-6 miles) thick. They are composed of mafic (i.e., iron-magnesium) material that are created and fed at mid-ocean ridges by upwelling magma from the earth's interior and spread (i.e., rift) horizontally at an average rate of approximately 5 cm (2 inches) per year.

    2) Lighter, thicker, "fluffier" **continental plates** that are 25-70 km (15 to 40 miles) thick. They are composed of lighter, felsitic (i.e., calcium, potassium and sodium silicates), granite-like material and float like marshmallows on top of the hot chocolate of the earth's crust and mantle.

    As the plates move, jostle and collide with each other, the thinner, denser oceanic plates usually subduct, or slide, beneath the lighter continental plates, creating wrinkles of mountains chains (orogeny) and volcanoes on the land surface above, venting gas and magma through those volcanoes and precipitating earthquakes. The boundaries between two plates that move vertically past each other are called **dip slip** or **thrust faults**. The boundaries between two plates that move past each other horizontally are called **strike slip** or **transforms faults**. Continental drift was first proposed in 1912 by Alfred Wegener (1880-1930), but his theory was rejected by most scientists until the 1960s, when empirical evidence was gathered and presented to support continental drift and plate tectonics.

7. **The Standard Model** is the paradigmatic theory of particle physics, the "theory of almost everything." It describes the three fundamental forces, or interactions (the electromagnetic , strong and weak nuclear forces), but not gravitation nor dark energy. Particles on subatomic scales have oscillating or wave-like properties and are described as being carriers of energy, or "force carriers." The energy or excitations of a wave in a field are quantized, that is, quantum waves convey discrete bundles, packets or quanta of energy, in which energy is emitted or absorbed in discrete steps rather than continuously. Subatomic behavior is probabilistic rather than deterministic, and is governed by

indeterminacy, superposition and entanglement (*qq.v.* in Concepts).

The Standard Model contains a virtual zoo of subatomic particles, which are divided, roughly, into two main categories:

1) **Fermions** are elementary particles that make up the basic, ordinary matter of the universe and include:

   (a) **Quarks** (pronounced "kworks") come in six "flavors" (up, down, charm, strange, top and bottom) and combine to form protons (generally, two up and one down) and neutrons (one up and two down), which are bound together in the nucleus of the atom by the carriers of the strong force called gluons (see Bosons below).

   (b) **Leptons** are electrons, muons, tauons and neutrinos.

2) **Bosons** are wave-like force carriers, or "virtual" messenger particles that convey force via discrete quanta or bundles of energy, or "excitations" of force fields, and mediate interactions between particles. These include:

   (a) **Photons**, which have no mass but convey electromagnetic force (including visible light) and mediate interactions between charged particles by exchanging photons.

   (b) **Gluons**, which have no mass but mediate the strong nuclear interactions, which bind quarks together in the nucleus by exchanging (emitting and absorbing) gluons between them.

   (c) **W and Z bosons**, which mediate the weak nuclear interactions between quarks and leptons and are responsible for a type of radioactive decay.

   (d) **Higgs bosons**, which confer mass on particles.

   (e) In addition, there may be hypothesized **gravitons**, which mediate gravitational interactions between particles by exchanging (emitting and absorbing) gravitons.

There are also many other exotic and evanescent particles in the subatomic menagerie, including pions, kaons, hyperons, and J/psi particles, as well as three versions of neutrinos and two dozen different combinations of three-quark baryons, and antiparticles for each of the fermions (which have identical masses but opposite charges to their counterparts).

8. **Human Genes** are the basic units of inheritance. They provide the instructions for building (from twenty or so amino acids) the thousands of proteins that are used in building and maintaining the

body's structures and functions. Genes consist of four chemical compounds that are joined and arranged as base pairs (adenine-thymine and cytosine-guanine), which are located on discrete segments on the double stranded DNA molecules called chromosomes.

In the nucleus of each cell in the human body are 23 pairs of chromosomes. One chromosome in each pair is contributed by the father and one is contributed by the mother. The 23rd pair of chromosomes consists of an X chromosome contributed by the mother and either an X or Y chromosome contributed by the father. If the 23rd pair consists of two X chromosomes (XX), the child is a female; if the 23rd pair consists of one X and one Y chromosome (XY), the child is a male.

Each chromosome consists of a long, double-stranded molecule of DNA (deoxyribonucleic acid), similar in shape to a twisted rope ladder, which is called a "double helix." The half-rung and rail on each side of the ladder is called a nucleotide, and it consists of one of four types of chemicals called bases (adenine, cytosine, guanine and thymine) plus a phosphate-sugar backbone. The nucleotide/half-rung with the base adenine (A) only joins or bonds with the nucleotide/half-rung thymine (T) on the opposite side of the ladder to form a complete rung, or base pair; and the nucleotide cytosine (C) only pairs with guanine (G) on the opposite side of the ladder to form a complete rung or base pair. Thus, the chromosome, or DNA molecule, consists of two very long, parallel strands of nucleotides (say, AACGTC on one strand and TTGCAG on the opposite strand) which are joined to form a twisted rope ladder of base pairs (in this case, A-T, A-T, C-G, G-C, T-A and C-G).

The "genome," or total DNA for each person, consists of the 46 chromosomes that reside in the nucleus of every human cell, which are made up of approximately 3 billion base pairs (A-Ts, T-As, C-Gs and G-Cs), of which only 20,000 are genes that actually encode, or provide instructions for building, the thousands of different types of proteins that are used for building and maintaining the body's structures and functions.

Thus, a gene is a relatively small segment or sequence on the DNA strand that codes or provides instructions for creating a specific protein or a set of proteins (which are chains of amino acids), which are the basis for a every biological structure, function, process and trait. The gene does not create these proteins directly, but indirectly through a process of transcription (or copying) and recombination in which a section of the DNA molecule is unzipped and the bases on one strand are copied to a messenger molecule, or mRNA, by means of a reverse or mirror image of the original DNA segment (in the transcription process, another base, uracil, or U, is substituted for thymine, or T, in the mRNA). The RNA message, or transcript, is then transported from the nucleus of the cell to the ribosome in the main body of the cell where it is used as a template by the protein-making machinery to translate the code into the actual sequence of amino acids to make proteins, which are used by the cell to perform its functions.

For example, the genetic code on the DNA segment for the amino acid phenylalanine is the three nucleotide sequence (or "condon") TTT, and the genetic code for the amino acid arginine is the condon AGG. The DNA gene sequence TTTAGGTTT is copied and transported by the mRNA to the ribosome where it is used as a template for linking, or translating, the amino acids arginine and phenylalanine into the correct sequence to form a specific protein for a specific function.

The long, non-protein-coding sections of the DNA molecule were once thought to be "junk DNA," and RNA was thought to be a passive messenger of transcripts, but it is now known that the noncoding DNA sections and the RNA messengers play a critical role in regulating gene activity, or "gene expression," which is described in more detail in 10. Epigenetics/Gene Expression below.

9. **Mutations/Genetic Variants** are permanent, inheritable changes to one nucleotide or a sequence of nucleotides on the DNA molecule, which are caused by random, spontaneous changes, environmental factors (including chemical and radiation) and transcription errors. In the process of cell division and recombination, DNA is transcribed or copied, and, in the process, errors can occur, such as duplications, insertions, deletions,

inversions and translocations of nucleotides and segments of nucleotides. These errors are called genetic variants, mutations or SNPs (single nucleotide polymorphisms) and occur at an infrequent but fairly standard rate.

In most cases, these mutations and transcription errors do not occur on the sections of DNA molecule that code for proteins, but when they do, they can create traits or predispositions which produce a beneficial, harmful or neutral effect on that organism in its adaptation to its environment, its survival and its propagation. Duplications of long sequences of DNA are known to be associated with the evolution of new genes and functions. These genetic variants are the driving engine of evolution and natural selection, and even a very small advantage conferred by a genetic variation can be magnified very quickly and widely throughout the population if it increases the host's chances of reaching adulthood and transmitting the new trait through its altered gene or gene expression to its offspring.

For example, the gene variant that conferred the advantage of lactase persistence (that is, the ability of adults to digest lactose, or milk sugar) provided a new food source of milk and dairy products for those who possessed the gene variant and had access to domesticated, milk-producing animals. This allowed them to be better nourished than their conspecifics without the variant (especially during times of food shortages), to live longer and produce more offspring, and, thus, to spread the variant throughout the population.

10. **Epigenetics/Gene Expression** involves the non-protein-coding sections of the DNA molecule, which were once thought to be "junk DNA," and messenger RNAs, which were once thought to be passive transcribers, but are now known to play a critical role in gene expression. These regulate if, when and for how long a gene is "expressed," or turned on or off in the organism's development. Regulating gene expression allows the developing organism to respond relatively rapidly and dynamically to changes in the environment, without altering the underlying gene structure. Although the mechanisms are not precisely understood, it is known that gene expression is influenced by such environmental factors as stress, changes in the food supply, environmental pollution and

parental behavior. See 11. Adaptive/Developmental Plasticity for example.

11. **Adaptive/Developmental Plasticity** refers to the relationship between an organism and its environment, which is a dynamic and interactive one and is guided by the epigenetic mechanisms that regulate the expression of its genes, which allows the organism to adapt in response to changes in the environment, rather than passively waiting for mutations to randomly occur over very long time-frames. Gene regulation/expression allows environmental factors, within certain parameters and constraints, to be incorporated into the organism's biological template, or genome, and expressed in its phenotype. For example, studies have shown that:

1) Bacteria that were cultured and studied in the laboratory were able to alter the expression of a critical enzyme, under the pressure of starvation, which allowed them to digest lactose, the only food that had been provided to them.

2) In the presence of larger prey, the timing and duration of the gene regulating the size of the jaw of juvenile snakes was modified to allow those snakes to develop larger jaws which allowed them to eat the larger prey.

3) The expression of the genes governing the morphology of a finch's beak are adjustable over generations to allow the species to specialize and adjust as the relative types of food supplies shift, from, say, insects to nuts to flower nectar.

4) Female Western bluebirds living in areas where there is greater competition for nesting sites produce more androgen in their eggs, lay eggs that hatch earlier and produce sons who are more aggressive in exploring other territories.

5) The pups of mother rats who fail to lick and groom them grow up to be timid, fearful and excessively sensitive to stress, as a result of the chemical suppression of a gene that regulates glucocorticoid receptors.

6) It has been shown that that in humans, a variant on a single gene, combined with a stressful or abusive upbringing, can precipitate anti-social behavior.

7) The expression of a gene that governs the lightness or darkness of skin color was modified fairly recently in human evolution toward paleness in those groups who migrated to northern latitudes, which has less sunlight. Paler skin permitted the

greater absorption of sunlight and facilitated the synthesis of
Vitamin D and the absorption of calcium, especially in women,
who need greater amounts of Vitamin D and calcium for
bearing children.

12.   **Genetic Markers, Paleo-/Archaeogenetics and Human
Migration Patterns** refer to the fact that human origins and
prehistoric human migrations can now be traced through genetic
markers, or signatures, by using unique variants in the DNA to
identify and track specific haplogroups (i.e., those population
groups who have a common ancestor and share unique and specific
patterns of genetic variants), which allows geneticists and
historians to determine the origins, history, movement and
relationships among various population groups. L. Cavalli-Sforza,
Steve Olson, Colin Renfrew, Brian Sykes, Spencer Wells.

Most genes are shuffled and mixed (or recombined) in
kaleidoscopic fashion from generation to generation through sexual
reproduction. However, mutations, or genetic variants that occur
on the Y chromosome (which is passed down from father to son)
and on the non-coding mitochondrial DNA (or mtDNA, which
lies outside the cell nucleus and is inherited only through the
mother), are generally passed down intact, thus, serving as critical
genetic markers, or signatures, which provide a method for tracing
lines of descent and constructing genetic trees linking individuals
to groups (haplogroups) and groups to related groups. Because
variants occur at a given rate, geneticists can map the progression
of the mutations or variants on the Y chromosome and the MtDNA
to identify and determine when and where variant haplogroups rose
and separated from the parent population and to trace their
subsequent movements. For example:
1)   Anatomically modern humans rose approximately 200,000
      years ago in Africa, although there was some interbreeding
      later outside of Africa between modern humans and residual
      populations of Neanderthals in the Middle East as well as with
      the Denisovans, a now extinct species of hominins, in South
      Asia.
2)   The extraordinary genetic homogeneity and lack of genetic
      diversity among modern humans compared to that of other
      primate groups suggests a population bottleneck, which may
      have occurred as a result of the eruption of the supervolcano

Mt. Toba in Sumatra approximately 70,000 years ago. The multi-year volcanic winter following the eruption may have resulted in the near extinction of the human race; fewer than 20,000 may have survived the event, from whom all modern humans are descended.

3) The out-of-Africa migration of modern humans, which occurred approximately 60,000 years ago from the Horn of Africa, consisted of one or two small groups (of, perhaps, 150 to 1,000 individuals) from whom all non-Africans are descended. The migrations occurred in one or more waves and along two separate routes, which can be traced through the gene variants left by the pioneer haplogroups: (a) an early eastern route that may have occurred around 55,000 years ago along the southern coast of Asia to Australia and (b) a migration north from the Middle East into Central Asia, which then spit around 45,000 years ago, with one group heading west to colonize Europe and a second group heading east to populate Asia, and, then, 14,000 years ago, the North and South American continents.

4) The spread of farming from the Middle East into Europe approximately 8,000 years ago can be mapped and traced through human genetic variants, as well as linguistic and archeological evidence. See 9. Neolithic/Agricultural Revolution in Anthropology Details.

11. SOCIOLOGY

CONCEPTS AND PHRASES:

Acculturation: the cultural changes that occur to an individual or a
group as a result of contact with another cultural group: (1)
assimilation occurs when an individual or group adopts the
language, cultural norms, values and behaviors of the dominant
group; (2) **biculturalism** occurs when the individual or group
adopts the norms of the dominant culture but also preserves its own
culture. See Cultural diffusion, Enculturation, Melting pot and
Socialization in Concepts.

Agency: the capacity to make free, independent decisions and choices.
See Reflexivity in Concepts.

Alienation: the estrangement of an individual from others, from what
is meaningful in life and/or from the sense of self; also, the
disassociation of the individual from God (Soren Kierkegaard), the
laborer from the product of his or her labor (Henry David Thoreau,
Karl Marx) and the citizen from the community. Alienation is
characterized by a sense of powerlessness, meaninglessness,
anomie/normlessness (Emile Durkheim), and social isolation and
self-estrangement (Melvin Seeman).

Anomie ("normlessness"): a condition in which there is a breakdown
between the individual and the traditional social bonds, norms of
behavior and connections with support groups, such as families,
communities and churches. The isolated, rootless, alienated
individual in an anonymous, impersonal, indifferent society is said
to be in a state of anomie. See 13. Durkheim in Details.

Antagonistic cooperation: the only basis for society, according to the
tenets of Social Darwinism, in which social behavior is governed
by the struggle for existence, competitive individualism and the
survival of the fittest. William Graham Sumner. See Cash nexus
in Concepts, Thomas Hobbes in Quotations, 3. Adam

Smith/Classical/Free Market Economics in Economics Details and 25. Social Darwinism in American History Details.

Ascribed status: a social condition in which an individual's social identity is defined at birth by its' gender, race, class, parental occupation and social rank; versus **achieved status**, in which an individual's social position or role is earned through its' abilities and efforts. Ralph Linton. See Meritocracy in Concepts.

Behavioral/population sink: the thesis that increased population densities lead to increased social pathologies, aggression and personality disorders. (Paradoxically, in the laboratory experiments from which these conclusions were drawn, there was plenty of food and water available to the laboratory animals in less populated parts of the experimental area, but most of them chose to congregate in the more densely populated areas.) John B. Calhoun. See 15. Urbanization in American History Details.

Bourgeoisie: approximately, the middle class. The term is derived from the French term for "walled market town" and, historically, was associated with the rise of chartered medieval towns, whose citizens ("burghers") enjoyed more privileges than the serfs, who lived in villages and were subject to more feudal restrictions. The interests of these merchants and craftsmen sometimes clashed with those of the feudal, landed aristocracy and, thus, the urban middle class served as a historical force for political liberalization until the Industrial Revolution, when the term shifted to industrialists and financiers. In Marxist theory, it refers to the capitalist ruling class, that is, the social class who owns the means of production and exploits the working class. Marxists differentiate between the *haute bourgeoisie* of financiers and industrialists and the *petite bourgeoisie* of professionals, white-collar workers, shopkeepers and small business owners. Today the term *bourgeois* is commonly applied to a wide range of socio-economic groups including the nouveau riche, the upper-middle class, the middle class and the lower-middle class. At various times, the term has also been used pejoratively to refer to those who are materialistic, conventional and conformist and who strive for social advancement and the conspicuous display of wealth, learning and culture. See 20. Class Structure in Details.

Bureaucratization/rationalization: a fundamental attribute of modern, industrialized societies, according to Max Weber, in which organizations are characterized by their large scale, hierarchical structure, specialization and division of labor, rules and regulations, impersonal relationships, etc. Weber; Robert Wiebe, William Tilden. See 14. Max Weber and 24. Information Technology/Metaphor of the Machine in Details.

Cash nexus: the approximate term used by Karl Marx to describe the system of social relationships that prevails in modern, market-driven economies. These relationships are characterized by anonymous, impersonal market forces, economic individualism, "naked self-interest" and personal profit over social responsibility, which replaced the tight-knit communities, social networks and ethical norms (of fairness and mutuality) of traditional societies. Karl Marx, E. P. Thompson, Henry David Thoreau, Alexis de Tocqueville. See Antagonistic cooperation, Commodification and Sense of community in Concepts, Karl Marx in Quotations and 11. Ferdinand Tönnies/*Gemeinschaft* versus *Gesellschaft* in Details.

Caste system: a closed social system of rigid, hereditary stratification in which marriage or mobility between castes is prohibited.

Civil religion: a mixture of nationalistic and Judeo-Christian symbols, rituals, traditions and practices that are used in secular celebrations, e.g. religious invocations at Presidential inaugurations and state funerals, the national anthem at sporting events, pledges of allegiance to the flag, and the veneration of the Founding Fathers, military veterans and past wars. According to Jean-Jacques Rousseau, these ritualistic expressions of patriotism and nationalism serve as a form of social cement. Robert Bellah.

Class: a group sharing the same social and economic status. Also, a set of hierarchical categories that is used to define social stratification based on socio-economic and other criteria, usually wealth and income, but also hereditary rank, the relationship to the means of production (David Ricardo, Karl Marx), and education, status, prestige and power (Max Weber). James Harrington, James Madison, David Ricardo, Karl Marx, Max Weber; Fred Block, William Domhoff, Herbert Gutman, Lewis Lapham, Kevin Phillips, E. P. Thompson. The relationship between class and gender is examined by Dorothy Cobble, Judith Newton, Deborah Rosenfelt and Beverly Skeggs. See 20. Class Structure and 21. Social Classes in Details.

Class basis of ideas: the doctrine that ideas are conditioned or determined by the social and economic environment in which they arise; that ideology reflects the economic interests of the dominant

class. See Cultural hegemony in Concepts and 11.
Counterarguments to Economic/Technological Determinism in
Economics Details.

Class conflict/class warfare: see Benjamin Franklin, James
Harrington, Thomas Jefferson, Abraham Lincoln, James Madison
and Karl Marx in Economics Quotations and 7. Karl Marx/
Dialectical Materialism in Details.

Class consciousness: an individual's awareness of the social classes to
which it and others belong, based on their income, occupation,
birth, education, status, etc., as well as their economic and class
interests. See 20. Class Structure in Details.

Classless society: the purported goal of communism, which was
partially based on Marx's reading of anthropologist Lewis Henry
Morgan's studies on egalitarian hunter-gatherer societies such as
the Iroquois of North America.

Class signifiers/class imagery: signs, symbols and rituals that evoke
mental images of class, status, power, prestige and wealth, or the
lack thereof. These include class-specific rituals, manners,
language, codes, schooling, clothing, eating habits, body types,
behaviors and preferences. Martin Bulmer and David Lockwood.
See Status symbols in Concepts.

Cohort: members of the same generation or age group. See Theory of
Generations in Concepts and 35. American Generational Cycles in
American History Details.

Commodification: the transformation of ideas, human beings, works
of art, sexual relationships, nature, animals, etc. into products with
assigned economic values that can be bought and sold in the
marketplace. Karl Marx, Friedrich Engels. See Consumer culture
and Fetishism of Commodities in Concepts.

Conspicuous consumption/conspicuous waste: see Consumer culture
in Concepts and 12. Thorstein Veblen in Details.

Consumer culture: one in which individuals are preoccupied with the
acquisition of material goods and the enhancement of personal
beauty, youth and status. The concept is reflected in Alexis de
Tocqueville's materialism (1835-1840), Karl Marx's fetishism of
commodities (1867), Thorstein Veblen's conspicuous consumption
and conspicuous waste (1899) and Christopher Lasch's culture of
narcissism (1979). Modern consumerism is associated with
industrialization and mass production, a rising middle class, status
symbols, advertising and globalization, and is accompanied by
threats to the sustainability of the natural environment. See

Commodification, Culture of narcissism and Status symbols in Concepts.

Convergence theory: that, because of technological developments, capitalism and socialism have merged and been superseded by the new technocratic, bureaucratic state. Daniel Bell, John Kenneth Galbraith, Clark Kerr, Max Weber. See End of ideology in Concepts.

Critical theory: a term that is applied to two different, but overlapping, schools of thought: (1) Neo-Marxist sociological criticism, which is a synthesis of Kant, Hegel, Marx, Weber and Freud and is concerned with forms of social dominance and transformation and (2) critical literary criticism, which is concerned with textual analysis, explanations and meanings. See 9. Cultural Materialism in Details and 4. Post-structuralism in Literary Concepts Details.

Cross-cultural studies: those that study human behavior across several cultures in order to (1) identify common, as well as unique, cultural traits; (2) differentiate universal from relative or variable values and behaviors and (3) reveal the researcher's own, unrecognized, and, perhaps, unconscious, cultural assumptions. See Reflexivity in Concepts.

Cultural diffusion: the transfer of cultural practices and techniques from one group to another, usually through direct contact, imitation, intermarriage, trade or common media. In anthropology, for example, there is a great deal of debate about whether farming spread from Anatolia to Europe approximately 8,000 years ago through cultural diffusion or by colonization and the physical displacement of the original hunter-gatherers by Neolithic farmers from the Middle East.

Cultural hegemony: the doctrine that cultural norms and values are socially constructed and imposed by the dominant class, but are perceived to be universally true by the general population; that the dominant ideology at any given time of the ruling elite (e.g., patriarchy, emperor worship, slavery, feudalism, the divine right of kings, laissez-faire capitalism, Social Darwinism, dialectical materialism, the cult of personality) causes the general population to falsely believe in the universality and immutability of that world view, to accept their subordinate status and to act in ways which are antithetical to their own self-interest; Antonio Gramsci; versus **post-hegemonic synthesis**, which ascribes free will, agency, autonomy and reflexivity, or self-awareness, to individuals as they make their political and cultural choices, and sees cultural hegemony in layered social structures rather than as a monolithic value system. Peter Berger and Thomas Luckmann, Anthony Giddens, Raymond Williams. See Reflexivity and Stratigraphic model in Concepts.

Cultural imperialism: the imposition of one culture's ideas, values and behaviors on another. Commonly, it refers to the Westernization of traditional, pre-industrial cultures with secular humanism, market-driven capitalism, materialism and consumerism.

Cultural materialism: see 9. Cultural materialism in Details.

Cultural phenotypes: the observable traits of a cultural group; ideal or modal personality types; national character traits. Max Weber, Margaret Mead, Geoffrey Gorer, William Tilden. Various personality modalities and typologies are described in Psychology Details.

Cultural relativity: the belief that each culture is unique, has its own values and moral imperatives and should be understood in its own terms; versus **ethnocentrism** (*q.v.* in Concepts). Ruth Benedict, Franz Boas, Bronislaw Malinowski, Margaret Mead. See Max Weber in Quotations.

Cultural stereotypes: oversimplified perceptions, expectations, generalizations and beliefs, usually negative and prejudicial, about, usually, but not always, ethnic or marginalized social groups.

Cultural symbols/icons: objects or persons of great cultural or popular significance, such as a national flag, a historical document, a pop star, a can of soup, an automobile, a weapon, a sports hero or a building. See Vernacular tradition in American History Concepts.

Culture: see 2. Culture in Details.

Culture of narcissism: a culture whose members are characterized by both self-love and self-doubt, as well as by materialism and consumerism, self-indulgence, self-absorption, hedonism, a sense of entitlement, the cultish veneration of youthfulness, an indifference to history and a fear of aging and death. Christopher Lasch, Alexis de Tocqueville. See Consumer culture and Hedonistic solipsism in Concepts.

Culture of poverty: the thesis that poverty is not simply the lack of resources, but a system of values that perpetuates itself through the socialization of successive generations; that the poor have a "strong feeling of marginality, of helplessness, of dependency, of not belonging. . . of powerlessness, a widespread feeling of inferiority, of personal unworthiness." Oscar Lewis, Michael Harrington.

Culture wars: the "culture struggle" (*kulturkampfe*) between those who hold opposing sets of values, assumptions, ideals and world views. In the United States during the 20th Century, for example, there was intense public debate over such polarizing social issues as the prohibition of alcohol, women's right to vote, science and evolution, isolationism, foreign military intervention, racial segregation, dissent and disloyalty, nuclear testing, fluoridation, racial integration, school busing, gender discrimination, abortion, homosexual rights, pornography, recreational drug use, economic inequality, global warming, immigration, health insurance, gun control, etc. The rhetoric is often fierce and fulminous, but, over time, public discourse is eventually modulated, resolved through reform or displaced by other issues. Patrick Buchanan, James Hunter.

Decentered self: the theory that knowledge is derived from one's relationships with others and from one's social systems, and not from the individual mind acting as an autonomous knower. Jacques Lacan. See Sociological assumption in Concepts and 1. Sociology in Details.

Demographics: the quantitative study of population groups and their attributes and trends; the classification and profiling of social groups by age, gender, race, income, education, political affiliation and other factors, often for marketing or political purposes and for formulating social policies and allocating services and resources.

Diachronic: studies that focus on the origins, history and development of a subject over a period of time; versus **synchronic**: studies that focus on the structure and functions of a subject at a given point in time. Ferdinand de Saussure.

Disembourgeoisment: the displacement and downward mobility of individuals and families from the middle class. See Downward mobility, Economic inequality/concentration of wealth and Status anxieties in Concepts and 22. Social Mobility in Details.

Disenchantment: the loss of magic, mystery, spirituality and "sublime values" in modern, rational, secular, bureaucratic society. Friedrich Schiller, Max Weber.

Dominance/status hierarchies: the predominant form of social organization in many animal species, which is said to promote order and stability, if not equity and justice, within the group. See

Class, Class signifiers/class imagery, Cultural hegemony and Status symbols in Concepts and 20. Class Structure in Details.

Downward mobility: in postindustrial America, the decline of the middle class, which is associated with globalization, the offshore outsourcing of jobs, economic recession, de-unionization, regressive taxation, economic inequality and the concentration of wealth. Jacob Hacker and Paul Pierson, Paul Krugman, Kevin Phillips, Thomas Piketty, Joseph Stiglitz. See *Disembourgeoisment*, Economic inequality/concentration of wealth, Great Gatsby curve and Status anxieties/displaced social groups in Concepts and 22. Social Mobility in Details.

Dunbar's number: the thesis that the maximum effective size of stable, cohesive social groups is 150 individuals (with a range of 100 to 250), which is the typical size of hunting-gathering clans, military companies and other traditional social groups. It is said to be the maximum number of people with whom a single individual can maintain personal, face-to-face relationships, which is cognitively limited by the size of the neo-cortex. Thus, large, modern, complex, hierarchical organizations and nation-states are constrained by this tribal and cognitive parameter. Robin Dunbar, Malcolm Gladwell.

Economic elitism versus **political egalitarianism**: two conflicting and contradictory sets of values in American political and social thought: (1) the former accepts the concentration of wealth and plutocracy, while (2) the latter celebrates equality and individual opportunity. Kevin Phillips. See 15. Elites/Oligarchies in Details and Donor class, Patronage, Plutocracy and Super PACs in Political Science Concepts.

Economic inequality/concentration of wealth: the redistribution of wealth upwards. Wealth and income are major factors in defining an individual's socioeconomic status. Economic inequality (1) is linked to social, racial and gender inequality; (2) has a powerful, negative effect on social mobility and (3) constraints access to political power and social resources and services, such as education, medical care, legal representation. In the United States, the top 1% of households accounts for over 30% of all income and holds 40% of all assets. There is greater economic inequality in the United States than in any other democracy in the developed world. According to Oxfam, eighty-five of the world's wealthiest individuals have a combined wealth equal to that of the bottom

50% of the world's population (or, 3.5 billion people). Jacob Hacker and Paul Pierson, Paul Krugman, Kevin Phillips, Thomas Piketty, Joseph Stiglitz. See Great Gatsby curve in Concepts and 22. Social Mobility in Details.

Economic/technological determinism: see 10. Economic/ Technological Determinism and 11. Counterarguments in Economics Details.

Embourgeoisment: the upward mobility of the working class; also, the assumption of middle-class values, aspirations and behaviors by the working class. See *Disembourgeoisment* and Downward mobility in Concepts and 22. Social Mobility In Details. .

Enculturation: the process by which an individual learns and absorbs the accepted norms, values and behavior of its culture. See Acculturation and Socialization in Concepts.

End of ideology: the thesis by some historians and social scientists that political ideologies in the United States are irrelevant and exhausted, and that public policy will be driven, instead, by technocratic issues. Daniel Bell. See Convergence theory in Concepts.

Ethnocentrism: judging other cultures by one's own cultural value system; viewing the behavior and values of other cultures as inferior; versus cultural relativity (*q.v.* in Concepts) and functionalism. See Xenophobia in Concepts and Max Weber in Quotations.

Ethos (Greek for "character"): the character and spirit of a culture that is reflected in its values, ideals and beliefs. See Moral code and Symbolic code in Concepts.

Feminism: see Gender roles, Patriarchy and Sexism in Concepts and 35. Feminism in American History Details.

Folk culture: the vernacular objects and practices of small, isolated, often, rural groups, that are rooted in a sense of community and a specific sense of place, and the knowledge of which is usually passed down through oral tradition. See Popular culture in Concepts.

Folkways: the customs, standards, conventions and norms of a culture that govern, for example, its attitudes, behavior, etiquette, greetings and dress. See Ethos, Manners and mores and Symbolic code in Concepts.

Functionalism/structural functionalism: see 18. Structural Functionalism in Details.

Gang: a group of, almost, exclusively male individuals with a leader, an organizational structure and a set of rules and rituals that claims a territory and engages in violent and illegal activity. Street gangs share many features of hunter-gatherer foraging and raiding bands that compete against other male bands for resources, mates, spoils, defense of territory, revenge, etc. Bands are characterized by the symbols and rituals of identification and bonding, which intensify the solidarity of the in-group and dehumanize the out-group. See Narcissism of small differences in Concepts and Male coalitional violence in Anthropology Concepts.

Garden cities: planned, satellite communities containing homes, retail shops, public parks and light industries, which are surrounded by green belts and linked to a larger central city by transportation networks. Ebenezer Howard, Kenneth Jackson, William Morris, Lewis Mumford, John Stilgoe. See Suburbanization in American History Concepts.

Gemeinschaft versus ***gesellschaft***: the traditional, pre-industrial, relational "community" versus the modern, industrial, transactional "society." See 11. Ferdinand Tönnies in Details.

Gender roles: the social roles, identities, norms, behaviors and attitudes assumed by, and expected of, males and females in a particular culture. According to various theories, the roles are said to be fixed or fluid, and socially constructed or biologically determined. Gender roles may be derived from the division of labor involving reproduction and child care, the means of subsistence, gender dimorphism, patriarchy; warfare, etc. Post-essential feminist theory maintains that gender roles are socially constructed rather than biologically determined or derived from an essential, universal female identity. Cynthia Epstein, Beth Hess and Myra Ferree, Judith Newton, Rosemarie Tong. See Patriarchy and Sexism in Concepts; Pair-bonding and Sexual contract in Anthropology Concepts; Essentialism and Post-essentialism in Religion/Philosophy Concepts and 35. Feminism in American History Details.

Gentrification: the upscale transformation of poor, working class neighborhoods by more affluent newcomers. The process is often accompanied by increased rents and property values and the partial or complete displacement of the original inhabitants, including minorities, artists and counter-culturalists.

Global village: see 23. Marshall McLuhan in Details.

Great Gatsby curve: a graph that depicts the declining social mobility and increasing income inequality in the United States. Miles Corak, Alan Krueger, Thomas Piketty, Joseph Stiglitz. See Economic inequality/concentration of wealth and Downward mobility in Concepts and 22. Social Mobility in Details.

Haute bourgeoisie: the upper-middle class. See Bourgeoisie in Concepts and 20. Class Structure and 21. Social Classes in Details.

Hedonistic solipsism: a term applied to the obsessive, contemporary cultural practice of using personal electronic devices in preference to face-to-face human contact and social relationships.

Holism: the concept that social systems function as integrated wholes and should be viewed as such, rather than as a collection of individual parts. Jan Smuts.

Ideal types: Max Weber's classification of social-political leadership and authority into the following categories: (1) charismatic, (2) traditional (e.g. monarchy) and (3) rational-legal (the modern bureaucratic state). See Cultural phenotypes in Concepts, 14. Max Weber in Details and various personality modalities and typologies in Psychology Details.

Identity: the defining features of an individual's character and personality, both as the individual perceives itself and as others perceive it; also, the sense of selfhood as a distinct personality, with a sense of uniqueness as well as a sense of affiliation within a larger, concentric superset of social groups, from which are derived one's family, gender, cohort, ethnic, class, cultural, national, human and spiritual identities. See Looking glass effect in Psychology Concepts.

Idiographic: studies that focus on specific, individual cases; versus **nomothetic**: studies that focus on broad social patterns and trends, use empirical methods and quantitative data to demonstrate causal relationships, and draw generalizations and conclusions about social groups and classes. Gordon Allport, Allan Johnson.

Individualism: an American cultural value and trait. It is associated with self-reliance, social and geographical mobility, the ideal of the self-made man and the distrust of collective action. The term was coined by Alexis de Tocqueville in his *Democracy in America* (1835-40), which he defined as the "feeling which deposes each citizen to isolate himself from the mass of his fellows and withdraw. . . . . He gladly leaves the greater society to look for itself." See Antinomian personality in American History Concepts and 3. Alexis de Tocqueville, 11. Frederick Jackson Turner/Frontier Thesis, 21. New England Transcendentalism in American History Details and Narcissism of small differences in Sociology Concepts. For economic individualism, see Objectivism, Positive central state versus laissez-faire individualism and Rugged individualism in Concepts and 4. Conservatism: Laissez-faire/Economic Individualism in Political Science Details.

Intelligentsia: intellectuals as a social class, such as writers, thinkers, teachers, scholars, academicians, men and women of letters; also, public intellectuals engaged in public discourse and discussions about public policy issues. The term was originally applied to 19th Century Russian reformers and, later, used more broadly to describe intellectuals and thinkers as a class by Max Weber and others. See 14. Max Weber in Details, Anti-intellectualism in American History Concepts, Republic of letters in Literary Concepts and 27. 18th Century Enlightenment in Philosophy/Religion Details.

Intersectionality: the interrelationship of gender, race, class, sexual orientation and age and its impact on social identities and oppression. Patricia Hill Collins and Kimberlé Crenshaw.

Kinship groups: extended family groups that are based on blood and marriage; the basic social unit of pre-industrial societies.

Legislation cannot change folkways or mores: an argument used by Social Darwinists, states' rights advocates, libertarians and social conservatives to defend the status quo and to counter the efforts of reformers working for civil rights and social justice. William Graham Sumner. See Ethos, Folkways, Social engineering and Symbolic code in Concepts and 25. Social Darwinism and 26. Reform Darwinism in American History Details.

Leveling upward: a belief in collective upward mobility and rising living standards through technological improvements, greater access to education and health care, etc. Ralph Linton, Arthur Schlesinger.

Life style: a set of signs, symbols and behaviors that reflect an individual's or a group's attitudes, values and identity; it includes the individual's wealth, income, dress, living and consumption patterns, social relationships, etc. See Class signifiers/class imagery, Subculture and Status symbols in Concepts.

Literacy: the ability to read and write. High literacy rates are associated with the transmission of cultural knowledge, individual self-determination (especially for women) and scientific, social, cultural and economic development.

Longitudinal studies: those in which the same subjects are observed over long periods of time, in some cases decades or, even, life-times.

Lumpen proletariat (a term derived from the German word for "rag"): the underclass, i.e., those outside the formal, legal economy. It includes the homeless, the chronically unemployed, beggars, prostitutes, petty criminals, addicts, drug dealers, gamblers and bootleggers. See 20. Class Structure and 21. Social Classes in Details.

Managerial revolution: a society in which the ruling elite of corporate executives and managers achieves social dominance, political power and privilege by controlling the means of production. James Burnham. See 15. Elites/Oligarchies in Details.

Manners and mores: culturally-specific norms, behaviors, conventions, customs, moral codes, etc. Harriet Martineau, William Graham Sumner. See Ethos, Folkways and Symbolic code in Concepts.

Mass society: the central focus of a school of thought that is critical of modern society for its weak communal ties, *anomie*, alienation, ignorance, passivity, mindless conformity, cultural mediocrity, materialism, "crowd psychology," "mob rule" and manipulation by, and receptivity to, demagogues and mass movements. See 16. Mass Society and 17. Erich Fromm in Details.

Material culture: the tangible material objects produced by a culture, as well as the underlying social relationships associated with those objects. Also, the economic/productive and sexual/reproductive relationships that form the basis of a society's substructure or material base, according to the precepts of cultural materialism. See 9. Cultural Materialism in Details.

Mechanical solidarity: a central characteristic of traditional, small-scale pre-industrial societies, according to Emile Durkheim, in which social cohesion was derived from a homogenous population with similar backgrounds who performed similar rituals and similar tasks; versus **organic solidarity**: a central characteristic of modern, industrial societies, in which social bonds are derived from the economic interdependence and reliance members with diverse interests and specialized tasks must place on each other. See 13. Emile Durkheim in Details.

Medium is the message: Marshall McLuhan's thesis that the medium by which information is conveyed is as important as the content that it conveys; that the evolution of communications technology has affected both human cognition and social organization. In McLuhan's paradigm, (1) **oral cultures** (pre-alphabetic/tribal) were superseded by (2) **print cultures** (characterized by individualism, fragmentation and linear logic), which are now being displaced by (3) **electronic media**, which have re-established aural and oral cultures and shared tribal identities, as well as global networks of virtual communities. See 23. Marshall McLuhan and 24. Information Technology/Metaphor of the Machine in Details.

Melting pot: a popular metaphor for the assimilation and homogenization of immigrant groups in the United States, notwithstanding the class, racial and ethnic prejudice and exclusionary barriers that were directed against them. An alternative metaphor of the "salad bowl" more accurately represents the diversity, multiculturalism and unique contributions of ethnic groups. See Assimilation in Concepts and 14. Immigration in American History Details.

Meritocracy: a government or society that is led by an educated, professional, technocratic class whose position and status is based on achievement, effort and talent rather than on birth or wealth. It is analogous to Thomas Jefferson's **natural aristocracy of talent** versus an **artificial aristocracy of birth and wealth**. The concept is based on the assumption that society should provide equal opportunities for all and special privileges for none, which was a cardinal principle of Jeffersonian and Jacksonian Democracy in the first half of the 19th Century. See Ascribed status, Pluralism and Technocracy in Concepts and 22. Social Mobility in Details.

Metaphor of the machine: see 24. Information Technology/Metaphor of the Machine in Details and Cult of efficiency and Mass production in Economics Concepts.

Middle class: a term which was first used in 1830s. See Bourgeoisie in Concepts and 20. Class Structure and 21. Social Classes in Details.

Military-industrial-university-media complex: the central thesis of a school of thought that political and economic power in the United States is exercised in concert by an interlocking power elite of political, corporate, military, academic and media leaders, who share a common world view and move easily between institutions. The complex originated in the massive public military expenditures and research and development projects during World War II and the Cold War of the 1950s and 1960s. President Dwight Eisenhower first identified the complex and named its first two components. Jane Mayer, C. Wright Mills. See Power elites in Concepts, 15. Elites/Oligarchies in Details and Permanent warfare economy/military Keynesianism in Economics Concepts.

Moral code: the symbolic system of norms and values which govern a society. See Ethos and Symbolic code in Concepts.

Moral economy: a normative economic and social order in which there is a balance between private acquisitiveness and social responsibility, between economic individualism and social justice. It seeks to recapture the values, cohesiveness and sense of belonging which were intrinsic to traditional societies before they were displaced by anonymous, impersonal market forces, economic individualism and social anomie. See Cash nexus and Sense of community in Concepts; 11. Ferdinand Tonnies/*Gemeinschaft* in Details and Moral capitalism in Economics Concepts. E. P. Thompson, Alexis de Tocqueville.

Multiculturalism: ethnic and cultural pluralism; the recognition and appreciation of the values and contributions made by multiple ethnic and cultural groups; versus ethnocentrism. David Hollinger. See Assimilation versus biculturalism, Ethnocentrism, Melting pot and Pluralism in Concepts.

Narcissism of small differences: the urge to exaggerate the minor differences between similar individuals or groups in order to preserve a sense of uniqueness, separation and otherness. Freud used the term to suggest that human aggression is innate. The concept is often applied to groups with adjoining territories who are constantly at war with each other, such as the Protestants and Catholics in Northern Ireland, the Palestinians and Israelis in the West Bank, and the Crips and the Bloods in East Los Angeles. The sense of uniqueness and superiority, and the feelings of antipathy and envy directed at those who are virtually similar, may be derived from the fact that the "other" is unconsciously perceived as a sexual or resource competitor. Sigmund Freud; Ernest Crawley, Glen Gabbard. See Gangs and Tribalism in Concepts and Male coalition violence and Territoriality in Anthropology Concepts.

National character: see 2. American Cultural Values and Traits, 3. Alexis de Tocqueville and 11. Frederick Jackson Turner/Frontier Thesis in American History Details.

Nationalism: the identification with, and sense of belonging to, a nation-state or a national, ethnic or cultural group. See 19. Origins of American Nationalism in American History Details.

Nature-nurture continuum: the spectrum, or range, of complex interactions between (1) nature (that is, hereditary, biological and genetic factors) and (2) nurture (environmental, relational, and social systems) and the extent to which each determines, conditions or influences human behavior. The continuum is influenced by the degree of agency, autonomy and free choice exercised by the individual between those two poles. See Agency, Reflexivity, Social psychology, Social structure, Sociobiology, Sociological assumption and *Tabula rasa* in Concepts and 1. Sociology in Details.

Nuclear family: a husband, a wife and their biological children, all of whom live in a single household; versus **extended family**: a blood-related group, which may include the immediate family as well as grandparents, aunts, uncles, and/or cousins, who or may not live in the same household or nearby; versus **postmodern family**: the traditional nuclear family of two married parents who live with their biological children, or families with a single parent, step-parents, unmarried parents, same-sex parents, couples without children or extended families of multiple generations who may live in the same household.

Oral versus **written cultures**: see 23. Marshall McLuhan in Details.

Oral tradition: in non-literate societies (i.e., those without a written language, or whose members cannot read or write), the primary method for transmitting knowledge and cultural traditions from generation to generation, using stories, speeches, songs, poems and folktales.

Paradigm: a model, a conceptual framework, a pattern of ideas, a mindset, a world view. Thomas Kuhn.

Patriarchy (Greek for "rule of the father"): a social system of male privilege and female subordination, in which nearly all economic and legal power is held by men. See Sexism in Concepts.

Peer group/nurture assumption: Judith Rich Harris' thesis that the critical, formative determinates of a child's personality, in addition to genetic factors, are the child's peer groups, rather than its home environment, parents, teachers, other adults or society at large. See Theory of generations in Concepts.

Pluralism: economic, political, cultural, ethnic and religious diversity; the coexistence of, and the influence exerted by, diverse and competing economic, political, social, ethnic and religious groups, which allows each group to contribute to the marketplace of ideas and prevents the monopoly of any one point of view. When the influence is wielded asymmetrically by a few powerful groups, the system is described as **elite pluralism**. According to some cultural materialists, the ideology of democratic pluralism, of society being held together by common norms and the promise of equal opportunity, is a myth, a pretense, an "illusion of control," a social construct of the ruling class. Stuart Hall, Joseph Stiglitz. See 15. Elites/Oligarchies in Details.

Popular culture: folk, popular and mass cultures, which are often described in terms of their opposition to elite or high culture ("highbrow," "middlebrow" and "lowbrow" are derived from the pseudo-scientific study of phrenology in late 19th Century). Herbert Gans, Clifford Geertz, John Kouwenhoven, Dwight Macdonald, Bernard Rosenberg and David Manning, Jane and Michael Stern, Alexis de Tocqueville, James Twitchell. See Popular Culture in Art Concepts for examples.

Positivism: a school of philosophy that views science as the definitive source of knowledge, in which truth is derived from the application of scientific methods and empirical techniques to all natural phenomena, including human society and social behavior. It is one of the foundations of modern sociology. See 1. Sociology and 4. Auguste Comte/Positivism in Details.

Post-Enlightenment: a term applied to the 20th and 21th Centuries, a period that is said to be characterized by the erosion of the Enlightenment values of reason, order, optimism, secularism and faith in science, human progress and social improvement. The *zeitgeist* is thought to be the result of world wars, mass movements, totalitarianism, genocide, the threat of nuclear annihilation and the rise of religious fundamentalism. See 4.

Sigmund Freud in Psychology Details and 16. Mass Society and 17. Erich Fromm in Details.

Post-hegemonic synthesis: see Cultural hegemony versus post-hegemonic synthesis in Concepts.

Post-hoc perceptual bias: the thesis that people often cannot imagine the probability or consequences of a harmful action until after it has occurred. It is reflected in the disparity between the enormous personal and economic losses incurred by society from dysfunctional, anti-social and criminal behavior, and the small investment made by society in identifying and preventing the causes. Prevention and proactive intervention are hindered by social inertia, indifference, denial and fatalism, as well as by post-hoc perceptual biases.

Post-industrial urbanism: see Mike Davis in Selected References.

Post literacy: see 23. Marshall McLuhan in Details.

Potlatch: status-related gift-giving and redistributive feasts, which were practiced by certain indigenous cultures in which status was achieved or affirmed by periodically giving away one's wealth. Philanthropy is a modern analogue and exhibits a similar status-related component. Ruth Benedict, William Tilden.

Power elite: an interlocking political, corporate, military, academic and media elite, who share a common world view and move easily between institutions. Jane Mayer, C. Wright Mills. See Military-industrial-university-media complex in Concepts, 15. Elites/Oligarchies in Details and Permanent warfare economy in Economics Concepts.

Pre-industrial societies: see 11. Ferdinand Tonnie/*Gemeinschaft* and 13. Emile Durkheim/mechanical solidarity in Details and Anthropology Concepts, Quotations and Details.

Privatism and the fall of the public man: the withdrawal of citizens from public involvement. Richard Sennett, Philip Slater. See Individualism in Concepts, Culture of contradictions and Pursuit of loneliness in American History Concepts and 3. Tocqueville in American History Details.

Professional/technocratic class: a social class that is defined by its higher education, specialized knowledge, professional standards, autonomy, independence and prestige and in which status is achieved rather than ascribed. Eliot Freidson, Max Weber. See Intelligentsia, Meritocracy and Technocracy in Concepts.

Proletariat: originally, a Roman social class whose members owned no property; the term now refers to wage laborers or the industrial working class; versus peasants (agricultural laborers and small land owners), the bourgeoisie, petite bourgeoisie, *salariat* and haute bourgeoisie. Karl Marx. See Bourgeoisie and *lumpen proletariat* in Concepts and 21. Social Classes in Details.

Prosocial behavior: behavior that is intended to benefit others. It may be motivated by empathy, altruism or anticipated reciprocity and may be associated with parental nurturing, trust, social cooperation and the maternal hormone oxytocin. Patricia Churchland, Philip Kitsch, Donald Pfaff, Frans de Waal. See Social psychology in Concepts and Group-level selection, Mirror neurons and Theory of mind in Anthropology Concepts and 5. Social Intelligence/Social Brain Hypothesis in Anthropology Details.

Public opinion: the aggregate attitudes of the public on the common issues of the day. It wasn't until the rise of the public sphere (*q.v.* in Concepts) in the 18th Century Enlightenment that what average people thought about public issues became important to those who governed. Public opinion's influence on public policy and its vulnerability to manipulation by interest groups and the media is the subject of many studies. James Bryce, Benjamin Ginsberg, Jill Lepore, Walter Lippmann, Paul Starr, Alexis de Tocqueville.

Public sphere: the arena of public discourse. Beginning in the 18th Century Enlightenment, the "realm of communication was marked by new arenas of debate, more open and accessible forms of urban public space and sociability, and an explosion of print culture" (Jürgen Habermas). There were "rational, critical and genuinely open discussion of public issues" in coffeehouses, book stores, lecture halls and libraries. The media in the public sphere were associated with the rise of popular literacy, the democratic diffusion of knowledge, political debate and cultural pluralism. Jurgen Habermas, James Melton, Paul Starr. See 27. 18th Century Enlightenment in Philosophy/Religion Details. For the impact of technology and electronic social media on the public sphere, see Virtual communities in Concepts and 24. Information Technology in Details.

Racism: the personal, institutional and, often, legally-sanctioned prejudice by one race or ethnic group against another. Historically, in the United States, it was manifested in chattel slavery, the forced removal of Native-Americans to reservations, violence, exclusion, racial segregation, xenophobia, deportations, job discrimination,

lynchings, disenfranchisement, anti-Semitism, internment and
ethnic and religious profiling.

Reflexivity: self-awareness; an individual's recognition of the
personal, social and environmental influences that shaped it, as
well as the individual's autonomous ability to change and re-shape
its own views and norms; the circular relationship between cause
and effect. "Man is both knowing subject and the object of his
own study" -- Michel Foucault. See Agency in Concepts.

Rites of passage: religious and cultural ceremonies and rituals that
formally recognize the transitions in the physical state and social
status of an individual as it passes through the various stages of
life, including birth, childhood, puberty, initiation into adulthood,
marriage, child-bearing and death.

*S*alariat: those members of the proletariat who receive a fixed salary
rather than hourly wages for their labor.

Science of human relationships: see Franklin Roosevelt in
Quotations.

Self-fulfilling prophecy: "a false definition of the situation evoking a
new behavior which makes the original false conception come
true," such as a bank run or a belief in the inevitability of war; the
circular relationship between an expectation and a self-validating
behavior. Robert Merton.

Sense of community: the feelings of belonging, interdependence and
shared sense of values and commitment to common goals among
members of a group; versus alienation, isolation and anomie. See
Alienation, Anomie, Cash nexus and Privatism and the fall of the
public man in Concepts, 11. Ferdinand Tonnies/*Gemeinschaft* in
Details and John Winthrop in American History Quotations.

Sexism: the conscious and unconscious prejudice and discrimination
directed against members of a gender, primarily women, as
expressed in various forms, including language, stereotyping,
objectification, patriarchy, condescension, sexual harassment,
segregation, disenfranchisement, legal and economic dependency,
job discrimination, unequal pay, domestic violence, suppression of
sexuality, prohibition of family planning techniques, genital
mutilation, honor killings and sex-selected abortion. See Gender
roles and Patriarchy in Concepts and 35. Feminism in American
History Details.

Shame versus **guilt cultures**: the former are associated with outward
sanctions involving public embarrassment, humiliation and

dishonor from violating social norms, while the latter are associated with private remorse resulting from self-directed blame and violations of internal moral standards. Shame cultures are manifestations of outer-directed behavior patterns and personality types, while guilt cultures are manifestations of inner-directed behavior and personality types. Ruth Benedict, David Reisman.

Social contract: the doctrine that society is a contractual relationship between its members based on their free will and mutual consent. Also, the expectations by members of a society that, under the terms of the social contract, they have the responsibility to be good, lawful, productive citizens and it, society, in turn, has a reciprocal responsibility to protect its members' natural rights and insure that their basic human needs are met, such as an education, a decent living and health care. Thomas Hobbes, Thomas Jefferson, John Locke, Jean-Jacques Rousseau.

Social engineering: the organized attempt to change individual behavior on a large scale, usually through governmental policies, but also through social pressure and moral suasion. The prohibition of the sale of alcohol and the war on drugs are two failed examples; the war on drunk driving and the campaigns against smoking and childhood obesity are two somewhat more successful ones. Edward Ross, Lester Ward. See Legislation cannot change folkways and Technocracy in Concepts; 6. John Stuart Mill/Utilitarianism in Details and 26. Reform Darwinism in American History Details.

Socialization: the process by which a child, through the influence of its family, peers, school, church, the media, etc., absorbs the values, norms, skills and behaviors necessary to define its identity and become a functioning member of society. See Enculturation in Concepts.

Social mobility: the upward and downward movement of individuals, families and groups from one socioeconomic stratum to another. See *Disembourgeoisment*, Economic inequality, *Embourgeoisment*, Downward mobility and Great Gatsby curve in Concepts and 22. Social Mobility in Details.

Social psychology: the study of human behavior in its social context. It is based on the assumption that human behavior is inherently relational, that is, that it is shaped and/or determined by its social environment, or, to paraphrase Eric Fromm, the psychic structure as it is defined by the social structure. Since society is "an intricate web of multiple relations between individuals" (George Simmel), and, since all individuals belong to groups (family, friends, neighbors, cohort, school-mates, church members, business associates, community members, citizens), their behavior is shaped and conditioned by those groups. "The individual mind can exist only in relation to other minds with shared meanings" (George Herbert Mead). See 1. Sociology and 18. Structural Functionalism in Details.

Social structure: the organized pattern of social relationships that make up a society. These include social institutions, economic organizations, class systems, social networks, cultural expectations, norms, social roles, etc. Individuals are embedded in and conditioned by those social structures. Emile Durkheim, Ellen Langer, Karl Marx, Robert Merton, Talcott Parsons, Alexis de Tocqueville, Max Weber, Daniel Wegner. See Agency, Cultural hegemony, Nature-nurture continuum and Sociological assumption in Concepts and 1. Sociology and 18. Structural Functionalism in Details.

Sociobiology: a school of scientific thought that maintains that individual and social behavior is largely inherited, that is, that it is the product of genes and natural selection. Inherited behaviors include those associated with gender, aggression, territoriality, mating, reciprocal altruism, social cooperation, intelligence, anxiety/stress-response, introversion, etc. Steven Pinker, Edward O. Wilson.

Socioeconomic status: an individual's position, class or rank in a stratified society. See Class, Class signifiers, Dominance/status hierarchies and Status symbols in Concepts and 20. Class Structure and 21. Social Classes in Details.

Sociological assumption: the thesis that human behavior is inherently relational, that is, that it is shaped and/or determined by its social environment and its web of relationships; versus the **nominalist** view that society is a collection of separate, autonomous, independent individuals. See Agency, Individualism and Nature-nurture continuum in Concepts and Margaret Thatcher in Quotations and 1. Sociology in Details.

Sports: in anthropological and sociological terms, a form of tribal rivalry; ritualized warfare; a demonstration of totemism and territoriality; the symbolic expression of competitive capitalism; the opiate of the masses; the latter-day equivalent of Roman circuses. See Totemism and Tribalism in Concepts and Sexual selection and Territoriality in Anthropology Concepts.

Stake-in-society: the 17th and 18th Century political doctrine that only those who have an economic stake in society, specifically the ownership of "real" or landed property, should be allowed to govern it. Property qualifications provided the means for protecting the **"better and wiser sort"** from majority rule and government by the **"meaner sort."** John Locke. See Class structure in colonial America and Stake-in-society in American History Concepts.

Status: the honor and prestige associated with an individual's rank or position in society, which may be ascribed or achieved (*q.v.* in Concepts). See Class, Class signifiers, Dominance/status hierarchies and Status symbols in Concepts and 14. Max Weber, 20. Class Structure and 21. Social Classes in Details.

Status anxieties/displaced social groups: the anxieties associated with the decline in social status of one group (say, working class white males without a college education) relative to other groups (say, immigrants, women, minorities, white collar workers, public employees, the college educated). Status anxieties have been identified as a causal factor in, and the dynamic basis of, both reform and reactionary movements. Daniel Bell, David Donald, Richard Hofstadter, George Mowry. See *Disembourgeoisment*, Economic inequality/concentration of wealth, Downward mobility in Concepts and 22.Social Mobility in Details and 28. Populism and 29. Progressivism in American History Details.

Status symbols: time-bound indicators of social status and wealth. Examples include luxury homes, expensive automobiles, trophy spouses, jewelry, artwork, designer clothing, travel and leisure time, vacation homes, state-of-the-art electronic devices, books, memberships, publications, awards, titles, pale skin, tanned skin, conspicuous consumption and waste, as well as inconspicuous consumption, patrician frugality and anti-status symbols (an older car; rumpled, off-the-rack clothing; disheveled hair, a partially knotted tie, etc.). Martin Bulmer and David Lockwood. See Class signifiers/class imagery in Concepts.

Stratigraphic model: a conceptual, hierarchical paradigm with biology at its base and successive economic, social, psychological and cultural layers; versus **webs of significance**, a conceptual model in which all domains are inter-linked without vertical ranking. Clifford Geertz.

Subculture: a self-identified subgroup within the dominant culture that practices a different lifestyle and uses specific signifiers, such as language, codes, rituals, clothing, accessories, body markings and other symbols to identify and indicate membership in the group. In the United States, subcultures include beats, bikers, body-builders, bondage enthusiasts, climbers, counter-culturalists, country-and-western music fans, cowboys, gangstas, gothics, grungers, gun enthusiasts, heavy metalists, hillbillies, hip-hoppers, hippies, hoodies, hunters, LGBTs, New Ageists, nudists, pot-heads, preppies, punks, rappers, RVers, skate-boarders, skiers, skinheads, square-dancers, surfers, survivalists and swingers. See Tribalism in Concepts.

Suburbanization: see Suburbanization in American History Concepts and David Brooks, Kenneth Jackson, John Stilgoe in Selected References.

Superstructure: according to the tenets of cultural materialism, art, ideology and religion and social, cultural, political and legal institutions, which are said to be driven by changes in the economic/technological base or material substructure. For examples and counter-arguments, see 10. Technological/Economic Determinism and 11. Counterarguments in Economics Details.

Symbolic code: a culture's system of prescribed values, beliefs, ideals, mores, folkways and traditions; the rules, rituals, canons, commands, conventions, legislation and social codes that govern a society. Alfred North Whitehead. See Ethos, Folkways and Moral code in Concepts.

Symbolic groups: those that are identified by their social, political and ideological significance as much as by their economic and class interests, although some control the opinion- and decision-making institutions of society. Examples include antebellum Southern plantation owners, post-Civil War captains of industry, Wall Street financiers, Main Street businessmen, family farmers, urban professionals, college students, blue-collar workers, ethnic groups, retired persons, military veterans, religious groups, sports celebrities, NRA members, soccer moms, LGBTs, etc. Daniel Bell.

Tabula rasa: John Locke's theory that the mind at birth is a blank slate or tablet and, thus, that all men are created equal. It laid the intellectual foundation for natural rights, political democracy and social improvement. Its inherent environmentalism runs counter to the tenets of structuralism and sociobiology. See Nature-nurture continuum and Sociobiology in Concepts.

Technocracy: (1) a government in which public policy and decision-making is guided by professional experts, administrators, scientists, engineers and specialists and by the application of scientific methods to social issues; (2) a meritocracy based on education, training and talent, which is similar to Jefferson's natural aristocracy of talent, rather than an artificial aristocracy of birth and wealth and/or (3) an economy that is driven by technological innovations. Jacques Ellul, Walter Lippmann, Lester Ward, Max Weber.

Technological determinism: a school of thought that asserts that economic and technological changes in the material environment, or substructure, drive changes in the social, political, cultural, religious, ideological and legal superstructure. It is often identified with Marxism, but, although the two overlap, it has an independent history and is not necessarily driven by class dialectics. For examples and counter-arguments, see 10. Technological/Economic Determinism and 11. Counterarguments in Economics Details.

Technology: see 3. Technology in Details.

Theory of generations: that a distinctive consciousness and perspective is shared by members of the same generation, or cohort, of young people reaching maturity at the same time in response to the major political, cultural and historical events of their youth, which, in turn, shapes how they respond to later events and become agents of history themselves. Karl Mannheim, Arthur M. Schlesinger, Jr., William Strauss and Neil Howe. See 35. American Generational Cycles in American History Details.

Totemism: among hunter-gathering groups, the veneration of an animal or plant as the symbolic or spiritual ancestor or emblem of a group, clan or tribe. The modern use of an animal or plant (e.g., an eagle, bear, lion, dove, lily, rose or maple leaf) as an emblem to represent a kingdom, dynasty, nation-state, corporation, school or sports team is a vestige of this tribal expression.

Tribalism: the sense of unity, common identity and loyalty among members of a tribal group. Hunter-gatherer tribes are usually described as open, cooperative and egalitarian, but are also associated with ethnocentrism, xenophobia, territoriality and inter-tribal violence. The level of violence among tribal groups is the subject of debate. See Male coalitional violence, Narcissism of small differences, Nesting instinct and Territoriality in Anthropology Concepts and 12. Violence and Human Nature (the Hobbes-Rousseau Dichotomy) in Anthropology Details.

Underclass: see Lumpen proletariat in Concepts and 21. Social Classes in Details.

Urbanization: see 15. Urbanization in American History Details and Gunther Barth, Mike Davis, Carl Degler, Lewis Mumford in Selected References.

Utilitarianism: the doctrine that public policies should seek to achieve the greatest happiness, or the least harm, for the greatest number of people. Jeremy Bentham and John Stuart Mill. See 6. John Stuart Mill/Utilitarianism in Details.

Variety/plasticity of human cultures: the wide range of cultural practices and behaviors in pre-literate societies, which anthropologists have documented and which attest to the adaptability and diversity of human cultures, as opposed to linear, monistic theories of biological or material determinism. Ruth Benedict, Franz Boas, Margaret Mead. See Cultural relativity in Concepts and Max Weber in Quotations.

Virtual communities: those that are created through Internet technology and electronic social media. According to Marshall McLuhan, modern technology has created a global village in which print culture has been superseded by the electronic media of an oral, tribal culture, which is characterized by its collective identity, electronic interdependence and shared sense of community. The 18th Century "republic of letters" was the first virtual, international community. See Public Sphere in Concepts; 23. Marshall McLuhan and 24. Information Technology in Details and 27. 18th Century Enlightenment in Philosophy/Religion Details.

Westernization: the absorption of modern, secular, commercial and individualistic values by traditional, agrarian, pre-industrial societies.

Winner-take-all societies: societies in which disproportionately high rewards are given to the very elite in the corporate, financial, legal, entertainment and sports worlds; the hyper-concentration of wealth and prestige, with the very, very few getting very, very much and the many getting relatively little. Robert Frank, Jacob Hacker and Paul Pierson, Paul Krugman, Kevin Phillips, Thomas Piketty, Joseph Stiglitz. See Economic inequality/concentration of wealth and Great Gatsby curve in Concepts and 22. Social Mobility in Details.

Working class: E. P. Thompson, David Montgomery. See 21. Social Classes in Details.

Xenocentrism/xenophilia: valuing other cultures more highly than one's own.

Xenophobia: the fear and/or hatred of outsiders and other cultures. See Ethnocentrism in Concepts.

Yuppies: young, urban professionals. David Brooks.

QUOTATIONS:

- *Societies are not made of sticks and stones, but of men whose individual characters, by turning the scale one way or another, determine the direction of the whole.* -- Plato.

- *The whole must of necessity be prior to the part.* -- Aristotle.

- *During the time men live without a common power to keep them all in awe, they are in that condition which is called war; and such a war as is of every man against every man. . . . The life of man* [in a state of nature is] *solitary, poor, nasty, brutish, and short.* -- Thomas Hobbes.

- *The first man who, having fenced in a piece of land, said "This is mine," and found people naïve enough to believe him, that man was the true founder of civil society. From how many crimes, wars, and murders, from how many horrors and misfortunes might not any one have saved mankind, by pulling up the stakes.* -- Jean-Jacques Rousseau.

- *The history of all hitherto existing society is the history of class struggles.* -- Karl Marx.

- *It is not the consciousness of men that determines their existence, but on the contrary, their social existence determines their consciousness.* -- Marx.

- *"Culture" is a finite segment of the meaningless infinity of the world process, a segment on which human beings confer meaning and significance. . . . The transcendental presupposition of every cultural science lies not in our finding a certain culture or any "culture" in general to be valuable but rather in the fact that we are cultural beings, endowed with the capacity and the will to take a deliberate attitude toward the world and to lend it significance.* -- Max Weber.

- *There is no absolutely "objective" scientific analysis of culture . . . All knowledge of cultural reality . . . is always knowledge from particular points of view.* -- Weber.

- *Today, we are faced with the preeminent fact that, if civilization is to survive, we must cultivate the science of human relationships -- the ability of all peoples, of all kinds, to live together and work together, in the same world, at peace.* -- Franklin Roosevelt.

- *There is no such thing as society: there are individual men and women, and there are families.* -- Margaret Thatcher.

- *For most of the past two centuries, the Left has been identified with science and against obscurantism; we have believed that rational thought and the fearless analysis of objective reality (both natural and social) are incisive tools for combating the mystifications promoted by the powerful -- not to mention being desirable human ends in their own right. The recent turn of many "progressive" or "leftist" academic humanists and social scientists toward one or another form of epistemic relativism betrays this worthy heritage and undermines the already fragile prospects for progressive social critique. Theorizing about "the social construction of reality" won't help us find an effective treatment for AIDS or devise strategies for preventing global warming. Nor can we combat false ideas in history, sociology, economics and politics if we reject the notions of truth and falsity.* -- Alan Sokal.

SOCIOLOGY DETAILS: (1) Sociology, (2) Culture, (3) Technology, (4) Auguste Comte/Positivism, (5) Alexis de Tocqueville, (6) John Stuart Mill/Utilitarianism, (7) Karl Marx/Dialectical Materialism, (8) Economic/Technological Determinism, (9) Cultural Materialism, (10) Lester Ward, (11) Ferdinand Tönnies, (12) Thorstein Veblen, (13) Emile Durkheim, (14) Max Weber, (15) Elites/Oligarchies, (16) Mass Society, (17) Erich Fromm, (18) Structural Functionalism, (19) Conflict Theory, (20) Class Structure, (21) Social Classes in the United States, (22) Social Mobility, (23) Marshall McLuhan and (24) Information Technology/Metaphor of the Machine.

1. **Sociology** is the study of human society and social behavior. It applies scientific methods to the study of human behavior and

focuses on the dynamics and behavior patterns of social groups and institutions. Sociology is based on the assumption that human behavior is inherently relational, that is, that it is shaped and conditioned by its social environment. Since society is "an intricate web of multiple relations between individuals" (George Simmel), and, since all individuals belong to social groups (family, neighborhood, peers, school, church, business, community, country), their behavior is shaped and conditioned by those groups. "The individual mind can exist only in relation to other minds with shared meanings" (George Herbert Mead), or, to paraphrase Erich Fromm, the psychic structure as defined by the social structure. Auguste Comte, Emile Durkheim, Karl Marx, Herbert Spencer, Alexis de Tocqueville, Lester Ward, Max Weber.

2. **Culture** is a set of learned and shared behaviors, norms, values, assumptions, beliefs, ideals, mores, folkways, customs, traditions, social roles, symbols, language, laws and institutions that are held in common by a particular social group.

3. **Technology** is the use of organized knowledge, tools, machines, techniques and methods for practical purposes.

4. **Auguste Comte** (1798-1857)/**Positivism** is a school of thought that views science as the definitive source of knowledge, in which truth is derived from the application of scientific methods and empirical techniques to all natural phenomena, including human social behavior. It (1) uses quantitative methodologies, (2) seeks to be objective and value-neutral and (3) attempts to avoid both metaphysical speculation and the examination of internal or introspective mental states that cannot be observed directly by the senses and measured objectively (although many internal mental states can now be observed directly and in real time by using the magnetic resonance imaging [MRI] of cognitive and behavioral neuroscience). Positivist studies have been criticized for failing to account for observer bias, for discounting non-quantifiable observations and for ignoring internal mental states and the non-material aspects of human experience. See Religion of humanity in Philosophy/Religion Concepts.

5. **Alexis de Tocqueville** (1805-1859): See 3. Alexis de Tocqueville in American History Details.

6. **John Stuart Mill** (1806-1873)/**Utilitarianism** is the philosophy that (1) every action should be judged by its utility, that is, whether it increases happiness, usefulness and satisfaction, and (2) social policies should seek to achieve the greatest happiness, or the least harm, for the greatest number of people (an idea that was first advanced by Jeremy Bentham). Mill was an advocate of Comte's "religion of humanity" (i.e., secular humanism) and was an early supporter of women's rights and an opponent of slavery. He believed that each individual has the right to act as he or she wants, as long as those actions do not harm others. He maintained that poverty is caused by social forces, not character flaws.

7. **Karl Marx** (1818-1883)/**Dialectical Materialism** is an economic, social and political philosophy which asserts that:
   1) Societies change in dialectical stages because of class conflict, i.e., the struggle between socio-economic classes (for example, between the landed aristocracy and the urban bourgeoisie, and between the bourgeoisie and the industrial proletariat).
   2) The mode of production consists of (a) the factors of production (land and other natural resources, labor, capital and technology) and (b) the (social) relations of production (e.g., slavery, feudalism, capitalism).
   3) Changes in the economic/technological base or substructure drive changes in the superstructure (that is, art, ideology and religion, and social, cultural, political and legal institutions).
   4) The dictatorship of the bourgeoisie (the capitalist class) will inevitably be destroyed by its internal contractions and ever greater financial crises, and will be replaced by the dictatorship of the proletariat (the working classes), which will lead, eventually, to a classless, stateless society of pure communism.

   It is also associated with the following concepts:
   5) The alienation of the laborer from the product of his or her labor (the worker becomes an appendage of the machine).
   6) Commodification and the fetishism of commodities (*q.v.* in Concepts).
   7) Cultural hegemony (*q.v.* in Concepts).

Marxist theory is identified with economic/technological determinism but it is not coterminous with it. It has informed cultural materialism and various forms of Neo-Marxism, including

Marxist humanism, which is more democratic, evolutionary and less deterministic than orthodox Marxism. Karl Marx, Friedrich Engels; Louis Althusser, Antonio Gramsci.

8. **Economic/Technological Determinism** is the theory that changes in the economic/technological base, or substructure, drive changes in the superstructure (art, ideology, religion and social, cultural, political and legal institutions). It is often identified with Marxism, but, although the two overlap, it has an independent history and is not necessarily driven by class dialectics. **The theory of differential social change, or cultural lag** (W. F. Ogburn in Stow Persons), is a corollary of economic/technological determinism that asserts that various components of the superstructure change at varying rates and lag behind changes in the economic/technological base. For examples and counterarguments see 10. Economic/Technological Determinism and 11. Counterarguments in Economics Details.

9. **Cultural Materialism** is a synthesis of Neo-Marxism and Neo-Freudianism, according to which the material culture, or base, consists not only of economic/productive modes and relationships but also sexual/reproductive ones. It originated in the Frankfurt School of social theory, which was founded in the 1920s and which, in the face of European totalitarianism, sought to modify classical Marxism by shifting away from its positivism, materialism, and determinism.

Cultural materialism (1) incorporates insights from Immanuel Kant, G. W. F. Hegel, Karl Marx, Max Weber (rational-legal-bureaucratic domination), and Sigmund Freud (the repression and irrationality inherent in rationalized, technocratic society); (2) modifies the one-to-one relationship between the base and the superstructure; (3) recognizes the role of human agency, reflexivity and critical awareness in the power of social transformation; (4) views consciousness as conditioned, rather than determined, by the social structure, and (5) focuses on class, politics, race and gender and marginalized groups. Cultural materialism has informed historical studies (the Annales School and the New Social/Cultural history, for example), cultural studies, critical theory, feminism, and studies of mass culture, authoritarianism and the rise of totalitarianism. Theodor Adorno, Walter Benjamin, Sigmund

Freud, Erich Fromm, Jürgen Habermas, Stuart Hall, Marvin Harris, Max Horkheimer, Herbert Marcuse, Karl Marx, E. P. Thompson, Raymond Williams. See Cultural hegemony versus Post-hegemonic synthesis in Concepts.

10. **Lester Ward** (1841-1931) proposed that **biological ("genetic") evolution**, which is blind and wasteful, has been replaced by purposeful, **social ("telic") evolution**, in which humans can collectively plan and control their own destinies, reform society and end social injustice through collective action and the positive liberal state. See 26. Reform Darwinism in American History Details, Group-level selection in Anthropology Concepts and 5. Social Intelligence/Social Brain Hypothesis in Anthropology Details.

11. **Ferdinand Tönnies** (1855-1936) developed the dichotomous social categories of: (1) *Gemeinschaft* **("community")**, which describes the social organization that was characteristic of pre-industrial societies, which were homogenous and based on a shared sense of community, personal relationships, cooperation, traditional values, mutual obligations and ascribed status and (2) *Gesellschaft* **("society")**, which describes the social organization that is characteristic of modern, industrialized societies, which are heterogeneous and based on competitive, impersonal relationships, the specialization and division of labor, individual self-interest and achieved status. See Cash nexus in Concepts and Emile Durkheim's distinction between mechanical and organic solidarity in 13. Details.

12. **Thorstein Veblen** (1857-1929) proposed that wealth is not a badge of social superiority, nor proof of the elect nor an emblem of the "fittest," as Calvinists and Social Darwinists asserted, but rather that the leisure class is pecuniary, avaricious and predatory and driven by invidious distinctions to conspicuous consumption and conspicuous waste. See 26. Reform Darwinism in American History Details.

13. **Emile Durkheim** (1858-1917) was one of the founders of sociology and a proponent of scientific rationalism. He developed the concepts of (1) *anomie* (*q.v.* in Concepts) and (2) healthy versus pathological cultures. He proposed that seemingly personal

and individual acts are conditioned by the social context in which they occur; for example, suicide rates are higher in Protestant than in Roman Catholic cultures because the former have less social cohesion and value individual autonomy and self-determination. Durkheim developed and contrasted the social categories of **mechanical solidarity**, which was characteristic of pre-industrial societies, in which social cohesion was derived from a homogenous population with similar backgrounds who performed similar rituals and similar tasks; with **organic solidarity**, which is characteristic of modern, industrial societies, in which social bonds are derived from the economic interdependence and reliance members with diverse interests and specialized tasks must place on each other. See Ferdinand Tönnies's distinctions between *Gemeinschaft* and *Gesellschaft* in 11. Details.

14. **Max Weber** (1864-1920) was one of the founders of sociology, who:
    1) Stressed the importance of culture, religion and ideas over economic and material conditions, and proposed that the former are the driving force in history; that, for example, a religious ideology (in this case, the Protestant ethic of industry and frugality) laid the foundation for an economic system (capitalism).
    2) Developed a system to define social stratification based on education, status, prestige and power, as well as on class. His four-class model includes the upper class, the white collar/professional class, the petite bourgeoisie and the working class.
    3) Identified the rationalization and bureaucratization of modern society, which is characterized by its large scale, hierarchical structure, specialization and division of labor, experts, written rules and regulations and impersonality and the dictatorship of the bureaucracy.
    4) Defined and classified political leadership and authority as (a) charismatic, (b) traditional and (c) rational-legal.
    5) Identified and defined four personality types: (a) goal-rational, (b) value-rational, (c) emotion-rational, and (d) traditional (custom/habit-driven).
    6) Identified the intelligentsia as a social category of professional experts and specialists.

7) Developed the concepts of *charisma* (the "gift of grace") and *verstehen* ("insight").

8) Borrowed Friedrich Schiller's term "disenchantment" to describe the loss of magic, mystery, spirituality and "sublime values" in modern, rational, secular, bureaucratic society.

15. **Elites/Oligarchies** are the subject of a school of thought that asserts that social and political systems are controlled by elites, who maintain their power through force, manipulation, ideology, the need for united action against a perceived enemy and the apathy of rank-and-file members. According to Robert Michels' **"iron law of oligarchy,"** every organization is ruled by an elite, and representative democracy is merely a façade to legitimize a particular elite in which the "dominion of the elected over the electors" is inevitable and cannot be prevented. In the United States, according to C. Wright Mills, the power elite consist of an interlocking political, economic, academic, military and media directorate, who share a common world view and move easily between institutions. Jane Mayer, Robert Michels, C. Wright Mills, Vilfredo Pareto. See Cultural hegemony, Military-industrial-university-media complex and Power elite in Concepts.

16. **Mass Society** is the subject of a school of thought that is critical of modern society for its atomistic "individualism," weak communal ties, *anomie*, alienation, ignorance, passivity, mindless conformity, cultural mediocrity, materialism, "crowd psychology" and manipulation by, and receptivity to, demagogues and mass movements. Emile Durkheim, Erich Fromm, Salvador Giner, Gustave Le Bon, C. Wright Mills, José Ortega y Gasset, Alexis de Tocqueville.

17. **Erich Fromm** (1900-1980) proposed, in *Escape from Freedom* (1941), that the freedom of modern man from the web of medieval restrictions and the customs and traditions of pre-industrial societies has created a sense of alienation, isolation, *anomie* and anxiety, which causes some to escape or abandon their freedom by seeking the purposefulness, emotional certainty and security, provided by totalitarian groups and religious movements. See True Believers in Political Science Concepts.

18. **Structural Functionalism** is a school of sociological thought that (1) proposes that society is a system of social structures, institutions, patterns, functions and shared ways of thinking (norms, values, customs and traditions) that regulate social relationships and provide a stable, cohesive and, mostly, harmonious way of achieving its goals and meeting the needs of its members; (2) offers the organic analogy of society as a complex system whose parts work together to promote the coherence and stability of the whole; (3) focuses on social roles and advocates the socialization, adaptation and adjustment of the individual to the larger organism; (4) allows that the solidarity and stability of the whole is, sometimes, but necessarily, achieved at the expense of the subordination and inequality of some of its parts. Talcott Parsons, Robert Merton. See Sociological assumption in Concepts.

19. **Conflict Theory** is a school of sociological thought that stands in opposition to structural functionalism's paradigm of harmony and consensus. Conflict theory (1) focuses on inequality and power differentials in social structures, which are created through conflict and the "unequal distribution of power and resources in society"; (2) analyzes cultural hegemony, ideology and other means by which power elites seek to repress the un-empowered, maintain social control and perpetuate the status quo and (3) is informed by feminist, post-structural and postcolonial theories. Lewis Coser, Ralf Dahrendorf, James Madison, Karl Marx, C. Wright Mills. See 7. Karl Marx/Dialectical Materialism in Details; 5. Conflict Schools of American Historiography and 7. Counterarguments to American Exceptionalism in American History Details and 4. Post-structuralism in Literary Concepts Details. James Harrington, Benjamin Franklin, Jean- Jacques Rousseau, Thomas Jefferson, James Madison, Abraham Lincoln and Karl Marx in Economics Quotations.

20. **Class Structure** is a set of hierarchical categories that is used to define social stratification and is based on social, economic and other criteria, usually wealth and income, but also hereditary rank, the relationship to the means of production (David Ricardo, Karl Marx) and education, status, prestige and power (Max Weber). The three-strata model divides society into the working class, middle class and upper class. Weber's four-class model includes the upper class, the white collar/professional class, the petite

bourgeoisie and the working class. Fred Block, William Domhoff, Herbert Gutman, Michael Harrington, Lewis Lapham, James Madison, Karl Marx, Kevin Phillips, David Ricardo, E. P. Thompson, Max Weber. Issues involving class and gender are the focus of feminist critical theory and are discussed by Dorothy Cobble, Judith Newton, Deborah Rosenfelt and Beverly Skeggs.

21. **Social Classes in the United States**, according to one model, consist of:
    1) The **upper class**: the top 1% of the population, which is composed of top-level executives, financiers, entrepreneurs, heirs and celebrities, some of whom received an Ivy League education.
    2) The **upper-middle class**: 15% of the population, which is composed of salaried professionals and middle-level managers, many of whom possess graduate degrees.
    3) The **lower-middle class**: 30% of the population, which is composed of semi-professionals, lower-level managers and supervisors, teachers, small businessmen and skilled craftsmen, many of whom have some college education.
    4) The **working class**: 30% of the population, which is composed of clerical and blue-collar workers, most of whom have a high school education.
    5) The **working poor**: 12% of the population, which is composed of service, low-end clerical and blue-collar workers, most of whom have some high school education.
    6) The **underclass**: 12% of the population, who have limited or no participation in the formal economy, but some participation in the informal or underground economy and often depend on governmental assistance.
    W. Lloyd Warner, Dennis Gilbert.

22. **Social Mobility** is the upward and downward movement of individuals, families and groups from one socioeconomic stratum to another. In the United States:
    1) 60-70% of the business elite in 19th Century were born into families in the upper or upper-middle classes.
    2) Currently, approximately 60% of those in the upper fifth of income were born into families in the upper two fifths of income.

3) Only 8% of those born into families in the lower fifth of income rose to the top fifth in income.

Markus Jantti, Alan Krueger, C. Wright Mills in Richard Hofstadter, Thomas Piketty, Gary Solon, Joseph Stiglitz, David Zimmerman. See *Disembourgeoisment*, Economic inequality, *Embourgeoisment*, Downward mobility and Great Gatsby curve in Concepts.

23. **Marshall McLuhan** (1911-1980) proposed that:
   1) The medium is the message; that is, that the medium by which information is conveyed is as important as the content that it conveys, and that the evolution of communications technology has affected both human cognition and social organization. For example, although it has no inherent content, the electric light bulb has exercised a profound influence over society. McLuhan's thesis is challenged by Henry David Thoreau's assertion that inventions such as the electrical telegraph are but "an improved means to an unimproved end."
   2) Technology has created a global village in which the individualism, fragmentation and linear logic of the "hot" print culture has been superseded by the "cool" electronic media of an oral, tribal culture, which is characterized by its collective identity, electronic interdependence and shared sense of community.
   3) "Hot" media (such as books and movies), which are high definition and low participation (since they demand attention but engage only one sense) have been displaced by "cool" media (such as television), which are low definition and high participation (since they demand conscious participation).

McLuhan also developed the concepts of:
   4) The typographical man ("schizophrenia may be a necessary consequence of literacy").
   5) The world-wide web (the global electronic brain, as it were).
   6) The phrase "tune in, turn on and drop out."

See Marshall McLuhan in Art Quotations and Literary Concepts Quotations.

24. **Information Technology/Metaphor of the Machine** is the dominant paradigm of modern society, in which the machine symbolizes society's total organization and rationalization, the total integration of the parts into the whole and the relentless

application of reason to the end of productivity. In this model, the individual is seen in functional terms, not as end in itself, and industrial civilization is seen to embody a transformation of scale, a style of thought and an ethos of more, further, faster, richer, quicker.

The obsession with speed, order and rationality, which is characteristic of industrial society, has reached its apotheosis in the Information Age of computer technology and systems analysis. Henry Adams' 19th Century metaphor of the machine and his principle of acceleration have been validated by the exponential growth of electronic-based information systems during the last fifty years in which simple binary logic is used to process information at nanosecond speeds. This has enabled small lap-top boxes and hand-held personal devices to provide sophisticated data analysis, desktop publishing, interactive social media and instantaneous access to global databases containing the subtotal of virtually all recorded human experience (down to the genetic level) through a pervasive electronic nexus embracing nearly every aspect of human life and social structure.

According to one school of thought, computer technology has fostered the breakdown of social and political hierarchies and has led to the decentralization of power. Internet technology and social media have created peer-to-peer networks and virtual communities, which promote participatory government, electronic interdependence, a communal economy and a sense of shared humanity (John Naisbitt). This global consciousness renders nation-states less relevant and challenges their scope and power. On the other hand, the centralization and consolidation of information in vast, global networks and "cloud" databases facilitates and deepens the commercial and governmental surveillance of personal online transactions and communications and makes it easier for nation-states and corporations to observe and track the intimate details of the lives of nearly every citizen on the globe. Henry Adams, Jacques Ellul , James Gleick, Marshall McLuhan, Lewis Mumford, John Naisbitt, Dennis Strong, F. W. Taylor, William Tilden, Alvin Toffler, Max Weber. See Mechanomorphism in Philosophy/Religion Concepts.

SELECTED REFERENCES

Aaron, Daniel. *Men of Good Hope: A Story of American Progressives.* Oxford: Oxford University Press, 1961.

Adams, Henry. *The Education of Henry Adams.* Boston: Houghton Mifflin Company, 1918.

Adams, James Truslow. *The Founding of New England.* Boston: Little, Brown and Company, 1921.

Adorno, Theodor, et al. *The Authoritarian Personality.* New York: Harper and Brothers, 1950.

Alexander, June Granatir. *Daily Life in Immigrant America, 1870-1920.* Chicago: Ivan R. Dee, 2007.

Anderson, Terry. *The Movement and the Sixties.* New York: Oxford University Press, 1995.

Aptheker, Herbert. *American Negro Slave Revolts.* New York: International Publishers, 1943.

Armstrong, Karen. *The Battle for God: A History of Fundamentalism.* New York: Knopf, 2000.

Bakan, Joel. *The Corporation: The Pathological Pursuit of Profit and Power.* New York: Simon and Schuster, 2005.

Baptist, Edward. *The Half Has Never Been Told: Slavery and the Making of American Capitalism.* New York: Basic Books, 2014

Barry, John M. *Roger Williams and the Creation of the American Soul: Church, State and the Birth of Liberty.* New York: Viking, 2012.

Barth, Gunther. *City People: The Rise of Modern City Culture in Nineteenth-Century America.* New York: Oxford University Press, 1980.

Beard, Charles and Mary. *The Rise of American Civilization.* New York: The Macmillan Company, 1930.

Becker, Carl. *The Heavenly City of the Eighteenth Century Philosophers.* New Haven: Yale University Press, 1932.

Bell, Daniel. *The End of Ideology.* New York: The Free Press, 1962.

_____, ed. *The Radical Right.* Garden City, New York: Doubleday and Company, 1963.

Bellah, Robert. *Broken Covenant: American Civil Religion in a Time of Trial.* Chicago: University of Chicago Press, 1992.

Benedict, Ruth. *Patterns of Culture.* Boston: Houghton Mifflin, 1934.

Benson, Lee. *The Concept of Jacksonian Democracy: New York as a Test Case.* Princeton, New Jersey: Princeton University Press, 1961.

Bentley, Michael, ed. *Companion to Historiography.* London: Routledge Press, 1997.

Berle, Adoph and Gardiner Means. *The Modern Corporation and Private Property.* New York: The Macmillan Company, 1933.

Berlin, Ira. *The Making of African America: The Four Great Migrations.* New York: Viking Penguin, 2010.

Bernstein, Barton, ed. *Towards a New Past: Dissenting Essays in American History.* New York: Random House, 1967.

Blassingame, John. *The Slave Community: Plantation Life in the Antebellum South.* New York: Oxford University Press, 1972.

Boorstin, Daniel. *The Lost World of Thomas Jefferson.* New York: Henry Holt and Co., 1948.

Bourke, John Gregory. *Scatologic Rites of All Nations.* Washington, D. C. 1891.

Branch, Taylor. *Parting of the Waters: America in the King Years, 1954-1963.* New York: Simon and Schuster, 1988.

Bridges, William. "Family Patterns and Social Values in America, 1825-1875." *American Quarterly.* XVII (Spring, 1965): 3-11.

Brinton, Crane. *The Anatomy of Revolution.* New York: Prentice-Hall, 1938.

Brown, Harrison. *The Challenge of Man's Future.* New York: Viking, 1954.

Brown, Norman O. *Life Against Death: The Psychoanalytical Meaning of History.* New York: Alfred A. Knopf, 1959.

Bryan, Frank *Real Democracy: The New England Town Meeting and How It Works.* Chicago: University of Chicago Press, 2004.

Bryce, James. *The American Commonwealth.* New York: Macmillan, 1893.

Calvin, William. *The Ascent of Mind: Ice Age Climates and the Evolution of Intelligence.* New York: Bantam Books, 1990.

Campbell, Joseph and Bill Moyers. *The Power of Myth.* New York: Doubleday, 1988.

Carr, E. H. *What is History?* Cambridge: Cambridge University Press, 1961.

Cavalli-Sforza, Luigi and Francesco Cavalli-Sforza. *The Great Human Diasporas: The History of Diversity and Evolution.* Reading, Massachusetts: Perseus Books, 1995.

Chase, Richard. *The American Novel and Its Tradition.* New York: Anchor Books, 1957.

Chernow, Ron. *Alexander Hamilton.* New York: Penguin Books, 2004.

Cobble, Dorothy Sue. *Dishing It Out: Waitresses and their Unions in the Twentieth Century.* Urbana: University of Illinois, 1991.

Cohen, Lizabeth. *Making a New Deal: Industrial Workers in Chicago, 1919-1939.* Cambridge: Cambridge University Press, 1990.

Conner, Clifford. *A People's History of Science: Miners, Midwives, and "Low Mechanicks."* New York: Nation Books, 2005.

Conniff, Richard. *The Natural History of the Rich: A Field Guide.* New York: W. W. Norton and Company, 2002.

Conzen, Michael, ed. *The Making of the American Landscape.* New York: Routledge, 1990.

Cott, Nancy. *Bonds of Womanhood: 'Woman's Sphere' in New England, 1780-1835.* New Haven: Yale University Press, 1977.

Cronin, William. *Changes in the Land: Indians, Colonists, and the Ecology of New England.* New York: Hill and Wang, 1983.

Crossan, John Dominic. *The Historical Jesus: The Life of a Mediterranean Jewish Peasant.* New York: HarperCollins, 1992.

Cuddon, J. A. *A Dictionary of Literary Terms and Literary Theory.* Cambridge: Basil Blackwell, 1991.

Cunliffe, Barry, ed. *The Oxford Illustrated History of Prehistoric Europe.* Oxford: Oxford University Press, 1994.

Dabbs, James McBride and Mary Goodwin Dabbs. *Heroes, Rogues and Lovers: Testosterone and Behavior.* New York: McGraw-Hill, 2000.

Daniels, Roger. *Coming to America.* New York: HarperCollins, 1990.

Davis, Mike. *Dead Cities and Other Tales.* New York: The New Press, 2002.

Degler, Carl. *Out of Our Past: The Forces that Shaped Modern America.* New York: Harper and Row, 1959.

D'Emilio J. and E. B. Freedman. *Intimate Matters: A History of Sexuality in America.* New York: Harper and Row, 1988.

Diamond, Jared. *The Third Chimpanzee: The Evolution and Future of the Human Animal.* New York: HarperCollins, 1992.

_____. *Guns, Germs, and Steel: The Fates of Human Societies*. New York: W. W. Norton, 1998.

Donald, David. *Lincoln Reconsidered: Essays on the Civil War Era*. New York: Vintage Books, 1961.

Douglass, Frederick. *Narrative of the Life of Frederick Douglas*. 1845

Du Bois, W. E. B. *The Souls of Black Folk*. New York: New American Library Classics, 1995.

Durkheim, Emile. *Emile Durkheim: Selected Writings*. Ed. Anthony Giddens. London: Cambridge University Press, 1972.

Ehrich, Eugene. T*he Harper Dictionary of Foreign Terms*. New York: Harper and Row, 1990.

Ehrlich, Paul. *The Population Bomb*. New York: Ballantine Books, 1972.

Eliot, T. S. *The Wasteland and Other Poems*. New York: Harcourt, Brace and World, Inc., 1930.

Elkins, Stanley. *Slavery: A Problem in American Institutional and Intellectual Life*. Chicago: University of Chicago Press, 1959.

Ellul, Jacques. *The Technological Society*. New York: Alfred Knopf, 1967.

Emerson, Ralph Waldo. *The Heart of Emerson's Journals*. Ed. Bliss Perry. Boston: Houghton Mifflin Company, 1926.

_____. *The Selected Writings of Ralph Waldo Emerson*. Ed. Brooks Atkinson. New York: The Modern Library, 1940.

Epstein, Barbara. *Politics of Domesticity: Women, Evangelism, and Temperance in Nineteenth Century America*. Middletown, Connecticut: Wesleyan University Press, 1981.

Erikson, Erik. *Childhood and Society*. New York: W.W. Norton, 1963.

Fagan, Brian. *People of the Earth: An Introduction to World Pre-History*. Boston: Little and Brown, 1977.

Fenn, Elizabeth. *Encounters at the Heart of the World: A History of the Mandan People*. New York: Hill and Wang, 2014.

Ferguson, Niall. *Colossus: The Rise and Fall of the American Empire*. New York: Penguin Group, 2004.

Ferris, Timothy. *The Whole Shebang: A State-of-the-Universe(s) Report*. New York: Simon and Schuster, 1997.

Fields, R. Douglas. *Why We Snap: Understanding the Rage Circuit in Your Brain*. New York: Dutton, 2016.

Fischer, David Hackett. *Albion's Seed: Four British Folkways*. New York: Oxford University Press, 1989.

Fisher, Helen. *The Sex Contract: The Evolution of Human Behavior.* New York: William Morrow and Company, 1982.

Foner, Eric. *Reconstruction: America's Unfinished Revolution, 1863–1877.* New York: Harper and Row, 1988.

Franklin, Benjamin. *The Autobiography of Benjamin Franklin.* Ed. Max Farrand. Berkeley: University of California Press, 1949.

Franklin, John Hope. *From Slavery to Freedom: A History of Negro Americans.* New York: Alfred Knopf, 1966.

Freud, Sigmund. *The Standard Edition of the Complete Psychological Works of Sigmund Freud.* Ed. and trans. James Strachey. London: The Hogarth Press and the Institute of Psychoanalysis, 1953-1966.

Fromm, Erich. *Escape from Freedom.* New York: Holt, Rinehart and Winston, 1941.

Foner, Eric, *Free Soil, Free Labor, Free Men: The Ideology of the Republican Party Before the Civil War.* New York: Oxford University Press, 1995

Gaddis, John Lewis. *The United States and the Origins of the Cold War, 1941-1947.* New York: Columbia University Press, 1972.

Galbraith, John Kenneth. *American Capitalism, The Concept of Countervailing Power.* Boston: Houghton Mifflin, 1952.

_____. *The Affluent Society.* Boston: Houghton Mifflin, 1958.

Gallagher, Catherine and Stephen Greenblatt. *Practicing New Historicism.* Chicago: University of Chicago Press, 2001.

Gay, Peter. *The Enlightenment: The Rise of Modern Paganism.* New York: W. W. Norton, 1995.

Geertz, Clifford. *The Interpretation of Cultures.* New York: Basic Books, 1973.

Genovese, Eugene. *The Political Economy of Slavery: Studies in the Economy and Society of Slave South.* New York: Vintage, 1965.

_____. *Roll Jordan, Roll: The World the Slaves Made.* New York: Pantheon Books, 1974.

George, Henry. *Progress and Poverty.* New York: Random House, 1879.

Gilbert, Felix. *The Beginnings of American Foreign Policy: To the Farewell Address.* New York: Harper and Row, 1965.

Gleick, James. *Isaac Newton.* New York: Pantheon Books, 2003.

_____. *The Information: A History, A Theory, A Flood.* New York: Pantheon, 2011.

Goldman, Eric. *Rendezvous with Destiny: A History of Modern American Reform.* New York: Alfred A. Knopf, 1952.

Gombrich, E. H. *The Story of Art.* New York: Phaidon, 1966.

Goodwyn, Lawrence. *The Populist Movement: A Short History of the Agrarian Revolt in America.* Oxford: Oxford University Press, 1978.

Gordon, Linda. *Woman's Body, Woman's Right: Birth Control in America.* New York: Penguin, 1977.

Gorer, Geoffrey. *The American People: A Study in National Character.* New York: W.W. Norton and Co., 1964.

Grandin, Greg. *The Empire of Necessity: Slavery, Freedom, and Deception in the New World.* New York: Henry Holt and Company, 2014.

Greider, William. *One World, Ready or Not: The Manic Logic of Global Capitalism.* New York: Simon and Schuster, 1997.

Greenberg, Amy. *Wicked War: Polk, Clay, Lincoln and the 1846 U. S. Invasion of Mexico.* New York: Alfred A. Knopf, 2012.

Gutman, Herbert G. *The Black Family in Slavery and Freedom, 1750-1925.* New York: Vintage, 1976.

Hahn, Steven. *A Nation Under Our Feet: Black Political Struggles in the Rural South from Slavery to the Great Migration.* Cambridge: Belknap Press, 2005.

Hall, Calvin S. *A Primer of Freudian Psychology.* New York: Signet, 1955.

Hallett, Hilary A. *Go West, Young Women!: The Rise of Early Hollywood.* Berkeley: University of California Press, 2013.

Handlin, Oscar. *The Uprooted: The Epic Story of the Great Migrations that Made the American People.* Boston: Little, Brown and Company, 1973.

Harrington, Michael. *The Other America.* New York: Penguin, 1966.

Harris, Marvin. *Our Kind: Who We Are, Where We Came From, Where We Are Going.* New York: Harper and Row, 1989.

Hartz, Louis. *The Liberal Tradition in America.* New York: Harcourt, Brace and World, 1955.

Hawley, Amos. *Human Ecology: A Theoretical Essay.* Chicago: University of Chicago Press, 1986.

Hays, Samuel P. *The Response to Industrialism, 1885-1914.* Chicago: University of Chicago Press, 1957.

Heilbroner, Robert. *The Worldly Philosophers: The Lives, Times and Ideas of the Great Economic Thinkers.* New York: Simon and Schuster, 1961.

Hicks, John. *The Populist Revolt.* University of Minnesota Press, 1931.

Higham, John. *Strangers in the Land: Patterns of American Nativism, 1860-1925*. New Brunswick, New Jersey: Rutgers University Press, 1955.

Hirsch, E. D., Jr. *Cultural Literacy: What Every American Needs to Know*. Boston: Houghton Mifflin Company, 2002.

Hofstadter, Richard. *The American Political Tradition and the Men Who Made It*. New York: New York: Alfred A. Knopf, 1948.

_____. *The Age of Reform: From Bryan to F.D.R.* New York: Alfred A. Knopf and Random House, 1955.

_____. *Social Darwinism in American Thought*. Boston: Beacon Street Press, 1955.

Horney, Karen. *The Neurotic Personality of Our Time*. New York: W. W. Norton, 1937.

Hulbert, Ann. *Raising America: Experts, Parents and a Century of Advice About Children*. New York: Alfred Knopf, 2003.

Hunt, Lynn, ed. *The New Culture History*. Berkeley: University of California Press, 1989.

Israel, Jonathan. *Democratic Enlightenment: Philosophy, Revolution, and Human Rights 1750-1790*. Oxford: Oxford University Press, 2011.

Jackson, Kenneth. *The Crabgrass Frontier: The Suburbanization of the United States*. Oxford: Oxford University Press, 1985.

Jacobs, Wilbur. *Dispossessing the American Indian: Indians and Whites on the Colonial Frontier*. New York: Scribner and Sons, 1972.

Jefferson, Thomas. *The Life and Selected Writings of Thomas Jefferson*. Ed. Adrienne Koch and William Peden. New York: Random House, 1944.

Johannsen, Robert. *To the Halls of Montezuma: The Mexican War in the American Imagination*. Oxford: Oxford University Press, 1985.

Johnson, Allan G. *The Blackwell Dictionary of Sociology: A User's Guide to Sociological Language*. Malden, Massachusetts: Blackwell Publishers, 1995.

Jones, Ernest. *Papers on Psycho-Analysis*. London: Bailliere, Tindall and Cox, 1913.

Jordan, Winthrop. *White over Black: American Attitudes toward the Negro*. Chapel Hill, North Carolina: University of North Carolina Press, 1968.

Josephson, Matthew. *The Robber Barons: The Great American Capitalists 1861-1901.* New York: Harcourt, Brace and World, 1934.

Jung, Carl. *The Basic Writings of C. G. Jung.* Ed. Violet De Laszlo. New York: Modern Library, 1959.

Kazin, Michael. *The Populist Persuasion: An American History.* New York: Basic Books, 1995.

_____. *American Dreamers: How the Left Changed a Nation.* New York: Alfred Knopf, 2011.

Katz, Jonathan. *Gay American History.* New York: Thomas Y. Crowell Publishing, 1976.

Kennan, George. *American Diplomacy, 1900-1950.* New York: The New American Library, 1951.

Kessler-Harris, Alice. *Out to Work: A History of Wage-Earning Women in America.* New York: Oxford University Press, 1982.

Killinger, John. *Hemingway and the Dead Gods: A Study of Existentialism.* University of Kentucky Press, 1960.

Klingberg, Frank. *Cyclical Trends in American Foreign Policy Moods.* University Press of America, 1983.

Kolko, Joyce and Gabriel. *The Limits of Power: The World and United States Foreign Policy, 1945-1954.* New York: Harper and Row, 1972.

Kouwenhoven, John. *Made in America: The Arts in Modern Civilization.* New York: Doubleday and Company, 1948.

Kramer, Paul and Frederick Holborn. *The City in American Life from Colonial Times to the Present.* New York: Capricorn Books, 1970.

Kristeva, Julia. *The Kristeva Reader.* Ed. Toril Moi. Oxford: Basil Blackwell, 1986.

Krutch, Joseph Wood. *The Modern Temper.* New York: Harcourt, Brace and World, 1929.

La Feber, Walter. *America, Russia and the Cold War, 1945-1967.* New York: John Wiley and Sons, 1968.

Lapham, Lewis. *Money and Class in America: Notes and Observations on Our Civil Religion.* New York: Ballantine Books, 1989.

Lasch, Christopher. *The New Radicalism in America, 1889-1963: The Intellectual as a Social Type.* New York: Random House, 1965.

_____. *The Agony of the American Left.* New York: Random House, 1966.

_____. *The Culture of Narcissism: American Life in An Age of Diminishing Expectations.* New York: W. W. Norton and Company, 1979.

Laurie, Bruce. *Artisans into Workers: Labor in Nineteenth-Century America.* New York: Hill and Wang, 1989.

Lawrence, D. H. *Studies in Classic American Literature.* New York: The Viking Press, 1923.

Leakey, Richard and Roger Lewin. *Origins Reconsidered: In Search of What Makes Us Human.* New York: Doubleday, 1992.

Le Bon, Gustave. *The Crowd.* New York: Viking Press, 1963.

Leuchtenburg, William. *The Perils of Prosperity, 1914-32.* Chicago: University of Chicago Press, 1958.

_____. *Franklin D. Roosevelt and the New Deal, 1932-1940.* New York: Harper and Row, 1963.

Levin, Lawrence W. *Black Culture and Black Consciousness: Afro-American Folk Thought from Slavery to Freedom.* New York: Oxford University Press, 1977.

Lewis, Thomas, Fari Amini and Richard Lannon. *A General Theory of Love.* New York: Random House, 2000.

Lewis, R. W. B. *The American Adam: Innocence, Tragedy, and Tradition in the Nineteenth Century.* Chicago: University of Chicago Press, 1955.

Linton, Ralph. *The Tree of Culture.* New York: Vintage Books, 1958.

Lipset, Seymour Martin. "The Sources of the Radical Right." *The Radical Right.* Ed. Daniel Bell. Garden City, New York: Doubleday and Company, 1963. 207-371.

MacLean, Paul D. *The Triune Brain in Evolution.* New York: Plenum Press, 1990.

Mann, Charles. *1491: New Revelations of the Americas Before Columbus.* New York: Random House, 2005.

Marcus Aurelius. *Meditations.* New York: Penguin Books, 1964.

Marcuse, Herbert. *Eros and Civilization: A Philosophical Inquiry into Freud.* Boston: Beacon Press, 1955.

Marx, Karl. *Handbook of Marxism.* Ed. Emile Burns. New York: Random House, 1935.

Marx, Leo. *The Machine in the Garden: Technology and the Pastoral Ideal in America.* New York: Oxford University Press, 1964.

May, Ernest. *Imperial Democracy: The Emergence of America as a Great Power.* New York: Harcourt, 1961.

May, Henry F. *The End of American Innocence: A Study of the First Years of Our Own Time, 1912-1917*. New York: Alfred A. Knopf, 1959.

Mayer, Henry. *All on Fire: William Lloyd Garrison and the Abolition of Slavery*. New York: St. Martin's Griffin, 1998.

Mayer, Jane. *Dark Money: The Hidden History of the Billionaires Behind the Rise of the Radical Right*. New York: Doubleday, 2016.

McClure, Samuel M., David I. Laibson, George Loewenstein and Jonathan Cohen. "Separate Neural Systems Value Immediate and Delayed Monetary Rewards." *Science*. 306 (15 October 2004): 503-507.

McGirr, Lisa. *Suburban Warriors: The Origins of the New American Right*. Princeton: Princeton University Press, 2001.

McLuhn, Marshall. *Understanding the Media: The Extensions of Man*. New York: McGraw-Hill, 1964.

Mead, Margaret. *And Keep Your Powder Dry*. New York: William Morrow and Co., 1943.

Merton, Robert. *Social Theory and Social Structure*. New York: Free Press, 1968.

Meyers, Marvin. *The Jacksonian Persuasion: Politics and Belief*. Stanford: Stanford University Press, 1957.

Miller, Perry. *Jonathan Miller*. New York: Dell Publishing, 1949.

_____. *Errand into the Wilderness*. Cambridge: Belknap Press, 1956.

Mills, C. Wright. *The Power Elite*. New York: Oxford University Press, 1956.

Moller, Herbert. "Sex Composition and Correlated Culture Patterns of Colonial America." *The William and Mary Quarterly*. II (1945): 113-153.

Montgomery, David. *The Fall of the House of Labor: The Workplace, the State, and American Labor Activism, 1865-1925*. Cambridge: Cambridge University Press, 1987.

Morgan, Edmund and Helen. *The Stamp Act Crisis: Prologue to Revolution*. Chapel Hill: University of North Carolina Press, 1953.

Mowry, George. *The Era of Theodore Roosevelt and the Birth of Modern America, 1900-1912*. New York: Harper and Row, 1962.

Mumford, Lewis. *The City in History: Its Origins, Its Transformations, and Its Prospects*. New York: Harcourt, 1961.

Newton, Judith and Deborah Rosenfelt, eds. *Feminist Criticism and Social Change: Sex, Class and Race in Literature and Culture.* New York: Methuen, 1985.

Newton, Judith. *Starting Over: Feminism and the Politics of Cultural Critique.* Ann Arbor: The University of Michigan Press, 1994.

Olson, Steve. *Mapping Human History: Discovering the Past Through Our Genes.* Boston: Houghton Mifflin Company, 2002.

Olmstead, Kathryn. *Real Enemies: Conspiracy Theories and American Democracy, World War I to 9/11.* Oxford: Oxford University Press, 2009.

O'Neill, William. *Everyone Was Brave: A History of Feminism in America.* Chicago: Quadrangle, 1971.

Ortega y Gasset, José. *The Revolt of the Masses.* New York: W. W. Norton and Company, 1930.

Parkman, Francis. *Complete Works.* Centenary Edition. Boston: Little, Brown and Co., 1925.

Parrington, Vernon Louis. *Main Currents in American Thought.* New York: Harcourt, 1939.

Persons, Stow. *American Minds: A History of Ideas.* New York: Holt, Rinehart and Winston, 1958.

Philbrick, Nathaniel. *Mayflower: A Story of Courage, Community, and War.* New York: Penguin, 2006.

Phillips, Kevin. *Wealth and Democracy: A Political History of the American Rich.* New York: Random House, 2002.

_____. *American Theocracy: The Peril and Politics of Radical Religion, Oil, and Borrowed Money in the 21th Century.* New York: Penguin, 2006.

Pierson, George. "The M-Factor in American History." *American Quarterly.* XIV (Summer, 1962): 275-289.

Piketty, Thomas. *Capital in the Twenty-First Century.* Arthur Goldhammer, Trans. Cambridge: Harvard University Press, 2014.

Pinker, Steven. *How the Mind Works.* New York: W. W. Norton, 1997.

_____. *The Better Angels of Our Nature: Why Violence Has Declined.* New York: Viking Penguin, 2011.

Potter, David. *People of Plenty: Economic Abundance and the American Character.* Chicago: University of Chicago Press, 1954.

Potts, Malcolm and Thomas Hayden. *Sex and War: How Biology Explains Warfare and Terrorism and Offers a Path to a Safer World.* Dallas: Benbella Books, 2008.

Ram Dass. *The Only Dance There Is*. Garden City, New York: Anchor Books, 1970.

Reisman, David, et. al. *The Lonely Crowd*. New Haven: Yale University Press, 1950.

Reynolds, David S. *John Brown: Abolitionist*. New York: Alfred Knopf, 2005.

Rogers, Daniel T. *Age of Fracture*. Cambridge: Harvard University Press, 2011.

Rohmann, Chris. *A World of Ideas: A Dictionary of Important Theories, Concepts, Beliefs, and Thinkers*. New York: Random House, 1999.

Rorabaugh, W. J. *The Alcoholic Republic: An American Tradition*. New York: Oxford University Press, 1979.

Rosen, Ruth. *Lost Sisterhood: Prostitution in America, 1900-1918*. Baltimore: Johns Hopkins University Press, 1982.

_____. *The World Split Open: How the Women's Movement Changed America*. New York: The Penguin Group, 2000.

Rosenberg, Bernard and David Manning White, eds. *Mass Culture: The Popular Arts in America*. New York: Macmillan, 1964.

Rosenberg, Harold. *The Tradition of the New*. Cambridge, Massachusetts: Da Capo Press, 1959.

Rossiter, Clinton. *The First American Revolution*. New York: Harcourt, Brace and World, 1953.

Rostow, Walt Whitman. *Stages of Economic Growth*. New York: Cambridge University Press, 1960.

Roszak, Theodore. *The Making of a Counter Culture*. Garden City, New York: Doubleday and Company, 1969.

Ruiz, Ramón Edwardo, ed. *The Mexican War: Was It Manifest Destiny?* New York: Holt, Rienhard and Winston, 1963.

Russell, Bertrand. *A History of Western Philosophy*. New York: Simon and Schuster, 1945.

Samuelson, Paul A. *Economics: An Introductory Analysis*. New York: McGraw-Hill, 1962.

Schlesinger, Jr., Arthur. *The Age of Jackson*. Boston: Little and Brown, 1945.

_____. *The Cycles of American History*. Boston: Houghton Mifflin Company, 1986.

Schlosser, Eric. *Reefer Madness: Sex, Drugs, and Cheap Labor in the American Black Market*. New York: Houghton Mifflin Company, 2003.

Schneider, Herbert. *The Puritan Mind*. Ann Harbor: University of Michigan Press, 1930.

Schumacker, E. F. *Small is Beautiful: Economics as if People Mattered*. New York: Harper and Row, 1973.

Self, Robert O. *All in the Family: The Realignment of American Democracy since the 1960s*. New York: Hill and Wang, 2012.

Shipler, David. *The Working Poor: Invisible In America*. New York: Vintage, 2005.

Skeggs, Beverly. *Formations of Class and Gender: Becoming Respectable*. Thousand Oaks, California: SAGE Publications, 1997.

Sklar, Martin. *The Corporate Reconstruction of American Capitalism, 1890-1916*. Cambridge: Cambridge University Press, 1988.

Slater, Phillip. *The Pursuit of Loneliness: American Culture at the Breaking Point*. New York: Beacon Press, 1970.

Smith, Adam. *The Wealth of Nations*. New York: Modern Library, 1937.

Smith, Henry Nash. *Virgin Land: The American West as Symbol and Myth*. Cambridge: Harvard University Press, 1950.

Snow, C. P. *The Two Cultures*. Cambridge: Cambridge University Press, 1959.

Stampp, Kenneth. *The Peculiar Institution*. New York: Vintage Books, 1956.

Starr, Paul. *The Creation of the Media: Political Origins of Modern Communications*. New York: Basic Books, 2004.

Steinberg, Ted. *Down to Earth: Nature's Role in American History*. New York: Oxford University Press, 2002.

Stephanson, Anders. *Manifest Destiny: American Expansionism and the Empire of the Right*. New York: Hill and Wang, 1995.

Stiglitz, Joseph, *The Price of Inequality*. New York: W. W. Norton, 2012.

Stilgoe, John. *Borderland: Origins of the American Suburb, 1820-1939*. New Haven: Yale University Press, 1988.

Strauss, William and Neil Howe. *Generations: The History of America's Future, 1584-2069*. New York: William Morrow and Company, 1991.

Thernstrom, Stephan. *Poverty and Progress*. Cambridge: Harvard University Press, 1964.

Thompson, E. P. *Working Class: The Making of the English Working Class*. New York: Alfred Knopf, 1963.

Thompson, Warren. *The Population Problem*. New York: McGraw-Hill, 1953.

Thoreau, Henry David. *The Portable Thoreau*. Ed. Carl Bode. New York: Viking Press, 1947.

Thornton, Russell. *American Indian Holocaust and Survival: A Population History Since 1492*. Norman, Oklahoma: University of Oklahoma Press, 1990.

Thorpe, Rebecca U. *The American Warfare State: The Domestic Politics of Military Spending*. Chicago: The University of Chicago Press, 2014.

Tilden, William W. *Crown's Children: Freud's Anal Typology as an Organizing Concept in American Historiography*. Berkeley: Plaine Style Press, 2010.

_____. "American Cultural Traits." *The Journal of Psychohistory* 40, No. 3 (Winter 2013): 193-221.

Timberlake, James. *Prohibition and the Progressive Movement, 1900-1920*. Cambridge: Harvard University Press, 1963.

Tocqueville, Alexis de. *Democracy in America*. Ed. Phillips Bradley. New York: Alfred A. Knopf, 1945.

Tong, Rosemarie. *Feminist Thought: A Comprehensive Introduction*. Boulder, Colorado: Westview Press, 1988.

Tracy, Sarah and Caroline Acker. *Altering American Consciousness: The History of Alcohol and Drug Use in the United States, 1800-2000*. Boston: University of Massachusetts Press, 2004.

Trilling, Lionel. *The Liberal Imagination: Essays on Literature and Society*. New York: The Macmillan Company, 1950.

Turner, Frederick Jackson. "The Significance of the Frontier in American History." *The Frontier in American History*. New York: Henry Holt and Company, 1920.

Twitchell, James. *Carnival Culture: The Trashing of Taste in America*. New York: Columbia University Press, 1992.

Tyler, Alice Felt. *Freedom's Ferment: Phases of American Social History from the Colonial Period to the Outbreak of the Civil War*. New York: Harper and Row, 1944.

Veblen, Thorstein. *The Theory of the Leisure Class*. New York: The Modern Library, 1934.

Wade, Richard. *The Urban Frontier*. Chicago: University of Chicago Press, 1964.

Ward, John William. *Andrew Jackson: Symbol for an Age*. New York: Oxford University Press, 1962.

Webb, Walter Prescott. *The Great Frontier*. Austin, Texas: University of Texas Press, 1964.

Weber, Max. *The Protestant Ethic and the Spirit of Capitalism*. Trans. Talcott Parsons. New York: Charles Scribner's Sons, 1958.

Weinberg, Albert. *Manifest Destiny: A Study of National Expansionism in American History*. Baltimore: Johns Hopkins Press, 1935.

Wells, Spencer. *The Journey of Man: A Genetic Odyssey*. Princeton: Princeton University Press, 2002.

White, Richard. *Railroaded: The Transcontinentals and the Making of Modern America*. New York: W. W. Norton, 2011.

Wiebe, Robert. *The Search for Order, 1877-1920*. New York: Hill and Wang, 1967.

Wilentz, Sean. *Chants Democratic: New York City and the Rise of the American Working Class, 1788-1850*. Oxford: Oxford University Press, 1984.

Wilkerson, Isabel. *The Warmth of Other Suns: The Epic Story of America's Great Migration*. New York: Random House, 2010.

Williams, Raymond. *Culture and Society: 1750-1950*. New York: Columbia University Press, 1958.

Williams, William Appleman. *The Tragedy of American Diplomacy*. New York: Dell, 1962.

Wilson, Edmund. *Axel's Castle: A Study in the Imaginative Literature of 1870 to 1930*. New York: Charles Scribner's Sons, 1931.

Wilson, Edward O. *Sociobiology: The New Synthesis*. Cambridge: Harvard University Press, 1977.

Wittke, Carl. *We Who Built America: the Saga of the Immigrant*. New York: Prentice Hall, 1939.

Wright, Louis B. *Culture on the Moving Frontier*. New York: Harper and Row, 1955.

Zinn, Howard, ed. *New Deal Thought*. New York: Bobbs-Merrill Company, 1966.

Zunz, Olivier. *Why the American Century?* Chicago: Chicago University Press, 1998.

Made in the USA
Middletown, DE
12 June 2016